Literary Taste, Culture and Mass Communication

Volume 6

THE SOCIOLOGY OF LITERATURE

Literary Taste, Culture and Mass Communication

Volume 6

THE SOCIOLOGY OF LITERATURE

edited by

Peter Davison/Rolf Meyersohn/Edward Shils

CHADWYCK-HEALEY CAMBRIDGE
SOMERSET HOUSE TEANECK, NJ

Chadwyck-Healey Ltd
20 Newmarket Road
Cambridge CB5 8DT
ISBN 0 85964 041 8

Somerset House
417 Maitland Avenue
Teaneck, NJ 07666
ISBN 0 914146 49 1

Library of Congress Cataloging in Publication Data
Main entry under title:

The sociology of literature

(Literary taste, culture and mass communication; v. 6)
    Bibliography: p.
    1. Literature and society — Addresses, essays,
lectures. I. Series.

AC1.L79 vol. 6 [PN51] 301.16'1s [801'.3] 77-90614

British Library Cataloguing in Publication Data

Literary taste, culture and mass communication.
    Vol. 6: The sociology of literature

    1. Arts and society — Addresses, essays and
    lectures.
    I. Davison, Peter II. Meyersohn, Rolf III.
    Shils, Edward Albert IV. Sociology of
    literature

    700   NX180.S6

Printed in England

Contents

Introduction

As several references in the contributions to this volume make plain, the sociological approach to the study of literature may be said to have begun with Madame de Staël's *De la littérature considéré dans ses rapports avec les institutions sociale* Paris 1800 (see Milton C. Albrecht, p. 105; Ian Watt, p. 121; Robert Escarpit, p. 139; Jacques Leenhardt, p. 149; and W. Witte, p. 211) and her *De l'Allemagne* Paris 1813 (see Witte, p. 211), and to have been given particular impetus by another French writer, Hippolyte Taine, whose "famous triad", as Wellek and Warren describe it (p. 34), of *race, milieu,* and *moment* recurs frequently in these contributions, and by Karl Marx, whose influence, far more than any specific writings on the subject, profoundly affected the study of the relationship of literature and society. This volume appropriately includes, therefore, not only reviews of the development of the study of the relationship of literature and society and a few practical examples, but also some references which look back over past centuries. As in so much else, the past can provide an illuminating perspective for contemporary work.

At one extreme there have been those who have, like Wellek and Warren's "vulgar Marxist", posited a too-direct, too-simple, relationship of literature and society; at the other, those whom Kenneth Burke describes as concerned to erect barriers about literature as a special pursuit (p. 293). It is curious that many scholars overlook a subtlety in Marx's approach which Wellek and Warren are at pains to point out, quoting from his introduction to *The Critique of Political Economy*:

> Certain periods of highest development of art stand in no direct relationship with the general development of society, nor with the material basis and the skeleton structure of its organization. Witness the example of the Greeks as compared with the modern nations or even Shakespeare. (p. 36)

It is even strange though that those who might least be expected to accept the "vulgar Marxist" approach of direct relationship between the world of art (whether it be literature, film, or television), and society, seem to accept that position *in toto*, in arguing for direct influences in the legislature and courtroom. Perhaps they might be advised to have in mind not only the reservations of Marx and Engels, but, for example, the Payne studies (mentioned by Albrecht, pp. 113—114), which state, among other things, that influence "is selective, being determined primarily by an individual's background and needs".

A sociological approach to literature is patently difficult because it must attempt to reconcile the mass of people, made up of individuals, with the mass of literature, itself individual, even unique. When the individual person is related to the individual work — we have the literary critic confronting a specific work; once the work, its author, and readers are put into a social context, not only are the imponderables and variables complex (as Meyersohn says, "The traces left by our contemporaries are so vast that no amount of ordering can group them into proper categories", p. 5), but, often enough, specialised interests (which can easily become entrenched positions) direct the manner of interpretation and therefore dictate the result. The extreme position can be held by those who believe that the function of literature is solely didactic or hedonistic or "art for art's sake",[1] but a belief in the function of literature as approximating however loosely to Horace's *dulce et utile* cannot wholly ignore sociological implications.

The contributions to this volume are, as usual in this series, chosen and juxtaposed to prompt insights into the problems raised but, for convenience, they have been arranged in five groups. It must be stressed that the groupings are a convenience for the reader; they are not watertight compartments and, furthermore, there is deliberately some anticipation of issues raised in other volumes of this series. For example, Charles Glicksberg's "Literature and Society" could well have been placed in volume 10 or volume 11, but it usefully, in the context of this volume, brings home the social pressures which the author may face, and it also claims that the "politics of the writer, however explicit outside of his art, plays [*sic*] no significant role inside his work" (pp. 94ff).

The volume begins with two introductions or "overviews": one by two literary scholars (thought chiefly the work of Réné Wellek, whose discipline is comparative literature), and one by a sociologist, Rolf Meyersohn, who has worked chiefly in America but who was also visiting Fulbright Professor at the Centre for Contemporary Cultural Studies, Birmingham, England in 1967—68, a formative time in the development of that Centre.

Meyersohn brings out very acutely the differences in approach to literature by the sociologist and the literary critic. This is readily seen (at the risk of oversimplification) in the way a literary work may be used by the sociologist as the source of data so that its value *qua* literature may be ignored. Indeed, there is what he calls "the very difficult notion that great literature might be less useful than kitsch or at least no more useful" (p. 7) and compare Wellek and Warren's reference to Taine, p. 24 . That this might be so can be seen in part by considering some of the implications raised in the Introduction to volume 8 in the discussion of English patriotic songs and

---

1   Louise Rosenblatt whose "Toward a Cultural Approach to Literature" is reproduced here also wrote *L'Idée de l'art dans la littérature anglaise* Paris 1931.
has always seemed to me a sort of wild poetic justice that MGM films should have borne the motto, *Ars gratia artis!*

comparing those songs with, if not "great literature", at least a worthy and recognisable work of dramatic art, John Osborne's *The Entertainer*. (But see Goldmann, p. 171, premise 4, referred to below.)

On the other hand, Richard Hoggart argues in "Literature and Society" in volume 9 (and this Meyersohn readily acknowledges in his footnote 9), that the techniques of social science cannot recreate the complexity of "what an unskilled labourer feels on his pulses every day of the week". It is no slight to either scholar to suggest that such an exchange, which I take to be not untypical of those engaged in considering the sociology of literature from sociological and literary critical points of view, is rather like two people playing tennis — but in different courts; or like certain Pinter dialogues. Perhaps another way of putting this is to suggest that the literary scholar making a sociological approach to literature will tend to apply his sociological techniques to explain further within the world of the work of literature and will use those techniques evaluatively; the sociologist, however, will work outwards from his "data" in order to help him better to explain (rather than evaluate?) the nature of society.

Wellek and Warren, though literary scholars, do not hesitate to concede that "a large majority of the questions raised by literary study are, at least ultimately or by implication, social questions" (p. 23). Their approach is delicately balanced. They succinctly dispose of claims that literature directly mirrors society (p. 24) but accept that the "writer is not only influenced by society but influences it. Art not merely reproduces life but also shapes it" (p. 31). They believe that literature can be used as a social document "to yield the outline of history", and they give as one of their examples the Prologue to *The Canterbury Tales* — but compare Watt, p. 127, and Witte, p. 209. Despite that, they are doubtful if we can precisely define the influence of a book on its readers (pp. 31—32). It is difficult enough to tell whether *Gone With the Wind* has "changed Northern readers' attitudes towards Mrs Stowe's war", much more difficult to make analyses which are concerned with "literature in the broadest sense, and society in the broadest", for "the appeal must be made to the experience not of the connoisseur alone but to that of the human race" (p. 31). Further, no study will be of value if it takes for granted the idea that literature is simply a mirror of life (p. 32), and it is always necessary to take into account the writer's artistic method.

The relation between literature and society they classify as: (i) The sociology of the writer, the profession of literature, its institutions and economic basis; also into this class goes a writer's extra-literary pronouncements; (ii) Social content, implications and purposes of the work of literature; (iii) The social influence of literature (pp. 24—25). But the degree to which literature is determined by or dependent upon its relationships to society "will enter into all the divisions of our problem" (p. 25).

Although they take into account many of the approaches suggested elsewhere in this volume, e.g. those of Taine, Marx, De Bonald, Mannheim, Kohn-Bromstedt, and sometimes specific instances (suicide and Goethe's *The*

Sorrows of Werther springs to mind), it is worth noting their remark that "it seems impossible, however, to accept a view constituting any particular human activity the 'starter' of all the others" (p. 34).

A pointed criticism of Wellek and Warren is to be found in the contribution reproduced here by J. Leenhardt, p. 153.

The USA

The next group of articles brings together some of the more general considerations of the problems posed by the sociology of literature as discussed in American journals in the past forty or so years. The first article suggests, directly and indirectly, something of the ferment associated with the social interpretation of literature in the mid-thirties. Everett Hunt's contribution was made to a symposium on literature and society and he is particularly concerned with the work and approach of Granville Hicks. Hicks was the editor of *New Masses* at the time and the issue of *English Journal* in which Hunt's article appears is immediately followed by Hicks's address, "Literature and Revolution", given at the College Conference on English in the Central Atlantic States on 1 December 1934. In the year that the two papers were published, 1935, Hicks was dismissed from his teaching post on political grounds, causing a furore over the issue of academic freedom. His *The Great Tradition* (not to be confused with F.R. Leavis's study of George Eliot, Henry James and Conrad) offers a Marxist interpretation of American literature since the Civil War.

Everett Hunt disagrees with Hicks's assertion that social interpretation tells us "what we most want to know" (p. 53), especially one suspects, if it is an interpretation dominated by "the narrowness of the Marxian formula for criticism", for he suggests that "the restraints of Puritanism are mild compared with the Marxian formula" (p. 51). Nevertheless, Hunt *does* think that "the world attitude of the author seems to me to be the most truly liberal way of teaching" (p. 52) provided it is not identified with the class struggle. He also believes the student would be well advised to be sent back to Taine (see, for example, Wellek and Warren p. 34, Mueller, p. 61; Albrecht, p. 107; Watt, p. 122; Witte, p. 211), but, in undergraduate teaching, it is "the work of art itself" that should be kept in the foreground. He concludes by repeating a view expressed on p. 53: "Literature does have an effect on conduct, and that it is possible to discriminate — if not too dogmatically — between good and bad effects".

John Mueller, after remarking that until then (1935) social scientists had paid little attention to the fine arts, analyses the romanticists' perception of the artists' and scientists' role (p. 58), the solution of formalism as a means of repudiating realistic fidelity — so that art is seen as independent of the "experience in the exterior world", and the effect of natural science on romanticists and idealists. He then suggests that there is a dislocation between "conspicuous events" and "prevailing art taste" but that obsession with the concept of the *Zeitgeist* has blinded critics "to the seething cultural process" within what they took to be homogenous unity (p. 63). Art is not, he argues, the product of the "times", nor of society, but rather "the creation of the respective groups of which the largest society is composed".

Alexander Kern outlines the application of the sociology of knowledge to literary study in order that literature might be better explained and interpreted, though he does not suggest it as an aid to evaluation (p. 78). Louise Rosenblatt, concerned to reinforce international understanding by "moral solidarity at home", and clearly much influenced by the conclusion of hostilities and hopes for world peace and cooperation in the post-war world, argues that the study of the literature of other nations will enable Americans to eliminate their prejudices against foreigners and their own provincialism (which characteristic she mentions several times). Charles Glicksberg describes the pressures on writers to take political responsibility, a debate carried on in the English press a little later in the 1950s by Eugène Ionesco and the critic, Kenneth Tynan (see Further Reading).

The first of the two articles by Milton C. Albrecht reproduced here, "The Relationship of Literature and Society", takes Mueller's article in this volume as its starting point and analyses some of the studies based on the three hypotheses that literature reflects society; that it influences society; and that it helps preserve the *status quo*. Albrecht touches on several then recent developments — the growing interest in popular art forms (and he refers among others to Ruth Inglis's article reproduced here); the idea that popular literature and films might reflect stress patterns and emotional needs of their audiences; attempts to prescribe artistic production or prevent its circulation; and attempts to isolate the supposed beneficial effects of literature and film. A fascinating aspect of the debates and theories reviewed by Albrecht is the sense of *déjà vu*. Explanations for the popularity of Elizabethan revenge tragedy have something in common with the suggestion that films reflect stress patterns and the emotional needs of society (e.g. revenge on stage as a proxy for that forbidden in life); it has been argued also by scholars of the drama of the Elizabethan period that certain dramatists reflected or even prompted changes in attitudes to women, kingship, and class consciousness; and the alleged ill-influence of popular art, especially the drama, was argued out in the sixteenth and seventeenth centuries in ways not wholly dissimilar from those which see children as "moulded by movies" and "movie-made criminals" (pp. 113–114). Finally in this section Ian Watt reinforces the arguments of Wellek and Warren.

The Continent of Europe
In view of the interest in the relationship of literature and society in France and the important influence on American thought in this field by scholars such as Adorno, Horkheimer and Marcuse, it is wholly appropriate that some contribution from the Continent of Europe should be included here.

The work of Robert Escarpit, Director of the Centre de Sociologie des Faits Littéraires, like that of Lucien Goldmann, is well known, and the extracts from their work serve only to represent their contributions to thinking on this subject. Escarpit briefly answers the question, "why a sociology of literature?" and then gives an outline of the development of the subject, starting with Madame de Staël but extending it, in a particularly European context, sketching the very great amount of work now being done in Europe in this field. Looked at from the continent of Europe in 1958, it is interesting that Escarpit can declare that, "an authentic sociology of literature is being born", referring to "encouraging response" from a number of countries — including all but one, America! The explanation for this is doubtless to be found in the article by Jacques Leenhardt: "The enormous American production of sociological works obviously comprises numerous 'notes' on literature but these notes do not all compensate for the general dearth which is so obvious in this field" (pp. 152–153) and see also the paper by Raymond Williams, pp. 258–265.

Lucien Goldmann and Jacques Leenhardt both taught the sociology of literature in the École Pratique des Hautes Études in Paris, Goldmann being Director of Studies. Goldmann was also Director of the Centre for the Sociology of Literature of the Free University of Brussels. Though now well known, this was once not the case as Raymond Williams notes in his tribute to Goldmann reproduced later in this volume, for he states that when he was writing *The Long Revolution* (1961) he did not know of the work of Lukács or Goldmann (Williams, p. 264).

Leenhardt gives a historical review of the development of literature and sociology but he usefully fills in certain details not referred to by others and offers a much more sharply critical assessment, especially of American work. He places in the tradition such scholars as Leo Löwenthal, George Lukács, Karl Mannheim, Theodor Adorno, J.M. Guyau, and Goldmann. He concludes by suggesting two lines of research, one of which would be an "empirical and strictly sociological" study of the conditions operating between creative groups and individuals (p. 164), and the "second direction that research should take would lead to a more scrupulous reading of texts" (p. 165).

Lucien Goldmann, influenced by George Lukács, outlines the alternative to the kind of research commonly undertaken which is concerned

> with the content of literary works and the relationship between that content and the collective consciousness, that is to say the ways in which men think and behave in daily life (p. 170).

Such work, he argues, is often regarded as of little value to those concerned with literature, even if it is not rejected outright. He therefore offers what is tantamount to a *modus operandi* for the research worker. He begins by noting the five most important premises of genetic structuralist sociology. Of particular interest in view of what has been said above (see Meyersohn, p. 7) is that "the very peaks of literary creation may not only be studied quite as well as average works, but are even found to be particularly suitable for positive research" (p. 131). It will be seen, also, that this approach involves taking into consideration "the conscious intention of the author". Goldmann gives a number of examples of works examined and concludes by suggesting a mode of extending this research method, taking as a starting point Julia Kristeva's study on Bakhtin (p. 189).

The final study in this section originated in Czechoslovakia. Vladimír Karbusicky begins with a very firm opening statement: "No one can deny that a work of art stems from reality and that it has an influence on society" (p. 195). Karbusicky is very critical of the general application of information theory to the study of the sociology of literature and offers a much more complex model (figure 2) to illustrate the relationships of "sphere of creation", "sphere of institutional influence", and "sphere of aesthetic experience". It will be noted that this allows for the perceiver's experience, including social experience, which takes account of Albrecht's argument that "influence is not a simple cause-effect relationship, as commonly assumed; it is selective, being determined primarily by an individual's background and needs" (Albrecht p. 114).

Great Britain

Each of the articles in the fourth group originally appeared in Britain and, though not all by British scholars, each is clearly addressed to the British reader. W. Witte's article is a relatively early defence of the sociological approach to literature and should be read in the light of the then increasingly strong concern for studying "the poem on the page" — itself a reaction from investing a work with biographical and other external elements in textual reading. Witte argues that a sociological approach does not conflict but complements and is essential if a work has social or economic conditions or political events for its theme.

L.C. Knight's inaugural lecture was given just over thirty years ago and a decade after the appearance of his seminal study *Drama and Society in the Age of Jonson*. Although he spoke of the past (and it is partly to remind readers concerned with the twentieth century of the valuable work done on the relationship of literature and society in the earlier centuries that this study has been included), he did not hide his conviction that "the kind of enquiry I have in mind has an intimate bearing on our present unavoidable preoccupation with the social forms of to-day and to-morrow" (p. 221). He argues that literature is the basis on which the social historian should build and that the study of society should be evaluative. This is reminiscent of a passage in *Drama and Society in the Age of Jonson*:

> The claim that I am making is that the essential life of a period is best understood through its literature; not because of what that literature describes, but because of what it embodied. If this is so the whole of Elizabethan and Jacobean literature should be considered in a study of this kind (Chapter 5).

The sub-title to Edward Shils's witty and rightly caustic review of the lack of development of sociology in Britain despite the pioneering work of the English "social explorers" (see Further Reading and contrast Hunt writing of the United States in 1935, where departments of literature were "shrinking rapidly before the increased enrolments in social science . . . ", p. 49), suggests that the future of sociology in Britain is really a problem associated with the development of British society itself. Looking back after nearly twenty years one can see how accurate was that assessment. Despite the very considerable expansion of higher education, the strategic importance of the two ancient universities seems almost as great in academic and socio-political terms now as then and the effect of their willingness to prompt or stunt growth ripples its way throughout our institutions. Sociology has, of course, grown very considerably since 1960, at least as an undergraduate subject in many institutions, but whether the hopes for sociology suggested on pp. 250–51, and prompted also by Knights's inaugural lecture at Leeds and Richard Hoggart's appointment at Birmingham (see his inaugural lecture reprinted in volume 5) have been fully realised, I doubt. If they have not, the reason may only in part be the social and financial troubles of the past decade, both of which have conspired against academic adventurousness. The "undeveloped heart", of which Shils writes on p. 242, or perhaps a certain superficial sentimentality which is sometimes its substitute, still plays a significant role.

Raymond Williams's tribute to Lucien Goldmann explains and places his contribution to the study of sociology of literature (especially in a British context) and perceptively reviews the way in which such studies have developed (or rather, failed to develop) in Britain. He points to the very vigorous work in literary criticism in Britain, especially in Cambridge between the wars, and the effect of its vanquishing a Marxian approach to literature: that English scholars, in effect, cut themselves off from the work of men such as Lukács and Goldmann. He points (as did Shils in *On the Eve*) to the "historic failure to develop British social studies in any adequate way", to the absence of an intellectual centre for current work, to the provincialism of much literary and social study in Britain, and of the desperate need for a new theory (pp. 259–60). The problem in seeking such a theory, he argues, is that it must be sought in fields of study inimical to the English literary critical tradition.

Very interestingly he begins his paper by commenting on the limitations of "the ordinary language" thought appropriate for intellectual discussion in Britain: "a framing of ideas within certain polite but definite limits". This limitation he associates with "certain restrictions and deadlocks in the larger society" (and note again the sub-title to Shils's contribution, p. 258). Thus, there is a need for a "highly specialised and internal vocabulary" that will enable a "break to be made with the English bourgeoisie", so satisfying a demand for "alternative procedures and styles" (pp. 258–59), as if, rather belatedly, the social and literary critic were following the example of the creative writers, as described by Martin Turnell. A trifle paradoxically, the last part of Williams's paper is a lucid account of Goldmann's method.

Williams's paper was published in 1971 and since then there has been some attempt in Britain to develop an internal vocabulary for work of this kind. Its success has been limited and its reception sometimes unkind. Thus, on 7 July, 1978, the *Times Literary Supplement* carried a review by Geoffrey Marshall of *Policing the Crisis: mugging, the state, and law and order* by Stuart Hall, Charles Critcher, Tony Jefferson, John Clarke, and Brian Roberts. This made great play with the language in which the book was written. It was followed shortly afterwards in the *Times Higher Education Supplement* (28 July, 1978) by a defence of the Centre for Contemporary Studies, Birmingham (whence the book originated), by Peter David who, though he described the review as ungenerous, went on to admit that one could see the reviewer's point:

> Much of the output of the Birmingham University centre is written in an unhappy mixture of journalism and sociology which baffles the lay reader. Things are never said or expressed but "articulated"; and events don't occur at particular times but at "conjunctures".

The problem of an appropriate language that will express resistance to outworn structures is still acute and one senses that "bafflement of the bourgeoisie" might be the aim rather than lucid articulation of new theories and approaches using a new vocabulary. Ironically, David's suggestion that the Centre's language owes much to journalese is, unwittingly, even more cruel than Marshall's sarcasm.

Special Applications

The final section of this volume is devoted to six fairly short applications of sociology to literature and the writer. Ruth Inglis's "Objective Approach" is evaluated by Albrecht and although he finds the basic hypothesis ("that literature, mainly fiction and biography in 'popular' forms, reflects social 'facts' ") "the most mechanistic version of all" of the ways of studying the relationship of literature and society, he does admit that "the results have been somewhat profitable" (p. 110). Albrecht in his second article reproduced in this volume is concerned specifically with the reflection theory and in studying how cultural norms and values of the American family are reflected in short stories in six large-circulation magazines in 1950. He also includes the journal studied by Ruth Inglis, *The Saturday Evening Post*. Their conclusions are not, in general terms, dissimilar.

The extract from Kenneth Burke's *The Philosophy of Literary Form*, begins with an analysis of proverbs as "strategies for living" which he then suggests might be extended "to encompass the whole field of literature", the most complex and sophisticated works of art being considered as if they were "proverbs writ large". This approach would, he argues, not only give fresh insights into the organisation of literary works but would automatically break down the barriers erected about literature as a specialised pursuit. He admits that that might outrage good taste but good taste had now become inert. Some forty years on, Burke reads as freshly and provocatively as ever, suggesting that, despite the development of many of the approaches advanced in this volume, the barriers erected about the study of literature are still pretty firmly in place and there are still many of those about "who take the division of faculties [and departments?] in our universities to be an exact replica of the way in which God himself divided up the universe" (p. 294).

Albert Votaw, writing just after the end of the 1939—45 war, sees the literature of violence as a reaction to the experience of the concentration camp — a nightmare realised out of the nineteenth century dream of the perfection of science which would enable man to control his environment but now does so in order that he might exterminate himself. Votaw, was, of course, writing before the flood of fictional detectives and spies who "lived out in the cold". Martin Turnell, in contrast to Votaw, starts with a much earlier period, the seventeenth century, and shows how the writer has become alien to his class. He has some particularly interesting things to say about the development of the idea in literature of the bourgeoisie. The artist instead of aiming to "glorify the existing order" (p. 325) now aims to shape and change society rather than preserve its *status quo*. Like Charles Glicksberg, Turnell argues that "a writer's responsibility as a writer is paramount" (pp. 329—30).

The volume concludes with an article on the impact of mass media on society. This should be read in conjunction with volume 2 *Mass Media and Mass Communication*. Becker is concerned with the impact of the media on the dissemination of information, especially in styles of self-presentation by American politicians; the impact of mass media on attitudes; on culture; and finally on social structures. It is the third element that is particularly relevant in the context of this volume. He argues that though the mass media have not had a negative effect upon our culture, indeed their effect may have been beneficial, it is possible they could have been "more positive" (p. 367).

If there is one thing certain in the varied approaches to the sociology of literature suggested in this volume it is that, as Rolf Meyersohn puts it, "acquaintance leads to a greater feeling of relative ignorance" (p. 10).

PETER DAVISON

Further Reading

A number of the contributions to this volume review work in the field and provide many references to further reading in footnotes and bibliographies. Nevertheless, it might be helpful to separate out a few of the works referred to and to add one or two more titles. The major nineteenth-century works are listed first and these are followed by studies written in this century in alphabetical order of author's surnames.

Nineteenth Century

Madame de Staël's *De la littérature considérée dans ses rapports avec les institutions sociale* was published in Paris in 1800. It appeared in English as *A Treatise of Ancient and Modern Literature* 1803 and *The Influence of Literature upon Society* 1812. Her novel *Delphine* 1802 is imbued with her sociological interests. Robert Escarpit wrote an account of Madame de Staël's analysis of English institutions (her companion volume to *De l'Allmagne* 1810 on England was not completed) *L'Angleterre dans l'oeuvre de Madame de Staël* 1954.

Hippolyte Taine's four-volume *Histoire de la littérature anglaise* 1863–64 (translated as *History of English Literature* 1871) contains in its introduction an account of his approach to the study of literature (and see Albrecht p. 107 fn. 19).

Marx's influence on the study of literature and society is much more pervasive than his writings on the subject, but some direct discussions are to be found in *Marx and Engels on Literature and Art* ed. S. Baxandall and S. Morawski St. Louis 1973; or K. Marx and F. Engels *Literature and Art*, New York 1947.

Twentieth Century

R.D. Altick *The English Common Reader: a social history of the mass reading public, 1800–1900* Chicago 1957.

Julien Benda *La trahison des clercs* 1927; translated as *The Treason of the Intellectuals* 1928.

Elizabeth and Tom Burns eds. *Sociology of Literature and Drama* Harmondsworth 1973, contains an interesting introduction and a useful bibliography.

David Daiches *Literature and Society* London 1938. See also his *Critical Approaches to Literature* London 1956: ch. 18: "Criticism and Sociology"; and ch. 19: "Criticism and the Cultural Context".

Hugh D. Duncan *Language and Literature in Society* Chicago 1953. Contains a bibliographical guide to the sociology of literature.

Robert Escarpit *Sociologie de la littérature* Paris 1958; transl. E. Pick as *Sociology of Literature* Lake Erie College Studies Ohio 1965.

Robert Escarpit " 'Creative Treason' as a Key to Literature" *Yearbook of Comparative Literature* no. 10; reprinted in E. & T. Burns *Sociology of Literature and Drama* 1973.

E. Goblot *La barrière et le niveau* Paris 1925.

J.S.R. Goodlad *A Sociology of Popular Drama* London 1971.

A.L. Guérard *Literature and Society* New York 1935.

Granville Hicks *The Great Tradition* New York 1933.

Richard Hoggart "The Literary Imagination and the Sociological Imagination" (1967) in *Speaking to Each Other* London 1970. This was first given as a talk to the Sociology Section of the British Association. See also his "Literature and Society" in volume 9.

Eugène Ionesco *Notes et contre-notes* Paris 1962; transl. Donald Watson as *Notes and Counter Notes* London 1964; for "The London Controversy" with Kenneth Tynan, Philip Toynbee, and Orson Welles.

L.C. Knights *Drama and Society in the Age of Jonson* London 1937.

Ernst Kohn-Bramstedt *Aristocracy and the Middle-Classes in Germany: social types in German literature 1830–1900* London 1937. This edition has an introduction "The sociological approach to literature" by G.P. Gooch.

Diana Laurenson and Alan Swingewood *The Sociology of Literature* London 1972.

F.R. Leavis *The Common Pursuit* London 1952 for "Literature and Society" and "Sociology and Literature".

F.R. Leavis *Education and the University: a sketch for an "English school"* London 1943; for, as L.C. Knights puts it, practical suggestions as to how explorations into related fields of inquiry might be made without losing one's way "in the soft-soil of half-knowledge".

Queenie D. Leavis *Fiction and the Reading Public* London 1932; New York 1965.

George Lichtheim *Lukács* (Fontana Modern Masters) London 1970.

Leo Löwenthal *Literature and the Image of Man: sociological studies of the European Drama and Novel 1600–1900* Boston 1957.

Leo Löwenthal *Literature, Popular Culture and Society* Englewood Cliffs 1961.

Karl Mannheim *Ideology and Utopia: an introduction to the sociology of knowledge* transl. L. Wirth and E. Shils London 1954.

Herbert Read *Art and Society* London 1967.

Levin L. Schücking *Die Soziologie der litterarischen Geschmacksbildung* Munich 1923; enlarged edn, Leipzig 1931; transl. E.W. Dickes as *Sociology of Literary Taste* London 1944.

George Steiner "George Lukács and his devil's pact" (1960) and "Literature and post-history: in honour of George Lukács" (1965) in his *Language and Silence* London 1967.
Bernice Slote ed. *Literature and Society* Lincoln Nebraska 1964.
George Thomson *Aeschylus and Athens: a study of the social origins of drama* London 1941.
George Thomson *Marxism and Poetry* New York 1946.
Ian Watt *The Rise of the Novel* Berkeley 1957.
Réné Wellek and Austin Warren "The Function of Literature" in *Theory of Literature* New York 1949.
Raymond Williams *Culture and Society, 1780–1950* London 1958.

A useful selection from the reports of the early British social explorers (see Edward Shils *On the Eve* p. 239), is conveniently to be found in *Into Unknown England 1866–1913* ed. Peter Keating Manchester and London 1976. There is a bibliography of primary and secondary works.

PETER DAVISON

Literary Taste, Culture and Mass Communication

Sociology and Cultural Studies: Some Problems
Rolf Meyersohn

from

Occasional Papers no. 5, Birmingham University
Centre for Contemporary Cultural Studies, 1969.

In the development of empirical sociology, its practitioners have inadvertently adopted a view of society which, even though it helped generate and verify some sociological theories about a society, has relied on a conception of its members as respondents. Human beings, adult and adolescent, bright and stupid, rich and poor (often selected on those criteria) have been asked to answer questions by professional question-askers, called interviewers, who relied on a respondent's essential good nature, his interest in the idea of progress, occasionally his desire to earn a little money or receive a reward for being a patient answerer. The questions and answers have been used to make statements about the world. Apart from the question of whether the respondents were telling the truth — a question that turned out on the whole not to be worth asking, for the respondents did by and large tell the truth — the problem arose whether the interview situation imposed a view of the world that distorted, not the truth as such, but the setting in which the truth was spoken. For sociologists, who have at least as much sensitivity to the concept of role as actors, realized that interviewers and respondents were playing roles that changed the situation in such a way that many kinds of questions were answered even if truthfully, then truthfully only within the role setting in which they were asked. As respondents they told the truth, but whether this truth held for humans as observers, as participants, as citizens, as workers, could not be determined. Humans when interviewed behave as respondents, and it has been in this context that questions are answered. To say this is not to say that the material collected has not been valuable or does not continue to be valuable. But it has limits, as does every method.

Over the course of time all kinds of methods have been developed that have done more than involve people as respondents — and also less. In recent years there has been explicit attention paid to so-called "unobtrusive measures", and the drawing of inferences from what can be observed, overheard, estimated, without actually asking the objects of this attention any questions. Perhaps the classic example is Robert Lynd, wandering around Muncie, Indiana, early in the morning and simply noting that in working-class areas the lights in houses went on about an hour earlier than in middle-class areas.[2] Gene Webb, more modern than Lynd, provides far sneakier examples of unobtrusive measures in his book of that name.[3] The philosophy of science underlying this kind of research is that society as such is a kind of laboratory where, if eyes, ears, cameras and tape recorders are kept open, one can pick up clues to reality, undistorted by the intervention of new roles such as respondent and interviewer.

Anthropologists, however, have never thought that their subjects would be merely respondents. They were seen as informants or observers, and the anthropologist, although he remained an outsider, nonetheless became a kind of participant, or participant-observer. That the anthropologist changed something about the quality of life in his village was never doubted; indeed the anthropologist hoped that through the change created by his presence he might learn something about the society (even if on occasion he did not live to tell the tale — if the natives had interesting if extreme reactions to strangers).

Recently anthropologists have begun to use some of the interviewing techniques that sociologists had employed (I am thinking of some of the work of Bernard Cohen of the University of Chicago who has interviewed Indian villagers and their families in an effort to determine the processes of industrialization; or of Manning Nash who has studied some similar problems in Mexico); sociologists have increasingly used participant observation techniques, and by now the tools whereby the different social scientists gather their data are far less clearly associated with any particular discipline than had been true in the past; the questionnaire survey is by now perhaps more common in political science — where it was discovered only recently — than in any other social science.

Yet the notion persists that interview situations provide the most objective climate — demographers, social scientists who work with Census material, are apt to think their data are "hard", largely because they were obtained in larger number. Probably the interview situation is still the most popular tool of the sociologist. In Holland or Finland or Germany, and in most American universities, a "methods" course in sociology continues to train students in the mysteries of questionnaire building, interviewing, coding and analysis. Yet practitioners rely on all kinds of other ways of testing and generating sociological hypotheses, concepts and theories. These different conceptions of society as consisting of respondents, of informants, of participant observers co-exist nonetheless. Out of each of them there has been built up some knowledge of our world, of the nature of society.

Yet the social world consists of more than its inhabitants, and society of more than the groups constituting it. Humans leave traces behind as they pursue their work, their play, their lives. These material traces of humanity are most easily made real for inquiries into the past; archaeology, paleontology, branches of history are indisputable domains of social science, even if in the one case the data seem so hard that its practitioners are often seen as natural scientists, in the other so soft that they are considered members of the humanities (historians had for some time been able to choose their citizenship in the one or the other domain). The traces left by our contemporaries are so vast that no amount of ordering can group them into proper categories. Yet the word culture is used to describe them, and cultural analysis attempts to interpret their meanings.

Most sociologists do cultural analysis of one sort or another. Peter Blau looked at the records kept by unemployment insurance supervisors to compare work in various organizational arrangements;[4] Coleman, Katz, and Menzel looked at pharmaceutical prescription records of the physicians in Peoria, Illinois to verify the earliest date of introduction of a new drug.[5] These are primitive examples. Records kept for one purpose or another, indeed the essential documents recording the transactions between physician, patient, and pharmacist, or between the clerk, his supervisor and his client, are rather uninteresting cultural analysis because they are so unambiguously instrumental; they leave little room for expression of human qualities. One prescription looks like another, even if one doctor's handwriting is less legible than another's. When James Coleman examined the senior-year books of the ten high schools he studied, the cultural analysis was less primitive, for he used these books to "get a feel" for the cultural climate of these schools.[6] What kinds of persons were picked as class president, what was mentioned about them, what sorts of emphasis was placed on academic achievement as against athletic prowess as against social success and glamour? The cultural analysis was limited to be sure, to helping him become more sensitized to the places he was about to study directly.

The kind of cultural analysis conducted with pharmaceutical prescriptions or high school year-books is limited too, because the domain is clearly restricted to a single institutional framework. Prescriptions are easily analysable and their meaning grasped because it is known in advance why they were written, for whom, and for what purpose; the institutional framework consisted of distinct and unambiguous roles, pharmacist, physician, patient. No difficulty here in establishing audiences, or representativeness, and the question of symptomatics was strictly medical. The high school year-books, too, are written within and for a self-contained world.

I think, by the way, that cultural analysis, the techniques of critical reading, have not sufficiently explored these simpler tasks; if only to develop the techniques, the analysis of documents, of cultural traces, in situations where the other elements are very clearly understood, helps beginners — that is, us — to comprehend and validate what we read.

Cultural analysis, in the sense in which I have been using it, relies on the assumption that the documents examined are in some direct or indirect way related to the social structure in which the documents occur; their analysis is designed to help illuminate that social structure. Because this use of cultural materials regards them as a source for data, the literary or artistic merits of the documents are slighted, for these belong to another domain, which here would be regarded as irrelevant. To use an analogy: in his analysis of hysteria, Freud used case material from a young woman; she might have been very beautiful or might have expressed herself magnificently in describing her free-associations; but these aspects were not relevant to the symptomatology. To cite a fellow sociologist, Sanford Dornbush: "The artistic act is sui generis, but that does not preclude the meaningful search for its context. Understanding about light rays and prisms does not make the sunrise less beautiful."[7] There are two implications in this use of cultural material, even literature, which must be explored. First the very difficult notion that great literature might be less useful than kitsch or at least no more useful. The high school year-book written by seniors from a small town in southern Illinois, still semi-literate, was as useful to Coleman as the one written by seniors from a snappy upper-middle class suburb of Chicago. It may ultimately be true that "a good writer can give us a sense of the formative but largely submerged currents in an age's life,"[8] but sociologists are not ready to deal with the structure of society on this level. In using cultural material as data to characterise aspects of the social structure, sociologists select, not on the basis of literary or artistic merit, but on the basis of relevance to that structure. Hence the intrinsic power, "their power as works of literature"[9] is ignored. Weber's use of Ben Franklin's *Autobiography* is, as Alan Shuttleworth points out,[10] extreme-ly selective.

A second implication in using literature as cultural material is that once the literary and artistic merit is ignored, and the criterion of relevance for the theoretical framework of the inquiry is taken seriously, then the class of data to which these documents belong looks very different from the way it looks to the literary student. Unlikes are lumped together, and the sociologist rummages through a variety of materials that the purist would regard as unrelated; indeed, their lumping might be regarded as sacrilege. It is often for this reason that sociologists are regarded as illiterate. They ignore the social distance between literature and other writing.

So far I have stressed the importance of considering cultural materials, literature and other data, in terms of the ways in which they can and have been used to illuminate a variety of social structures. The efforts to use literature to characterize society, as mass society, as alienating society, as post-industrial society, have not been altogether successful, because they have been premature in their efforts. That majestic example of a successful content analysis, *The Protestant Ethic, and The Spirit of Capitalism,* was also, after all, as Merton said "a prime example of theorizing in the middle range; it deals with a severely delimited problem — one that happens to be exemplified in a particular historical epoch with implications for other societies and other times; it employs a limited theory about the ways in which religious commitment and economic behaviour are connected; and it contributes to a somewhat more general theory of the modes of interdependence between social institutions"[11] (p.63)

Even when whole epochs are characterized, the data we need from literature are limited; were we to test Marx's proposition that "the end of an epoch repeats in comical form what at the beginning is enacted as hectic tragedy . . . that mankind could bid farewell to outlived forms not with nostalgia but with gaiety"[12], how simple-minded our classification scheme for literature need be! Perhaps the problem we have is that for the present sociology is not prepared to use all the data that literature can represent and can offer. Our conception of the world, and our ways of studying the world are limited. We try to be scientific and empirical, to add to the knowledge that exists, and to test our hypotheses logically and rationally. The subject has been sub-divided, in part by problem areas, such as delinquency, old age, and medical sociology, in part by processes, such as social stratification, bureaucracy, and social organization. Either way, the modes of research and of confirmation of findings rely on data that appear to be more direct than cultural analysis of literary materials. Possibly, there will be, to begin with, more and more utilization of cultural analysis in the way that Coleman or Blau has proceeded.

For most sociologists society does not constitute a topic of daily concern. Except for a few sociologists or a few occasions, most of the attention is paid to the study of component parts which are not well understood. It is therefore awkward to talk about society as it relates to some other aspect of life, let us say, literature. On this grand level very few statements of meaning or worth can be made.

The sociological techniques that have emerged, even under renewed and consistent attack, are designed for the examination of entities smaller than "society", for society as such cannot be studied and perhaps not even discussed meaningfully. Probably the most successful books in sociology are those that talk about society at the end and not the beginning of the inquiry. That model both for my colleagues here at the Centre as well as for my colleagues in sociology, Weber's *Protestant Ethic,* concerns itself with certain problems in a certain period of time in a certain kind of society, problems having to do with the relationship between two component parts of that society, the structure of ideas and the structure of interests. Weber did not talk about society; he talked about widely distributed religious beliefs among one emerging segment of society.

The point is important because of our tendency to think that we make hypotheses about society or rather that we take them seriously. We do not. We make hypotheses about far more limited aspects of society. We don't attempt to discuss society as such. When sociologists consider the problem of confronting data, of making and testing hypotheses, they have already assigned themselves a limited task, limited to examining certain relationships under certain conditions. It is thus not relevant to consider that sociologists are interested in society; they are, as a physicist is interested in nature or a literary critic in literature; his daily bread is earned with smaller pieces. Dahrendorf, in attacking grand theory-making in the social systems approach, wrote: "It is certainly true that physics deals with nature, and yet physicists would hardly see an advance in calling nature a system and trying to analyze it as such."[13]

This is not the occasion to review the debate between grand

theorists and theorists of the middle-range. If the facts of 20th-century sociology throughout the world are taken to define the problem, then certainly middle-range sociology has become the dominant mode, the distinguishing feature of current sociology. Like literary criticism, in which there is a kind of "random access"[14] to works written since Homer, grand theory can confirm itself by writings of Greek philosophy or medieval scholasticists as easily as with writings of Weber or Hegel. Much of sociology has developed without such grand theory-making. In part this has happened because there is too much to do without reading the "speculators", in part because the compelling nature of social life leads sociologists to pursue what they are already acquainted with, for acquaintance leads to a greater feeling of relative ignorance.

Cultural studies, however, also include a second domain; this might be called the sociology of culture, of sociology, of knowledge. If prescriptions are used by doctors for patients, what are works of fiction used for, or sociological studies? This question is altogether different from the one asked earlier. The material is used not to characterize a particular social structure, but to comprehend the relationship between the documents, their authors, and their publics; no propositions about society as a whole are tested, but rather an unfolding of the communication and interaction processes is attempted. The process is not used as illustration, as indication of the state of the world, but as a province of inquiry for its own sake, because it is a vital kind of communication. This process may be what Ian Watt meant when he described as one category of inquiry in the relationship between literature and society that of studying the social functions of literature, how far literary values correspond to social values.[15]

The social structure is here seen as including the writer and the written documents. It is not a trace left by humans engaged in other enterprises, but is deliberate. Hence the novel is to be taken seriously as a novel and the plight of the novelist is taken seriously as a real problem. One would have to consider such statements as Roland Barthes': "In front of the virgin sheet of paper, at the moment of choosing the words which must frankly signify his place in History, and testify that he assumes its data, he (the writer) observes a tragic disparity between what he does and what he sees . . . Writing . . . is a blind alley because society itself is a blind alley . . . Literature becomes the Utopia of language".[16]

Such a "job description" becomes documentation to be examined in an institutional analysis of the arts. Such analysis needs to be carried out not only for the sociology of literature, music and the mass media, but for sociology itself — sociology after all is also comprised of a body of written works. John Rex has attempted a beginning along these lines:

> In the main the problems investigated by sociologists are those which have arisen in the course of philanthropic work or in the struggle for some social reform. In England, for example, there are many who would regard Charles Booth's studies of the incidency of poverty among different groups in London as the starting point of empirical social investigation in their society. The assumption behind this appears to be that when argument occurs about social reform, the task of the sociologist is to collect the objective facts. But however valuable the collection of such information may be from a moral point of view, it is still necessary to ask whether it is at all relevant to sociology, i.e., whether it tells us anything about the *nature* of "society", or about the *social relations* which exist between men . . . The mere fact of differing income levels does not tell us in what sense those on the same level constitute groups, or whether any such groups can be thought of as constituting a "class structure".

> It may however be argued that work of this kind is sociologically relevant in three ways. Firstly, it may be claimed that the facts of differential income distribution and differential life-chances are themselves important facts about the class-system. Secondly, it may be said

that these facts are facts about the relation between our economic system and family and community life. Thirdly, in showing that the facts were at variance with commonly-accepted myths, the social investigators could claim to have drawn attention to an important set of facts in the sociology of knowledge. . . . it is true that knowledge of a man's income enables us . . . to know what he may expect of other people in a market situation. But even here everything depends upon our knowledge of the social significance of money . . . But facts about income distribution (taken as) facts about the class system (means) that possession of a certain income assigns a man a place not so much in a market situation as in some sort of status-hierarchy. . . . The sociological significance of the research is thought to lie not in the facts taken in themselves but in the implications we are supposed to read into them. The difficulty is that these implications are by no means unambiguous.[17]

Although the ultimate goal of the social sciences is the study of society, the division of labour that has taken place within this set of disciplines has led to many different sub-goals. Indeed, the "harder" the discipline, the further removed it is from this ultimate goal. Experimental social psychologists are interested in exposing the processes of attitude formation, for example. Their work keeps them too busy to think about the connection with the study of society that their findings might produce. Political sociologists are interested in the relationship between certain kinds of political beliefs and social action, as for example, voting behaviour. Is that a direct confrontation with the study of society? No. The confrontation is indirect. On the one hand, social scientists are interested in uniformities of behaviour in which a particular society and its norms, values, structure, might be seen as no more than "environmental influence"; on the other hand, social scientists are studying behaviour within a particular society in which they take for granted the state of the world as it is.

But there are of course social scientists whose main interest is the study of society. They attempt to make statements that describe particular societies and compare them to other societies, or the past of the particular society. Yet even here, the study of society is limited to those aspects that social theorists consider relevant to their theories. There seems to be a general feeling among theorists that the "explanation" of particular societies is less important than the revelation of certain processes which may only be a small aspect of the whole society's operation. In recent years sociological theorists have been concerned with social stratification, for example. Yet this realm of social life is hardly the only important realm that characterizes society. If that is true, do social scientists really study the nature of society? Yes, but only if one believes that the nature of society is revealed — partially, at least — by the segments that happen to be the focus of study.

Perhaps a better answer is that those social scientists who are explicitly interested in the study of societies do study society. In that sense, there is no difference between social scientists and literary scholars. The difference comes rather in the modes by which society is revealed to them. There is no doubt that social scientists are more concerned with a larger number of sub-groups, or sub-systems, the literary scholars with the "critical incident"; the one makes more of rules, the other of the exceptions. Whereas social scientists rely on the interplay between hypotheses and data to expose varieties of patterns within a society, the literary scholar relies more on the *apercu,* the salient observation, to expose these patterns. But no work of fiction reveals processes of society directly. These processes are revealed only in *interpretations* of the work of fiction; interpretations that might turn the work of fiction into a better expose of society than any work of social science could be. Yet fiction, like fact, does not speak for itself in conversations about society. It has to be discovered and interpreted. Hence it is the literary critic not the creator of fiction who acts like the social scientist. The writer of fiction, like any other human being, organizes his own experience, including his fantasies, into conscious thought. He may do it better, he may create a work of art; but it is only in its interpretation that the nature of society is revealed. If the writer of fiction had wanted to expose society directly, he would not have written fiction.

I think much of the Centre's work rests on the premise and promise that the interconnections between literature and the popular arts and society can be established. I consider this an eminently worthwhile goal, and a great ideal. To be sure when idealism becomes institutionalized, there are always social costs. These were well described by Richard Hoggart's discussion of the reception of the Pilkington Report;[18] not only those of the Commission's own idealism, those of a reasoned approach to a social institution, but also the social costs of the BBC's idealism, of a broadcast service that is founded on pluralistic rationalities. The institutionalization creates costs in part because what emerges as a creative force becomes, necessarily, routine; because what begins small grows large, and size, as we all know, has its own consequences; and finally, because things never work out as planned. Such social costs could as well be applied to the Centre and to cultural studies. But as with the BBC and with the Pilkington Report, the costs are meaningful precisely because the credit is good.

Postscript

Several further ideas have emerged as a result of the discussion following the presentation of the paper. These are presented here without acknowledgement to the particular Seminar member who might have inspired them; this is not rudeness but an effort to protect the audience from misrepresentation.

(1) *The novelist as theorist.* What distinguishes great from ordinary literature is not the quality of data but the "theory" of society underlying the work. The data — the record of interaction, the description of family life, the inventory of objects, the leisure activities, the ways in which a servant girl might spend stolen money — such records might be found anywhere. Some might be recorded more faithfully by great novelists. They are invaluable in providing a record of the times; though fictional, they serve as data much as interview data, or historical documents serve. They can be used as an aid in the formulation of a theory about an age or a period. This, however, is only one use of Literature as a resource for cultural analysis. Another, richer use is in the *theory* of society revealed in Literature. This theory of society is translated into concrete episodes by the novelist; whereas for sociologists, society is something abstract, a generalized concept of one sort or another (see below for an elaboration of this point) for the novelist, society exists in the social actions of the characters created. They embody the novelist's conception or theory of society. The theory may be unconscious or it may be very deliberate; it is not really important which it is. If the novel is Literature, then the coherence and "concentration of meaning" contained within it permits the reader to be able to draw it out. The novel can therefore be treated as containing a theory of society, and the "data" — that is, the novel on one level — can be used to build this theory. The structure of the society, the social actions of the individuals, the links between these two can all be drawn out. This then is another use of literature.

(2) *The literary critic as sociological theorist.* The kind of work that this kind of drawing out entails can best be done by

a literary critic. Clearly a great deal of digging is needed for the novel must be read in order to find out about society, that is, to comprehend the novel's theory of society. This is not the natural way to read the novel, for what is involved is the total concentration on this problem to the exclusion of others. This difficulty was described by Leavis:

> "There seems to be a general view that anyone can read a novel; and the uses commonly made of novels as evidence, sociological or other would seem to illustrate that view. Actually, to use as evidence or illustration the kinds of novel that are most significant and have most to offer requires an uncommon skill, the product of a kind of training that few readers submit themselves to. For instance, the sociologist can't learn what Jane Austen has to teach about the part played by the family in the life, individual and social, of her time, so different in this respect from ours, without being, in reading her, a much more intelligent critic than any professional authority he is likely to have gone to for guidance. Nor, without being an original critic, adverted and sensitized by experience and the habit of critical analysis, can the social psychologist learn what Conrad has to teach about the social nature of the individual's 'reality'. "
> (Scrutiny, XII, p.11.)[19]

The important point is that the novel does not speak for itself. When reading Jane Austen, one does not automatically make generalizations about "the part played by the family in the life of her time" — only if this area of interest is specified beforehand, does this theme emerge. It may even be that the novelist says in a preface that the novel is about this theme; yet only the critic can determine the validity of the statement, since the novel, as a work of fiction is not *about* anything, at least not in the way that a research study is "about" something; it tells a story. It does not deal with problems in the way that a social science investigation deals with problems. The critic's task, in the enterprise described here, is to translate the novel from a tale about people into a social document and to make the novelist into a social theorist. In this translation, the critic introduces abstractions, concepts that generalize and categorize. Here the link between literary criticism and sociology becomes most apparent, for the concepts introduced are often identical.

(3) *Abstraction in sociology.* Although sociologists would agree that they are essentially interested in studying the relationship between man and society, there is considerable disagreement about the aspects of man that really interest them. Many things human are, if not alien, then at least irrelevant to them; to be relevant, the things human must be interpersonal and they must be capable of being related to a larger realm, sometimes known as "social system", "social structure", "social institution", etc. The relationship between the interpersonal and this larger realm must be susceptible to specification. For this reason certain concepts are introduced that specify this connection; most prominent among them is the concept of social role. Writes Dahrendorf, "At the point where individual and society intersect stands *homo sociologicus,* man as the bearer of socially predetermined roles. To a sociologist the individual *is* his social roles, but these roles, for their part, are the vexatious fact of society. In solving its problems, sociology necessarily takes social roles as its elements of analysis; its subject matter is the structure of social roles."[20] The introduction of a broad linking concept, such as role, enables the sociologist to bring in additional concepts that specify the rules by which these roles are played; an example is the concept of *norms.* The particular words employed here are not necessarily those used by all sociologists, but the over-all strategy outlined is probably fairly accurate. It is of course impossible to generalize about the ways in which sociologists move among the three basic areas of focus, that is, (a) the individual, (b) the society, and (c) the link between them. Some sociologists are mainly concerned with the relationship between (a) and (b), others between (b) and (c); some attempt to remain on the level of social structure and appear to forget about individuals, even the partial individuals described above. The point is that abstractions such as these provide sociologists with the framework for the analysis of society and societies.

REFERENCES

1. Paper presented at Graduate Seminar, Centre for Contemporary Cultural Studies, University of Birmingham, May 14, 1968.

2. *Middletown* (New York: Harcourt Brace, 1929).

3. Gene Webb et al., *Unobtrusive Measures; Nonreactive Research in the Social Sciences.* (Chicago: Rand McNally, 1967).

4. Peter M. Blau, *The Dynamics of Bureaucracy* (Chicago: University of Chicago Press, 1955).

5. James Coleman, Elihu Katz, and Herbert Menzel, *Medical Innovation* (Indianapolis: Bobbs-Merrill, 1966).

6. This procedure was not reported. See James S. Coleman, *Adolescent Society* (New York: Free Press, 1961) for account of findings of this study.

7. "Content and Method in the study of the Higher Arts," in Robert N. Wilson, editor, *The Arts in Society* (Englewood Cliffs, N. J.: Prentice-Hall, 1964), pp. 365-72, at 366.

8. Richard Hoggart, "Literature and Society", *American Scholar,* 1966, 35, 277-89, at 279.

9. *Ibid.,* p. 277. Richard Hoggart argues convincingly that good literature provides an insight into an age not gained through other means, and that social science techniques cannot recreate the complexity of "what an unskilled labourer feels on his pulses every day of the week". (Ibid., p. 278). I am arguing that social science is attempting to organize insights into structures that go beyond those of the individual, even the artist and writer, and hence relies on literature as a source of information, a record of transactions between different members of society. The complex feelings of even an unskilled labourer are not simulated in such an effort, but are subsumed.

10. He writes: "He (Max Weber) does not rest content with pointing to those features of the text (of Franklin's Autobiography) which concern him. He does not allow the text to speak for itself (as Leavis, at a certain point, would): he insists on speaking for the text. He produces his own explicit, summary characterization of the qualities in Franklin's writing which interest him, and from that point on the text is of no further interest." "Max Weber and the 'Cultural Sciences'," *CCCS,* Occasional Papers No. 2, p. 27.

11. Robert K. Merton, "On Sociological Theories of the Middle Range", in his *On Theoretical Sociology* (New York: Free Press, 1967), pp. 39-72, at p. 63.

12. Cited in Hans Gerth and C. Wright Mills, *Character and Social Structure,* (London: Routledge & Kegan Paul, 1954), p. 57.

13. "Out of Utopia: Toward a Reorientation of Sociological Analysis", American Journal of Sociology, 1958, 64, 115-127; reprinted in Ralf Dahrendorf, *Essays in the Theory of Society* (London: Routledge & Kegan Paul, 1968), pp. 107-128, at 118).

14. The image of random access is derived from Derek Price who discussed the difference between work in the humanities and sciences in terms of the importance that first-hand acquaintance with the "classics" plays. "The cumulating structure of science has a texture full of short-range connections like knitting, whereas the texture of a humanistic field of scholarship is much more of a random network with any point being just as likely to be connected with any other." "The scientific foundations of science policy", *Nature,* April 17, 1965, 206, 233-8, cited in Merton, *op. cit.,* p. 27. Clearly, social science is somewhere in between, as suggested by the patterns of citations in the three domains. In the physical sciences, represented by such journals as *The Physical Review* and the *Astro-*

physical Journal some 60% to 70% of the citations refer to publications appearing within the preceding five years. In the humanities, represented by such journals as the *American Historical Review, Art Bulletin,* and the *Journal of Aesthetics and Art Criticism,* the corresponding figures range from 10% to 20%. In between are the social sciences, represented by such journals as the *American Sociological Review,* the *American Journal of Sociology,* and the *British Journal of Psychology,* where from 30% to 50% of the citations refer to publications of the preceding five years. *Ibid.,* p. 29.

15. "Literature and Society", in Robert Wilson, *op. cit.,* pp. 300-314.

16. Roland Barthes, *Writing Degree Zero,* translated by Annette Lavers and Colin Smith (London: Jonathan Cape, 1967) pp. 92, 93, 94.

17. John Rex, *Key Problems of Sociological Theory* (London: Routledge & Kegan Paul, 1961) pp. 28 ff.

18. See Richard Hoggart, "The Difficulties of Democratic Debate", pp. 197-212.

19. F. R. Leavis, "Literature and Society", *Scrutiny,* 1943, 12, 11.

20. Ralf Dahrendorf, "Homo Sociologicus: On the History, Significance, and Limits of the Category of Social Role", in his *Essays in the Theory of Society,* (London: Routledge & Kegan Paul, 1968) pp. 19-87, at 24-25.

Literature and Society
René Wellek and Austin Warren

from

Theory of Literature by René Wellek and Austin Warren.
Jonathan Cape, London, 1949.

LITERATURE AND SOCIETY

*

LITERATURE is a social institution, using as its medium language, a social creation. Such traditional literary devices as symbolism and metre are social in their very nature. They are conventions and norms which could have arisen only in society. But, furthermore, literature 'represents' 'life'; and 'life' is, in large measure, a social reality, even though the natural world and the inner or subjective world of the individual have also been objects of literary 'imitation'. The poet himself is a member of society, possessed of a specific social status: he receives some degree of social recognition and reward; he addresses an audience, however hypothetical. Indeed, literature has usually arisen in close connexion with particular social institutions; and in primitive society we may even be unable to distinguish poetry from ritual, magic, work, or play. Literature has also a social function, or 'use', which cannot be purely individual. Thus a large majority of the questions raised by literary study are, at least ultimately or by implication, social questions: questions of tradition and convention, norms and genres, symbols and myths. With Tomars, one can formulate:

> Esthetic institutions are not based upon social institutions: they are not even part of social institutions: they are social institutions of one type and intimately interconnected with those others.[1]

Usually, however, the inquiry concerning 'literature and society' is put more narrowly and externally. Questions are asked about the relations of literature to a given social situation, to an economic, social, and political system. Attempts are made to describe and define the influence of society on literature and to prescribe and judge the position of literature in society. This sociological approach to literature is particularly cultivated by those who profess a specific social philosophy. Marxist critics not only study these relations between literature and society, but also have their clearly defined conception of what these relations should be, both in our present society and in a future 'classless' society. They practise evaluative, 'judicial' criticism, based on non-literary political and ethical criteria. They tell us not only what were and are the social relations and implications of an author's work but what they should have been or ought to be.[2] They are not only students of literature and society but prophets of the future, monitors, propagandists; and they have difficulty in keeping these two functions separate.

The relation between literature and society is usually discussed by starting with the phrase, derived from De Bonald, that 'literature is an expression of society'. But what does this axiom mean? If it assumes that literature, at any given time, mirrors the current social situation 'correctly', it is false; it is commonplace, trite, and vague if it means only that literature depicts some aspects of social reality.[3] To say that literature mirrors or expresses life is even more ambiguous. A writer inevitably expresses his experience and total conception of life; but it would be manifestly untrue to say that he expresses the whole of life – or even the whole life of a given time – completely and exhaustively. It is a specific evaluative criterion to say that an author should express the life of his own time fully, that he should be 'representative' of his age and society. Besides, of course, the terms 'fully' and 'representative' require much interpretation: in most social criticism they seem to mean that an author should be aware of specific social situations, e.g. of the plight of the proletariat, or even that he should share a specific attitude and ideology of the critic.

In Hegelian criticism and in that of Taine, historical or social greatness is simply equated with artistic greatness. The artist conveys truth and, necessarily, also historical and social truths. Works of art furnish 'documents *because* they are monuments'.[4] A harmony between genius and age is postulated. 'Representativeness', 'social truth', is, by definition, both a result and cause of artistic value. Mediocre, average works of art, though they may seem to a modern sociologist better social documents, are to Taine unexpressive and hence unrepresentative. Literature is really not a reflection of the social process, but the essence, the abridgement and summary of all history.

But it seems best to postpone the problem of evaluative criticism till we have disengaged the actual relations between literature and society. These descriptive (as distinct from normative) relations admit of rather ready classification.

First, there is the sociology of the writer and the profession and institutions of literature, the whole question of the economic basis of literary production, the social provenance and status of the writer, his social ideology, which may find expression in extra-literary pronouncements and activities. Then there is the problem of the social content, the implications and social purpose of the works of literature themselves. Lastly, there are the problems of the audience and the actual social influence of literature. The question how far literature is actually determined by or dependent on its social setting, on social change and development, is one which, in one way or another, will enter into all the three divisions of our problem: the sociology of the writer, the social content of the works themselves, and the influence of literature on society. We shall have to decide what is meant by dependence or causation; and ultimately we shall arrive at the problem of cultural integration and specifically at how our own culture is integrated.

Since every writer is a member of society, he can be studied as a social being. Though his biography is the main source, such a study can easily widen into one of the whole milieu from which he came and in which he lived. It will be possible to accumulate information about the social provenance, the family background, the economic position of writers. We can show what was the exact share of aristocrats, bourgeois, and proletarians in the history of literature; for example, we can demonstrate the predominant share which the children of the professional and commercial classes take in the production of American literature.[5] Statistics can establish that, in modern Europe, literature recruited its practitioners largely from the middle classes, since aristocracy was preoccupied with the pursuit of glory or leisure while the lower classes had little opportunity for education. In England, this generalization holds good only with large reservations. The sons of peasants and workmen appear infrequently in older English literature: exceptions such as Burns and Carlyle are partly explicable by reference to the democratic Scottish school system. The role of the aristocracy in English literature was uncommonly great – partly because it was less cut off from the professional classes than in other countries, where there was no primogeniture. But, with a few exceptions, all modern Russian writers before Goncharov and Chekhov were aristocratic in origin. Even Dostoyevsky was technically a nobleman, though his father, a doctor in a Moscow Hospital for the Poor, acquired land and serfs only late in his life.

It is easy enough to collect such data but harder to interpret them. Does social provenance prescribe social ideology and allegiance? The cases of Shelley, Carlyle, and Tolstoy are obvious examples of such 'treason' to one's class. Outside of Russia, most Communist writers are not proletarian in origin. Soviet and other Marxist critics have carried out extensive investigations to ascertain precisely both the exact social provenance and the social allegiance of Russian writers. Thus P. N. Sakulin bases his treatment of recent Russian literature on careful distinctions between the respective literatures of the peasants, the small *bourgeoisie*, the democratic intelligentsia, the *déclassé* intelligentsia, the *bourgeoisie*, the aristocracy, and the revolutionary proletariat.[6] In the study of older literature, Russian scholars attempt elaborate distinctions between the many groups and sub-groups of the Russian aristocracy to whom Pushkin and Gogol, Turgenev and Tolstoy may be shown to have belonged by virtue of their inherited wealth and early associations.[7] But it is difficult to prove that Pushkin represented the interests of the impoverished landed nobility and Gogol those of the Ukrainian small landholder; such a conclusion is indeed disproved by the general ideology of their works and by the appeal the works have made beyond the confines of a group, a class, and a time.[8]

The social origins of a writer play only a minor part in the questions raised by his social status, allegiance, and ideology; for writers, it is clear, have often put themselves at the service of another class. Most court poetry was written by men who, though born in lower estate, adopted the ideology and taste of their patrons.

The social allegiance, attitude, and ideology of a writer can be studied not only in his writings but also, frequently, in biographical extra-literary documents. The writer has been a citizen, has pronounced on questions of social and political importance, has taken part in the issues of his time.

Much work has been done upon political and social views of individual writers; and in recent times more and more attention has been devoted to the economic implications of these views. Thus L. C. Knights, arguing that Ben Jonson's economic attitude was profoundly medieval, shows how, like several of his fellow dramatists, he satirized the rising class of usurers, monopolists, speculators, and 'undertakers'.[9] Many works of literature – e.g. the 'histories' of Shakespeare and Swift's *Gulliver's Travels* – have been reinterpreted in close relation to the political context of the time.[10] Pronouncements, decisions, and activities should never be confused with the actual social implications of a writer's works. Balzac is a striking example of the possible division; for, though his professed sympathies were all with the old order, the aristocracy, and the Church, his instinct and imagination were far more engaged by the acquisitive type, the speculator, the new strong man of the *bourgeoisie*. There may be a considerable difference between theory and practice, between profession of faith and creative ability.

These problems of social origins, allegiance, and ideology will, if systematized, lead to a sociology of the writer as a type, or as a type at a particular time and place. We can distinguish between writers according to their degree of integration into the social process. It is very close in popular literature, but may reach the extremes of dissociation, of 'social distance', in Bohemianism, with the *poète maudit* and the free creative genius. On the whole, in modern times, and in the West, the literary man seems to have lessened his class ties. There has arisen an 'intelligentsia', a comparatively independent in-between class of professionals. It will be the task of literary sociology to trace its exact social status, its degree of dependence on the ruling class, the exact economic source of its support, the prestige of the writer in each society.

The general outlines of this history are already fairly clear. In popular oral literature, we can study the role of the singer or narrator who will depend closely on the favour of his public: the bard in ancient Greece, the *scop* in Teutonic antiquity, the professional folk-tale teller in the Orient and Russia. In the ancient Greek city-state, the tragedians and such composers of dithyrambs and hymns as Pindar had their special, semi-religious position, one slowly becoming more secularized, as we can see when we compare Euripides with Aeschylus. Among the courts of the Roman Empire, we must think of Virgil, Horace, and Ovid as dependent on the bounty and goodwill of Augustus and Maecenas.

In the Middle Ages, there are the monk in his cell, the troubadour and *Minnesänger* at the court or baron's castle, the vagrant scholars on the roads. The writer is either a clerk or scholar, or he is a singer, an entertainer, a minstrel. But even kings like Wenceslaus II of Bohemia or James I of Scotland are now poets – amateurs, dilettantes. In the German *Meistersang*, artisans are organized in poetic guilds, burghers who practise poetry as a craft. With the Renaissance there arose a comparatively unattached group of writers, the Humanists, who wandered sometimes from country to country and offered their services to different patrons. Petrarch is the first modern *poeta laureatus*, possessed of a grandiose conception of his mission, while Aretino is the prototype of the literary journalist, living on blackmail, feared rather than honoured and respected.

In the large, the later history is the transition from support by noble or ignoble patrons to that afforded by publishers acting as predictive agents of the reading public. The system of aristocratic patronage was not, however, universal. The Church and, soon, the theatre supported special types of literature. In England, the patronage system apparently began to fail early in the eighteenth century. For a time, literature, deprived of its earlier benefactors and not yet fully supported by the reading public, was economically worse off. The early life of Dr Johnson in Grub Street and his defiance of Lord Chesterfield symbolize these changes. Yet a generation earlier, Pope was able to amass a fortune from his translation of Homer, lavishly subscribed by nobility and university men.

The great financial rewards, however, came only in the nineteenth century, when Scott and Byron wielded an enormous influence upon taste and public opinion. Voltaire and Goethe had vastly increased the prestige and independence of the writer on the Continent. The growth of the reading public, the founding of the great reviews like the *Edinburgh* and the *Quarterly*, made literature more and more the almost independent 'institution' which Prosper de Barante, writing in 1822, claimed it to have been in the eighteenth century.[11]

As Ashley Thorndike urged, the

outstanding characteristic of the printed matter of the nineteenth century is not its vulgarization, or its mediocrity, but rather its specialization. This printed matter is no longer addressed to a uniform or homogeneous public: it is divided up among many publics and consequently divided by many subjects, interests, and purposes.[12]

In *Fiction and the Reading Public*, which might well be considered a homily on Thorndike's text, Q. D. Leavis[13] points out that the eighteenth-century peasant who learned to read had to read what the gentry and the university men read; that the nineteenth-century readers, on the other hand, are properly spoken of not as 'the public' but as 'publics'. Our own time knows still further multiplications in publishing lists and magazine racks: there exist books for 9 to 10-year-olds, books for boys of high-school age, books for those who 'live alone'; trade journals, house organs, Sunday-school weeklies, Westerns, true-story romances. Publishers, magazines, and writers all specialize.

Thus a study of the economic basis of literature and of the social status of the writer is inextricably bound up with a study of the audience he addresses and upon which he is dependent financially.[14] Even the aristocratic patron is an audience and frequently an exacting audience, requiring not only personal adulation but also conformity to the conventions of his class. In even earlier society, in the group where folk-poetry flourishes, the dependence of the author on the audience is even greater: his work will not be transmitted unless it pleases immediately. The role of the audience in the theatre is, at least, as tangible. There have been even attempts to trace the changes in Shakespeare's periods and style to the change in the audience between the open-air Globe, on the South Bank, with its mixed audience, and Blackfriars, a closed hall frequented by the higher classes. It becomes harder to trace the specific relation between author and public at a later time when the reading public rapidly expands, becomes dispersed and heterogeneous, and when the relationships of author and public grow more indirect and oblique. The number of intermediaries between writers and the public increases. We can study the role of such social institutions and associations as the *salon*, the café, the club, the academy, and the university. We can trace the history of reviews and magazines as well as of publishing houses. The critic becomes an important middle-man; a group of connoisseurs, bibliophiles, and collectors may support certain kinds of literature; and the associations of literary men themselves may help to create a special public of writers or would-be writers. In America especially, women who (according to Veblen) provide vicarious leisure and consumption of the arts for the tired businessman have become active determinants of literary taste.

Still, the old patterns have not been completely replaced. All modern governments support and foster literature in various degrees; and patronage means, of course, control and supervision.[15] To overrate the conscious influence of the totalitarian state during the last decades would be difficult. It has been both negative – in suppression, book-burning, censorship, silencing, and reprimanding, and positive – in the encouragement of 'blood and soil' regionalism or Soviet 'socialist realism'. The fact that the state has been unsuccessful in creating a literature which, conforming to ideological specifications, is still great art, cannot refute the view that government regulation of literature is effective in offering the possibilities of creation to those who identify themselves voluntarily or reluctantly with the official prescriptions. Thus, in Soviet Russia, literature is at least in theory again becoming a communal art and the artist has again been integrated into society.

The graph of a book's success, survival, and recrudescence, or a writer's reputation and fame is mainly a social phenomenon. In part it belongs, of course, to literary 'history', since fame and reputation are measured by the actual influence of a writer on other writers, his general power of transforming and changing the literary tradition. In part, reputation is a matter of critical response: till now, it has been traced chiefly on the basis of more or less formal pronouncements assumed to be representative of a period's 'general reader'. Hence, while the whole question of the 'whirligig of taste' is 'social', it can be put on a more definitely sociological basis: detailed work can investigate the actual concordance between a work and the specific public which has made its success; evidence can be accumulated on editions, copies sold.

The stratification of every society is reflected in the stratification of its taste. While the norms of the upper classes usually descend to the lower, the movement is sometimes reversed: interest in folklore and primitive art is a case in point. There is no necessary concurrence between political and social advancement and aesthetic: leadership in literature had passed to the *bourgeoisie* long before political supremacy. Social stratification may be interfered with and even abrogated in questions of taste by differences of age and sex, by specific groups and associations. Fashion is also an important phenomenon in modern literature, for in a competitive fluid society, the norms of the upper classes, quickly imitated, are in constant need of replacement. Certainly the present rapid changes of taste seem to reflect the rapid social changes of the last decades and the general loose relation between artist and audience.

The modern writer's isolation from society, illustrated by Grub Street, Bohemia, Greenwich Village, the American expatriate, invites sociological study. A Russian socialist, Georgi Plekhanov, believes that the doctrine of 'art for art's sake' develops when artists feel a

hopeless contradiction between their aims and the aims of the society to which they belong. Artists must be very hostile to their society and they must see no hope of changing it.[16]

In his *Sociology of Literary Taste*, Levin L. Schücking has sketched out some of these problems; elsewhere, he has studied in detail the role of the family and women as an audience in the eighteenth century.[17]

Though much evidence has been accumulated, well-substantiated conclusions have rarely been drawn concerning the exact relations between the production of literature and its economic foundations, or even concerning the exact influence of the public on a writer. The relationship is obviously not one of mere dependence or of passive compliance with the prescriptions of patron or public. Writers may succeed in creating their own special public; indeed, as Coleridge knew, every new writer has to create the taste which will enjoy him.

The writer is not only influenced by society: he influences it. Art not merely reproduces life but also shapes it. People may model their lives upon the patterns of fictional heroes and heroines. They have made love, committed crimes and suicide according to the book, be it Goethe's *Sorrows of Werther* or Dumas's *Musketeers*. But can we precisely define the influence of a book on its readers? Will it ever be possible to describe the influence of satire? Did Addison really change the manners of his society or Dickens incite reforms of debtors' prisons, boys' schools, and poorhouses?[18] Was Harriet Beecher Stowe really the 'little woman who made the great war'? Has *Gone with the Wind* changed Northern readers' attitudes towards Mrs Stowe's war? How have Hemingway and Faulkner affected their readers? How great was the influence of literature on the rise of modern nationalism? Certainly the historical novels of Walter Scott in Scotland, of Henryk Sienkiewicz in Poland, of Alois Jirásek in Czechoslovakia, have done something very definite to increase national pride and a common memory of historical events.

We can hypothesize – plausibly, no doubt – that the young are more directly and powerfully influenced by their reading than the old, that inexperienced readers take literature more naïvely as transcript rather than interpretation of life, that those whose books are few take them in more utter seriousness than do wide and professional readers. Can we advance beyond such conjecture? Can we make use of questionnaires and any other mode of sociological inquiry? No exact objectivity is obtainable, for the attempt at case histories will depend upon the memories and the analytic powers of the interrogated, and their testimonies will need codification and evaluation by a fallible mind. But the question, 'How does literature affect its audience?' is an empirical one, to be answered, if at all, by the appeal to experience; and, since we are thinking of literature in the broadest sense, and society in the broadest, the appeal must be made to the experience not of the connoisseur alone but to that of the human race. We have scarcely begun to study such questions.[19]

Much the most common approach to the relations of literature and society is the study of works of literature as social documents, as assumed pictures of social reality. Nor can it be doubted that some kind of social picture can be abstracted from literature. Indeed, this has been one of the earliest uses to which literature has been put by systematic students. Thomas Warton, the first real historian of English poetry, argued that literature has the 'peculiar merit of faithfully recording the features of the times, and of preserving the most picturesque and expressive representation of manners';[20] and to him and many of his antiquarian successors, literature was primarily a treasury of costumes and customs, a source book for the history of civilization, especially of chivalry and its decline. As for modern readers, many of them derive their chief impressions of foreign societies from the reading of novels, from Sinclair Lewis and Galsworthy, from Balzac and Turgenev.

Used as a social document, literature can be made to yield the outlines of social history. Chaucer and Langland preserve two views of fourteenth-century society. The Prologue to the *Canterbury Tales* was early seen to offer an almost complete survey of social types. Shakespeare, in the *Merry Wives of Windsor*, Ben Jonson in several plays, and Thomas Deloney seem to tell us something about the Elizabethan middle class. Addison, Fielding, and Smollett depict the new *bourgeoisie* of the eighteenth century; Jane Austen, the country gentry and country parsons early in the nineteenth century; and Trollope, Thackeray, and Dickens, the Victorian world. At the turn of the century, Galsworthy shows us the English upper middle classes; Wells, the lower middle classes; Bennett, the provincial towns.

A similar series of social pictures could be assembled for American life from the novels of Harriet Beecher Stowe and Howells to those of Farrell and Steinbeck. The life of post-Restoration Paris and France seems preserved in the hundreds of characters moving through the pages of Balzac's *Human Comedy*; and Proust traced in endless detail the social stratifications of the decaying French aristocracy. The Russia of the nineteenth-century landowners appears in the novels of Turgenev and Tolstoy; we have glimpses of the merchant and the intellectual in Chekhov's stories and plays and of collectivized farmers in Sholokhov.

Examples could be multiplied indefinitely. One can assemble and exposit the 'world' of each, the part each gives to love and marriage, to business, to the professions, its delineation of clergymen, whether stupid or clever, saintly or hypocritical; or one can specialize upon Jane Austen's naval men, Proust's *arrivistes*, Howells's married women. This kind of specialization will offer us monographs on the 'Relation between Landlord and Tenant in Nineteenth-Century American Fiction', 'The Sailor in English Fiction and Drama', or 'Irish-Americans in Twentieth-Century Fiction'.

But such studies seem of little value so long as they take it for granted that literature is simply a mirror of life, a reproduction, and thus, obviously, a social document. Such studies make sense only if we know the artistic method of the novelist studied, and can say – not merely in general terms, but concretely – in what relation the picture stands to the social reality. Is it realistic by intention? Or is it, at certain points, satire, caricature, or romantic idealization? In an admirably clear-headed study of *Aristocracy and the Middle Classes in Germany*, Kohn-Bramstedt rightly cautions us:

Only a person who has a knowledge of the structure of a society from other sources than purely literary ones is able to find out if, and how far, certain social types and their behaviour are reproduced in the novel. . . . What is pure fancy, what realistic observation, and what only an expression of the desires of the author must be separated in each case in a subtle manner.[21]

Using Max Weber's conception of ideal 'social types', the same scholar studies such social phenomena as class hatred, the behaviour of the parvenu, snobbery, and the attitude towards the Jews; and he argues that such phenomena are not so much objective facts and behaviour patterns as they are complex attitudes, thus far better illustrated in fiction than elsewhere. Students of social attitudes and aspirations can use literary material, if they know how to interpret it properly. Indeed, for older periods, they will be forced to use literary or at least semi-literary material for want of evidence from the sociologists of the time: writers on politics, economics, and general public questions.

Heroes and heroines of fiction, villains and adventuresses, afford interesting indications of such social attitudes.[22] Such studies constantly lead into the history of ethical and religious ideas. We know the medieval status of the traitor and the medieval attitude towards usury, which, lingering on into the Renaissance, gives us Shylock and, later, Molière's *L'Avare*. To which 'deadly sin' have later centuries chiefly assigned the villain; and is his villainy conceived of in terms of personal or social morality? Is he, for example, artist at rape or embezzler of widows' bonds?

The classic case is that of Restoration English comedy. Was it simply a realm of cuckoldom, a fairyland of adulteries and mock marriages as Lamb believed? Or was it, as Macaulay would have us believe, a faithful picture of decadent, frivolous, and brutal aristocracy?[23] Or should we not rather, rejecting both alternatives, see what particular social group created this art for what audience? And should we not see whether it was a naturalistic or a stylized art? Should we not be mindful of satire and irony, self-ridicule and fantasy? Like all literature, these plays are not simply documents; they are plays with stock figures, stock situations, with stage marriages and stage conditions of marriage settlements. E. E. Stoll concludes his many arguments on these matters:

> Evidently this is not a 'real society', not a faithful picture even of the 'fashionable life': evidently it is not England, even 'under the Stuarts', whether since or before the Revolution or the Great Rebellion.[24]

Still, the salutary emphasis upon convention and tradition to be found in writing like Stoll's cannot completely discharge the relations between literature and society. Even the most abstruse allegory, the most unreal pastoral, the most outrageous farce can, properly interrogated, tell us something of the society of a time.

Literature occurs only in a social context, as part of a culture, in a milieu. Taine's famous triad of *race*, *milieu*, and *moment* has, in practice, led to an exclusive study of the milieu. Race is an unknown fixed integral with which Taine operates very loosely. It is often simply the assumed 'national character' or the English or French 'spirit'. *Moment* can be dissolved into the concept of milieu. A difference of time means simply a different setting, but the actual question of analysis arises only if we try to break up the term 'milieu'. The most immediate setting of a work of literature, we shall then recognize, is its linguistic and literary tradition, and this tradition in turn is encompassed by a general cultural 'climate'. Only far less directly can literature be connected with concrete economic, political, and social situations. Of course there are interrelationships between all spheres of human activities. Eventually we can establish some connexion between the modes of production and literature, since an economic system usually implies some system of power and must control the forms of family life. And the family plays an important role in education, in the concepts of sexuality and love, in the whole convention and tradition of human sentiment. Thus it is possible to link even lyric poetry with love conventions, religious preconceptions, and conceptions of nature. But these relationships may be devious and oblique.

It seems impossible, however, to accept a view constituting any particular human activity the 'starter' of all the others, whether it be the theory of Taine, who explains human creation by a combination of climatic, biological, and social factors, or that of Hegel and the Hegelians, who consider 'spirit' the only moving force in history, or that of the Marxists, who derive everything from the modes of production. No radical technological changes took place in the many centuries between the early Middle Ages and the rise of capitalism, while cultural life, and literature in particular, underwent most profound transformations. Nor does literature always show, at least immediately, much awareness of an epoch's technological changes: the Industrial Revolution penetrated English novels only in the forties of the nineteenth century (with Elizabeth Gaskell, Kingsley, and Charlotte Brontë), long after its symptoms were plainly visible to economists and social thinkers.

The social situation, one should admit, seems to determine the possibility of the realization of certain aesthetic values, but not the values themselves. We can determine in general outlines what art forms are possible in a given society and which are impossible, but it is not possible to predict that these art forms will actually come into existence. Many Marxists – and not Marxists only – attempt far too crude short cuts from economics to literature. For example, John Maynard Keynes, not an unliterary person, has ascribed the existence of Shakespeare to the fact that

we were just in a financial position to afford Shakespeare at the moment when he presented himself. Great writers flourished in the atmosphere of buoyancy, exhilaration, and the freedom of economic cares felt by the governing class, which is engendered by profit inflations.[25]

But profit inflations did not elicit great poets elsewhere – for instance, during the boom of the twenties in the United States – nor is this view of the optimistic Shakespeare quite beyond dispute. No more helpful is the opposite formula, devised by a Russian Marxist:

Shakespeare's tragic outlook on the world was consequential upon his being the dramatic expression of the feudal aristocracy, which in Elizabeth's day had lost their former dominant position.[26]

Such contradictory judgements, attached to vague categories like optimism and pessimism, fail to deal concretely with either the ascertainable social content of Shakespeare's plays, his professed opinions on political questions (obvious from the chronicle plays), or his social status as a writer.

One must be careful, however, not to dismiss the economic approach to literature by means of such quotations. Marx himself, though on occasion he made some fanciful judgements, in general acutely perceived the obliqueness of the relationship between literature and society. In the Introduction to *The Critique of Political Economy*, he admits that certain periods of highest development of art stand in no direct relation with the general development of society, nor with the material basis and the skeleton structure of its organization. Witness the example of the Greeks as compared with the modern nations or even Shakespeare.[27]

He also understood that the modern division of labour leads to a definite contradiction between the three factors ('moments' in his Hegelian terminology) of the social process – 'productive forces', 'social relations', and 'consciousness'. He expected, in a manner which scarcely seems to avoid the Utopian, that in the future classless society these divisions of labour would again disappear, that the artist would again be integrated into society. He thought it possible that everybody could be an excellent, even an original, painter. 'In a communist society there will not be any painters, but at most men who, among other things, also paint.'[28]

The 'vulgar Marxist' tells us that this or that writer was a bourgeois who voiced reactionary or progressive opinions about Church and State. There is a curious contradiction between this avowed determinism which assumes that 'consciousness' must follow 'existence', that a bourgeois cannot help being one, and the usual ethical judgement which condemns him for these very opinions. In Russia, one notes, writers of bourgeois origin who have joined the proletariat have constantly been subjected to suspicions of their sincerity, and every artistic or civic failing has been ascribed to their class origin. Yet if progress, in the Marxist sense, leads directly from feudalism via bourgeois capitalism to the 'dictatorship of the proletariat', it would be logical and consistent for a Marxist to praise the 'progressives' at any time. He should praise the bourgeois when, in the early stages of capitalism, he fought the surviving feudalism. But frequently Marxists criticize writers from a twentieth-century point of view, or, like Smirnov and Grib, Marxists very critical of 'vulgar sociology', rescue the bourgeois writer by a recognition of his universal humanity. Thus Smirnov comes to the conclusion that Shakespeare was the 'humanist ideologist of the *bourgeoisie*, the exponent of the programme advanced by them when, in the name of humanity, they first challenged the feudal order'.[29] But the concept of humanism, of the universality of art, surrenders the central doctrine of Marxism, which is essentially relativistic.

Marxist criticism is at its best when it exposes the implied, or latent, social implications of a writer's work. In this respect it is a technique of interpretation parallel to those founded upon the insights of Freud, or of Nietzsche, or of Pareto, or to the Scheler–Mannheim 'sociology of knowledge'. All these intellectuals are suspicious of the intellect, the professed doctrine, the mere statement. The central distinction is that Nietzsche's and Freud's methods are psychological, while Pareto's analysis of 'residues' and 'derivatives' and the Scheler–Mannheim technique of the analysis of 'ideology' are sociological.

The 'sociology of knowledge', as illustrated in the writings of Max Scheler, Max Weber, and Karl Mannheim, has been worked out in detail and has some definite advantages over its rivals.[30] It not only draws attention to the presuppositions and implications of a given ideological position, but it also stresses the hidden assumptions and biases of the investigator himself. It is thus self-critical and self-conscious, even to the extreme of morbidity. It is also less prone than either Marxism or psychoanalysis to isolate one single factor as the sole determinant of change. Whatever their failure at isolating the religious factor, the studies of Max Weber in the sociology of religion are valuable for their attempt to describe the influence of ideological factors on economic behaviour and institutions – for earlier emphasis had been entirely upon the economic influence on ideology.[31] A similar investigation of the influences of literature on social change would be very welcome, though it would run into analogous difficulties. It seems as hard to isolate the strictly literary factor as the religious factor and to answer the question whether the influence is due to the particular factor itself, or to other forces for which the factor is a mere 'shrine' or 'channel'.[32]

The 'sociology of knowledge' suffers, however, from its excessive historicism; it has come to ultimately sceptical conclusions despite its thesis that 'objectivity' can be achieved by synthesizing, and thus neutralizing, the conflicting perspectives. It suffers also, in application to literature, from its inability to connect 'content' with 'form'. Like Marxism, preoccupied with an irrationalistic explanation, it is unable to provide a rational foundation for aesthetics and hence criticism and evaluation. This is, of course, true of all extrinsic approaches to literature. No causal study can do justice to the analysis, description, and evaluation of a literary work.

But the problem of 'literature and society' can obviously be put in different terms, those of symbolic or meaningful relations: of consistency, harmony, coherence, congruence, structural identity, stylistic analogy, or with whatever term we want to designate the integration of a culture and the interrelationship among the different activities of men. Sorokin, who has analysed the various possibilities clearly,[33] has concluded that the degree of integration varies from society to society.

Marxism never answers the question of the degree of dependence of literature on society. Hence many of the basic problems have scarcely begun to be studied. Occasionally, for example, one sees arguments for the social determination of genres, as in the case of the bourgeois origin of the novel, or even the details of their attitudes and forms, as in E. B. Burgum's not very convincing view that tragi-comedy 'results from the imprint of middle-class seriousness upon aristocratic frivolity'.[34] Are there definite social determinants of such a broad literary style as Romanticism, which, though associated with the *bourgeoisie*, was anti-bourgeois in its ideology, at least in Germany, from its very beginning?[35] Though some kind of dependence of literary ideologies and themes on social circumstances seems obvious, the social origins of forms and styles, genres and actual literary norms have rarely been established.

It has been attempted most concretely in studies of the social origins of literature: in Bücher's one-sided theory of the rise of poetry from labour rhythms; in the many studies by anthropologists of the magic role of early art; in George Thomson's very learned attempt to bring Greek tragedy into concrete relations with cult and rituals and with a definite democratic social revolution at the time of Aeschylus; in Christopher Cauldwell's somewhat naïve attempt to study the sources of poetry in tribal emotions and in the bourgeois 'illusion' of individual freedom.[36]

Only if the social determination of forms could be shown conclusively could the question be raised whether social attitudes cannot become 'constitutive' and enter a work of art as effective parts of its artistic value. One can argue that 'social truth', while not, as such, an artistic value, corroborates such artistic values as complexity and coherence. But it need not be so. There is great literature which has little or no social relevance; social literature is only one kind of literature and is not central in the theory of literature unless one holds the view that literature is primarily an 'imitation' of life as it is and of social life in particular. But literature is no substitute for sociology or politics. It has its own justification and aim.

1. See bibliography, section 1.
2. See Morris R. Cohen's excellent discussion, 'American Literary Criticism and Economic Forces', *Journal of the History of Ideas*, 1 (1940), pp. 369–74.
3. On De Bonald, see Horatio Smith, 'Relativism in Bonald's Literary Doctrine', *Modern Philology*, XXXII (1934), pp. 193–210; B. Croce, 'La letteratura come "espressione della società"', *Problemi di estetica*, Bari 1910, pp. 56–60.
4. Introduction to *Histoire de la littérature anglaise* (1863): 'Si elles fournissent des documents, c'est qu'elles sont des monuments', p. xlvii, Vol. 1 of second ed., Paris 1866.
5. See e.g. Havelock Ellis, *A Study of British Genius*, London 1904 (rev. ed., Boston 1926); Edwin L. Clarke, *American Men of Letters: Their Nature and Nurture*, New York 1916 ('Columbia Studies in History, Economics, and Public Law', Vol. 72); A. Odin, *Genèse des grands hommes*, two vols., Paris 1895.
6. Sakulin, N. P., *Die russische Literatur*, Wildpark–Potsdam 1927 (in Oskar Walzel's *Handbuch der Literaturwissenschaft*).
7. e.g. D. Blagoy, *Sotsiologiya tvorchestva Pushkina* (The Sociology of Pushkin's Creation), Moscow 1931.
8. Herbert Schoeffler, *Protestantismus und Literatur*, Leipzig 1922. Questions of social provenance are obviously closely related to questions of early impressions, of the early physical and social milieu of a writer. As Schoeffler has pointed out, the sons of country clergymen did much to create the British pre-Romantic literature and taste of the eighteenth century. Having lived in the country, almost literally in the churchyard, they may well have been predisposed to a taste for landscape and graveyard poetry, for ruminations on death and immortality.
9. L. C. Knights, *Drama and Society in the Age of Jonson*, London 1937 and Penguin Books 1962.
10. Lily Campbell, *Shakespeare's Histories: Mirrors of Elizabethan Policy*, San Marino 1947; Sir Charles Firth, 'The Political Significance of Swift's *Gulliver's Travels*', *Essays: Historical and Literary*, Oxford 1938, pp. 210–41.
11. Prosper de Barante, *De la littérature française pendant le dix-huitième siècle*, Paris, third ed., 1822, p. v. The preface is not to be found in the first edition, of 1809. Barante's theory is brilliantly developed by Harry Levin in 'Literature as an Institution', *Accent*, VI (1946), pp. 159–68. Reprinted in *Criticism* (ed. Schorer, Miles, McKenzie), New York 1948, pp. 546–53.
12. Ashley H. Thorndike, *Literature in a Changing Age*, New York 1921, p. 36.
13. Q. D. Leavis, *Fiction and the Reading Public*, London 1932.
14. Some work on these questions: Alfred A. Harbage, *Shakespeare's Audience*, New York 1941; R. J. Allen, *The Clubs of Augustan London*, Cambridge, Mass. 1933; Chauncey B. Tinker, *The Salon and English Letters*, New York 1915; Albert Parry, *Garrets and Pretenders: a History of Bohemianism in America*, New York 1933.

15. See Grace Overmyer, *Government and the Arts*, New York 1939. On Russia, see the writings of Freeman, Max Eastman, W. Frank, etc.

16. Georgi V. Plekhanov, *Art and Society*, New York 1936, pp. 43, 63, etc. Chiefly ideological discussions are: A. Cassagne, *La Théorie de l'art pour l'art en France*, Paris 1906, reprinted 1959; Rose R. Egan, *The Genesis of the Theory of Art for Art's Sake in Germany and England*, two parts, Northampton 1921-4; Louise Rosenblatt, *L'Idée de l'art pour l'art dans la littérature anglaise*, Paris 1931.

17. L. L. Schücking, *Die Soziologie der literarischen Geschmacksbildung*, Munich 1923 (second ed., Leipzig 1931. English tr., *The Sociology of Literary Taste*, London 1941); see Schücking, *Die Familie im Puritanismus*, Leipzig 1929.

18. See T. A. Jackson, *Charles Dickens, The Progress of a Radical*, London 1937.

19. Mrs Leavis, quoted in note 13; K. C. Link and H. Hopf, *People and Books*, New York 1946; F. Baldensperger, *La Littérature: création, succès, durée*, Paris 1913; P. Stapfer, *Des réputations littéraires*, Paris, 1893; Gaston Rageot, *Le Succès: auteurs et public – essai de critique sociologique*, Paris 1906; Émile Hennequin, *La Critique scientifique*, Paris 1882. The social effects of another art, the moving pictures, are judiciously studied by Mortimer Adler in *Art and Prudence*, New York 1937. A brilliant dialectical scheme of 'aesthetic function, norm and value as social facts' is to be found in Jan Mukařovský, *Estetická funkce, norma a hodnota jako sociální fakt*, Prague 1936.

20. Thomas Warton, *History of English Poetry*, London 1774, Vol. I, p. 1.

21. E. Kohn-Bramstedt, *Aristocracy and the Middle Classes in Germany*, London 1937, p. 4.

22. See André Monglond, *Le Héros préromantique, Le Préromantisme français*, Vol. I, Grenoble 1930; R. P. Utter and G. B. Needham, *Pamela's Daughters*, New York 1937. Also the writings of E. E. Stoll, e.g. 'Heroes and Villains: Shakespeare, Middleton, Byron, Dickens', in *From Shakespeare to Joyce*, Garden City 1944, pp. 307-27.

23. Charles Lamb, 'On the Artificial Comedy', *Essays of Elia*, 1821; T. B. Macaulay, 'The Dramatic Works of Wycherley, Congreve, Vanbrugh, and Farquhar', *Edinburgh Review*, LXII (1841); J. Palmer, *The Comedy of Manners*, London 1913; K. M. Lynch, *The Social Mode of Restoration Comedy*, New York 1926.

24. E. E. Stoll, 'Literature and Life', *Shakespeare Studies*, New York 1927, and several papers in *From Shakespeare to Joyce*, Garden City 1944.

25. John Maynard Keynes, *A Treatise on Money*, New York 1930, Vol. II, p. 154.

26. A. V. Lunacharsky, quoted by L. C. Knights, loc. cit., p. 10, from the *Listener*, 27 December 1934.

27. *Einführung zur Kritik der politischen Ökonomie* (1857, a manuscript which Marx abandoned and which was published in an obscure review in 1903. Reprinted in Karl Marx–Friedrich Engels, *Über Kunst und Literatur*, ed. M. Lipschitz, Berlin 1948, pp. 21-2. This passage appears to give up the

Marxist position altogether. There are other cautious statements, e.g. Engels's letter to Starkenburg, 25 January 1894. 'Political, legal, philosophical, religious, literary, artistic, etc., development is grounded upon economic development. But all of them react, conjointly and separately, one upon another, and upon the economic foundation' (Marx–Engels, *Selected Works*, Vol. 1, p. 391). In a letter to Joseph Bloch, 21 September 1890, Engels admits that he and Marx had over-emphasized the economic factor and understated the role of reciprocal interaction; and, in a letter to Mehring, 14 July 1893, he says that they had 'neglected' the formal side – the way in which ideas develop. (See Marx–Engels, *Selected Works*, Vol. 1, pp. 383, 390.) For a careful study see Peter Demetz, *Marx, Engels und die Dichter*, Stuttgart 1959.

28. From *Die Deutsche Ideologie* (1845–6), in Karl Marx and F. Engels, *Historisch-kritische Gesamtausgabe* (ed. V. Adoratskij), Berlin 1932, Vol. v, pp. 21, 373.
29. A. A. Smirnov, *Shakespeare: A Marxist Interpretation*, New York 1936, p. 93.
30. Max Scheler, 'Probleme einer Soziologie des Wissens', *Versuch zu einer Soziologie des Wissens* (ed. Max Scheler), Munich and Leipzig 1924, Vol. 1, pp. 1–146, and 'Probleme einer Soziologie des Wissens', *Die Wissensformen und die Gesellschaft*, Leipzig 1926, pp. 1–226; Karl Mannheim, *Ideology and Utopia* (tr. L. Wirth and Z. Shils), London 1936 (reprinted New York 1955). Some discussions are: H. Otto Dahlke, 'The Sociology of Knowledge', in H. E. Barnes, Howard Becker, and F. B. Becker, *Contemporary Social Theory*, New York 1940, pp. 64–99; Robert K. Merton, 'The Sociology of Knowledge', *Twentieth-Century Sociology* (ed. Georges Gurvitch and Wilbert E. Moore), New York 1945, pp. 366–405; Gerard L. De Gré, *Society and Ideology: an Inquiry into the Sociology of Knowledge*, New York 1943; Ernst Gruenwald, *Das Problem der Soziologie des Wissens*, Vienna 1934; Thelma Z. Lavine, 'Naturalism and the Sociological Analysis of Knowledge', *Naturalism and the Human Spirit* (ed. Yervant H. Krikorian), New York 1944, pp. 183–209; Alexander C. Kern, 'The Sociology of Knowledge in the Study of Literature', *Sewanee Review*, L (1942), pp. 505–14.
31. Max Weber, *Gesammelte Aufsätze zur Religionssoziologie*, three vols., Tübingen 1920–21 (partially translated as *The Protestant Ethic and the Spirit of Capitalism*, London 1930); R. H. Tawney, *Religion and the Rise of Capitalism*, London 1926 and Penguin Books 1938 (new ed. with Preface, 1937); Joachim Wach, *The Sociology of Religion*, Chicago 1944.
32. See the criticism of Pitirim A. Sorokin, *Contemporary Sociological Theories*, New York 1928, p. 710.
33. P. A. Sorokin, *Fluctuations of Forms of Art, Social and Cultural Dynamics*, Vol. 1, New York 1937, especially chapter 1.
34. Edwin Berry Burgum, 'Literary Form: Social Forces and Innovations', *The Novel and the World's Dilemma*, New York 1947, pp. 3–18.

35. Fritz Brüggemann, 'Der Kampf um die bürgerliche Welt und Lebensauf-
fassung in der deutschen Literatur des 18. Jahrhunderts', *Deutsche Viertel-
jahrschrift für Literaturwissenschaft und Geistesgeschichte*, III (1925), pp. 94–
127.

36. Karl Bücher, *Arbeit und Rhythmus*, Leipzig 1896; J. E. Harrison, *Ancient
Art and Ritual*, New York 1913; *Themis*, Cambridge 1912; George Thomson, *Aeschylus and Athens, A Study in the Social Origins of the Drama*, London
1941, and *Marxism and Poetry*, London 1945 (a small pamphlet of great
interest, with application to Irish materials); Christopher Caudwell, *Illusion
and Reality*, London 1937; Kenneth Burke, *Attitudes toward History*, New
York 1937; Robert R. Marett (ed.), *Anthropology and the Classics*, Oxford
1908.

I. GENERAL DISCUSSIONS OF LITERATURE AND SOCIETY AND SOME BOOKS ON INDIVIDUAL PROBLEMS

BRUFORD, W. H., *Theatre, Drama and Audience in Goethe's Germany*, London 1950

DUNCAN, HUGH DALZIEL, *Language and Literature in Society, with a Bibliographical Guide to the Sociology of Literature*, Chicago 1953

DAICHES, DAVID, *Literature and Society*, London 1938
The Novel and the Modern World, Chicago 1939
Poetry and the Modern World, Chicago 1940

ESCARPIT, ROBERT, *Sociologie de la littérature (Que sais-je?)*, Paris 1958

GUÉRARD, ALBERT LÉON, *Literature and Society*, New York 1935

GUYAU, J., *L'Art au point de vue sociologique*, Paris 1889

HENNEQUIN, ÉMILE, *La C: itique scientifique*, Paris 1888

KALLEN, HORACE M., *Art and Freedom*, two vols., New York 1942

KERN, ALEXANDER C., 'The Sociology of Knowledge in the Study of Literature', *Sewanee Review*, L (1942), pp. 505–14

KNIGHTS, L. C., *Drama and Society in the Age of Jonson*, London 1937 and Penguin Books 1962

KOHN-BRAMSTEDT, ERNST, *Aristocracy and the Middle Classes in Germany: Social Types in German Literature, 1830–1900*, London 1937 (contains introduction: 'The Sociological Approach to Literature').

LALO, CHARLES, *L'Art et la vie sociale*, Paris 1921

LANSON, GUSTAVE, 'L'Histoire littéraire et la sociologie', *Revue de Métaphysique et morale*, XII (1904), pp. 621–42

LEAVIS, Q. D., *Fiction and the Reading Public*, London 1932

LERNER, MAX, and MIMS, EDWIN, 'Literature', *Encyclopedia of Social Sciences*, IX (1933), pp. 523–43

LEVIN, HARRY, 'Literature as an Institution', *Accent*, VI (1946), pp. 159–68. Reprinted in *Criticism* (eds. Schorer, Miles, McKenzie), New York 1948, pp. 546–53

LOWENTHAL, LEO, *Literature and the Image of Man, Sociological Studies of the European Drama and Novel, 1600–1900*, Boston 1957

NIEMANN, LUDWIG, *Soziologie des naturalistischen Romans*, Berlin 1934 (Germanische Studien 148)

READ, HERBERT, *Art and Society*, London 1937

SCHÜCKING, LEVIN, *Die Soziologie der literarischen Geschmacksbildung*, Munich 1923. (Second, enlarged ed., Leipzig 1931; English tr. *The Sociology of Literary Taste*, London 1941)

SEWTER, A. C., 'The Possibilities of a Sociology of Art', *Sociological Review* (London), XXVII (1935), pp. 441–53

SOROKIN, PITIRIM, *Fluctuations of Forms of Art*, Cincinnati 1937 (Vol. 1 of *Social and Cultural Dynamics*)

TOMARS, ADOLPH SIEGFRIED, *Introduction to the Sociology of Art*, Mexico City 1940

WITTE, W., 'The Sociological Approach to Literature', *Modern Language Review*, XXXVI (1941), pp. 86–94

ZIEGENFUSS, WERNER, 'Kunst', *Handwörterbuch der Soziologie* (ed. Alfred Vierkandt), Stuttgart 1931, pp, 301–38

II. SOME DISCUSSIONS OF THE ECONOMIC HISTORY OF LITERATURE

BELJAME, ALEXANDRE, *Le Public et les hommes des lettres en Angleterre au XVIIIᵉ siècle: Dryden, Addison et Pope*, Paris 1883 (English tr. *Men of Letters and the English Public*, London 1948)

COLLINS, A. S., *Authorship in the Days of Johnson*, New York 1927
  The Profession of Letters (1780–1832), New York 1928

HOLZKNECHT, KARL J., *Literary Patronage in the Middle Ages*, Philadelphia 1923

LÉVY, ROBERT, *Le Mécénat et l'organisation du crédit intellectuel*, Paris 1924

MARTIN, ALFRED VON, *Soziologie der Renaissance*, Stuttgart 1932 (English tr. *Sociology of the Renaissance*, London 1944)

OVERMYER, GRACE, *Government and the Arts*, New York 1939

SHEAVYN, PHOEBE, *The Literary Profession in the Elizabethan Age*, Manchester 1909

III. SOME MARXIST STUDIES OF LITERATURE AND DISCUSSIONS OF MARXIST APPROACH

BUKHARIN, NIKOLAY, 'Poetry, Poetics, and Problems of Poetry in the U.S.S.R.', *Problems of Soviet Literature*, New York, n.d., pp. 187–210 (reprinted in *The Problems of Aesthetics*, eds. E. Vivas and M. Krieger, New York 1953, pp. 498–514)

BURGUM, EDWIN BERRY, *The Novel and the World's Dilemma*, New York 1947

BURKE, KENNETH, *Attitudes towards History*, two vols., New York 1937

CAUDWELL, CHRISTOPHER, *Illusion and Reality*, London 1937

COHEN, MORRIS R., 'American Literary Criticism and Economic Forces', *Journal of the History of Ideas*, I (1940), pp. 369–74

DEMETZ, PETER, *Marx, Engels und die Dichter. Zur Grundlagenforschung des Marxismus*, Stuttgart 1959

FARRELL, JAMES T., *A Note on Literary Criticism*, New York 1936

FINKELSTEIN, SIDNEY, *Art and Society*, New York 1947

FRÉVILLE, JEAN (ed.), *Sur la littérature et l'art,* two vols., Paris 1936 (contains relevant texts on Marx, Engels, Lenin, and Stalin)

GRIB, V., *Balzac* (tr. from Russian; Critics' Group Series), New York 1937

HENDERSON, P., *Literature and a Changing Civilization*, London 1935
  The Novel of Today: Studies in Contemporary Attitudes, Oxford 1936

ISKOWICZ, MARC, *La Littérature à la lumière du matérialisme historique*, Paris 1926

JACKSON, T. A., *Charles Dickens. The Progress of a Radical*, New York 1938

KLINGENDER, F. D., *Marxism and Modern Art*, London 1943

LIFSHITZ, MIKHAIL, *The Philosophy of Art of Karl Marx* (tr. from Russian; Critics' Group Series), New York 1938

LUKÁCS, GEORG, *Balzac und der französische Realismus*, Berlin 1951
  Beiträge zur Geschichte der Ästhetik, Berlin 1954
  Der historische Roman, Berlin 1955 (English tr. London 1962)
  Der russische Realismus in der Weltliteratur, Berlin 1949
  Essays über Realismus, Berlin 1948
  Deutsche Realisten des 19. Jahrhunderts, Bern 1951
  Goethe und seine Zeit, Bern 1947
  Karl Marx und Friedrich Engels als Literaturhistoriker, Berlin 1948
  Schriften zur Literatursoziologie (ed. Peter Ludz), Neuwied 1961 (with bibliography)
  Thomas Mann, Berlin 1949

MARX, K., and ENGELS, F., *Über Kunst und Literatur* (ed. M. Lifschitz), Berlin 1948

NOVITSKY, PAVEL J., *Cervantes and Don Quixote* (tr. from Russian; Critics' Group Series), New York 1936

PLEKHANOV, GEORGI, *Art and Society* (tr. from Russian; Critics' Group Series), New York 1936; new enlarged ed. London 1953

SAKULIN, N. P., *Die russische Literatur*, Potsdam 1930 (in series *Handbuch der Literaturwissenschaft*, ed. O. Walzel) (tr. from Russian)

SMIRNOV, A. A., *Shakespeare* (tr. from Russian; Critics' Group Series), New York 1936

SMITH, BERNARD, *Forces in American Criticism*, New York 1939

THOMSON, GEORGE, *Aeschylus and Athens. A Study in the Social Origin of the Drama*, London 1941
  Marxism and Poetry, London 1945

TROTSKY, LEON, *Literature and Revolution*, New York 1925

The Social Interpretation of Literature
Everett L. Hunt

from

English Journal, no. 24, 1935.

THE SOCIAL INTERPRETATION OF LITERATURE[1]

EVERETT L. HUNT

An economic dogma as a basis for literary criticism is no worse, I suppose, than a theological or a psychological one, and Mr. Hicks's book, *The Great Tradition*, is an example of how much order can be obtained when one tosses such a hypothesis into the midst of discordant facts. Unfortunately, the most vigorous critics of Marxian economics are the economists themselves. With departments of literature shrinking rapidly before the increased enrolments in social science, it seems doubtful if we shall rehabilitate literature as a study by filching a doctrine so largely discredited, and by justifying our claim to it by proposing to put the emotional drive of literature behind it. We may succeed only in suggesting that if literature is economics teaching by example, it ought to be taught by really competent economists.

For me, Mr. Hicks's most persuasive argument is that under the inspiration of a belief in the dictatorship of the proletariat, established by revolution, teachers, critics, and writers of literature may experience a rebirth of ardor and aspiration. We are worn and confused; at times it seems that there is little health in us. A simple doctrine, hardly subject to disproof, which orders all our conflicts, divides our writers neatly into schools, explains all their failures, and fills us with a long unfelt glow, is not to be lightly rejected. We have to admit the presence of pessimism and frustration among writers who have not found the faith, even as Arnold and Clough and other poets of mid-nineteenth century doubt admitted a loss of buoyancy. But the revolutionaries deceive themselves when they tell us that their ardor comes from facing reality. They face modern poverty with the light of heaven in their eye. The revolution is to them what the lions were to the early Christians—a means of passage to a better world. Just as the Christian theologians delighted to lay the dark

[1] Contributed to a symposium on "Literature and Society" at the College Conference on English in the Central Atlantic States.

colors on this vile world in order to direct attention to heaven, so the revolutionary indictment of the present order is not meant to keep us face to face with reality, to encourage the patient planning of practicable remedies; rather its effect is to blind us to human nature, to paralyze the critical examination of cause and effect, and to sweep us into apocalyptic visions. The aftermath of false hopes is the price of such exaltation. Mr. Hemingway's bull-fights seem to Mr. Hicks an ignoble example of escapism. They last only an afternoon, and they lead only to more bull-fights. How long the revolution might last and what it might lead to, no one knows, but I suggest that even a very long bull-fight may fail to create a lasting zeal.

Just as the joy of battle and the hope of victory make the revolutionary impatient of the slow work of planning, so his hatred of the petty bourgeoisie blinds him to any possible merits of the middle class as a basis for society. For the proletariat he is full of what he calls altruism, for the bourgeoisie he has only blind fury; and yet, he tells us, our literature is to be regenerated by his joy in facing reality.

I am not suggesting that as citizens we should join the Republican party, that we should close our eyes to the evils of capitalism, or that writers should refrain from arousing public indignation over the injustices of our economic order. Not at all. But let the indignation take action guided by trained and competent social servants, not by literary critics crying "On with the revolution."

Even if we believed that an equitable distribution of property might eventually result from the revolution, such an event would be only the tuning of the strings of an orchestra in preparation for the concert. It would not tell us what the good life is, it would not solve problems of composition, it would not give aesthetic values, it would tell us nothing about the literary masterpieces of the future. Suppose that we could by class warfare establish a society in which all men had the economic security, the leisure, and the intelligence of the best university faculty in the country. Would the value and destiny of such individuals encourage literary men to glorify the revolution and enjoy it forever? Would we by a Platonic censorship root out the writers of the Ecclesiastes of the future, of the Rubaiyats, of Wessex novels, of Shropshire Lads? Would we compel our writers to say that growing old is a delight, that freedom from Victorian morality has made passion an eternal pleasure, that tragic flaws had disappeared with capitalism, that romanticism became absurd when the far away and long ago capitulated to the here and now, that all our moments were adjured to stay because so fair, or that desire had ceased to outrun achievement? When we survey the problems that have led sensitive human spirits to create the literature of the world we must conclude, I think, that the most successful of economic revolutions would not greatly change the problems of criticism.

The narrowness of the Marxian formula for criticism deprives us of much literature of the past, and, so far as it is followed by writers of the future, confines them to a strait-jacket. According to a rival social formula, one employed by Mencken, Lewisohn, Van Doren, and others, our literature is to be valued according to its success in escaping the restraints of Puritanism. But the restraints of Puritanism are mild compared with the Marxian formula. The Puritans who branded Hester Prynne with the scarlet letter are outdone in their zeal for righteousness by the critics who have escaped from Victorian morality only to condemn American writers for living abroad, to denounce a poet for retiring from the world over such a trifle as disappointed love, to pass a zoning ordinance forbidding American authors to practice their trade on the prairies, in the desert, in New England hills, throughout the rural south, or anywhere but in the centers of industrialism. The artistic delights these critics permit themselves are those of a pioneer loading his wagon for the Oregon trail. They justify it, some of them, on the ground of the impending crisis, and assert that the limitations are only temporary. But history is a succession of crises; once we intolerantly denounce all treatment of past times and distant places, all retreat into the inner self, all skepticism and melancholy as enfeebling artistic luxuries interfering with the revolution, we shall return again to the mentality of the early Christians preparing for the second coming.

It may be well to increase the social awareness of writers, to encourage them to live in the present. I am inclined to agree with Tolstoy that the great writers have been contemporary in the sense that they have been conscious of something new and something important. But to insist upon praising the strength and worth of the proletariat, to demand an optimistic faith in the revolution, is to compel authors to write by formula and to substitute rhetoric for art.

This is a peculiarly unfortunate attitude if we are to have a successful dictatorship of the proletariat, for under it art must assume an importance little dreamed of now. Now we waste our powers on getting and spending, on religion, on romantic love and the family, on patriotism. Much of our art mirrors these activities. After the revolution these interests are to disappear, or are to be transformed beyond recognition. We shall be left, apparently, with art and friendship. If art is then to fill our lives, to banish all the hateful feelings of the petty bourgeoisie, to expand all the naturally good impulses of the proletariat it will need all the richness and variety that life and imagination can give it. Such an art can never be explained or produced by any one formula.

After so much of disagreement with the preceding paper, I want to express approval of some of the premises on which the conclusions were founded. Anyone who has gone through the controversy over Matthew Arnold's "criticism of life" knows how inadequate that formula has been found. In the face of all that, I am willing to subscribe to it, for purposes of teaching, at least. I hope teachers will always recognize the large element of enjoyment in literature, beyond all explaining or interpreting, and will to some extent leave students alone to enjoy. But so far as the intellectual processes of teaching are concerned, a discussion of the world-attitude of the author seems to me to be the most truly liberal way of teaching. Students who aspire to be writers may prefer to approach literature in a strictly professional way, studying literary technique as a way of acquiring professional skill. Candidates for the doctoral degree may find it necessary to obey the philological requirements of the director of the dissertation, and, of course, may profit largely by doing so. But the study of technique and of philology have often threatened the liberal character of undergraduate instruction. In teaching undergraduates I am, as Mr. Hicks seems to be, most interested in the attempt to produce an imaginative realization of the world-attitude of the great writers. I want to agree most heartily with Mr. Hicks that this will never be brought about by continuous instruction in the technique of writing. I imagine that Mr. Hicks would agree that such methods often fail to produce even proficiency.

I also join Mr. Hicks in subscribing to such of Mr. Richards' writings as he has cited, insisting that literature does have an effect on conduct, and that it is possible to discriminate—if not too dogmatically—between good and bad effects. I have been particularly interested in the fact that Mr. Richards has become discouraged in his attempts to defend his early naturalistic scheme of values, has announced his abandonment of any effort to make a systematic statement of them. In this I think he is wise, but the failure of a rationalistic explanation of values need not prevent us from experiencing them.

I will go further with Mr. Hicks and agree that the so-called eternal interests of literature cannot be successfully treated in abstraction, and that in practice they have been best treated by writers who were alive to contemporary interests. I do not agree that contemporary interests must be related to the proletariat, and I object to the identification of world-attitude with attitude toward the class struggle.

Part of our present enthusiasm for the social interpretation of literature comes from weariness with concentration on literary sources, with a too complete separation from any significant interests in our own living. As such it partakes almost of the nature of revolt, and as such I welcome it. But it is not new, even to academic minds. It is old enough to have had its excesses chastened. Taine has been even more discredited than he deserves. May I say a word in passing for sending students to him? But I must emphasize what Mr. Hicks asserted in the early part of his paper only to obscure in the later part, namely, that all methods of interpretation must be used. I must deny his statement that social interpretation tells us "what we most want to know." There is no one approach that will tell us what we "most want to know" about literature. Wordsworth's recreancy as a lost leader is to me one of the least significant things about him. Tom Sawyer is more interesting to me than Mark Twain's state of mind as he contemplated the capitalism of his later years. So far as our study and teaching are concerned with ex-

plaining authors, the social approach must be in the nature of pro-
legomena to interpretation. After we have explained the social background of our author we are merely ready to begin the study of his
individual genius. Whether the social background or the individual
genius is more important to us, it is impossible to say. In many
cases it may be neither, but rather the work of art itself. For undergraduate teaching I would suggest that the work of art be kept in the
foreground. Our knowledge and understanding, as William James
said, grow like grease spots on the table cloth. Spreading from their
centers they eventually meet. In our desire to banish immaturity
from our students' minds, to explain everything to them and to our
colleagues, to be leaders in the world of thought, to produce an
effect on society, let us not entirely forget our humbler function of
subordinating ourselves to our authors, of helping to lodge good
books in students' minds; once a good book has had an opportunity to do its work on a student's mind, its influence will spread, it
will lead him to enjoy or to endure life in ways often unsuspected by
ourselves.

Is Art the Product of Its Age?
J.H. Mueller

from

Social Forces, vol. 13, no. 3, March 1935.

Is Art the Product of Its Age? by J.H. Mueller
copyright © The University of North Carolina Press.

IS ART THE PRODUCT OF ITS AGE?

JOHN H. MUELLER

Washington, D. C.

EVER since the decline of the theory of instinct as the explanation of human behavior, the sociologist has proceeded on the principle of the interrelation, potential or actual, between the various aspects of culture. While the social scientist has, accordingly, studied the major social institutions and the more or less conspicuous items of behavior in society, one prominent human activity has remained foreign to his area of research. This is the field of the fine arts. Not since the ascendancy of the social evolutionist has serious attention been accorded them by the American social scientist, unless we except the researches of a few ethnologists and anthropologists such as Boas[1] and his pupils.[2] Consequently there has been very little cross-fertilization between the social sciences and the field of aesthetics; and as a result there still prevails a lively controversy as to the very adaptability of scientific methods to the study of the arts.[3] One version of this issue revolves around the question whether, and to what extent, art is conditioned by the epoch.

This question would immediately elicit self-confident replies from those sufficiently interested and informed to venture an answer. As is the case, however, in all matters which touch aesthetic issues, the answers would diverge in accordance with the principles of the respective schools of thought. There are those who assert the independence of the art work of the vicissitudes of temporal affairs and claim for it a status beyond time and circumstance. How could one otherwise explain the enduring fame of the masters? Others, to the contrary, would contend that, since art is obviously made by man, even though in a "creative" capacity, it would necessarily reflect mundane interests. A third school would effect a compromise dividing, as well as it can, a given aesthetic product into its component parts, form and content—and the many variations of this dichotomy—and assert that while the content is conditioned by ephemeral factors, its form, if a great work of art, would be valid for all time. Finally, one may append another category of opinion: there is a relation, but the direction of flow of cause and effect is merely another version of the hen-and-egg conundrum. "Competent" authorities would seem to be available in support of each of these positions.

ROMANTICISM AND PHILOSOPHY

Conceptions of beauty, like those of religion and morals, usually undergo universalization on the part of their protagonists. It would seem, therefore, at the outset that if the universality of great art is admitted, it would already imply a negative answer to our query. If intrinsic worth is accorded to a masterpiece of Homer or Bach, if Shakespeare is the poet "for all time," if Beethoven belongs to all nations, their qualities could not be dependent upon adventitious changes in the social order. Therefore, to Roger Fry, art seems as "remote from actual life as the most useless mathematical the-

[1] Franz Boas. *Primitive Art*, Cambridge, 1927.

[2] Ruth L. Bunzel. *The Pueblo Potter, A Study of Creative Imagination in Primitive Art*, New York, 1929.

[3] See, for example, Thomas Munro. *Scientific Method in Aesthetics*, New York, 1928. Luther Anderson. *Aesthetics and Determinism*, American Magazine of Art, March, 1933, p. 127.

orem."[4] According to Schoen, "since the art work is inherent in value it also transcends time and place. The inherent, the intrinsic has neither chronology nor geography, but belongs to all epochs and all localities."[5]

The logical sanction for this supposed permanence of the work of art in the face of fluctuating circumstance was derived from philosophy in the form of the theory of the dualistic universe. Although usually associated with Plato and Plotinus, it flowered most abundantly, as far as our present issue is concerned, with the romantic revolt of the nineteenth century. This alliance of romanticism and Kantian metaphysics constituted in one form or another the prevailing philosophy of art almost until the opening of the present century.

Briefly expressed, according to the romanticist, the artist possessed intuitive powers to experience directly the supersensual world, while the scientist, by the aid of reason, analyzed merely the physical universe. Science was thereby relegated to an inferior order of intellectual merit while the artist, through his faculty of clairvoyance and imagination, discerned the Truth—with a capital "T". Schiller,[6] Shelley,[7] Schopenhauer,[8] and others promulgated this doctrine which was finally to place music, because of its abstraction and most distant resemblance to the world of the senses, at the pinnacle of the hierarchy of the arts. Art had no material function associated with the physical universe, but constituted a revelation of ultimate reality. Art existed for "art's sake" and served, in fact, as a refuge from the physical frustrations of the perceptual world instead of being conditioned and formed by it. Beauty was itself the prototype rather than the imitation of physical nature.

But the discrepant tastes, so patent to every historical observer, could not but be embarrassing to the pretensions of the universalist. While music, because of its abstract quality, was perhaps more easily accommodated to the principle, the pictorial and literary arts were somewhat more recalcitrant. "Formalism" presented a happy solution. Taking a leaf from the book of music, which was purely the "concord of sweet sounds," artists began to repudiate realistic fidelity which had been the ideal since the days of the Greek golden age, and concentrated upon what was thought to be those permanent and common qualities of objects, namely pure form. The last vestige of physical reality was to be eliminated by declaring subject matter entirely irrelevant, and asking the observer to react to the "unity of harmony of formal relations."[9] This school of thought, although not restricted to the graphic arts, nevertheless today finds its most enthusiastic sponsors among critics of painting and sculpture, prominent among whom are Roger Fry,[10] Clive Bell,[11] Herbert Read,[12] and George H. Opdyke.[13] "The logical extreme of such a method," in the words of Mr. Fry, "would undoubtedly be to give up all resemblance to natural form and to create a purely abstract language of form—a visual music—and the later works of Picasso

[4] Roger Fry. *Vision and Design*, London, no date, p. 199.

[5] Max Schoen. *Art and Beauty*, New York, 1932, p. 127.

[6] Friedrich Schiller. *Ueber die ästhetische Erziehung des Menschen*, especially letters, 2, 12, and 26.

[7] Percy B. Shelley. *Defence of Poetry*, Boston, 1891.

[8] Arthur Schopenhauer. *On the Metaphysics of the Beautiful and on Aesthetics*, in *Selected Essays*, Ernest Bax, ed., London, 1914.

[9] Herbert Read. *The Anatomy of Art*, New York, 1932, p. 4.

[10] *Op. cit.*

[11] *Art*: New York, 1913.

[12] *Op. cit.*

[13] *Art and Nature Appreciation*, New York, 1932.

show this clearly enough. I would suggest that there is nothing ridiculous in the attempt to do this." The consumer is expected "to be moved by the pure contemplation of spatial relations of plastic volumes *independent of his experience in the exterior world*, through his aesthetic sensibilities."[14] It follows as a corollary that "if we consider this special spiritual activity of art, we find it no doubt open at times to influences from life, but in the main self-contained—we find the rhythmical sequences of change determined much more by its own internal forces than by external forces . . . . the rhythms of life and of art are distinct, and as often as not play against each other."[15]

In order that these semblances of permanent reality could be appreciated by the human being, human nature had to be endowed with a parallel duality. So the substratum of human nature, it is said, consisted of the "constant factors"[16] which made the whole world kin. Since "human nature never changes," "the deeper traits of mankind are themselves unaffected by rapidly altering outward conditions."[17] So long as a work of art speaks to these feelings, it will surmount the threatening ravages of time.

To the accusation that such reasonings smack of *a priori* rationalization, even the most ecstatic romanticist and the most tenacious philosophical idealist may, and does, seek refuge in the empirical evidence that "great" art does survive the culture epoch which gave it birth. Posterity has been kind to Homer, Shakespeare, Bach, and Beethoven who are enjoyed and appreciated today in many cases even more deeply than by their own contemporaries. They thereby demonstrate their right to the claim that they appeal to permanent values, however critics may diverge on the principles of explanation.

To this, however, the determinist has his retort. Although, to be sure, certain masters are still cultivated today by especially trained patrons, a more penetrating analysis of historical criticism will disclose the fluctuating renown of even the greatest geniuses. Plato's rejection of the Homeric poems is an early instance.[18] "Gothic" was a vulgar epithet directed at a cumbersome architecture, which was only subsequently accepted, and now once again disparaged.[19] The masterpieces of Greek sculpture are today suffering the same fate at the hands of an influential coterie of modernists who decry the slavish subservience of art to realistic nature, which has been the standard since the days of the Renaissance, and hail with delight the emancipation from the incubus of classic models.[20] Contemporary observation would indicate that Goethe, once the idol of cultured literacy, is even now passing into eclipse; for the mild and even indifferent enthusiasm of otherwise intelligent Germans on the occasion of the centenary of his death (1932) was a keen disappointment to traditionalists and academicians.[21] The idolatry of Beethoven is likewise waning, as critical estimates of his merits on the occasion of the centenary of his death (1927) would indicate.[22] Bach was forgotten for a century and then revived by Mendelssohn. Nor has Shakespeare

---

[14] Fry, *op. cit.*, pp. 157–59.

[15] *Ibid.*, p. 6.

[16] Irving Babbitt. *On Being Creative*, Cambridge, 1932, p. 142.

[17] Helen H. Parkhurst. *Beauty*, New York, 1930, p. 261.

[18] *Republic*, Books III and X.

[19] Clive Bell. *Op. cit.*, pp. 144–45.

[20] See: Paul Guillaume and Thomas Munro. *Primitive Negro Sculpture*, New York. R. H. Wilenski. *Meaning of Modern Sculpture*, New York, 1932.

[21] Clifton Fadiman. "What is Left of Goethe?" *Nation*, June 16, 1932.

[22] *Music and Letters*, Vol. VIII, No. 2, April, 1927.

enjoyed any but vacillating fame.[23] In fact, so fickle is public acclaim, as taken through the ages, that taste has seemed to Mr. Kellett a veritable "whirligig" on which "we can never form a positive judgment, and every sentence of the critic should be preluded with a mental 'subject to reservation'."[24] Furthermore, even assuming the "permanence" of a work of art, we well know that the same work is in different epochs admired for widely different qualities.[25] With such caution thrust upon us, it requires considerable intellectual audacity to insist that any master "has stood the test of time," or that we, in the year 1935, located as we are between two eternities, hold the final judgment on any aesthetic issue.

Although such expressions of skepticism are far from convincing to the idealist, nevertheless there has arisen an increasingly quizzical attitude toward his pretensions. Pitted against the traditional system which has been dominated by philosophers and artists, and is still so influential in contemporary aesthetic theory, are the exponents of cultural determinism.

THE NATURAL SCIENCE MOVEMENT

Even before romanticism and formalism had gained the peak of dominance, there occurred a revolution in thought which was destined to challenge the primacy of traditional philosophical aesthetics. The natural science movement, which had already penetrated the physical sciences since Galileo and Newton, had now overtaken biology and social philosophy, and tended to discredit the metaphysical principles and the intuitional epistemology of romanticists and idealists as being incompatible with empirical methods.

Among the primary forces to shake the preeminent position of romanticism was the popularization of the theory of evolution which tended to divest man of his separate status and place him alongside the rest of nature, thereby undermining his claim to a "soul," his communion with ultimate reality, and kindred privileges. Thus Herbert Spencer left no place for the Kantian dogma that man could "know" ultimate reality without "understanding" it, but frankly posited the sphere of the unknowable. Instead of seeking the source of the arts in metaphysical reality, scholars now turned to more naturalistic phenomena. In the realm of art, attention was now directed to the prosaic studies of primitive art to determine its evolutionary development. Spencer himself speculated upon the origin of music in daily emotional speech;[26] Darwin saw aesthetic significance in the brilliant decorativeness of the male;[27] and Grosse, by his pioneer work in the beginnings of art, laid the basis for further investigations into the cultural factors in art phenomena.[28] Such scholars were not interested in the essence of Beauty. They assumed beauty as the physiologist assumes life. The artist was no longer a quasi-priest who was the interpreter of God and Nature, as set forth by Goethe;[29] art was no longer the incarnation of the "absolute spirit" of Hegel,[30] nor the "objectification of the Will" of Schopen-

[23] Augustus Ralli. A History of Shakespearean Criticism, London, 1932.

[24] Kellett, E. E. The Whirligig of Taste, New York, 1929, p. 80.

[25] See Frank Chambers. Cycles of Taste, Cambridge, 1928. I. A. Richards. Principles of Literary Criticism, New York, 1928, ch. XXVI.

[26] Herbert Spencer. Origin and Function of Music, in Essays, New York, 1910.

[27] Charles Darwin. Origin of Species, ch. IV.

[28] Ernest Grosse. Beginnings of Art, New York, 1897.

[29] Zueignung.

[30] Vorlesungen über die Aesthetik, Leipzig, 1842.

hauer.[31] Scholars of the modern stripe were intent upon analyzing the craft of man as a product of human ingenuity, in a particular biological, social, and geographic setting. That the evolutionary theories have been discarded is of no import compared to the significance of the inauguration of a new method of approach.

The growing interest in exact, comparative historiography likewise contributed to the new point of view. History assumed a social emphasis. Paced by such culture historians as Taine who purported to demonstrate the determinate relation of "race, milieu and the moment" and who made "no attempt to do more than explain art according to natural laws" without the aid of metaphysics,[32] it was only natural that scholars should strive to correlate art with the particular setting in which it arose. In this, incidentally, they were only catching up with Montesquieu who had previously applied the principle to legal institutions.

In the meantime physical science was conspiring to deflate the status of the queen of the fine arts: Music. Far from accepting its apotheosis of Pater and Browning,[33] or accepting the explanation of its power and charm as due to its perfect symbolism of the Ultimate, Helmholtz,[34] to the great distress of contemporary aestheticians, was searching its secrets in terms of vibrations and their effect upon the physiological organism. Similarly Fechner established his laboratory and in the 1870's published his psychological studies in which he frankly declared his intention of studying the fine arts inductively "from below" rather than deductively "from above."

CULTURAL DETERMINISM

Paradoxically enough, romanticism, which had received from Kant and Hegel the philosophical sanction of timelessness, contributed, itself, to the destruction of that principle. Emancipated from acknowledged authority and the model of the ancients, the protesting groups broke up into many schools, which fact tended to discredit them all. Each artist "copied nature" in his own manner. To Wordsworth it meant trees and mountains; to Zola, the dramatization of a slumming expedition and the "scientific" transcription of social relations; to the impressionists, Monet and Manet, unconventional subjects and color effects. Critical opinion was becoming so diverse that it was straining the principle of unity. In recent decades, with more penetrating studies, this has become all the more apparent. Locke,[35] tracing the romantic period in music, showed how it was conditioned by the social forces in Germany and France; Mumford[36] has performed an analogous task for architecture; Calverton,[37] using the Marxian approach, has related the literature of England and America to the class ideologies of those countries; Strzygowski[38] has sketched the diffusion of Christian art along the trade routes and "commercial currents which are, in turn, determined by political forces." This relativistic interpretation was similarly enunciated by Keppel and Duffus in their report for the Committee

[31] Op. cit.

[32] H. Taine. Lectures on Art, New York, 1889, 3rd ed.

[33] See Abt Vogler.

[34] H. von Helmholtz. On the Sensations of Tone, tr. by A. J. Ellis, 4th ed., New York, 1912.

[35] Arthur Locke. Music and the Romantic Movement in France.

[36] L. Mumford. Sticks and Stones; a Study of American Architecture and Civilization, New York, 1924.

[37] V. F. Calverton. Sex Expression in Literature, New York, 1926, and other works.

[38] Josef Strzygowski. Origin of Christian Church Art, p. 195.

on Social Trends, in which they frankly declare that "we cannot assign absolute values" to aesthetic theory.[39]

Although the relativistic interpretation of the existence of the varied standards of taste and its corresponding art forms has earned a certain acceptance in many quarters, it is still imperfectly understood.[40] After professing agreement to the general principle that "architecture is the reflection and expression of the culture and life of the time," Tallmadge still betrays doubts that that is always the case. "It is curious, for instance, that the Niagara limestone should be expressive of cultures as different as 1867 and 1927. Certainly the Gothic of France, born of medieval and unreflecting ecstasy, and reared in tortuous, unlighted, and unpaved streets, was not the proper garb for urbane and humanistic Italy with her cobble stone pavements."[41]

Such reservations are scattered throughout the literature on the history of art and hark back to the now outmoded folk-psychology or to the Hegelian *Zeitgeist*. At present, however, we recognize that the building of culture is a syncretic process, an accumulation of elements derived from manifold and otherwise alien sources. Just as there is no "pure" race so there is no "pure" culture. An indigenous culture[42] is purely hypothetical, depending upon the area in question conceived in both space and historical genesis. Diffusion is constantly occurring. How ostensibly inharmonious these elements may be is illustrated in the adoption of the nude figure in the graphic arts from Greek classicism during the Renaissance. This trait probably never would have arisen in western culture, as it never has arisen in oriental art, nor in Eskimo graphics. Even today, the convergent streams of Puritanism and classicism render it difficult to differentiate between art and indecency.[43]

Since culture is more than the overt phenomenon of social behavior, but includes beliefs, attitudes, and ideologies, the latter are frequently carried in migration more easily than bag and baggage. In fact, as often as not, art styles are introduced to new areas much like the plague— by a small number of infected carriers, as is well illustrated by the classic revival in America, which was given its impetus by the Chicago World's Fair of 1893 through the agency of a group of graduate architects recently returned from Paris where they had absorbed the teachings of the Beaux Arts. Similarly, Thomas Jefferson, a fine scholar as well as statesman, who had lived in Paris for five years as ambassador to the French court and had witnessed the construction of the Pantheon in Paris, and had consequently been infected by the classic virus which broke out in America after his return in the form of the capitol of Virginia, built according to the classic Roman model of the Maison Carrée at Nîmes, France.

To be sure, imitation is never exact, but an amalgamation of alien and provincial ingredients, which are, however, discerned only by the historically sophisticated. So America copied Greek models, even though it had to use tin and wood instead of marble; even though on the stately Corinthian pillars of the Capitol at Washington, D. C., were substituted, for the

[39] F. P. Keppel and R. L. Duffus. *The Arts in American Life*, New York, 1933, pp. 2–3.

[40] See, for example, the satirical article by Ernest Sutherland Bates. "American Virility and British Decadence," *Nation*, Oct. 18, 1933.

[41] Thomas E. Tallmadge. *The Story of Architecture*, New York, 1927, pp. 13–14.

[42] Architects commonly distinguish between indigenous and foreign architecture.

[43] For the early American reactions to the nude in art, see: Suzanne LaFollette. *Art in America*. New York, 1929, pp. 68–69.

graceful traditional Greek acanthus leaves, the ears of indigenous Indian corn, tobacco leaves, and cotton bolls. Good Presbyterians built churches during the first quarter of the nineteenth century in the style of pagan temples; and for the model of the central portion of the Pennsylvania station in New York, the architect sought out the tepidarium of the Imperial bath at Rome.

Similar analysis may be made of other cultures, but their array of fine arts will invariably testify to the extreme commixture of cultural elements even in the most provincial primitivity. If, therefore, by "product of the age" is meant "invented," then very few objects could be so accredited; if "reflection of the age" symbolizes its hopes, pretensions, aspirations or ideals, then the adaptation of the Greek colonnade to American circumstances is indeed a product of American life and culture.

Confusion has arisen likewise because of the expectation that conspicuous events be reflected in prevailing art tastes. This is by no means necessarily the case. During the Napoleonic wars, the violent storms of conquest passed right over the areas where literary activities were maintained unscorched by the heat of the conflict; the battle of Jena disturbed very little the dominant reading preferences of cultured Germans.[44]

Dominated by the concept of *Zeitgeist*, a term which served the Hegelians so well during the nineteenth century, critics were blind to the seething cultural process here delineated, but conceived of society as a homogenous unity, pervaded by a "spirit" which expressed itself consistently in its civilization. Such a conception of the spirit of the times would, indeed, suggest an incongruity in the repetitive appearance of Niagara limestone

in diverse cultures.[45] More accurately speaking, however, art is not the product of the "times", nor of society. These terms are too all-embracing. It is rather the product, the creation of the respective groups of which the larger society is composed. These groups may represent any conceivable interest in age, class, wealth, erudition, or sex, each displaying its characteristic taste preferences. The children with their fairy tales, the aristocracy with its opera, museums, and literature; the masses with their jazz—the innumerable groups all create, adopt, or perpetuate their own works of art. A German aesthetician,[46] with a characteristic flare for neologisms, refers to these groups as *Geschmacksträgertypen* (taste-carrier-types). It is only when we break up "society" into its component parts that the cultural determination of art forms becomes apparent.

There are those, however, who see the effective solution of our problem in neither of these extremes which have, respectively, rendered an unequivocal negative and affirmative reply to our original query. The compromise would divide the work of art into its two elements: form and content. Admitting what cannot be denied, namely that art epochs do present different fronts, and that only through familiarity with historical allusions can many works be made intelligible to modern mentality, some nevertheless assert that this objective aspect does not constitute the essence of art. It is alleged that when one has described or examined the works of art as have Taine, Calverton, and others, one has studied merely the materials, the outward husk, of art, not art itself. The materials, to be sure, reflect the times, but the fundamental feelings and emotions transmitted therein, to which the great artist appeals,

[44] L. L. Schücking. *Die Soziologie der literarischen Geschmacksbildung*, Berlin, 1931, p. 22.

[45] See *supra*, p. 370, of this issue.
[46] Schücking, *op. cit.*

and on which he relies to produce his effect, are elemental and eternal. "The ultimate values of art transcend the individual and his time and circumstance. . . . In expressing his intuition, the artist will use materials placed in his hands by the circumstances of his time."[47]

Closer insight will here disclose a false dichotomy of form and content, and arouse the suspicion that we have been misled by the easy analogy of the foundry. After all, only in Wonderland can the grin be separated from the Cheshire cat. To be sure, the fundamental emotions may be universal, but they cannot be communicated by telepathy; they must be made corporeal in a concrete situation. It is then found that a situation which would arouse vengeance in one culture may extract a peal of laughter in another. Succinctly put, the universality of an emotion would by no means guarantee the universality of a work of art. By the same logic, human nature is, and is not, uniform throughout mankind. As a formula of concepts, it may be "common to all mankind";[48] as a going concern, translated into concrete behavior as manifested in art, it is very much attached to time and space.

Among the more recent irreconcilables to the procedure of subordinating man to the laws of nature are the new humanists. The late Professor Irving Babbitt has stated: ". . . the great revolutionary task of the nineteenth-century thinkers was to put man into nature. The great task of twentieth-century thinkers is to get him out again; . . . a beauty that is relativistic and impressionistic finally becomes meaningless."[49] "Students of aesthetics may as well face the facts and recognize in determinism a theory that is hostile to art."[50]

However, the whirligig of taste, so fickle and capricious as it seems in the distribution of its favors, need not necessarily lead to such skepticism. Here the relativistic approach and a knowledge of elementary social science will inject meaning where aesthetic agnosticism would otherwise prevail. Tastes are not nearly so conglomerate and meaningless as the idealists would imply; for, beneath the diversities of standards there is a substructure of uniformity which itself makes social life possible and which will guarantee a certain comparable uniformity in aesthetic, moral, political, and other standards. Solipsism is not the alternative to absolutism. The work of art, and the group in which it has its being are related as plant and soil. To be sure, the social soil of America with its indoor assemblies and inclement weather does not nourish the classic style as did ancient Hellas with its outdoor worship and salubrious climate. But the migration of culture produces incompatibilities that are no greater than those produced by the migration of races.

The last stronghold of the idealists can also be captured. The formalistic types of art, such as music, also depend upon the mechanical inventions, instruments, the mutable habits of thought in harmony, and other psychological processes. Their cultivation depends upon distribution of surplus wealth, upon social organization, religious scruples, and other ingredients of culture which do not isolate such phenomena from any other feature of the culture complex.

Finally, the interaction between art and its epoch is not one-sided but reciprocal.

---

[47] Read, *op. cit.*, p. 223.

[48] The concept of universality needs clarification, but such elaboration would not be relevant at this point.

[49] Babbitt, *op. cit.*, pp. 132–33; 178–79.

[50] Luther Anderson, *op. cit.*

In a sense, the Wagnerian music-drama was a product of German nationalism of the nineteenth century, fertilized by the composer's erudition in Greek drama. At the same time, by establishing novel musical habits, it created the taste which finally approved it, and is even now, during the period of the recrudescence of German nationalist sentiments, enjoying a revival which makes it a powerful factor in social control. A work of art, therefore, is not the product of genius alone; it is a co-operative enterprise between author, audience, geography, philosophy of life and the innumerable winds of fashion which, as far as we are consciously concerned, blow whither they listeth. If art is still mysterious, so is the chemical reaction in the test tube. Everything, when pursued to its more profound implications, ends in mystery. Beauty is neither more nor less mysterious than is any other phenomenon in nature; tastes *can* be accounted for, and no taste is intrinsically superior to any other. With such a point of view, we shall no longer be interested in art, and its essence, but in the *arts* and their inter-relations as an activity of social man, toward the clarification of which the social sciences may well make a contribution.

The Sociology of Knowledge in the Study of Literature
Alexander Kern

from

The Sewanee Review, vol. 50, 1942.

Reprinted by permission of the author and *The Sewanee Review*.

THE SOCIOLOGY OF KNOWLEDGE IN THE STUDY OF LITERATURE

THE sociology of knowledge—that branch of sociology which deals with the effects of social and cultural backgrounds upon the forms of thought and expression—offers a fruitful technique for the correlation of literature and society. This technique aims at being more systematic, more objective, and more refined than previous attempts to use a knowledge of society in the interpretation of literary art.[1] Of course the interpretation of literature as part of the cultural pattern is nothing new, but this particular discipline, besides furnishing a method for those in search of a technique, offers a breadth of grasp and a hold on objectivity which have not been achieved by those who have attacked the problem from a particular political or economic viewpoint.

If, as is often contended, the best histories are those written with a bias, it is at least in part because the author sees invidious relations between groups he dislikes and their written expression. Yet the man with a bias is liable to the defects of his virtue. First, he may fail to see the connections between the thought and position of his own group, and may claim a superior validity for the ideas of his own class, as has been the case with Marx and his followers. Second, he may make serious errors in the overzealous application of his own preconceptions, as has Parrington on Thomas Hooker, or Babbitt on Wordsworth. Finally, such a scholar may isolate his one pet factor and claim that this factor is the cause of literature. But society is too complex for such a procedure.

More helpful is the widely accepted analogy of dynamic equilibria, as worked out by Willard Gibbs, applied to biology by L. J.

---

[1]Karl Mannheim, IDEOLOGY AND UTOPIA, translated by L. Wirth and E. Shils (New York, 1936). Chapter V and *passim* is the basic reference for this paper.

Henderson, and to society by Pareto. Gibbs found that in a closed system with a given number of variables the equations could be worked out so as to predict what effect the change of one variable would have upon the others. But in society, and especially in literature, the system is not closed, for we cannot follow the laboratory technique of excluding outside influences,[2] and even the number of variables is unknown. Thus the pursuit of one variable does not produce any causal connections, since an observable change in this factor may be merely an adjustment to a change in another. To the objection of Sorokin that the change of some factors not causally or functionally related to the rest will produce no or little change in the balance of the whole,[3] the answer may be made in passing that science takes this into account, since it is interested in the more significant changes and tries to allow for the results of the less important variables.

Accepting the concept of equilibria, the sociology of knowledge by its inclusiveness and refined technique, minimizes the defects of earlier attempts to link literature and society. It begins with the generally accepted assumption that thought is conditioned by society, and is unique only in carrying this assumption to its logical conclusion by pointing out that our own thought too is socially conditioned. On this postulate the whole elaborate structure of the sociology of knowledge is based. It claims that there is a large social content in the thought of any individual, and that many ideals and attitudes are absorbed in youth by even the greatest geniuses. This body of ideas is social in origin, and insofar as it was originally designed as a basis for group action, it is a rationalization of the group's interests. Thus the total ideology of the sociology of knowledge does not insinuate that the writer is trying to deceive, but seeks the relationships between certain thought forms and the cultural configurations in which they occur.

But the corollary that our own thought is suspect is what gives the sociology of knowledge its advantage in objectivity. Karl Mannheim goes so far as to point out that only in a time when

---

[2] E. Zilsel, "Physics and the Problem of Historico-sociological Laws", PHILOSOPHY OF SCIENCE, VIII (Oct., 1941), 569.
[3] P. A. Sorokin, SOCIAL AND CULTURAL DYNAMICS (New York, 1937), I, 14-22.

social forces are in such conflict that we are all challenged to examine the usually unconscious basis of our own thought, will the conception of total ideology arise. Indeed, he gets into deep water at this juncture by claiming that since society affects all thought, all knowledge is relative. He has of course been generally attacked for this untenable conclusion. The distinction between empirical and pragmatic truth made by the pragmatists, that between cognitive and non-cognitive knowledge made by the logical positivists, and that between a scientific proposition and an emotive statement made by the semanticists are still valid.⁴ That is, the truth of Einstein's general theory of relativity cannot be impugned by reference to the social factors which led him to formulate the problem, nor, as the Nazis claim, by the fact that he is a Jew.

But as Mannheim himself states, and all specialists claim, it is not necessary to accept his epistemology in order to apply his technique, which is the immediate subject of this paper. This process may be subdivided into a number of steps, not all of which need be applied to any one problem. First, select a period for study and pick the problem to be treated, setting up the leading concept and its opposite. Second, on the initial level of imputation analyze all the works involved, trace them to the central common idea, for example, trancendentalism, and produce a structural type which makes the *Weltanschauung* clear. Third, analyze the works and see to what extent they fit the construction. Blends and crossings of viewpoints within each work will be pointed out, and the actual history of the thought style will be charted. Fourth, on the level of sociological imputation, by going behind the *Weltanschauung*, seek to derive the structure and tendencies of thought style from the composition of the groups, classes, generations, occupations, sects, parties, regions, cliques, or schools which express themselves in that mode. Fifth, explain the direc-

---

⁴Charles Morris, FOUNDATIONS OF THE THEORY OF SIGNS, International Encyclopedia of Unified Science, I, No. 2 (Chicago, 1928), 40-41; Robert K. Merton, "Karl Mannheim and the Sociology of Knowledge," THE JOURNAL OF LIBERAL RELIGION, II (Winter, 1941), 134. Mannheim believes that objectivity can be achieved by synthesizing the vistas of several ideologies. While the practical value of such perspectives is tremendous, the question whether his epistemological generalizations are cogent still remains. Perhaps they show the effects of the philosophical atmosphere he breathed.

tion of development of the body of thought "through the structural situation and the changes it undergoes" and "through the constantly varying problems raised by the changing structure."

To make this general scheme meaningful it is necessary to explain each step in somewhat greater detail and to fill in some of the rather sketchily outlined steps of the process. Mannheim's formulation of the technique of the sociology of knowledge is designed to hold out the effects of prejudice as long as possible in the research process. A discussion of the constructed type will make this clear.

The first step in the construction of a type, a step which Mannheim does not himself distinguish from the second, is the selection of a concept and its opposite. It may at once be objected that this polarity is too simple, but by going from the general to the specific, later analyses produce all the necessary categories. Thus if one is dealing with transcendentalism, both Puritanism and Unitarianism would have to be adopted as contrasting thought forms and perhaps deism and materialism as well. More damning would be the contention that prejudice, which is to be so carefully excluded, operates at the very outset in the choice of the problem and the leading concepts. But this fact is of no methodological significance. One scholar will choose more fruitful subjects than another and will obtain more significant results, but the conclusions of both, if correctly obtained, will be equally true.

As for the second step, the construction of the type, this can be carried out with perfect objectivity. According to Professor Howard Becker,[5] this construct is not even an hypothesis, but rather an inductively derived heuristic fiction which is theoretically neither true nor false and to which given works will conform no more closely than they do to Professor René Wellek's similarly constructed period or movement.[6] Thus there should be no reason for falsely attibuting good or bad characteristics to the type, though some scholars do indeed have this difficulty. In theory their approval or hatred of romanticism should not prevent them from constructing the type objectively or at least hiring

[5]H. E. Barnes and H. and F. B. Becker (editors), CONTEMPORARY SOCIAL THEORY (New York, 1940), Ch. 2, "Constructive Typology."

[6]"Periods and Movements", in ENGLISH INSTITUTE ANNUAL, 1940 (New York 1941), 90-91.

someone else to do it. Once constructed, the type is useful in prediction. Given the type and a certain set of conditions there is at least a statistical likelihood, given the return of the conditions, that the results which held previously will follow. If, as has often been maintained from Aristotle to Bateson, history is interested in the uniqueness of the event, the sociology of knowledge, by trying to see whether configurations recur, shows the broader scope.

The third step of imputation, in which the works of a period are analyzed to see to what extent they actually fit the construction, to note the blends and crossings, and to chart the actual course of an idea, is also designed to produce objective results. Certainly the cross checking is more likely to be accurate than the technique of free, untested hypotheses, illustrated with carefully chosen examples, or of empathetic feeling into a period. By "controlled observation," that is, analysis and resynthesis, the course taken by a concept can be more accurately charted than by general impression.

However useful these three steps may be, it is the fourth, sociological imputation, which is the most distinctive and most significant. At the same time it demands the most thorough elaboration. In the first place Mannheim contends that not only the content, but the very structure of thought may be determined by the historico-social situation of the writer. A number of traits may be subject to this influence: (a) Words or concepts like *liberty* may have different meanings for different groups. (b) The absence of certain concepts may indicate the absence of social drives in that direction. Thus the idea of progress did not arise until the static society of the middle ages had been broken up. (c) Different groups have specially oriented categories. Conservatives are likely to be absolutists conceiving society as an organic, morphological whole; liberals are likely to be relativists and analytic rationalists. (d) Thought models are historico-socially oriented. Pragmatism can arise when the common sense middle class becomes intellectually dominant and respectable. (e) The degree of concreteness and abstractness of a theory may depend upon the social situation. Thus theoretical or moral justifications may cloak materialistic interests. Or an attitude may not be worked out because the contradictions within it would become apparent, as may have been the case with Emerson's thought. (f) An ontology itself is socially conditioned.

Thus it is clear that the place and dignity which authors enjoy in society may influence the nature of their output. Even more important than the group into which an author is born is the group with which he affiliates. This is true because authors tend to become "free" intellectuals, men who through insight and education are able to see through the traditions of their own group, and to ally themselves intellectually with any other sector of society. Certainly the shake-up of values produced by university experience is a widespread phenomenon. The artist too, may break loose from his own group, may become a theorist, like Burke for a superior class, or like Marx for the masses. This new attachment will become more important than the author's origin. Or to put it another way, the type of public to which the author addresses himself will tend to shape his work. The levels of taste in society and the social preconceptions of the various layers will influence the aesthetic and moral aims of the writer who is appealing, consciously or not, to the group view. A study of patronage and emolument systems will cast some light on the unstated assumptions of the authors. Some exploring has already been done, but there are still many blank areas on the map.

The fifth and last step in the process, the development of a body of thought through the structural situation as related to the country as a whole and to the changes in time, involves several points. First the importance of a given group is not the same in all countries. In the nineteenth century, the position of the landed gentry was different in Germany and England, for example.[7] Consequently the position of the group must be worked out before its attitude can be clarified and explained. Next, the relationship between groups is not constant. Thus American history may be taken as the decline of the landed aristocracy, and ultimately of agrarian interests. Finally, even if the balance of interests remains relatively constant, the issues and the ideologies are continually changing. *States rights,* for example, which was once the agrarian doctrine, has now become the slogan of

---

[7]E. Kohn-Bramstedt, ARISTOCRACY AND THE MIDDLE CLASSES IN GERMANY (London, 1937), 10.

the business and financial interests which it was originally intended to forestall.

This outline of the Mannheim technique will strike many as immediately applicable to society, but there may be doubts whether it is applicable to literature, or if applicable, whether it has any real advantages over other types of approach. Admittedly the connections between the social base and the literary superstructure are complex, intricate, and often concealed, while the relations upon the intellectual level are exceptionally strong. Nevertheless the author is a member of society. Certainly the content of prose and poetry, the products of living authors, will be influenced by the author's place in that society. That this is true of the novel is sufficiently obvious, and specific relationships could be multiplied. The author's attitudes, too, are amenable to the same approach. He may be accepting the situation or he may be reacting against it by trying to produce reforms, or by turning aside, like the priest and the levite, to absorb himself in nature, self-contemplation, or art for art's sake.

Once it is seen that this is a valid discipline in the study of literature, it becomes evident that the system has many advantages. In the realm of objectivity, besides offering a controlled procedure, it enables the scholar to bring to light the unarticulated forces operating in the history of thought, and it enables him to expose his own view and to allow for it. In the realm of completeness it is particularly superior. Other social approaches have been applied in a partial and sporadic fashion, but the sociology of knowledge aims at a systematic approach. Furthermore this system includes many factors, since it does not seek to explain all things on the basis of only one cause, but rather emphasizes the interaction between thought and the social structure. It follows the history of an idea in the intellectual realm, but not there alone, and in the social realm, but not there alone; it is the interconnections which are traced. Thus Whitman is developed not solely from Emerson and not solely from society, but from both. In this way the technique avoids the difficulties of economic determinism. On the assumption that the class system will not explain all thought, the sociology of knowledge refines on the older concepts by adding smaller but clearly distinguishable subdivisions such as generations and regional groups, which are certainly distinct enough in American society. And it escapes the difficulties of economic determinism in another way. Without minimizing the importance of economic factors, it recognizes with the American pragmatists the influence of "theoretical," that is, intellectual factors in producing change, and thus it prevents the question-begging of the crude application of the economic cause.

Furthermore it is useful in many fields of research. It is perhaps most easily applied in biographical studies of individuals to explain why the men thought as they did. For example, the apparent inconsistencies in Dr. Holmes become explicable when he is looked upon as fitting one of the sub-types set up in Veblen's THEORY OF THE LEISURE CLASS.

The study of forms is also amenable to this approach. There can be little doubt, for example, that the present cult of poetry which can be understood only with a key is the result of the general attitude that the poet is a dreamer who has nothing to say. Recognizing that the poet as seer is dead, the author intentionally contracts his audience and makes his work precious in order to build up his own dignity[8]. Literary scholars should also be encouraged by the success of art historians like Panofsky, Wind, Sorokin, and Shapiro who have charted the changes of forms and imputed them to the philosophies and social situations of the artists. Professor Bateson's contention that poetic types depend upon language may be referred back to the social changes which produced the linguistic changes. I have begun work on the transcendentalists, endeavoring to explain on the basis of this technique why they habitually express themselves in essays, short poems, and occasionally history, rather than in novels or long, dramatic poems. While my conclusions are not ready, it is already gratifying to discover how many fresh approaches are unearthed in the application of this methodology.

In the study of the history of ideas this technique is of major

---

[8]The problem is more complex than here suggested, not only because various types of obscurity must be isolated, but because obscurity itself must be explained partly by psychological factors, which are not the immediate subject of this paper. Mr. Kenneth Burke's brilliant analyses show how well the social and psychological approaches can be combined.

significance—perhaps of primary significance in the study of those transitional, unstable periods which accompany social change. In American literature, the rise and decline of movements like Puritanism, deism, transcendentalism, humanitarianism, realism, naturalism, imagism, the idea of progress, pre-first-World-War-pessimism, Marxism, the renaissance of metaphysical poetry, the growth of critical schools, the changing rôle of the aristocracy, and the cultural levels of the omnibus middle class—all these urgently need analysis from a social viewpoint.

The sociology of knowledge also aids intellectual history by indicating in what way literature can affect society. As has been pointed out, this system does not claim that all thought is socially determined. Thought patterns are part of the equilibrium of society, and a change of thought can change the entire balance of the equilibrium. Mannheim says that the special realm of this study is the interconnections between thought and society. Certainly there are links on the intellectual plane and one man's thought may influence that of another as Plato's did that of Aristotle. The thought of an individual may also influence that of a group, even to the extent of producing social change. This was true of UNCLE TOM's CABIN and of Montesquieu's doctrine of the separation of powers. Even exaggerated, simplified, or transformed ideas operate. Thus Jefferson was less democratic than his influence, Kant was not understood by the American transcendentalists, nor Hegel by many conscious proletarians. But lest it be thought that other influences are being ruled out, it is suggested that whether one's conception of romantic love is formed by Hemingway or Kathleen Norris depends upon one's own view of what seems suitable and true.

But after all, this methodology provides no panacea. It will not produce laws of causation; it will not be able to explain the temperament of an author; it will not even explain why a work is great literature. That depends upon the author's ability to appeal to a relatively unchanging core of human emotion. Not being universal, this technique cannot because of its grounds claim that other methods are invalid. Whether the approach to literature is individual or social it holds to be a question of method, not principle. The results may not be isomorphic, but when they are not collaborative or corroborative, they are at least not in conflict. Consequently this approach does not exclude the genetic, nor the historical, nor the aesthetic approach, as Dr. Bergmann and Dr. Spence make clear, but recognizes each of them as valid so far as it goes.[9] Nor will it eliminate the bias of the scholar; it gives him a controlled technique and even a way of recognizing his prejudices, but he is still human and may need forgiveness. There may even be a danger of the technique's leading a scholar into fields which properly belong to sociology, but this consequence is not inevitable or necessary, since the aim is not to produce a sociology of literature, but to use a sociological technique already developed to interpret literature.

To define the limitations of the sociology of knowledge is also to mark off its area of strength. One of its main values is that it offers a guide to the followers of those pioneers who first attacked literature from a particular social viewpoint. If this technique does not make these followers objective, its cross checking may at least prevent them from committing egregious blunders. Furthermore it may open up new insights, not only for those who have used similar techniques before, but also for those who have not. The application of the complete methodology will demand an amazingly thorough examination of all aspects of the problem, some of them newly disclosed, and this is a most exciting feature. Because it emphasizes the links between thought and society, it transcends either purely intellectual or purely social considerations by including them both. But because it cannot explain literary greatness it does not rule out criticism. If the scholar has actually been able to prevent his bias from interfering with his thought while he has been assembling and organizing his material, he feels all the more the desire to act as judge from the position of his own taste and principles. As Professor Harry H. Clark says, it is the duty of the scholar to explain, interpret, and evaluate.[10] But since we must understand what we judge, I suggest that the sociology of knowledge is of great value in performing the first two steps of this process.

---

[9] G. Bergmann and K. W. Spence, "Operationism and Theory in Psychology," PSYCHOLOGICAL REVIEW, XLVIII (Jan., 1941), 3.

[10] "Intellectual History", ENGLISH INSTITUTE ANNUAL, 1940 (New York, 1941), 123.

Toward a Cultural Approach to Literature
Louise M. Rosenblatt

from

College English, vol. 7, no. 8, 1946.

Toward a Cultural Approach to Literature

LOUISE M. ROSENBLATT[1]

PRESIDENT ROOSEVELT's warning that if civilization is to survive we must cultivate the science of human relationships—the ability of all peoples, of all kinds, to live together and work together in the same world, at peace"— has gained even more drastic urgency since it was written on the day before his death. International understanding and the moral and intellectual solidarity of all peoples must be achieved— under penalty of extinction if we fail. Educators have been especially alert to this need, and there has been a renewed concern to clarify the ways in which each field of study can better serve those ends. In the field of literature the need to acquaint American youth with the literary achievements of foreign peoples has been urged as an important means of eliminating provincialism and fostering sound international understanding. And, since international sympathies must be reinforced by moral solidarity at home, the study of foreign literatures has been urged, too, as a means of eliminating prejudice against people of various foreign ancestries within our own country.

An enveloping philosophy for the study of foreign literatures and a clear sense of the basic attitudes and insights that we seek to foster are essential. The crux of the problem lies in the development of attitudes toward cultural differences. It is not necessary to document here the existence, even among American

[1] Assistant professor, department of English, Brooklyn College, Brooklyn, N.Y.

college graduates, of attitudes of rejection or superiority toward those, abroad or at home, who diverge from accepted American norms. To be fruitful, the study of foreign literature should be permeated by consistent ways of thinking about cultural differences. In particular circumstances, with particular instructors and students, one or another type of course or series of texts may be desirable; but their effectiveness for fostering humane attitudes will depend on the concepts about people and cultures which make up the climate of thought within which the reading and study are carried on. The following remarks are an attempt to initiate discussion by sketching some of the ideas which should be implicit in any treatment of foreign literatures which seeks to serve our ultimate humanistic goals.

I

The anthropologists, through their study of primitive and modern societies, or, to use the anthropological term, cultures, have provided us with the ideological framework for our problem. They have reinforced our awareness of the amazing diversity of social patterns that men have created—strikingly different modes of behavior, types of personal relationships, ideas of good and evil, religious beliefs, social organizations, economic and political mechanisms, and forms of art. But the anthropologists find these differences evidence only of the extreme plasticity of the human creature. They have made us understand that men have fashioned these divergent patterns of living out of the raw materials of their common humanity, out of the common drives which all human beings share.

The scientific evidence is that race or any inherited physical traits cannot be recognized as causal factors in the diverse patterning of cultures. Each culture utilizes, at any time, only a limited number out of the vast range of potentialities possessed by the human creature. Everything from physical traits to the ability to dream dreams and see visions may receive different valuations in different societies, and a people may at different times in its history pour its personal and group life into widely contrasting molds. There will be many differences from individual to individual within a society, of course; but all will be shaped by reaction to the dominant pressures, the accepted habits, and the system of values, of that culture. There would be a great difference in the resulting personality, for example, according to whether the same human organism were born into a society which rewards gentleness, moderation, and co-operativeness or one that prizes aggressiveness, violence, and individualism. For each society develops some of the individual's latent possibilities and represses or rejects others.

Thus we come to see our American society as playing out one among the many modes of living that mankind has developed and as one among the many diverse cultural patterns man has evolved from his common drives and capacities. If we tend to feel that our ways have an inherent rightness and divine sanction, that, too, is an illusion that we share with individuals shaped by other cultures, which seem equally self-justified to them.

When the individual sees himself and all that he takes for granted in our American society as a product of the same process of cultural conditioning that has produced other personalities in very different types of society, he can acquire the objectivity necessary for meeting the impact of those differences. They will be recognized as variations on the common human theme and need not be met with blind and self-justified suspicion or fear or repugnance. The emotional rejection of differences can give way to intelligent reflection on them.[2]

Infused with this cultural approach, the study of foreign literature should indeed have a liberating effect. (I am assuming, of course, that any study of foreign literature will, above all, help the student to have direct, personal enjoyment of literary works as works of art.) Literature gives us concrete evidence of how differently men have phrased their lives in different societies. But literature, by its very nature, helps also to bridge those differences. For literature, which permits us to enter emotionally into other lives, can be viewed always as the expression of human beings who, in no matter how different the ways, are, like us, seeking the basic human satisfactions, experiencing the beauties and rigors of the natural world, meeting or resisting the demands of the society about them, and striving to live by their vision of what is important and desirable in life. Imaginative sharing of human experience through literature can thus be an emotionally cogent means of insight into human differences as part of a basic human unity.

[2] This statement of key ideas is necessarily sketchy. See Ruth Benedict, *Patterns of Culture* (Houghton Mifflin, 1934), and *Race: Science and Politics* (Viking Press, 1943), and the general works by Franz Boas, Ralph Linton, Bronislaw Malinowski, Margaret Mead, Robert H. Lowie, *et al.*

The ultimate human meaning of a work of literature, and especially a foreign work, is not that of a photographic document but emerges as we penetrate beneath the exotic social forms and themes to discover the structure of emotional relationships and moral emphases it embodies. Our delight in the picturesque or dramatic externals of foreign life, our interest in strange folkways, need not obscure our sense of the literary work as a crystallization of human emotions and aspirations, as a patterning of attitudes toward the world of man and nature. Sometimes these are explicit in the work, sometimes implicit, clothed in story and symbol. But always it is possible to reach through the literary work to the broader human patterns it reflects. Through the study of foreign literature, then, we are seeking to help our students to broaden their vision of the varied images of life, of the different patterns of values, of the contrasting habits of emotional response, that other peoples have created out of our common human potentialities. And these differences are to be seen as alternatives, beside which our way of life and our own system of values are to be placed.

Nor will the images of human behavior and personality encountered in literature fall into a neat hierarchy, with American society perched at the summit. It will not always be easy to decide in what direction the balance should fall, if these patterns are weighed in terms of their meaning for the fulfilment of human capacities. In some societies, as in the Greek or the feudal, men will be seen, for example, to have elaborated ideals of a different range of personal loyalties, a more exacting code of honor, than in our own, or to have envisaged stronger claims of friendship (cf. Pater's *Two Early French Stories*). Again, some societies tend to give greater prestige than we do to the artist and the intellectual. Or it may be necessary to make clear at what social cost certain types of elegance in art and manners, as in seventeenth-century France, were achieved. Moreover, in the same society—and in the same great work of art—high sensitivity on some points may coexist with great callousness on others. An acceptance of cruelty or violence, a view of the child as a little savage to be tamed, a suppression of women, and a glorification of brute power may be associated with much that we admire ethically and aesthetically. Perhaps such insights may lead to the question whether America, too, may not have cultural blind spots, juxtaposed to humane sensitivity at other points.

A concern with attitudes toward cultural differences gives special point to the literary scholar's interest in clarifying the relationship between the literary work and the society which produced it —and especially the relationship between the author and his audience. Of course, we know that literature is not a mere mirror of life. Literature is itself an integral part of a culture and has its own complex relationship to the rest of the cultural setting. A literary work often reflects only some one segment of the society, to which it may be addressed. If sometimes it offers a realistic description, at other times it may represent an escape from, or compensation for, actual conditions. And always it implies the temperament of the author—more or less at one with the dominant modes of thought and feeling in the society about him. It would be self-defeating, if in our zeal to find "characteristic" or "representative" foreign works we minimized these considerations and unwittingly reinforced the tendency to make hasty generalizations about foreign peoples.[3] Moreover, we are less insulated from the full human impact of the great masterpieces if we see how they often reflect only one part of the arc of a society.

Perhaps all of this sums up merely to insistence that we approach the literature of other peoples with the same concern for its intrinsic human meaning with which we approach our own literature today. The value of such intercourse with, and such an open mind toward, the cultural alternatives encountered through foreign literature of the past and present lies in the objectivity which it can foster. Such a comparative approach opens the path to escape from unquestioning acceptance of the familiar and from consequent crude prejudice against all other ways. If we are indeed seeking to foster international understanding, it must be based on such objectivity toward our own and other ways of life.

The same approach to differences can help to dissolve attitudes of rejection toward the minorities within our American society, who possess differentiating traits due to their national ancestry, their religious training, their segregation because of color, their belonging to one or another economic group. And the view of differences as alternatives due to environmental variations may lead even to the recognition that minority groups may possess some qualities, may follow some standards of behavior, such as habits of group aid, or may value some kinds of temperaments that, instead of being spurned as divergent from American norms, should be incorporated as an accepted part of the American pattern.

II

Awareness of the cross-fertilization of cultures is another insight militating against provincialism that can be fostered through the study of literature. Interchange from society to society has been one of the important factors in cultural growth and enrichment. Even among primitive cultures, the anthropologists point to those marginal peoples who have remained culturally impoverished and static because they were cut off from contact with other societies. The history of our Western civilization embodies a long series of such fructifying contacts. Within our own field of literature our problem is an embarrassment of riches in seeking to do justice to the intermingled cultural streams that have fed us. We must include at least the Hebrew, Greek, and Roman among the ancient literatures; the Middle Ages and the Renaissance must be presented as European developments with various influences from the East; and, in more recent times of national literatures, what a vast network of crosscurrents, of give-and-take across national frontiers!

Students of comparative literature remind us that, when such borrowings, such "influences," occur, it is because native conditions have created a favorable soil on which the foreign seed can be implanted. Each literature possesses, and continues to maintain, its own special characteristics, and the foreign influence may undergo a sea-change as it is incorporated into the new literary setting. Yet beneath the surface similar emotional needs and intellectual tendencies have made possible the transfusion of ideas, themes, or artistic forms.

[3] How disillusioning it was for many Frenchmen in 1870 to discover that the image of the romantic, sentimental, dreamy, contemplative Germans— based largely on the reading of German romantic literature—did not at all correspond to the full reality! See Fernand Baldensperger, *La Littérature: création, succès, durée* (Paris: Flammarion, 1927), p. 201.

This view of the intricate interpenetration of cultures both prevents a smug cultural egotism and permits a hopeful sense of possibilities for the future. No society is justified in the belief that it has produced the supermen toward which all history has been tending. We are not the supremely superior heirs who incorporate all that was good in the past. We see that peoples, at one time looked upon as barbarians and inherently inferior by the more advanced societies about them, have later, in the course of cultural interchange and growth, developed new and undreamed-of outlets for human capacities and have produced writers speaking across the barriers of language and time to their fellow-humans.

A reason frequently stated for studying the foreign works which have contributed to our own cultural heritage is that we shall thus inculcate a respect and sympathy for the peoples who produced these great writings: the Bible will demonstrate oneness in ethical and religious ideals with the Jews; Dante will lead to a sense of fraternity with the Italians; Homer, the Greeks; and so on. Such an increased appreciation and sympathy for specific peoples should surely be fostered.

But should there not be an equal emphasis on the fact of our common indebtedness to a multi-national, or multi-cultural, ancestry? The Bible, Homer, Shakespeare, Molière, Goethe, Ibsen, and the others are not only bonds between us and the people whose national pride they are. Such works are bonds also between us and all the other peoples they have enriched. The intermarriages of minds in the course of history have given us and other modern peoples many of the same cultural ancestors. Are not the Greek and Latin classics cultural links between us and the French, for example? And are not Shakespeare, Goethe, Ibsen, or the Bible, mediators among many cultures?

Indeed, when we look at the histories of literature as they now exist, we may well wonder if the nationalist obsession of recent centuries has not too strongly dominated our thinking and obscured the realities. Such revolutions have come about in the course of any national literature that an Englishman of the eighteenth century, for instance, might feel more at home with a French contemporary than with his own English descendant of the romantic period. Our national cultures are so complex, and include such a wide range of temperaments and philosophies, that an American poet today may find himself more akin to, say, a contemporary French poet than to another American poet. Fortunately, we do not always put nationalist categories first in treating literature. Courses in medieval literature and the Renaissance perforce cut across national and linguistic boundaries. Even in dealing with more recent times of intense nationalism, we are breaking away from distorting national compartmentalizations, to concentrate on great common movements of ideas and feeling, as in courses on the romantic movement, realism in fiction, the symbolist and post-symbolist trends. The study of different genres, drama, the short story, the novel, poetry, also leads us to move back and forth across national frontiers. More of this emphasis on parallel developments should permeate courses focused on American or English literature if we wish to present modern civilization as a co-operative enterprise transcending national frontiers. The evidence of the rich harvest of cultural interchanges in the past can be made the source of a receptive attitude toward such interchange with an ever-widening circle of peoples in the future.

The approach to cultural differences that has been sketched thus far is equally pertinent to the problem of affecting attitudes toward differences within our own society. Not only do we Americans share the general multiple indebtedness of our Western civilization, but we are living embodiments of a very special illustration of cultural intermingling. American history is coming to be understood more and more in terms of the interplay of peoples and patterns drawn from many lands. The period of zealous "Americanization," with its image of differences merged in the American melting pot, has given way to a growing realization of the fact that unity need not mean uniformity. The newer and more constructive image is that of an *orchestration*[4] of individual and group differences into a harmonious national unity. Differences can be welcomed as a national asset, a condition making for cultural fertility.

Teachers of English, both in the colleges and in the schools, may have to admit more than a small share of the responsibility for having perpetuated too narrow a conception of what is American. The tendency to overstress the so-called "Anglo-Saxon" elements in our culture is understandable. But without scanting this major aspect of our American literary tradition, we can do greater justice to the values in our life and literature that have resulted from the incorporation into our American society of people with varied traditions of behavior, feeling, and expression. The emphasis should not be on differences in themselves but rather on the fact that, out of this wealth

[4] Horace M. Kallen, *Culture and Democracy in the United States* (Boni & Liveright, 1924), p. 124.

of diverse temperaments and ways, we have laid the foundations for, and are together continuing to create, an integrated American culture. The special mark of this culture can be its flexibility, its fostering of a broad and fertile range of individual differences—some of which may be due to diversity of ancestry—within the framework of a creatively democratic society.

Given the complexity of the cultural picture, let us be especially careful that the study of foreign literature not lead to the mistaken notion that the label—English or French or Chinese or Polish—can be equated with any individual. The very laudable effort in the schools, at present, to stress the contributions of the various groups to our cultural heritage seems sometimes to fall into this error. Such labels denote broad cultural patterns, within which there can be great individual variations. The boy of Italian ancestry, for instance, may weary of having it assumed that he will take special pride in Dante and Leonardo da Vinci or that his schoolmates will value him more because of these great Italians. The boy may himself respond more to Homer or Walt Whitman—and they are as much his heritage as is Dante. Above all, we must remember that his Italian ancestry is only one of the factors in the complex process of cultural conditioning to which his life in America has exposed him. The concept of the interplay of cultural elements may thus help us to liberate ourselves from too rigid national or cultural categorizations and may permit us to look at individuals within our own and other cultures *as* individuals.

III

The comparative approach to cultures, the placing of our own beside the others, represents only the first step in the process of developing international and human understanding. Students, it may be objected, becoming acquainted with cultures extremely different from, yet in their own terms as valid as, our own, may lose their provincialism but retain only a sterile relativism, arguing that what is "good" in one culture may be "evil" in another. A similar confusion may result from the turning with equal enthusiasm from one great work to another in, let us say, a course in world literature. Nor do we wish to exchange the feeling of superiority of the smugly complacent American for the feeling of inferiority endured by another kind of American. A recurrent phenomenon in our country has been the intellectual or the artist who has reached out for the aesthetic riches of foreign lands and has become alienated from the American life about him.

The answer to these objections has been implicit throughout this discussion: the comparative approach, the awareness of cultural differences as cultural alternatives, to serve as a basis for a sound educative process, must be buttressed by an active sense of values. Only by turning a *critically* appreciative eye upon our own and other cultures, our own and other literatures, shall we avoid either excessive smugness or excessive humility. The fundamental criteria for such a critical attitude are provided by our democratic ideals. The belief in the value and dignity of the human being that has been the leaven throughout our history can be the foundation for such a system of values. Though we have in many ways fallen far short of our democratic ideals, the common awareness of those ideals has been our conscience and our goad. The fact that within our own society there are tendencies that some-

times frustrate and obstruct our democratic aspirations can be a reminder that in all cultures there are varied and often conflicting elements. There must be developed the kind of international understanding that respects the validity of other cultures and does not seek stupidly to impose our own but yet, at the same time, discriminates between those patterns that threaten and those that serve the democratic ideal and the mutually helpful relations among peoples. The problem becomes one of discriminating, in our own and other literatures, between those elements that nourish the sense of man's dignity and worth and those that, no matter how satisfying aesthetically, reinforce attitudes inimical to this view or reflect an authoritarian spirit. Thus the student is liberated imaginatively to look objectively upon his own and other societies and to envisage the possibility of even greater approximation toward our democratic goals.

If we claim that the study of literature has value for life today, if we believe that through such study we can contribute toward creation of the ways of thinking and feeling so sorely needed in our domestic and international life, we must make much more important than ever before this critical process based on a vital awareness of democratic values. These should not, of course, be made the subject of constant preachments. Nor need courses in literature include lectures on cultural anthropology. Such insights can usually be fostered in terms of specific literary works, for in their personal and human import lies a potent means for affecting attitudes. This will be accomplished through constantly recurring emphases, through the approach to literary works in terms of their underlying structure of emotional relationships and social values, and through a consistent attitude toward cultural differences. The ends we are so eager to serve can, I believe, be achieved when the study of foreign literature embodies such a critically comparative approach, based on the democratic system of values.

Literature and Society
Charles I. Glicksberg

from

Arizona Quarterly, vol. 8, no. 2. Summer 1952.

LITERATURE AND SOCIETY

By CHARLES I. GLICKSBERG

FOR quite some time there has been an insistent demand that the writer assume his political responsibilities and take an active interest in the complex problems of the world. The social implications of this militant aesthetic are unmistakable: the creative personality must abandon Axel's castle and grapple self-sacrificingly and single-mindedly with the hydra-headed evils of his age. Anyone who ventures to disagree with the apostles of this crusading aesthetic gospel is immediately judged guilty of supporting the cult of art for art's sake. Such footloose individualism is, of course, looked upon as the mark of the beast, the infallible sign of incipient fascism. Irresponsibility of this kind, it is charged, converts the artist into a rootless Bohemian, a man without organic ties in his own culture, orphaned and alienated, convinced of his own uniqueness and genius because fundamentally he is concerned only with his own ego.

The most strenuous advocates of this aesthetic creed have been the Marxists, who fanatically urge that the writer cannot escape his social, economic, and cultural environment. Only by affiliating himself with "the universal democratic humanism" that Communism makes possible will his life gain singleness of purpose and his work be infused with vital meaning. If in this new role he becomes a strident propagandist, that is a consummation devoutly to be wished, since all art is propaganda.

It is enormously revealing how in times of crisis everyone wants to recruit the writer—and recruit him, naturally, on the "right" side. No one ventures to explain how politics can vitalize and fructify art. Whereas it is fairly clear that art can illuminate the dusty arena of politics—statesmen can learn a great deal from reading, say, Plato, Goethe, Shakespeare, Shelley, or Whitman—

Charles I. Glicksberg, who teaches English at Brooklyn College and the New School, is the author of *Walt Whitman and the Civil War*.

it is not at all clear, despite the copious fulmination of the Communist press in England, Soviet Russia, and the United States, how the writer advances his art one iota by plunging head over heels into the troubled political issues of his time.

During the recent war when the people of the United Nations were making common cause against Germany, the writers spoke out vigorously in behalf of world democracy. Some, like Stephen Vincent Benét, Archibald MacLeish, Waldo Frank, and Lewis Mumford, did not have to be convinced of the necessity for taking affirmative action. Archibald MacLeish, for example, carried away by his realization of the frightful danger of the time, bitterly assailed the intellectuals for their aesthetic irresponsibility. Instead of perpetuating American democratic ideals, they found fault with their land, its crass materialism, its sordid and rapacious business ethics, its hideous industrialism and streamlined efficiency, blind to its positive virtues and its great heritage of freedom. He castigated writers like Hemingway and Dos Passos for sowing the seeds of distrust in the susceptible minds of the younger generation, indoctrinating them with a blighting nihilism so that they no longer believed in any moral principle or sense of purpose in life—a charge that is in part confirmed by the recent work of a young critic, John Aldridge, in *After the Lost Generation.*

This violent attack on the war novelists of the preceding generation was hysterical in the extreme. When men like Hemingway and Dos Passos composed their books they were engaged in a crusade against war and set down what they honestly believed was the truth. It is asking too much to expect writers to censor their critical intelligence, to sacrifice truth to the needs of political expediency and ideological faith. If they are men of profound talent and integrity, they cannot turn the current of belief on or off to suit the particular needs of the time. The truth of observation and feeling must come first. Even if their beliefs are denounced as heretical and dangerously negative, they cannot deny their gods.

The writers who were plunged into the maelstrom of the Second World War felt terribly alienated, if not lost. On far-flung battlefields, in lonely outposts of the Pacific, while flying long hours on reconnaissance in Africa or the Mediterranean, on board ship, men came face to face with the ultimate realities of life and achieved a deeper understanding of themselves in relation to the universe. Henceforth the poet was resolved to rid himself of conventions and false ideals; he would get down to the fundamental truth of being, and that truth, he found, was inescapably individual. The intoxicating vision of Marxism, the pipe dream of founding the classless State, went up in smoke. In "New Guinea Letter," Karl J. Shapiro points up this moral. Trapped in a jungle island hot with tropic vegetation, he wonders whether men are more nearly brothers and wryly arrives at negative conclusions. War solves no problems, it only creates new ones. Away with all drugs, he cries. Let us come down to solid earth, to enduring realities, to men as they are. With poignant disenchantment he declares:

> Give me a future you can't dream up,
> Men as they are, as they were begun
> With a nice right emphasis on Number One.
> Keep to the Left but if it gets hectic
> Take a powder on Papa and the dialectic.

Significantly enough, he concludes his poetic letter with a plangent plea for privacy, so that he may retrace his steps and find "The start of the maze within my mind,/The exquisite pattern of mankind."

With the end of the Second World War, the ideological emphasis strangely shifted. Communism, as represented by Soviet Russia, was now the enemy to be fought with every weapon in the arsenal of democracy. Again the writer was hastily summoned to takes sides in this conflict. One group hoarsely urged him to defend civil liberties, to support the waning cause of liberalism, to battle in behalf of the threatened First Amendment to the Constitution, to save civilization before the reactionaries seized power and imposed a fascist regime on the land of the free. With equal vehemence another group called for a holy war against the Communist menace. To add to the confusion of the already confused mind of the writer, there was the politics of the atomic bomb to consider.

It is therefore imperative to make clear what constitutes the legitimate function and place of the writer in society, his duty to himself as a writer and as a man, his relation to contemporary politics. As a writer he has but one compelling duty: to report the truth of human experience as honestly and completely as he can, without distortions, ideological preconceptions, or political bias. If he deals with life as he genuinely experiences it, his work will have all the political and psychoanalytic and sociological overtones that it needs to carry. There is no place in literature for overt political commitments, whether these be in the form of abstractions or categorical orthodoxies. The writer's function is not to label an emotion or stigmatize an attitude; it is not his job to divide people into political or economic groups but to reveal their essential humanity, to project life as sensuously and convincingly as possible. Since his allegiance to his art is primary and absolute, he belongs to no party and is therefore not hamstrung by party directives or class-conscious systems of aesthetics. He is above the battle only in the sense that he judges all the participants, whatever the political standard they work or fight under, by the same all-seeing, creative principle. His party is all of humanity, not a class, not even a nation. For his vision extends beyond all frontiers, sometimes even beyond the confines of life itself. Emphatically not a "class-man," he is concerned with all those on earth who struggle and suffer, strive and fail, as they journey, full of existential anxiety and guilt, to the end of night.

The politics of the writer, however explicit outside of his art, plays no significant role inside his work. Despite Shaw's stoutly proclaimed belief to the contrary, art is not primarily didactic. It never was. The argument that the writer is, like every individual, a product of his culture and therefore inevitably reflects the contradictions and crises of his age, is a truism that has little bearing on the issue at stake, for if everyone is conditioned by the environment then the question must be changed to read: What has the writer made of his environment? By what alchemical process of the imagination has he transformed the raw stuff of life into the enduring beauty and significance of art? Otherwise, why not read sociology or politics? Why not substitute the *Communist Manifesto* or *Das Kapital* or Lenin's revolutionary writings for works of poetry or fiction? It is encouraging to observe that the neo-romantics now reject the theory of the class war. The Russian Revolution opened the eyes of artists to the fruits of revolution that are effected by violence. Such "classless" societies do as much damage to the individual conscience as other forms of society, and they are as heavily impregnated with barbarism. Indeed, Alex Comfort, the most eloquent spokesman of the literary anarchists, is convinced that such collective totalitarianisms are even more repressive than the societies they have replaced.

The greater the writer the more difficult is it to state what politics he happened to hold. Such considerations are, from the point of view of aesthetics, idle and irrelevant. What political views did Shakespeare voice—and who particularly cares? Even with Shelley, his best poems are surely those in which there is no overt political preachment. *Prometheus Unbound* is memorable not because of any political message it preaches but because of the vision it communicates in soaring, impassioned verse of a more perfect humanity. And the best writers of our time belong to the same category of the essentially nonpolitical. What politics did Proust expound in *Swann's Way?* What political testament is to be found in Faulkner's novels, in Robinson Jeffers' or Robert Frost's poetry?

In the perspective of time we are able to see where the Marxist writers and critics and fellow travelers went astray during the feverish, Marxist-obsessed thirties. It is arrant romantic sentimentality to idealize the workers as proletarian heroes. It is equally absurd to expect the writers to play the role of Socialist saviors. If that is to be their aim, then they might as well give up their creative calling and, following the example set by such men as Ralph Fox and Christopher Caudwell, enroll in the army of Communism. But if they remain true to their art, they must realize that there is no correlation between orthodoxy or revolutionary fervor in politics and great or even good poetry. How explain the strange paradox that T. S. Eliot, whose political orientation is certainly ambiguous if not suspect, according to the Communist touchstone of value, has created poetry of a high order, while much of Mayakovsky's work is blatant progaganda? The failure of Marxists to formulate a vital, valid system of aesthetics lay in their rationalistic adherence to a rigid canon of dialectical materialism. Their cardinal sin was that they sought to confine the writer within the ideology of a class. Art, it is true, has its roots in society but it cannot be truly appraised solely in social, political, or economic terms. The object of the writer is to suggest the intrinsic quality of experience in all its immediacy and complexity. He probes beneath political abstractions and topical issues to the underlying, living reality, for his function is neither to propagandize nor to reform society but to report the truth of life as he sees it. Conflict is his native element, and the resolution of order out of chaos the secret of his art.

Russian theoreticians and "proletarian" writers did much to darken counsel and intensify the delirium of confusion. In *Art and Society,* George V. Plekhanov insisted that art is instinct with ideological content and cannot under any circumstances be divorced from it. During the period of civil and interventionist wars, Russia, instead of producing "pure proletarian" literature, whatever that might mean, turned out a motley crew of poets: postsymbolists, acmeists, imaginists, biocosmists, expressionists, lumonists, and nothingists as well as a host of so-called "proletarian" singers. Mayakovsky, who proclaimed himself a futurist, linked up his poetry with the October Revolution, regarding futurism as the most satisfying expression of proletarian culture. With exuberant energy he lyrically advertised the glorious achievements of Soviet Russia during the crtical years, supporting without qualification whatever the Communist Party declared was politically correct. It was this perversion of his undeniably great talent to political ends which led to his suicide. It was equally obvious that Soviet literary criticism, by propagandizing strenuously for the "collectivized" novel in which the masses rather than the individual played the part of the hero, was helping to black out the art of fiction.

Since 1939, the voices of disenchantment have swelled to a mighty chorus; the fellow travelers have recovered from their ideological madness. Malcolm Cowley, one of the disillusioned contributors to *Whose Revolution?*, points out that Communism is essentially an absolutist religion, like Catholicism, and rejects its simplified version of the individual as a mechanical, economic unit, driven by the primary need of self-preservation and governed by rational considerations alone. The future, he feels, cries aloud for a deep faith in life. A religious revival, he feels, is already under way. But whatever religion the West adopts, it will not be that of Marxist Communism. Perhaps the new religion, he speculates, will be the religion of humanity, a creed that would include "such words as freedom, equal opportunity, tolerance, human perfectibility, progress by reason and the sacredness of the individual. It is the faith instinctively held by most American liberals." But whatever society emerges out of the womb of the future, it will have to be sustained by some unifying religious faith.

And it is true that many of the intellectuals have given up the effort to achieve salvation through power-politics. Quite a number of them, as is evident in *Religion and the Intellectuals,* a symposium published by the *Partisan Review,* have gone over to religion. The conclusion they draw (and it offers a striking contrast to the messianic fanaticism of the thirties) is that either politics has failed dismally or, where it has succeeded, it has given rise to a monstrous system of totalitarian tyranny. Some writers, affiliating themselves with the philosophical anarchists and decentralists, no longer believe in mass action. Now, what they want to find out is the answer to such perennial questions as: What is the good life? What are the most important and enduring human needs, and how can these best be satisfied? In some cases, the process of disillusionment has been carried so far that the writers feel that society is the enemy of man. "The giant enemy of the next ten years," declares Alex Comfort in *Art and Social Responsibility*, "will not be a class but irresponsible society."

The writers revolted against Communism because it was a question of either holding fast to their integrity or betraying it, and they repudiated Communism rather than prostitute themselves as artists. They simply refused to be used as innocent pawns in an international game of chess. The alienation of serious-minded and highly gifted writers like André Gide, Arthur Koestler, Edmund Wilson, Herbert Read, D. H. Lawrence, W. H. Auden, Stephen Spender, Richard Wright, Max Eastman, Granville Hicks, Ignazio Silone, and Sidney Hook is not to be dismissed as a bad case of political turpitude or a failure of nerve. The writers have learned to their cost that in the elaboration of their art they must remain uncorrupted by political dogmas. Whatever duty they owe humanity does not transcend their duty to tell the truth. By virtue of his calling the writer rises above party interests and class categories. His primary allegiance to his art presupposes that he try to capture and communicate the flux of reality in all its refractory complexity and variousness.

Even the Surrealists, though they had at one time declared themselves Marxists, were forced to reject many of the aesthetic prescriptions of the Marxists. Art, they insisted, by educating the emotions and liberating the power of the unconscious, is a more potent revolutionary discipline than Marxists propaganda, since men are impelled by emotional rather than rational motives. André Breton's *Manifesto of Surrealism* announced that Surrealism would release the creative imagination of the artist by making a virtue of abnormality and converting madness into a form of freedom. Though Breton pretended that no contradiction was involved in adopting Communism, the ideological conflict that sprang up was inevitable. Though the Kharkov Conference tended to isolate, if not in effect to excommunicate the Surrealists, they defended themselves by quoting Lenin to the effect that enlarging the consciousness of the workers was in itself a dialectical achievement. There was no justification whatsoever, they argued, for writing poetry only on themes closely related to the class struggle. Hence they were exempt from the necessity of concerning themselves with political facts, and their work actually owes nothing to the inspiration of Marxist thought.

Even more significant as a test case is the career of Herbert Read. Even when he was actively trying to reconcile Surrealism with Marxism, he showed little patience with the arbitrary formulations of the Marxist theoreticians, for their conception of reality was politicalized whereas he would have reality retain its complex mysterious totality. The artist was fundamentally a disinterested person, and art, far from being a reflection of the dialectical process, was in itself a synthesis of the contradictions of reality and unreality. In *Poetry and Anarchism,* he threw off the last trammels of Marxist influence. Once he had believed that Soviet Russia was the realization of the highest social ideal; but the Stalinist dictatorship, the ruthless suppression of individual liberty, completed his disillusionment, and he embraced a new social ideal: anarchism. The poet as the dedicated agent of destruction in society must oppose all organized conceptions of the State. He draws no distinction between Fascism and Marxism. Both Marxist and Fascist states have done incalculable harm in that they deliberately exploit the poet for partisan ends. The poet cannot place allegiance to a party above allegiance to humanity as a whole.

In *Existentialism, Marxism and Anarchism,* Herbert Read points out that the Marxist is really more existentialist than the existentialists. Even the dialectical materialist is guilty of harboring some essence, of making subjective decisions and commitments. Man is shaped by more than his productive work; he also develops consciousness, and this means that subjective factors do enter into the warp and woof of the fabric of history. Only thus, argues Read, can the present moral and spiritual development of man be adequately explained. As an anarchist he insists that we must allow for spontaneous, creative growth, which can occur only in open society; such growth cannot take place "in a closed society such as the Marxists have established in Russia."

As George Orwell imaginatively demonstrates in his anti-utopian novel, *Nineteen Eighty-Four,* the history of the Revolution shows how history can be continuously and successfully falsified, so that black becomes white and no one is any the wiser. Under such circumstances, the Party is invariably right. Fortunately, the Party, no matter what desperate expedients it resorts to or what fiendish tortures it invents, cannot make a person believe, inwardly believe, that truth is falsehood and falsehood truth. It is only by remaining obdurately human, regardless of consequences, that the absolutism of the Party is broken.

The one writer who remained consistently human and who most vehemently repudiated the Marxist canons of orthodoxy was D. H. Lawrence, but he was in this respect born before his time. Only today is his vivifying, liberating influence making itself felt. In his intensely personal poetry he not only preached the need for transcending the limitations of the ego but also condemned the vulgar Communism which sought salvation in materialistic consummations. He believed not in wages or profits but in a religion of life. The only thing worth striving for is the oneness of the self, and that battle never ends. In short, Lawrence protests against restricting man to his occupational role, his proletarian or bourgeois status, since this grossly impoverishes life. Men should be spurred on, not by the goad of want or the lure of success, but by the desire to do what is meaningful, creative, organically satisfying. For Lawrence there is only one clue to the universe, and that is the individual soul. "Life consists in living individuals, and always did so consist, in the beginning of everything."

From D. H. Lawrence to Henry Miller and the Apocalyptic school represented by Dylan Thomas there is a direct line of descent. Their writing represents the revolt of the artist against extinction by the massive forces of industrialism, against a civilization in which life has no profound meaning, in which all values are convertible into cash, in which art is regarded as a luxury or perversion. Renouncing all collectivistic creeds, writers of this type create their own religion of art and affirm their faith in the integrity of the self. What the artist must do, if he is to protect his threatened individuality, is to remain adamant in his opposition to merging. Henry Miller carries this nihilist philosophy to its "logical" extreme. The cosmos lives on, the sun shines, the tides of the ocean rise and fall, and these have no concern with the political obsessions of mankind. The main thing is not to become involved in this collective madness but to remain steadfast, earth-rooted, pure in instinct. Henry Miller passionately expounds this creed of nonattachment and nonparticipation. In *Tropic of Cancer,* he declares: "My whole aim in life is to get near to God, that is, to get nearer to myself."

There is the existential motif that runs through a great deal of contemporary literature. Man stands alone in the universe, stripped of illusions, believing in nothing except his own absolute disillusionment. Some writers feel they owe society nothing and are determined to follow the law of their own instincts. The individual self, all that is original and truly creative, is the center and source of life.

Not until today have the implications of Julien Benda's book, *The Treason of the Intellectuals,* been fully grasped. The diagnosis he made of the condition of Western civilization, the betrayal by the intellectuals of the ideals they were supposed to uphold, the subordination of reason and justice to material interests and political passions, has been amply confirmed of late. Benda pleaded in vain for writers to transcend class interests and nationalistic prejudices. Though members of their nation, they must also stand apart from it, by virtue of their disinterestedness and of their concern for humanity as a whole, pursuing the truth regardless of utilitarian considerations, never betraying the ideal of universality. To be saved, we must turn to writers who are not infected with a maniacal lust for power, writers who practice the virtues of disinterestedness, detachment, and justice. The writer who conforms to the dictates of a party or of the State abdicates his true function, betrays his creative responsibility. The revolt against the Communist categorical imperative is made clear by Stephen Spender. In *The God That Failed,* he states that he could not accept "that it was necessary to deny to others the freedom to say what they believed to be true, if this happened to be opposed to the somewhat arbitrary boundaries to freedom laid down by the Proletarian Dictatorship." In short, his conscience revolted against the domination of his intellect by political categories and party edicts. Nor was he convinced that the dictatorship of the proletariat, once established, would cease and gradually give way to the classless society. Then he makes his statement of faith. It is highly significant in that it articulates the belief of many contemporary writers that to concentrate art exclusively on politics would mean the death of art:

"Because I do not believe that the central organizations of the Communists are capable of making a classless society, or indeed of doing anything except establishing the rule of a peculiarly vindictive and jealous bureaucracy, I do not feel that I should surrender my own judgment to theirs . . ."

The writers of the world are increasingly refusing to compromise their integrity and surrender their own judgment to that of any Party or political program.

The Relationship of Literature and Society
Milton C. Albrecht

from

American Journal of Sociology, 59, 1954.

THE RELATIONSHIP OF LITERATURE AND SOCIETY

MILTON C. ALBRECHT

ABSTRACT

In most theories of the relationship of literature and society reflection, influence, and social control are implied. Literature is interpreted as reflecting norms and values, as revealing the ethos of culture, the processes of class struggle, and certain types of social "facts." "Influence" is not strictly the reverse of reflection, since social stability and cultural ideals are involved. Social control, however, articulates closely with one version of reflection, though to a limited extent in complex, dynamic societies.

As Mueller pointed out fifteen years ago,[1] sociologists in the United States have paid little attention to literature and art; they, like other social scientists, have focused primarily on the instrumental aspects of social life.[2] Perhaps this is because practical social problems have grown so urgent—but, whatever the reason, some interest in the arts has persisted and in recent years has increased, however sporadically.[3] Of literary and social histories as well as of more limited investigations there are, of course, an untold number. Our purpose in this paper is to examine critically some of their characteristic viewpoints and theoretical assumptions. One hypothesis is that literature "reflects" society; its supposed converse is that literature influences or "shapes" society. A third hypothesis is that literature functions socially to maintain and stabilize, if not to justify and sanctify, the social order, which may be called the "social-control" theory.

The idea that literature reflects society is at least as old as Plato's concept of imitation.[4] Systematic application of the idea did not appear, however, until about a century and a half ago. The "beginning" might be said to be Madame de Staël's *De la littérature considérée dans ses rapports avec les institutions sociales*,[5] published in 1800, in which the author offered a social and historical interpretation of the literature of several nations. Her outlook was romantic and idealistic, expressed in terms of individual and social perfectionism. Apparently, the theory of reflection arose out of the spirit of nationalism spreading throughout Europe and from the environmentalism of seventeenth- and eighteenth-century thinkers.[6] In general, the idea is a manifestation of a change in man's perspective, crystallized during the nineteenth century in philosophies of history, in the formulation of the theory of evolution, and in the sociological conceptions of societies and their changing character through successive ages.[7]

The essential function of the reflection theory was to "explain" in social and historical rather than individual terms the quality and greatness of literature, as well as its content, style, and forms. In effect, it emphasized social and cultural determinism

[1] J. H. Mueller, "Is Art the Product of Its Age?" *Social Forces*, XIII (March, 1935), 367–76; "The Folkway of Art," *American Journal of Sociology*, XLIV (September, 1938), 222–38.

[2] Kingsley Davis, *Human Society* (New York: Macmillan Co., 1949), p. 392.

[3] Bibliographies may be found in A. S. Tomars, *Introduction to the Sociology of Art* (Mexico City, 1940), pp. 418–21; in H. E. Barnes and H. Becker, *Contemporary Social Theory* (New York: Appleton-Century Co., 1940), pp. 889–92; in James H. Barnett, *Divorce and the American Divorce Novel, 1858–1937* (Philadelphia, 1939), pp. 146 ff.; in Bernard Berelson and Morris Janowitz, *Public Opinion and Communication* (Glencoe, Ill.: Free Press, 1950). For many other sources see Hugh D. Duncan, "An Annotated Bibliography on the Sociology of Literature" (University of Chicago thesis, 1947).

[4] *The Republic*, in *The Works of Plato*, trans. B. Jowett (4 vols. in 1; New York: Dial Press, n.d.), II, 378 ff.

[5] 2 vols.; Paris, 1800. See also *De l'Allemagne* (Paris, 1813).

[6] Max Lerner and Edwin Mims, Jr., "Literature," in *Encyclopedia of the Social Sciences* (New York: Macmillan Co., 1933), IX, 538–39.

[7] Floyd N. House, *The Development of Sociology* (New York: McGraw-Hill Book Co., 1936).

instead of personal inspiration, and it became the broad orientation of innumerable works dealing with the arts. To be sure, other phrases were often used, such as "expression of society" or "mirror of life," but their meaning is practically identical with "reflection." These phrases were applied to nearly everything social and cultural as well as biological and geographical. At one time or another literature has been thought to reflect economics, family relationships, climate and landscapes, attitudes, morals, races, social classes, political events, wars, religion, and many other more detailed aspects of environment and social life.[8]

This diversity results, apparently, from the fact that literature embraces a wide variety of subject matter, representing "settings," behavior patterns, and ideas in their complex interrelationships. It has led some, like Mueller, to believe that the reflection theory is "too all-embracing" to be useful.[9] Nevertheless, it has traditionally been applied in a few major forms, sometimes stated explicitly but often merely implied or assumed—by literary and social historians as well as by sociologists and anthropologists. Probably the commonest conception has been that literature reflects predominantly the significant values and norms of a culture. As DeVoto says, "Literature is a record of social experience, an embodiment of social myths and ideals and aims, and an organization of social beliefs and sanctions."[10] These "social beliefs and sanctions" have usually included religious beliefs and customs, as manifested in myths and other art forms, both of primitive societies and of earlier historical periods of civilizations.[11] Boas finds, for example, that the conditions of life in a number of Indian tribes can be abstracted from their traditional tales: "Beliefs and customs in life and in tales are in full agreement."[12] Whether this is fully as true in complex civilizations such as our own seems less clear, and it is uncertain whether the situations used as vehicles for illustrating or emphasizing important social values are those actually occurring in a society or truly typical. On these questions there seems less general agreement, but the use of literature as an index of significant beliefs and values in a society has been widespread.[13]

In psychology a recent variant of this conception is that stories, at least as presented in movies, reflect the stress patterns and emotional needs of audiences, arising out of shared cultural and social life. Wolfenstein and Leites, for instance, believe that "the common day-dreams of a culture are in part the sources, in part the products of its popular myths, stories, plays and films."[14] As a consequence, the plots of the drama of a particular time or period show a distinctive configuration. Other investigators assume that a kind of collective unconscious is

[8] Cf. Lerner and Mims, *op. cit.*, p. 524. Franz Boas maintains (*General Anthropology* [New York: D. C. Heath & Co., 1938], p. 594) that "the contents of poetry are as varied as the cultural interests of the people." Henry Commager insists (*The American Mind* [New Haven: Yale University Press, 1950], p. 56) that imaginative literature could faithfully replace the documentary record of the contemporary scene.

[9] "Is Art the Product of Its Age?" *op. cit.*, p. 373.

[10] W. E. Lingelbach (ed.), *Approaches to American Social History* (New York: Appleton-Century Co., 1937), p. 54. Cf. David Daiches, *Literature and Society* (London: Victor Gollancz, 1938); Irwin Edman, *Arts and the Man* (New York: New American Library, 1949), pp. 122–29; Ruth Benedict, *Chrysanthemum and the Sword* (Boston: Houghton Mifflin Co., 1946), pp. 100–133; Hortense Powdermaker,

"An Anthropologist Looks at the Movies," *Annals of the American Academy of Political and Social Science*, CCLIV (November, 1947), 83–84.

[11] Consult E. Grosse, *The Beginnings of Art* (New York: Appleton, 1897); Y. Hirn, *The Origins of Art* (London, 1900); Jane Harrison, *Ancient Art and Ritual* (New York: Henry Holt & Co., 1913); Franz Boas, *Primitive Art* (Oslo, 1927); Herbert Read, *Art and Society* (New York: Macmillan Co., 1937); Susanne K. Langer, *Philosophy in a New Key* (New York: Penguin Books, 1948).

[12] *General Anthropology*, p. 600.

[13] See also studies of national character, surveyed by Otto Klineberg, *Tensions Affecting International Understanding* (New York: Social Science Research Council, 1950), pp. 49–58.

[14] Martha Wolfenstein and Nathan Leites, *Movies: A Psychological Study* (Glencoe, Ill.: Free Press, 1950), pp. 12–13.

reflected, or, in psychoanalytic terms, that literature presents a manifest and latent content, as in dreams, both derived from stresses in society, and both given symbolic meaning.[15] However, as Fearing states, there is no indication as to how makers of films gain access to the collective unconscious of a population for whom they are intended, or whether films actually carry the symbolic meanings to a mass audience.[16] Nevertheless, literature or motion pictures may present interpretive frames of reference, as Wolfenstein and Leites suggest, which have their counterpart in real-life attitudes. Although the relationship of movie or literary patterns to the larger culture is complex and not well understood, it is assumed that these patterns reflect in significant and characteristic ways the attitudes and shared experiences in society.[17]

By students of culture, literature and other arts have been used as reflections of the fundamental reality of a culture, variously called "culture mentality," "Weltanschauung," "spiritual principle," or "soul," and of the different stages in the development of a culture.[18] These conceptions are derived largely from Hegel and other historical philosophers of the early nineteenth century as well as from the sociologists, Comte and Spencer. Taine, for example, attempted to account for the characteristics of English literature and their historical changes by applying his famous triad: race, environment, and time. Although regarding "mind or spirit" as the master-idea inherent

in "race," he was enough of a positivist to look forward to the quantification of his formula for successful prediction of future literary trends.[19]

More recent representatives of this tradition, who are concerned with the unity and change of civilizations, include Spengler, Toynbee, and Sorokin. Of these, Spengler is the most closely identified with Hegelian thought, both in the principles of spirit and destiny and in regarding history as proceeding through phases of growth, maturity, and decay.[20] Other differences in ideology and method between these representatives lie beyond the scope of this article, but there are certain general agreements. All of them identify two main phases in the history of societies, called "culture" and "civilization" by Spengler,[21] "yin" and "yang" by Toynbee,[22] "ideational" and "sensate" by Sorokin, although the latter also distinguishes several mixed forms, of which the "idealistic" is a special type.[23] Each set of terms refers to contrasting types of societies, the one stable and slow to change, the other dynamic and rapid in change. Each society is characterized by a number of other qualities, which are reflected in literature and art. Toynbee finds that art styles more accurately establish the time span of a civilization, its growth and dissolution, than any other method of measurement.[24] Sorokin, however,

---

[15] J. P. Mayer, *Sociology of the Film* (London: Faber & Faber, 1946); Siegfried Kracauer, *From Caligari to Hitler* (Princeton: Princeton University Press, 1947); Parker Tyler, *Magic and Myth of the Movies* (New York: Henry Holt & Co., 1947).

[16] Franklin Fearing, "Influence of the Movies on Attitudes and Behavior," *Annals of the American Academy of Political and Social Science*, CCLIV (November, 1947), 76–78.

[17] Wolfenstein and Leites, *op. cit.*, pp. 295, 306–7.

[18] Cf. Radhakamal Mukerjee, "The Meaning and Evolution of Art in Society," *American Sociological Review*, X (August, 1945), 496: Art reveals "the soul of a culture and social milieu in a more significant manner than religion, science, and philosophy."

[19] H. A. Taine, *History of English Literature* (New York: Henry Holt & Co., 1886), pp. 1–21. For comment see Albert Guérard, *Literature and Society* (Boston: Lothrop, Lee & Shepard Co., 1935).

[20] Oswald Spengler, *The Decline of the West* (2 vols.; New York: A. A. Knopf, 1926–28), Vol. I, Introduction. Cf. G. W. F. Hegel, *Philosophy of History* (New York: Collier & Son, 1900), pp. 61–99, 115–34, 300–302.

[21] *Op. cit.*, I, 31–35.

[22] Arnold J. Toynbee, *A Study of History* (London: Oxford University Press, 1934–39), I, 201–4; III, 196 ff., 390; IV, 33–34. Dismissing Spengler's organic concept of cultures, Toynbee accepts the idea of dominant tendencies or bent (III, 382–90).

[23] Pitirim A. Sorokin, *Social and Cultural Dynamics* (4 vols.; New York: American Book Co., 1937–41), I, 55–102; IV, *passim*. He surveys various "phase" concepts of cultures in IV, 389 ff.

[24] *Op. cit.*, III, 378–79.

has described and elaborated on these qualities probably more systematically than either Spengler or Toynbee. According to him, in the literature and art which reflect ideational culture the subjects deal with persons and events of religious significance, the attitudes are ascetic, otherworldly, the style is symbolic, formal, and conventional, and the techniques are relatively simple. Sensate literature, on the other hand, selects secular, commonplace topics and events, is sensational and erotic, individualistic and skeptical; the style is sensual, realistic, and naturalistic and the techniques are elaborate and complex.[25] Tomars, although more sociological than cultural in orientation and avoiding the theories of change of the above trio, comes to almost identical conclusions as these expressed by Sorokin.[26]

This conception that reflection reveals the essential world outlook of a culture obviously overlaps the idea expressed earlier that it represents norms and values and the stress patterns, but reflection of ethos emphasizes the integrative character of cultures and their organization around dominant activities or beliefs—the concept of cultural focus recognized and developed by a number of anthropologists, though without the philosophic overtones so conspicuous in Spengler.[27] It is questionable whether literature and the arts are always as reliable indexes as usually assumed. Probably they are only one index among many, whose rele-

vance and significance vary with the society or culture.[28] Between literature and other cultural products there also seem to exist specific interrelationships, without any systematic attempt being made to designate the principles governing their interaction. Consequently, literature and other arts may be an index of cultural change, but they apparently cannot account for shifts in "mentality."[29] They are a symptom, not a cause. As such, they are passive, essentially static agents—a conclusion that hardly seems as inevitable as this formulation implies.

Another version of reflection derives from the dialectical materialism of Marx and his followers, who select the economic system rather than ethos or soul as the independent variable. Literature and art, along with other "ideologies," are determined by "the mode of production in material life,"[30] and by the ideas of the ruling class, which are in every epoch the ruling ideas.[31] But in the dialectical process, manifested in the class struggle, "art expresses the tendencies of a rising, and therefore revolutionary class."[32] The relationship of economic structure and ideological forms, however, is not causally direct and mechanical, as Engels points out.[33] Especially is this true of artistic greatness, which Marx admits has no direct rela-

[25] Sorokin, *op. cit.*, I, 679.

[26] *Op. cit.*, pp. 300–306, 392–95. See also Herbert A. Bloch, "Towards the Development of a Sociology of Literary and Art Forms," *American Sociological Review*, VIII (June, 1943), 310–20. Bloch presents a classification of literary patterns or themes which result when artists lack a common social idiom.

[27] Ruth Benedict, *Patterns of Culture* (New York: New American Library, 1948); Ralph Linton (ed.), *The Science of Man in the World Crisis* (New York: Columbia University Press, 1945), pp. 164–68; A. L. Kroeber, *Configurations of Culture Growth* (Berkeley: University of California Press, 1944), pp. 820–23, 826–28. Repudiating the idea of a master-plan, Kroeber uses the hypothesis that any notable cultural achievement presupposes adherence to a certain set of patterns which are limited and which may develop and become exhausted.

[28] Spengler regards the arts as "prime phenomena," while Sorokin includes other cultural aspects, all of which show essentially the same trends. In 1934 Elliott and Merrill regarded literature as probably "the most significant index" of social disorganization, but the latest edition of their text fails to mention literary indexes (Mabel Elliott and Francis Merrill, *Social Disorganization* [3d ed.; New York: Harper & Bros., 1950], pp. 45–48).

[29] Toynbee, *op. cit.*, IV, 52.

[30] Karl Marx and Friedrich Engels, *Literature and Art* (New York: International Publishers Co., 1947), p. 1. Cf. Louis Harap, *Social Roots of the Arts* (New York: International Publishers Co., 1949), p. 16.

[31] Karl Marx and Friedrich Engels, *The German Ideology* (New York: International Publishers Co., 1939), p. 39. Cf. Harap, *op. cit.*, pp. 39–40.

[32] Harap, *op. cit.*, p. 112; Marx and Engels, *Literature and Art*, pp. 25, 45, 52–55, 116.

[33] Karl Marx and Friedrich Engels, *Correspondence, 1846–1895* (New York: International Publishers Co., 1936), p. 475. Cf. Harap, *op. cit.*, pp. 10–11.

tion to either the degree of social development or the type of economic base.[34]

Among the numerous followers who have elaborated, interpreted, and applied these ideas are Veblen, Caudwell, Fox, Calverton, Parrington, and Hicks. Some are strict Marxists, others adapt and select Marx's ideas, of which the class influence on literature has been the most suggestive. Veblen shows the intrusion of economic motives, conspicuous waste, and expensiveness on the character of aesthetic objects.[35] Caudwell and Fox, dealing with poetry and the novel, respectively,[36] attempt to relate economic conditions and bourgeois ideas to the forms as well as the content of literature, and presume that artistic greatness will arise in a future classless society.[37] Parrington, a liberal rather than a Marxist, describes the economic background from which spring the regional and class differences that distinguish the main periods of American social and literary history.[38] More comprehensive and less doctrinaire than Calverton[39] or Hicks,[40] he traces the class and economic position of writers and shows how these "determine" their economic theories and their religious and political philosophies as well as the character and form of their literary productions.

One need not, of course, follow the Marxian system in investigating the influence of social classes on literature. Tomars, for example, adopting MacIver's concepts of corporate and competitive classes, describes and illustrates their differential influence on the subject matter and style of literature and other arts and examines interclass relationships as well.[41] More recently Gordon has been impressed by the accuracy with which novelists have represented the cultural traits that distinguish several social classes in the United States.[42]

In general, the Marxian orientation has been widely influential, though subject to a number of difficulties. Whether, for example, "proletarian" literature actually contributes to lower-class solidarity is questionable, and how in other respects it fosters the class struggle has not been systematically explored. Much of the Marxist writing is full of doctrinaire and negative judgments rather than thorough analysis or objective testing of hypotheses. The concept of classes seems of limited applicability to American society, and the system fails to include other types of groups from which certain variations of literary form and expression may be derived or to consider the influence on drama, for instance, of groups with conflicting or divergent interests.[43] The problem of how bourgeois writers and artists succeed in reflecting the ideas and aims of the proletarian class remains obscure. As for the notion that the classless society will provide the ultimate basis for the development of literary and artistic greatness, there is obviously no basis; it is either wishful thinking or hopeful propaganda—unless, of course, one accepts wholeheartedly the Marxian system. De-

[34] *Literature and Art*, pp. 18–19.

[35] Thorstein Veblen, *The Theory of the Leisure Class* (New York: Heubsch, 1924), pp. 126–66.

[36] Christopher Caudwell, *Illusion and Reality* (New York: International Publishers Co., 1947); Ralph Fox, *The Novel and the People* (New York: International Publishers Co., 1945).

[37] Caudwell, *op. cit.*, pp. 293–98; Fox, *op. cit.*, pp. 80, 125–26. Cf. Harap, *op. cit.*, pp. 168–82, and Lenin, in Clara Zelkin, *Reminiscences of Lenin* (New York: International Publishers Co., 1934), p. 13.

[38] Vernon L. Parrington, *Main Currents in American Thought* (3 vols. in 1; New York: Harcourt, Brace & Co. 1930). In method Parrington was influenced by both Taine and J. Allen Smith, from whom he derived the concept of economic determinism (III, vii).

[39] V. F. Calverton, *The Newer Spirit* (New York: Boni & Liveright, 1925); *The Liberation of American Literature* (New York: Charles Scribner's Sons, 1932).

[40] Granville Hicks, *The Great Tradition* (New York: Macmillan Co, 1933); *Figures of Transition* (New York: Macmillan Co., 1939).

[41] *Op. cit.*, pp. 141–223.

[42] Milton M. Gordon, "*Kitty Foyle* and the Concept of Class as Culture," *American Journal of Sociology*, LIII (November, 1947), 210–18.

[43] Levin L. Schücking points out how heterogeneous audiences influenced Elizabethan drama (*Sociology of Literary Taste* [London: Kegan Paul, 1944], pp. 11–13).

spite these and other limitations, the fact remains that Marx's concepts are dynamic and have focused attention on social rather than on the more strictly cultural aspects of literary reflection.

Within the last fifteen years several sociologists have explored or implied another variety of reflection which has arisen evidently from accumulated sociological data and a concern for social problems. Their basic assumption is that literature, mainly fiction and biography in "popular" forms, reflects social "facts": vocational and divorce trends, population composition and distribution. This hypothesis is perhaps the most mechanistic version of all, since it postulates that literary data somehow correspond to certain types of statistical data; that heroines in popular fiction, for example, are portrayed as having the same occupations, proportionately, as actually exist in society at a particular time.[44] Although the hypothesis seems hardly promising, the results have been somewhat profitable, for they indicate the direction of the distortion of statistical facts.[45] Story content, indeed, seems to be slanted in the direction of widespread interests and ideals. Inglis, for instance, discovers that popular fiction mirrors not actual jobs of women or their circumstances but rather "certain typical American attitudes and ideals."[46] Barnett and Gruen show that "divorce" novels are sensitive to "wide-spread attitudes toward marriage, love, and divorce."[47] These conclusions are largely in line with the first type of reflection described above, centering on norms and values, though dominant public interests and attitudes may not be identical with social norms.[48] Edgar Dale, for example, analyzing the content of fifteen hundred movies current in the twenties and early thirties, finds the distortion in the direction of sensational subjects, mainly crime, sex, and love, rather than desirable social values or even typical or "average" situations.[49] In this case the theory of emotional needs and stresses seems implied. Berelson and Salter, concerned with majority and minority Americans, observe that popular stories are biased in favor of the elite and the economically powerful—a bias which they believe to be characteristic in literary history.[50] In effect, therefore, they agree with Marx that the ideas of the ruling class are in every epoch the ruling ideas, although they emphasize ideas less than certain traits of hero and heroine. Statistical facts, then, are not reproduced in fiction. On the contrary, these studies, even though indirectly, support the argument for other types of reflection, described earlier.

In view of these several versions of reflec-

[44] Ruth Inglis, "An Objective Approach to the Relationship between Fiction and Society," *American Sociological Review*, III (August, 1938), 526–31. Cf. Leo Lowenthal, "Biographies in Popular Magazines," in *Radio Research, 1942–43*, eds. Paul Lazarsfeld and Frank Stanton (New York: Duell, Sloan, & Pearce, 1944), pp. 507–48. Lowenthal examines leading characters in popular biography in relation to a "cross section of socially important occupations."

[45] Guérard, like many literary critics, recognizes that *artistic* literature is "a dangerously distorting mirror," but he fails to perceive patterns in the direction of distortion (*op. cit.*, p. 20).

[46] *Op. cit.*, pp. 530–31. Cf. Richard and Beatrice Hofstadter, who show that Churchill's novels reflected humanistic values in revolt against acquisitive and business goals ("Winston Churchill: A Study of the Popular Novel," *American Quarterly*, II [spring, 1950], 12–28).

[47] James H. Barnett and Rhoda Gruen, "Recent American Divorce Novels, 1938–1945: A Study in the Sociology of Literature," *Social Forces*, XXVI (March, 1948), 332–37. Barnett's earlier survey shows more extensive use of divorce statistics and legislation and less awareness of "distortions," except a historical lag between "public attitudes" and their representation in fiction.

[48] Francis L. K. Hsu believes that literature is an index to repression in Western cultures as compared with suppression in Eastern cultures ("Suppression versus Repression," *Psychiatry*, XII [August, 1949], 224–27).

[49] *The Content of Motion Pictures* (New York: Macmillan Co., 1933). Like Inglis, Dale finds fictional representations favoring unmarried, youthful people and wealthy rather than poor. Barnett and Gruen (*op. cit.*) discover a bias toward professional people in urban settings.

[50] Bernard Bereleson and Patricia Salter, "Majority and Minority Americans: An Analysis of Magazine Fiction," *Public Opinion Quarterly*, X (summer 1946), 188.

tion, it would seem that the theory is not entirely useless but that more extensive investigation is needed. The reliability of literature and art as indexes of the state of society and culture might be checked against other indexes, so that the danger is avoided of deducing the "spirit of the age" from its art and then rediscovering it in its art[51]—the danger which DeVoto calls "the literary fallacy."[52] It seems evident, also, that to some extent the phrase "reflection of society" is a misnomer, since much of what literature presumably reflects is specifically cultural rather than social, as Sorokin explicitly states.[53] Marx and others have called attention to the influence of social classes, but many other social aspects might be explored. It is not clearly understood, for example, what social processes develop and sustain differences in aesthetic taste or determine what is called artistic greatness. At present the reflection theory seems to account for some of the content and certain broad aspects of literary and artistic styles, without coming to grips with the problem of what social conditions are responsible for the existence and popularity of specific literary and artistic forms. And inevitably it stresses the external product as an artifact, so that some investigators minimize or deny the possible role of the arts in social change.

Despite gaps and uncertainties, these general orientations show some possibilities of ultimate agreement. It should be kept in mind, also, that historically the reflection theory has done valuable service in challenging older insights and established traditions. It has directed attention to the social and cultural characteristics of literature in addition to its more narrowly formal aspects. It has emphasized the conception of artists as agents of social forces rather than as individual geniuses or great men with inventive imaginations. It has provided social and historical modes of analysis as alterna-

tives to exclusively biographical and aesthetic approaches and offered concepts of cultural relativism in place of absolutist aesthetic principles and social determinism in place of artistic individualism.

The historical emphasis on reflection has naturally tended to distract attention from the question of the influence of literature on society, but the two concepts have frequently been regarded as mutually influential or as opposite sides of the same coin.[54] Mukerjee holds that "art is at once a social product and an established means of social control."[55] Inglis, finding no evidence that popular literature "shapes" society, believes that it results in a measure of social control by supporting the status quo of American attitudes and ideals.[56] In brief, one can formulate the proposition that, if literature reflects, then it also confirms and strengthens cultural norms, attitudes, and beliefs.

This "social control" function of literature is suggested in the article by Berelson and Salter,[57] and Betty Wang finds that it applies to the folk songs of China.[58] More systematically and directly, however, it is supported by Warner and Henry's investigation of *Big Sister*, a radio serial drama.[59] They conclude that this drama is essentially a minor morality play adapted to a secular society. Psychologically, it does not just "entertain" its listeners, but it releases their antisocial impulses, anxieties, and frustra-

[54] See Barnett, *op. cit.*, p. 11; Paul Meadows, "Social Determination of Art," *Sociology and Social Research*, XXVI (March–April, 1942), 310–13.

[55] *Op. cit.*, p. 496.

[56] Inglis' use of "social control" as a form of "influence" seems to lead to some confusion. It seems preferable to restrict the term to its more limited and precise context.

[57] *Op. cit.*, p. 188.

[58] "Folk Songs as a Means of Social Control," *Sociology and Social Research*, XIX (September–October, 1934), 64–69; "Folk Songs as Regulators of Politics," *ibid.*, XX (November–December, 1935), 161–66.

[51] Schücking, *op. cit.*, pp. 4–5.

[52] Bernard DeVoto, *The Literary Fallacy* (Boston: Little, Brown & Co., 1944).

[53] *Op. cit.*, IV, 124–28.

[59] W. Lloyd Warner and William E. Henry, "The Radio Daytime Serial: A Symbolic Analysis," *Genetic Psychological Monographs*, XXXVII (February, 1948), 3–73.

tions and provides them with both a feeling of being instructed and a sense of security and importance. Socially the program promotes understanding of the ideals and values of family life, and it strengthens and stabilizes the basic social institution of our society, the family.[60]

Although no mention is made of Malinowski in this study, these conclusions recall his statements on the role of myth among the Trobriand Islanders. Myth comes into play, he says, "when rite, ceremony, or a social or moral rule demands justification, warrant of antiquity, reality, and sanctity."[61] Psychologically, myths help to still doubts and calm fears. Myths of death, for example, bring down "a vague but great apprehension to the compass of a trivial, domestic reality."[62] Myths of origin are not "explanations," as some anthropologists have thought, but ways of instruction in and justification of the social system. Such a myth "conveys, expresses, and strengthens the fundamental fact of the local unity of the group of people descendent from a common ancestress."[63] It thus contributes to social solidarity and supports the existing social order.

Malinowski's findings and those of Warner and Henry are apparently consistent and essentially the same, both in psychological and in social functions of certain types of literature. Both investigations uphold the theory of social control. It should be recognized, however, that *Big Sister* applies to only a single social institution, the family, whereas Trobriand myths affect the total society. Moreover, the radio listeners to *Big Sister* are confined to the "common man" of modern American society; they do not include career women from the upper middle class (the control group), for whom the program has little or no appeal. Presumably

these women would prefer programs expressing different values, as may other subgroups, such as members of the upper and lower classes. In short, different social classes or groups in our society may select and emphasize distinct social and aesthetic values, ranging from comic books to stories in the *New Yorker*, or from popular fiction to classical art.

In our complex society, then, as contrasted with Trobriand society, social control through literature may either be limited to those norms and values common to all groups or applied to class or group control, each class or group responding to the art and literature that confirms its own set of values, customs, and beliefs. In the latter case, if these sets are to some extent in conflict, one may logically expect literature in some degree to further their antagonism and thus contribute not to social solidarity but to intergroup conflict and to social disunity. Group differences, for example, may be exposed and attacked. Writers satirize businessmen and business ethics, opposing certain widespread social beliefs and practices. Or, as Marxian theory indicates, literature may tend to perpetuate the status quo of the "common man," yet operate simultaneously, though perhaps unintentionally, to confirm and strengthen an intrenched economic power elite. Maintaining the status quo in the family system and in other institutions at various social class levels may also help to impede or reduce social changes that are adaptive to new conditions, so that the literature which supports the older, traditional social forms may serve as a conservative rather than as a dynamic force.[64]

Some literature, however, may minimize

[60] *Ibid.*, p. 64.

[61] Bronislaw Malinowski, "Myth in Primitive Psychology," in *Magic, Science and Religion and Other Essays* (Glencoe, Ill.: Free Press, 1948), pp. 84–85.

[62] *Ibid.*, p. 113.

[63] *Ibid.*, p. 93; cf. pp. 85–89, 109.

[64] This conservative effect of literature may be conspicuous in periods of rapid social change, as seems demonstrated in L. K. Knight's *Drama and Society in the Age of Jonson* (London: Chatto & Windus, 1937) and in Walter Taylor's *The Economic Novel in America* (Chapel Hill: University of North Carolina Press, 1942). Conservative aspects of radio programs are pointed out by Paul Lazarsfeld in *Print, Radio, and Film in a Democracy*, ed. Douglas Waples (Chicago: University of Chicago Press, 1942), pp. 66–78.

or reconcile intergroup conflict, like humor for different racial groups,[65] and some may contribute to social mobility, which is an important cultural value in our society. Literature and art, as Fearing states, may reveal to an individual a wide variety of patterns of behavior which he may accept or reject.[66] In either case, his awareness of the range of possibilities, the degree of freedom for action, would be increased, the areas of significant meanings enlarged, and his horizon expanded. It seems possible that, if accepted, some of the new values would promote social mobility rather than reconciling one to his "place."[67]

In these and probably other ways the social control theory seems inadequate for explaining a number of direct and "hidden" social effects of literature in a complex society—effects that await further testing. Nevertheless, recognition and support of this theory, particularly by Malinowski and the Warner-Henry study, indicates its importance to students of the general problem of the function of literature and art in society. Its significance is increased by the fact that it articulates so closely with what is probably the commonest version of reflection, so that each tends to reinforce the other and to uphold in part the proposition stated earlier.

The concept of social control, then, may well be considered as separate and distinct from the influence theory which emphasizes literature as "shaping" society. Actually, the idea of literature as shaping or molding society seems to have taken two broad forms, depending on whether the influence has been regarded as beneficial or detrimental to society. Both are obviously value

judgments rather than theories, but they have been widely held. The theory, for instance, that some literature, if not all, tends to disrupt or to corrupt society has been a hardy perennial in the history of Western civilization. Its traditional form was set by Plato in *The Republic*, where he feared that the fundamental laws of the state would be altered by shifts in modes of "music."[68] This concept was later adopted by the Christian church, remained current throughout the Middle Ages, and found its strongest expression in sixteenth-century Catholicism and in Puritanism.[69] Today, in similar fashion, the Soviet Union strictly controls the character of aesthetic output, while in the United States censorship is more limited.[70] All such measures have been direct attempts to prescribe artistic production or prevent its circulation, on the assumption that some works extend and perpetuate values antithetical to an emerging social order, as in Russia, or introduce and display values disruptive of an existing social order, as in the United States.

This was the orientation of the series of investigations on movies sponsored in the 1930's by the Payne Fund and of a number of more recent independent studies. Since many of these are well known, we shall confine our discussion to a few aspects. In general, it was assumed that people, especially children, are more or less passive and can easily be swayed by the stimuli of the movies or other artistic forms to act in given directions, usually toward immoral or criminal behavior. A popular account pictured children as "molded by movies," as "movie-made criminals," though a few were influ-

---

[65] Milton Barron, "A Content Analysis of Intergroup Humor," *American Sociological Review*, XV (February, 1950), 88–95; Richard Stephenson, "Conflict and Control Functions of Humor," *American Journal of Sociology*, LVI (May, 1951), 569–75.

[66] *Op. cit.*, p. 74.

[67] Cf. Richard Wright, *Black Boy* (10th ed.; New York: World Publishing Co., 1945), pp. 217–22, 226–28: "I hungered for books, new ways of looking and seeing. . . . It had been my accidental reading of fiction and literary criticism that had evoked in me vague glimpses of life's possibilities."

[68] *Op. cit.*, pp. 140, 186–87.

[69] Lerner and Mims, *op. cit.*, pp. 537–38.

[70] For Soviet control of the arts see Tomars, *op. cit.*, pp. 299–301, 370–71; Max Eastman, *Artists in Uniform* (New York: A. A. Knopf, 1934), pp. 33–38; Juri Jelagin, *Taming of the Arts* (New York: E. P. Dutton & Co., 1951), p. 76. For American censorship see Ruth A. Inglis, *Freedom of the Movies* (Chicago: University of Chicago Press, 1947); Charles A. Siepmann, *Radio, Television and Society* (New York: Oxford University Press, 1950).

enced to adopt more ideal attitudes and goals.[71]

The bulk of the evidence from the Payne studies, however, is to the contrary. That movies do have measurable effects on attitudes of children Thurstone and Peterson clearly demonstrate,[72] and that conduct may also be affected is evident from several of the investigations.[73] But the influence is not a simple cause-effect relationship, as commonly assumed; it is selective, being determined primarily by an individual's background and needs.[74] A person may focus on particular items such as hair or dress styles, manners, methods or robbery, or courtship techniques, but opposing forces may also be present to cancel or modify the effect of these influences. The consensus of all these studies seems to be that movies have differential effects depending on movie content, on an individual's needs, and on his social and cultural background.[75] When Hulett attempted to discover the net effect of a commercial motion picture, *Sister Kenny*, upon public opinion in a whole community rather than on specific individuals, he obtained negative results.[76]

It must be admitted that the larger question of the negative impact of films on society or culture is still unanswered, to say nothing of the influence of literature or art. The complexity of the problem as yet defies adequate testing, although certainly the naïve assumption of a one-directional type of influence is thoroughly discredited, at least among social scientists. Among laymen and some "experts" the idea persists and has again found expression recently concerning television.

The very persistence of the idea that movies or other forms of literature and art are socially disruptive apparently indicates an enormous respect for the power of artistic media—a respect deeply intrenched in tradition. The conception also seems to manifest fears which arise and become widespread during periods of rapid social and cultural change, when a society is more or less disorganized. When underlying causes of change are obscured or unrecognized, pervasive anxieties seem to find one outlet by attacking movies or other artistic forms, or by curbing their publishers and producers. That this process is a channeling if not a displacement of anxiety seems possible, but it leaves unresolved the problem of the extent to which artistic products may not only reflect social change but also contribute to it.

If the detrimental effects of movies or literature on society are still undetermined, the beneficial effects are even less so, though the traditional claims have been many and exceedingly great. Historically, one such claim refers to the "moral" value of literature, already dealt with in connection with the social control theory, but the effects of the arts beyond their social control function may more appropriately be classified as influence in "shaping" society, a power which Toynbee and others have denied to the arts.

When one examines various claims, they prove to be a curious mixture. Albert Guérard, for example, states that literary works have set fashions, such as a "fatal pallor," and that Goethe's *Werther* was "responsible for" a wave of suicides.[77] He be-

[71] Henry J. Forman, *Our Movie Made Children* (New York: Macmillan Co., 1935), *passim*.

[72] Ruth C. Peterson and L. L. Thurstone, *Motion Pictures and the Social Attitudes of Children* (New York: Macmillan Co., 1933).

[73] Herbert Blumer, *Movies and Conduct* (New York: Macmillan Co., 1933); Herbert Blumer and Philip M. Hauser, *Movies, Delinquency, and Crime* (New York: Macmillan Co., 1933); Paul G. Cressey and Frederick M. Thrasher, *Boys, Movies, and City Streets* (New York: Macmillan Co., 1933).

[74] Mildred J. Weise and Steward G. Cole, "A Study of Children's Attitudes and the influence of a Commercial Motion Picture," *Journal of Psychology*, XXI (1946), 151–71.

[75] Paul G. Cressey, "The Motion Picture Experience as Modified by Social Background and Personality," *American Sociological Review*, III (August, 1938), 516–25.

[76] J. E. Hulett, Jr., "Estimating the Net Effort of a Commercial Motion Picture upon the Trend of Local Public Opinion," *American Sociological Review*, XIV (April, 1949), 263–75.

[77] *Op. cit.*, p. 337.

lieves that literature has produced the conceptions of national types and that literary ideas preceded and "guided" political movements and reforms.[78] Similar claims have been made about particular works such as *Uncle Tom's Cabin* and *The Jungle*, by Upton Sinclair, which is supposed to have "brought about" the reform of the packing houses in 1906. In fact, however, these claims have not been substantiated.[79] Essentially, they rest on the same kind of simplified notion of causation as those for the "bad" influence of the movies.

Some of these so-called "influences," indeed, are mainly problems of cultural diffusion as related to social change, which have been dealt with by both Tomars and Sorokin, among others. Tomars has concentrated on interclass currents and fashions of art in a competitive society as contrasted to a corporate society.[80] Sorokin has more comprehensively stated some approximate uniformities of spatial displacement, mobility, circulation, and diffusion of cultural phenomena, including literature and art.[81] Again, both emphasize the complexity of such processes. As Sorokin points out, whether literary or art forms "penetrate" another social class or a different culture involves a number of conditions, which include at least the degree of "refinement" and complexity of a work, the nature of the culture or subculture being "influenced," the type of communication system being used, and sometimes the amount and character of coercion or force that is applied.[82] The diffusion of certain types of literature or art may,

then, be involved in social change. However, whether literature or any other kind of art "penetrates" first in time or more successfully than other cultural objects or ideas is doubtful; even if true, it is clearly not the function merely of the work of art itself.[83]

Much the same difficulty is encountered in other traditional assertions about the "shaping" influence of art, especially those pertaining to personal character and to ideal human existence. John Dewey, for example, insists that, when we enter into the spirit of Negro or Polynesian art, "barriers are dissolved, limiting prejudices melt away."[84] Developing this thought, Gotshalk declares that the fine arts are "an indispensable foundation of congruity of feeling or social solidarity between individuals and peoples."[85] Consistent with these judgments is the evaluation of the arts as the crowning achievement of civilization, the chief means of measuring the stature of a society, a symbol of its internal power and worth.[86]

These statements refer to the "highest" cultural ideals for individuals and for humanity, essentially the religious conception of brotherhood. Obviously they are not formulated in ways that would lend themselves to scientific test. Perhaps the arts help to perpetuate such ideals or contribute to their acceptance by other cultures. To the extent that they reinforce these values in our culture, they would presumably perform the social control function, though probably for certain elite groups more than for others. As Eastman points out, the present attempts at maintaining this supreme evaluation of the arts are primarily directed

[78] *Ibid.*, pp. 338–40.

[79] In *American Outpost* (New York: Farrar & Rinehart, 1932) Sinclair acknowledges that he is supposed to have helped clean up the stockyards but insists "this is mostly delusion." Donald Grant came to similar conclusions in "*The Jungle:* A Study of Literary Influence" (unpublished paper, University of Buffalo). Materials on *Uncle Tom's Cabin* are well known.

[80] *Op. cit.*, pp. 141–23.

[81] *Op. cit.*, IV, 197–289.

[82] *Ibid.*, pp. 202 ff.

[83] *Ibid.*, pp. 268–79, 282–88.

[84] *Art as Experience* (New York: Minton, Balch & Co., 1934), p. 334 ff. Cf. Albert R. Chandler, *Beauty and Human Nature* (New York: Appleton-Century Co., 1934), pp. 294–95; Daiches, *op. cit.*, p. 10.

[85] D. W. Gotshalk, *Art and the Social Order* (Chicago: University of Chicago Press, 1947), pp. 210, 212–13.

[86] Dewey, *op. cit.*, p. 345; Gotshalk, *op. cit.*, p. 203; Edman, *op. cit.*, p. 51; Auguste Rodin, *Art* (New York: Dodd, Mead & Co., 1928), pp. 7–9.

at preserving the high status of embattled men-of-letters, who seek to recapture the position they enjoyed in the past, when their association with religion and "superior" knowledge gave to the arts singular prestige. Today their position is being undermined by the encroachments of experimental science, once rated low in the social scale as "the vulgar pursuit of useful knowledge."[87]

To define the problem in this way would be to investigate the historical origins and the social structures that support and maintain the high cultural value placed on the arts—the fine arts especially, but popular arts as well—and to assess their effects on social behavior in many groups, in comparison to other kinds of cultural interest. Lundberg thinks that "social relations are today managed on the basis of what poets, play- wrights, journalists, preachers and radio commentators assume, on the basis of folklore, literature, and highly limited personal experience, to be principles of human nature and human relations."[88] Future research will no doubt determine the truth of this statement, and eventually we may also be able to trace more clearly the extent to which art has become, as Max Weber states, a cosmos of independent values, which are in dynamic tension with religion and which take over "the function of a this-worldly salvation," especially from the increasing pressures of theoretical and practical rationalism.[89]

UNIVERSITY OF BUFFALO

[87] Max Eastman, *The Literary Mind* (New York: Charles Scribner's Sons, 1932), pp. 36–53.

[88] George A. Lundberg, *Can Science Save Us?* (New York: Longmans, Green & Co., 1947), p. 63.

[89] H. H. Gerth and C. Wright Mills (eds.), *From Max Weber: Essays in Sociology* (New York: Oxford University Press, 1946), p. 342.

Literature and Society
Ian Watt

from

The Arts in Society, R.W. Wilson (ed.) Prentice-
Hall, Englewood Cliffs, NJ, 1964.

LITERATURE AND SOCIETY

Watt's elegant account of literature in social perspective might well serve as a paradigm for the sociological analysis of art. It is distinguished by an acute historical awareness, a catholicity of reference which dissuades us from an oversimplified version of the relations between literature and society. The sociologist, often too much inclined to take twentieth century industrial society as the measure of all things, can profit from this exposure to the rich variability of the artist's role, of literature's societal mirroring, of the functions of art.

Our understandable but dangerous enthusiasm for reading social history in literary works is properly bridled by Watt's analysis; he shows how seldom art may be construed as a direct, veridical rending of its creator's milieu, how often it must be seen as a partial, distorted, slanting image. As Kohn-Bramstedt wisely maintains:

. . . only a person who has a knowledge of a society from other sources than purely literary ones is able to find out if, and how far, certain social types and their behavior are reproduced in the novel. . . . What is pure fancy, what realistic observation, and what only an expression of the desires of the author must be separated in each case in a subtle manner.

Yet Watt does not discourage the social scientist, or try to bar his profane excursions into what some purist critics regard as the sacred territory of art. Rather, he challenges the investigator to be more alert, more perceptive, more ingenious in his efforts to tease out meaningful connections between art and environment. Above all, he implies, a social analyst must be himself sensitive to literary values and receptive to the nuances of artistic tradition and formal patterning.

Again, we are disabused of the assumption that literature is either prepotent or utterly ineffective as an agent for modifying attitudes or promoting social change. We simply have a paucity of reliable knowledge about the consequences of literary experience for human behavior. This may well be an area to which social science research can make substantial future contributions, as the sociologist refines his investigatory skills and as the exposure of large numbers of people to the arts presumably increases in both scope and intensity. As Watt maintains, literature is a social as well as a private phenomenon; whether the artist's ideology inclines him to exalt or dismiss the supposed social relevance of his work, that relevance is inescapable as long as man remains the symbolic animal —as long, that is, as he remains human.

LITERATURE AND SOCIETY

Ian Watt

Conscious interest in the relation between literature and society is quite recent, mainly because it depends on a considerable degree of historical, sociological, and literary awareness. The problem was not really opened up until the late seventeenth century, when the Ancients and Moderns controversy in England and France, a debate about whether the achievement of modern European literature was comparable to that of classical Greece and Rome, naturally led to wide historical and social comparisons; to the idea, for example, that epic poetry, which was then considered the supreme literary genre, perhaps really belonged to a special kind of society, and that this explained why, for all their efforts, the Renaissance writers of national epics had obviously failed to rival Homer or Virgil.

From then onward, and especially in Germany, literary scholarship gradually developed the concept of *Kulturgeschichte*—the systematic study of human culture as a whole from a historical and comparative perspective. At the end of the eighteenth century this perspective was much widened by the growing Romantic interest in folk tales and ballads, and by the work of such scholars as Bishop Percy, Herder, and the Grimm brothers, work which drew attention to the fact that there were long and important traditions of popular as well as of classical literary expression. Meanwhile, in France, De Bonald hit on the famous formula "literature is an expression of society" (1796), and in 1800 Madame de Staël published her *De La Littérature considérée dans ses rapports avec les institutions sociales*. In the same year, but in England, Wordsworth's historic "Preface" to the *Lyrical Ballads* announced that one of the aims of the new literary movement which we call Romanticism was to create works whose matter and manner were adapted to a much wider group than that for which their neoclassical predecessors had written, and to face the acute social and moral problems set up by the Industrial Revolution's "increasing accumulation of men in cities."

Since then a great deal has been written about the relations between literature and society, but the main categories of enquiry have remained fairly constant. To oversimplify, they may be reduced to three: most obviously, there is the particular social position of the writer, and the nature of his relation to his public; rather more widely and elusively, there is the question of how far literature is or ought to be a reflection of the society from which it springs;

finally, and most generally, there are the ultimate problems of the social function of literature, and of how far literary values correspond to social ones.

The Social Context of the Writer

Taine's formula for the key forces which determine the author's literary product was *race, moment, milieu;* but the most directly determining factor is probably one specific aspect of the author's particular social *milieu*—his institutional context as a writer: how he makes his living; how far he and his fellows constitute a separate occupational group; the nature of his audience, and of his own individual relation to it. In all these matters there would seem to be an almost infinite range of possibilities; and yet historically there are actually certain fairly well-established institutional patterns of authorship, patterns which are closely related to the social structure of the time.

When the invention of writing first made possible the permanent recording of human thought and feeling, literacy was confined to a small social caste. Consequently in Babylon, Egypt, and Palestine, for instance, if we can judge by what remains, writing was used mainly to record the political and religious traditions of the past and the laws and practices of the present. One can hardly talk as yet of literature or of authors as such, since there was no clearly differentiated literary product or specialized professional role; those who could write merely utilized their laborious skill on stone or clay or papyrus for important public purposes. In China, where the nature of the particular writing system developed made literate prowess difficult and highly valued, literary ability, tested through examinations, became the basis for the selection of the ruling bureaucracy; and it was from this mandarin class that most of the creative writers were drawn. The long formal association in China of an esoteric literature with a powerful administrative elite is an extreme case of the generally close relationship of literature with social power, an association which seems to be almost universal under bureaucratic forms of government, and whose long tradition has Chaucer as its earliest illustrious representative in England.

In the West the invention of the alphabet prevented reading and writing from remaining the exclusive possession of a small elite. In any case the rudiments of the literary profession as such seem to have developed long before, in various small pastoral and tribal societies. The Greek rhapsodist, the Welsh bard, the Icelandic *sagamann,* and the Anglo-Saxon *scop* all made their livings by reciting or singing the heroic deeds and other memorable exploits of the tribal leaders, in the halls and courtyards of the local chieftains: out of these miscellaneous and partly improvised narratives epic poems were eventually composed and written down. Modern opinion, discarding the generous democratic enthusiasms of earlier theorists about collective or folk authorship, now tends to regard Homer and his mainly anonymous Northern analogues as highly skilled professional authors working on the basis of existing traditional, and usually oral, materials. Some of the bards, of course, were merely professional reciters who added little of their own; but others were both authors and reciters. This combination was repeated in medieval Europe: while some troubadours, jongleurs, minstrels, and minnesingers were mainly performers, others, like Arnaut Daniel and Wolfram von Eschenbach, also became famous as original authors. The directness and intimacy of the relationship of the Homeric bard or the medieval troubadour with his audience has since been much admired by later writers: Vachel Lindsay, for example, revived the art of the wandering minstrel early in this century; and so, in their fashion, have many later poets on the campus touring circuit.

The supreme example of harmonious reciprocity between author and audience, however, is probably that afforded by Periclean Athens. In theory, at least, every male citizen there was in some sense a literary performer, speaking on public affairs in the market place or taking part as author or actor in the great dramatic festivals which were a free and indeed obligatory part of community life; the great tragedians, Aeschylus, Sophocles and Euripides were not so much members of a separate professional class as citizens who had outshone their fellows in the common pursuit of one of the recognized forms of civic glory. This kind of integration of the author in the whole social group has also had some modern approximations: in the late Middle Ages, for example, the mystery and miracle plays were written and performed by members of the various trade guilds, and were an essential part of town life.

In modern times the historical successor to the bard as professional author, at least in the West, was the recipient of patronage. The system had developed in Greece after the decline of Athens, and achieved its most illustrious form in Rome under Augustus. There Maecenas made his name the symbol of discriminating patronage on behalf of the sovereign, dispensing munificent rewards to such inspired celebrators of the glories of the regime as Horace and Virgil. Something similar seems to have developed in the early days of many secure, wealthy, and leisured aristocracies: in Renaissance Italy, for example, or in the France of Richelieu and Louis XIV.

Royal patronage was often succeeded by a more casual kind of patronage by the rich; in the Rome of Martial and Juvenal, for example, or in the England of Alexander Pope, we hear much of abuses of the system, with needy authors vying with each other to flatter whoever might be expected to repay them with rich food or gold coin. This kind of private patronage, however, was eventually superseded by that of the reading public in general. In the later days of Imperial Rome the presence of a huge leisured and literate class had combined with an abundance of cheap slave labor to produce something like the modern book trade: publishing houses with large staffs of well-trained slave copyists could turn out editions of several hundred by hand in a few days. But it was only with the invention of movable-type printing late in the fifteenth century, and the subsequent increase of popular literacy, that a reading public arose large enough to enable authors to rely entirely and directly on the sales of their works.

It took some time for this, our modern system, to replace other methods. At first, for example, the press was used primarily for making more widely available educational and religious texts: the spread of printing owes much to the Protestant stress on reading the Bible, especially in vernacular translations such as Martin Luther's. For several centuries, however, writers of secular literature found their support elsewhere. Thus Shakespeare depended on private and court patronage as well as on the boxoffice receipts of the theatrical company in which he was a shareholder, whereas most of his contemporaries sought noble patrons or combined literature with clerical careers; only a few unfortunate hacks relied entirely on writing for the market, producing popular, ephemeral, and ill-paid works for the booksellers. It was not until after the Copyright Act of 1709 that the author's ownership of his own literary works was legally assured; and then there slowly arose the modern system of royalties, where the author does not, as previously, sell his work outright to the bookseller, but receives an agreed percentage of sales.

The development of the royalty system in turn depended on a considerable scale of purchases by the public. This was made possible by the great expansion of middle-class leisure and literacy brought about by industrialism and urbanization toward the end of the eighteenth century. Later, the power press and other technological advances early in the nineteenth century made it possible to produce huge numbers of newspapers and magazines that were cheap enough for some working-class pockets, and thus led to the mass reading publics of today.

The complement of the mass public is the professional author. Evidence of the existence of a considerable group of professional writers, dependent wholly or mainly upon publishers for their living, is first reflected in the late seventeenth century by the frequent attacks of satirists on the starved hacks of Grub Street. By the middle of the eighteenth century the author by profession had finally secured somewhat more respectful recognition, and a good many writers, such as Dr. Johnson, were able to live very comfortably without recourse to patronage.

The economic dependence of authors on large sales, combined with social, and consequently educational, stratification, has had profound literary consequences. As early as the time of the Ptolemies, for instance, there existed quite separate classical and popular bodies of writing for the vast urban society of Alexandria; but as, with printing and modern industrialization, the reading public gradually expanded from the thousands of the eighteenth century to the millions of today, the ensuing literary stratifications became much more marked, and were more and more systematically exploited by the publishing industry. Some of the early nineteenth century writers in France and England were very much aware of the tendency: in 1859 Saint Beuve coined the phrase "industrial literature"—potboiling wordage produced to the specific requirements of mass journalism; and in 1881 John Ruskin attacked the "excitement of the lower passions" which characterized the works of the "railroad-station novelist." Today we have *Time* magazine, whose style and content are no longer those of the individual writer but are the hallmarks of a vast collective enterprise; whereas at the other extreme are the little magazines, produced by and for the "highbrows"—the word apparently dates only from 1908.[1] Characteristically, it is in the unremunerative pages of the highbrow quarterlies that many of the great masterpieces of our time have appeared, from Joyce's *Ulysses* to T. S. Eliot's *The Waste Land*.

The present social and economic context of authorship thus reflects certain features of modern society in general. There exists, for a few authors, the possibility of an unprecedentedly complete freedom of individual expression, but only for a minute, fragmented, and very special kind of audience; while there is an equally unprecedented and usually decisive pressure on the majority of professional writers to conform to the demands of the giant publishing organizations which offer glittering rewards for alertly docile service in entertaining the masses.

Literature as a Reflection of Society

There is a rather misleading simplicity about the word "reflects." In some senses all writing cannot but be a "reflection" of society, since it contains many elements which are socially derived. Language, to begin with, is a social product; and most writing—certainly most literature—is related to some established tradition or model of expression. More specifically, literary works usually reflect various surface features of the life of a society. Yet although the clothes and meals and customs described are rarely invented, they may not be those current at the time of writing; and since this is often true of more important matters, literature cannot be assumed to be necessarily a reliable reflection of the society of any specific period. Spenser, for example, "writ in no language" according to Ben Jonson, meaning that his language was an invented conglomerate of archaic and contemporary forms; so indeed was the society which the *Faerie Queene* described. Nor is Spenser an exceptional case: there is a very general tendency for well-established literary traditions to foster a conscious or unconscious archaism of matter or manner.

There are many other reasons why it is dangerous for the social historian to assume that any particular literary work is an accurate reflection of the author's society, although, of course, it may offer invaluable illumination or confirmation of matters known or surmised from other sources. Every individual's social experience is idiosyncratic in many ways, and if he is a writer this colors the selection and presentation of every social detail in his works. Thus Chaucer, in the "Prologue" to *The Canterbury Tales,* undoubtedly gives us our most vivid description of the society of his day; but it is in some ways a very incomplete and prejudiced description: seemingly he didn't care for merchants or tradesmen or ecclesiastical dignitaries, and wasn't much interested in the urban or rural proletariat. Yet actually the selections and exclusions may be not a matter of Chaucer's personal outlook on society at all, but merely the more or less accidental result of Chaucer's particular literary subject: the lowest orders of society could not afford to go on pilgrimages, and that happened to be what Chaucer was writing about. Certainly we can't assume from the character of the Wife of Bath that fourteenth century England contained no faithful married women; but at most that—as we should perhaps expect—their activities had less literary appeal.

Literary genres often reflect the social attitudes of the particular group which produced them, rather than that of the society which their content overtly portrays. Pastoral poetry, for example, does not tell us much about the economy or institutions of the Sicilian shepherds whose lives it pretends to describe, but it does reveal the taste for a fashionable kind of escape which arose in the later days of Greece and Rome among certain urban and leisured audiences. The influences of the author's particular social orientation in distorting his picture of social reality may not be conscious, but it is always present to some degree. Most of the court literature of the past made the nobles much more noble and the rustics much more rustic than they were in reality; while in the last hundred years the various radical, socialist, and communist movements have produced proletarian fiction in which the picture of the worker is a good deal more heroic or tragic than would probably be substantiated by objective sociological investigation.

Even the kinds of writing which aim at the most literal and detailed description of their society are far from being sociologically reliable mirror images of reality; for, quite apart from the influences of the social group, the author's own individual temperament and his personal ideology play a compelling, though usually unconscious, role. In Zola's novels, for example, the novelist's individual personality is continuously present, despite his resolute attempt at objective reporting; and in general the quasi-scientific Naturalist ideology, with its doctrine of the crushing influence of the environment, usually tended to produce fictional characters who were a good deal less crush-proof than the human average, and to place them in circumstances that were exceptionally crushing.

On the other hand the opposite position is also true: literature which makes no pretence whatever at reflecting social reality always does so in some form, however individual, abstract, or unrealistic that reflection may at first sight appear. *Alice in Wonderland,* for instance, or Kafka's *The Castle* are full of brilliant insights into the essence of the social world of their authors, but these insights only become manifest after a patient and imaginative interpretation of the fantasy or symbolism through which they are expressed.

Literature, then, reflects society, but it usually does so with various degrees of indirectness and selectivity. The particular "society" which it reflects is often equally difficult to determine; we hardly know, for instance, how far Homer describes the period of the Trojan War, and how far his own. Then again, as societies become larger and less homogeneous, they become more difficult to portray, merely because of their scale and complexity. Whatever the historical period may actually be, Homer at least gives us a sense of knowing and understanding a whole society; but no one could possibly attempt anything along the same lines for modern America, for example, if only because no single individual can have personal knowledge of more than a minute fraction of it.

Nor is the difficulty only a question of the scale and complexity of modern society as a literary subject matter; for this increased scale and complexity also modify the author's personal situation in society: he becomes more a member of a specialized social group and less a representative of the community in general.

In early eighteenth century England, for example, the interests and values of the middle class dominated the subject matter, the literary treatment, and the moral orientation of such novelists as Defoe and Richardson. But by the middle of the eighteenth century in France, and soon after in England, the professional writer tended to belong to a particular group of specialists, the intelligentsia, which regarded itself, and with some measure of justice, as somehow outside or above the class system as a whole. This feeling of separateness increased during the nineteenth century. In France, for example, the growing divorce of intellectuals and artists from established social institutions produced Bohemianism—a limbo as unrooted in any defined temporal or social environment as Shakespeare's Bohemia; whereas, in the United States, the even greater isolation of intellectuals produced, in the novels of Hawthorne and Melville, for instance, a more agonized anticipation of the social alienation of most great twentieth century writers.

The modern author, then, is in a problematic situation as regards his portrayal of society at large; and this, not only because of social fragmentation in general, or because of his personal ideological commitments, but also because of the drastic changes in the immediate social and economic context of authorship which have been referred to previously. Socially, the author belongs to a small professional group; economically, he depends directly on the modern publishing industry and their mass media. The author thus operates in a literary climate where the crucial decisions about the kind of social reflection he will create are based on an even lower estimate of what the public wants in the way of sexual and social fantasy than is probably the case.

Many successful writers, with more or less cynicism, provide the appropriate literary stimuli, stimuli which bear little recognizable relation to the shape of social reality. The great best-sellers of today, for example, are Mickey Spillane and Erskine Caldwell (whose *God's Little Acre* was the first novel to sell over ten million copies); what they most obviously have in common is a frantic primitivist revolt against social controls, especially those on sexual and aggressive impulses. This kind of revolt, and the amazing popularity of works which embody it, may well be tokens of some deep psycho-social breakdown; but we must not forget that there may be quite different explanations for the nature of such fiction, explanations which are based on the assumption that the success of this kind of fiction depends precisely on its not being a reflection of contemporary reality. For such works must, to begin with, be regarded as the particular modern embodiments of the age-old and almost universal tendency to enjoy imaginative gratifications of impulses which are largely denied in social life. Nor is the brutalized vulgarity with which these impulses are gratified in much contemporary writing necessarily a reflection of the prevalence of such impulses in contemporary society: it may only be the result of intensified commercial exploitation of an ever-increasing reading public.

This would be one example of how literature may be a reflection of its society only in a very special and indirect sense; and there are many other such examples. One can at least assert, however, that the writer always reflects his society in some way. However little, for example, he may intend to portray the reality of his time, he is inevitably responsive, directly or indirectly, to changing patterns, not only of mass fantasies, but of basic social values and goals. Thus, as Leo Lowenthal has demonstrated,[2] in the last decades the great majority of biographies in popular magazines have no longer dealt with "heroes" drawn from business, politics, or the professions, but with men and women in the world of popular entertainment.

The responsiveness of the author to the social patterns of his time cannot usually be so conveniently demonstrated: it is rarely susceptible of statistical analysis. But a reflection of social reality is always there, if we can find it; and not only in those writers, usually of the middle rank, who, like Trollope or Marquand, consciously set themselves the task of chronicling the average life of their time, but in every kind of writer, once we know how to interpret him. Mickey Spillane is not the Tolstoy of our era; but he belongs to it, and tells us something about it.

Social Function of Literature

Almost every society has its venerated classics—wisdom books, national epics, devotional hymns—which are taught to the young and which make available to the whole community a common background of knowledge, belief, and aspiration. It is always difficult, however, to assess the functional efficacy of such a literature, because there is obviously a particularly wide gap in the case of national and religious classics between public attitudes and private behavior. This gap has probably widened somewhat in modern times. Many recent studies of the social role of reading and of exposure to mass communications suggest mainly negative conclusions. Yet these are hardly final. That few people read the Bible does not disprove its importance as the source of much of our speech and our approved social and moral attitudes; then again, it is always difficult to decide whether the social values derive from the literary work, or vice versa; and in any case we should remember that the best literature by its very nature deals with matters of such delicate complexity that they can hardly be discussed except in their own terms, terms which render them virtually inaccessible to empirical study.

It is much easier, fortunately, to deal with the different ideas that have been held about what the social function of literature ought to be.

One extreme position is that associated with the Romantic poets, who tended to regard themselves as the lineal successors of the priests and the prophets: in their different ways Blake and Wordsworth and Shelley, for example, conceived of themselves as endowed by their private imaginative inspiration with the duty of leading humanity to a new and better world. Somewhat similar ideas about the function of literature as an innovating and reforming force are occasionally found earlier in such religious radicals as Milton, and also in such later political enemies of the institutions of their time as Voltaire, Rousseau, and the whole group of Encyclopaedists, writers whose often clandestine publications were an important factor in bringing about the French Revolution. Today, this conception of the reforming role of the writer survives in various forms; from the notion of the writer as a man of highly original moral, social, or literary beliefs, to the "fearless crusaders" of the newspapers.

At the other extreme is the idea that literature ought to limit its function to giving pleasure, whether through humor, wish-fulfillment, excitement, or intrinsic aesthetic perfection: in this idea, the doctrine of art for art's sake joins hands with the practice of the box office, and disregards not only the values inherent in any truthful report on social reality, but also the fact that an antisocial literature is itself a social reality with many important (and often deplorable) consequences.

The classical and perhaps the most defensible position on this issue is essentially a compromise: literature should instruct by pleasing—*delectando pariterque monendo*. "Pleasing" goes without saying, as long as we remember that there are many kinds and degrees of pleasure, some of them the reward of considerable effort. As for "instructing," the problem is more complicated. For one thing, a conscious didactic purpose may never have been a very useful thing for a writer: most primarily didactic or propagandist writing has little social effect, and, incidentally, succeeds even more rarely in being valuable as literature. It is also apparent that a didactic purpose is only possible to the writer if he accepts the major social, moral, and religious values of his society; and this acceptance has become less and less common of late. Here the effects of the individualist ideology of the last few centuries have been reinforced by the very widespread opposition of the modern intellectual elite to the predominantly Philistine and materialist values of its society in general. As a result, very few twentieth century writers have been able to follow the example of the many great writers of the past who endorsed the main social and moral orthodoxies of their time.

This discrepancy between past and present writers, however, is only partial, for, whatever they may themselves have intended, the works of Sophocles and Shakespeare, Goethe and Tolstoy, are essentially didactic only in the sense that our social and moral awareness is increased by imaginative participation in the works of those who have been supremely responsive to the realities of human experience: realities, of course, which always have a very important social component.

From this perspective the literary opposition between the Realist and Naturalist insistence on the liberal description of the actual social worlds, and the Parnassian and Symbolist reassertion of the artistic autonomy of imaginative creation, is seen to be a good deal less than absolute. For, although there is an age-old divergence between those who see man as essentially a social being, and those who insist on his individual uniqueness, the force of the contradiction begins to disappear the moment a writer puts pen to paper: as W. B. Yeats put it, "art is the social act of a solitary man."

It is a social act, however, of a very special kind, and one which reminds us that "literature and society" can be a misleading phrase in yet another way, because it suggests a more absolute distinction between the two terms than is actually the case. If only because, in one perfectly valid sense, literature *is* its own society: it is the subtlest and the most enduring means which man has devised for communicating with his fellows; and not the least of its functions is to give those who have learned its language something that no other society has ever afforded.

Bibliography

The subject is too vast and dispersed for reasonable documentation to be possible; and the following brief bibliography hardly scratches the surface. Still, the following are recommended on their particular topics.

Denney, Reuel, *The Astonished Muse* (Chicago: University of Chicago Press, 1957).

Duncan, Hugh D., *Language and Literature in Society* (Chicago: University of Chicago Press, 1953).

Edwin H. Miller, *The Professional Writer in Elizabethan England* (Cambridge: Harvard University Press, 1959).

Escarpit, Robert, *Sociologie de la littérature* (Paris: Presses Universitaires de France, 1958).

Hart, James D., *The Popular Book* (New York: Oxford University Press, 1950).

Hauser, Arnold, *The Social History of Art,* I and II (New York: Alfred A. Knopf, Inc., 1951).

Leavis, Queenie D., *Fiction and the Reading Public* (London: Chatto & Windus, Ltd., 1932).

Levin L. Schucking, *The Sociology of Literary Taste,* 1931, trans. E. W. Dickes (London: Kegan Paul, 1944).

Lowenthal, Leo, *Literature and the Image of Man . . . 1600-1900* (Boston: Beacon Press, 1957).

———, *Literature, Popular Culture and Society* (Englewood Cliffs, N.J.: Prentice-Hall, Inc., 1961).

Raymond Williams, *Culture and Society, 1780-1950* (London: Chatto & Windus, Ltd., 1958).

Thomas F. Marshall, with George K. Smart and Louis J. Budd, *Literature and Society, 1950-1955: Selective Bibliography* (Coral Gables, Fla.: University of Miami Press, 1956).

Literature and Society

[1] Mitford M. Mathews, *Dictionary of Americanisms;* "highbrow" and "lowbrow" were given wide currency, in a somewhat special sense, by Van Wyck Brooks in his essay *America's Coming of Age,* published in 1915.

[2] In "Biographies in Popular Magazines," *Radio Research 1942-1943,* Paul F. Lazarsfeld and Frank Stanton, eds. (New York: 1944); reprinted in *American Social Patterns,* William Petersen, ed. (Doubleday Anchor, New York: 1956), pp. 63-118.

Why a Sociology of Literature?
Robert Escarpit

from

The Sociology of Literature by Robert Escarpit.
Frank Cass, London.

Why a Sociology of Literature?

Literature and Society

EACH AND EVERY literary fact presupposes a writer, a book and a reader; or, in general terms, an author, a product and a public. By way of an extremely complex transmitting mechanism, a circuit of interrelationships is constituted. It combines art, technology and business, uniting well-defined individuals in a more or less anonymous though limited community.

The presence of artists poses psychological, moral and philosophic problems at all points of the circuit; their work raises esthetic, stylistic, linguistic and technical problems. Finally, the existence of a public implies historical, political, social and even economic problems. In other words, there are at least a thousand and one ways of exploring any literary fact.

It is difficult to study the threefold relationship of literature to individuals, to abstract forms and to diverse situations. It is not easy to picture tri-dimensional phenomena, especially when asked to write their history. For centuries, literary history has held— and still holds fast— to the study only of particular writers and their works, to a biographical and textual commentary. It has considered the aggregate context as a sort of decoration best left to the inquisitive mind of the political historian.

The absence of a real sociological perspective is evident in even the best traditional textbooks of literary history. Writers are sometimes conscious of a social dimension which they try to represent, but, lacking a rigorous method adapted to that end, they often remain immured in the classical framework of the man and his work. On such a two-dimensional screen the perspectives of history are obscured. Literary facts undergo distortions comparable to those of a world map which has no relief; as a map drawn by a schoolboy falsely shows an enormous Alaska overshadowing a tiny Mexico, so do twelve or fifteen years of Versailles in the seventeenth century overshadow sixty years of French literary life.

Those difficulties will never be completely eliminated. Even were a perfect delineation possible, it is essential that explorers of literature, whether biographers or commentators, historians or critics, attain a complete and undistorted view of all literary facts. If we wish to understand writers in our time, we cannot forget that writing is a profession— or at least a lucrative activity— practiced within the framework of economic systems which exert undeniable influences on creativity. We cannot forget, if we wish to understand literature, that a book is a manufactured product, commercially distributed and thus subject to the laws of supply and demand. We must see that literature is, among other things, incontestably, the production segment of the book industry, as reading is its consumption segment.

An Historical Account

Our notion of literature is recent and dates from the last years of the eighteenth century. Originally, we did not *make* literature; we *had* it. It was the distinguishing sign of well-educated people: for this notion we have substituted that of "general culture." For a contemporary of Voltaire, however, the world of "literature" opposed the world of the "public," or the people. This situation implies a cultural aristocracy and as a result, the problem of social relations between literature and society could scarcely emerge into consciousness.

An evolution began in the sixteenth century which picked up momentum in the eighteenth. On the one hand, knowledge became specialized; scientific and technical works tended to be progressively shut off from real literature, while the scope of literature diminished and tended to be restricted to that of a pastime. Doomed to this unwarranted position, literature tried to establish new organic relationships between itself and the community. What one may call "engaged" literature is the last of these attempts.

On the other hand, the same technical and cultural progress which accentuated the gratuitousness of literature enlarged the need for literature and increased the efficiency of communication between the consuming public and the book industry. With the invention of the printing press, the development of the book trade, the decline of illiteracy and, later, with the advent of audio-visual techniques, what used to be the privileged characteristics of an upper class of well-educated people became the cultural occupation of a relatively unrestricted middle-class élite. Then, in recent times, these became the way to improve the masses intellectually.

Both specialization and this wider distribution reached their critical points in the early eighteen hundreds. At that time, literature began to appreciate its social dimension. *De la littérature considérée dans ses rapports avec les institutions sociales*, by Madame de Staël, published in 1800, is doubtless the first attempt in France to join literature and society in a systematic study.

Madame de Staël defines her intentions in her prefatory discourse:

> I have undertaken the examination of what are the influences of religion, morals and laws on our literature, and of what is the influence of literature on religion, morals and laws.[1]

This undertaking extends to literature Montesquieu's treatment of the history of law: Madame de Staël, one of his intellectual disciples, wrote a *Spirit of Literature*. At a time when the words "modern" and "national" took on new meaning in the critics' vocabulary, an explanation of the diversity of literature in time and space by the variations and peculiar traits of human societies became inevitable.

The *Zeitgeist*, the spirit of an era, and the *Volksgeist*, the national spirit, were the two fundamental notions which appeared and took shape in Madame de Staël's circle of German friends. They are found again in the doctrine of Taine, divided according to the ternary formula of *race, milieu* and *moment*. The convergence of these three factors determines the literary phenomenon.

Taine lacked a clear idea of "human science." Half a century after him, Georges Lanson criticized this deficiency: "The analysis of poetic genius has nothing in common with the analysis of sugar but the name."[2] Taine's outline of *race, milieu*, and *moment* is too unpolished to embrace all the aspects of an infinitely complex reality. Above all, his methods are not adapted to the specificity of the literary fact: beyond some brutally transposed procedures from nature and science, he has access only to traditional methods of history and literary criticism (biographical analysis and textual commentary) with which to approach the material he is studying.

Yet the essence of Taine's doctrine survives. After Taine, neither historians nor critics could allow themselves — although they did sometimes— to ignore the fact that external

---

1. *De la littérature*, "Discours préliminaire," Paragraph 1.
2. "Méthodes de l'histoire littéraire," *Etudes Françaises*, Premier Cahier (January 1925), p. 23.

circumstances, notably social ones, have a bearing on literary activities.

Economics being a human science, more efficacy could have been expected from Marxism than from Taine's doctrine. The first Marxist theories, however, showed themselves to be extremely discreet on literary questions. The volume *Sur la littérature et sur l'art*, in which the writings of Marx and Engels appear jointly, is rather disappointing. It is only with Plekhanov, in the beginning of this century, that a real Marxist theory of literature is constructed, and it, of course, was sociological in nature. But later, anxiety for political efficiency led Soviet literary critics (and with them, Communist critics) to put less accent on literature than on social observation gleaned from literary works.

Vladimir Zhdanov defined his attitude in 1956:

Literature must be considered in its inseparable relation to social life, the background of those historical and social factors which influence the writer: this has always been the governing principle behind Soviet literary research. It is founded on the Marxist-Leninist method of perception and analysis of reality, and it excludes the subjective and arbitrary point of view which considers each book as an independent and isolated entity. Literature is a social phenomenon, the perception of reality through creative imagery.[3]

The methodological consequence of this attitude is obvious:

The principle of the historical method which is at the base of Soviet literary research has as its primary criterion for all works of art the degree of fidelity with which it represents reality in all its complexity.[4]

While the literary sociology applied by the Hungarian Georges Lucas and his disciple, the Frenchman Lucien Goldmann, also bears the Marxist stamp, it is perhaps less rigorous but more conscious of specifically esthetic problems.

The principal opposition to the Soviet sociological method was "formalism." The powerful formalist school, officially condemned in the nineteen-thirties, sought to apply a

---

3. "Some Recent Soviet Studies in Literature," *Soviet Literature*, No. 8 (Moscow, 1956), p. 141
4. *Ibid.*

science of esthetics to the forms and procedures of literary art.[5] In fact, it was only one aspect of a vast movement which had its origins in Germany and in which were combined the influences of Wilhelm Dilthey's neo-Hegelian philosophy, of philological criticism, and of *Gestalt* psychology. Throughout the world this *Literaturwissenschaft* or science of literature has been, from the nineteenth century up to our own time, one of the most serious obstacles to the appearance of a real sociology of literature.

The science of sociology, however, through Comte, Spencer, Le Play, Durkheim and others progressed towards complete autonomy. It bypassed literature, that complex domain of extremely uncertain data and definitions, for literature had been protected by an attitude of deference.

Sociological tendencies were expressed throughout the last half-century in the form of great, governing ideas, rather than in the form of one coherent method. They have sometimes joined with formalistic tendencies: L. L. Schüking and the sociology of taste, R. Wellek and the study of language as a social element in literature.[6] Comparative literature, the last-born of the literary sciences, has undoubtedly initiated the greatest number of interesting ideas.

The study of the huge theme of a collective consciousness, to which Paul Hazard devoted part of his work,[7] leads to that "history of ideas" which Lovejoy has made his specialty and which is now indispensable to a full understanding of literature. Jean-Marie Carré has oriented his pupils towards the problem of "mirages," a problem raised by the distorted view which one national group obtains of another through the influence of writers.[8]

Among governing ideas, one of the most fecund was certainly that of "generations." This idea was expressed in 1920 by François Mentré in his work, *Les générations sociales*. But the merit of being the first to elaborate this idea belongs to

---

5. Let us note, however, that between 1927 and 1930 there existed a "formalistic" sociology of literature. See Gleb Struve, *Histoire de la littérature soviétique* (Paris, 1946), pp. 226-229.

6. L. L. Schüking, *Die Soziologie der literarischen Geschmäcksbildung* (Leipzig, 1931). René Wellek and Austin Warren, *Theory of Literature* (New York, 1949).

7. *La crise de la conscience européenne* (Paris, 1935).

8. *Les écrivains français et le mirage allemand* (Paris, 1947).

Albert Thibaudet, whose revolutionary work, *Histoire de la littérature française de 1789 à nos jours,* appeared in 1937. It was the fundamental work by Henri Peyre, *Les générations littéraires,* published in 1948, which really demonstrated the sociological significance of "this problem of collective inspiration which is that of literary generations."[9] To these names one might add that of Guy Michaud; in his *Introduction à une science de la littérature,* which appeared in Istanbul in 1950, he was the first to launch explicitly— among a hundred other ideas— the idea of a literary sociology as we understand the term today.

Up to recent times, however, the absence of documentation made the *in vivo* study of sociological phenomena in literature practically impossible. How could one pretend to interpret the past when incapable of checking facts in the present? Fortunately, this situation has rapidly been improved in the ten years which followed the Second World War.

One must first mention the decisive role played by UNESCO: systematic censuses taken by its various divisions permitted the acquisition of previously inaccessible information about collective aspects of literature. In 1956, R. E. Barker's report, *Books For All,* although too fragmentary and conjectural in documentation, was nevertheless useful as a basis for work to come.

The book industry also timidly investigated standardization and market studies. I must regretfully say that the superstition of a "sixth sense" and, more particularly, commercial caution make France one of the most backward countries in accumulating information. The only official documentation on the book trade in France, excellent but desperately thin, is the *Monographie de l'édition* by Pierre Monnet, published in 1956 by the Cercle de la Librairie.[10] In 1960, The National Union of Publishers asked the Institute of Economic and Social Research to investigate reading and book practices in France. The very important results of this investigation have not been published commercially.[11] German publishers and bookstores regularly publish precise and

9. Henri Peyre, *Les générations littéraires* (Paris, 1948). It was Henri Peyre who, in 1950, urged me to undertake research in the sociology of literature.

10. First edition (1956), Second edition (1959), Third edition (1963).

11. See the bibliography at the end of this chapter.

abundant documentation under the title *Buch und Buch-handel in Zahlen*. In England, uncontested capital of the "capitalist" edition, partial studies are already numerous. This situation also prevails in new countries which are trying to make up their cultural lag (and are succeeding in their efforts) with the help of an intelligently planned book trade policy.

Thus we come to what in our time and the future will undoubtedly be the most efficient apparatus for research in literary sociology: namely, the necessity for planning in the book trade industry.

Towards a Book Industry Policy

What used to be the quest for individual wisdom, an attempt at self-knowledge, is now the search for aggregate wisdom. In literature, our societies seem, as a rule, to lack self-knowledge. The advancement of the masses, foretold over a century ago and now an inexorable reality in the last generation, has scarcely led to a rethinking of the material characteristics of political communities. Cultural traits have been neglected to a larger extent. Even though we talk a great deal about it, the notion of mass culture remains marked by a paternalistic and missionary zeal which masks its real lack of force. Thus a community of one million men has at its disposal a literary culture meant for a community of thousands.

So it is not surprising that this situation has troubled organizations interested in social welfare. In January of 1957, the magazine *Informations Sociales*, the organ of the "Union Nationale des caisses d'allocations familiales," devoted a special issue to a vast poll on "literature and the mass audience." The poll had the merit of bringing into the forefront almost all the problems of literary sociology, and its publication may be considered as a decisive step towards regulated research.[12]

An article by Gilbert Mury, "Is a Sociology of the Book Trade Possible?" is notable in that it justifies literary so-

---

12. The poll was based on a series of observations of unequal value. At the request of René Mongé, editor-in-chief of the magazine and initiator of the poll, I coordinated the results and commented on them.

ciology through the example of religious sociology. Deference to human values retarded the appearance of literary sociology and directly opposed religious sociology. But the same need to act, to elaborate a coherent design, which has always permitted believers to conquer their scruples, must conquer the reticence of literary purists.

> Not so long ago, all objective research on faith and religious practices was considered by excellent minds as an attack against mysticism. Today the Catholic episcopate is beginning such investigations in order to adapt itself to the reality of its pastoral movement . . . . It is certain that, from writers to book dealers, all men connected with the book trade would gain from the results of systematic studies of the public and, consequently, they would better envision new ways of reaching them.[13]

Gilbert Mury reminds us that salesmen have their place in the Temple of the Muses: having economic aspects which religion wishes to ignore, literature must be all the more open to sociological considerations. To see clearly is not simply a necessary action, it is also good business. But we need not necessarily limit ourselves to commercial considerations. Diderot writes in his "Lettre sur le commerce de la librairie:"

> A blunder which is always committed by those whose lives are governed by general maxims is the application of the manufacture of material to the publishing industry.

The sociology of literature must respect the specific nature of the literary fact. The tradesman may use literary sociology to his advantage, but it may also aid the reader by assisting traditional literary science, whether historical or critical, in the tasks which belong to it. These preoccupations remain indirectly those of literary sociology, but its role is only to express them at the social level.

Such a program demands vast research which surpasses the capacity of individuals or even of isolated groups. In the first edition of this book, published in 1958, I was able to present only a few results of a miniscule part of the stated

---

13. *Informations sociales* (January 1947), p. 64. Gilbert Mury, a professor of philosophy, is presently engaged in research on literary sociology dealing mainly with the behavior of the public.

problems. But that edition permitted me to enter into contact with researchers who shared my interest in the same problems and even to awaken enough curiosity to begin new research. Several publications have devoted space to this rereach;[14] various conferences have shown that specialists of criticism or literary history are adopting the sociological perspective more and more willingly.

There is now in Bordeaux a Center of Sociological Literary Facts and another is being created in Brussels. With the help of Penguin Books an institute of a similar nature has been founded in Birmingham. Encouraging response has been received from America, Germany, Italy, Japan, Africa and the socialist countries. An authentic sociology of literature is being born.

---

14. *Tendances*, No. 1 (1959). *Chronique sociale de France*, No. 1 (1959). *Esprit*, No. 4 (1960), etc.

Bibliography

Altick, R. D., *The English Common Reader*, Chicago, 1956.

Angoulvent, P., *L'Edition française au pied du mur*, Paris, 1960.

Dumazedier, J. and Hassenforder, J., *Eléments pour une sociologie comparée de la production, de la diffusion et de l'utilisation du livre*, Bibliographie de la France, Paris, 1963.

Escarpit, R., "Les Méthodes de la sociologie littéraire," *Actes du 11e Congrès de l'Association internationale de Littérature Comparée*, Chapel Hill, North Carolina, 1958.

———, "La sociologie de la littérature," Encyclopédie française, Vol. XVII, 1963.

———, " 'Creative Treason' as a Key to Literature," *Yearbook of Comparative and General Literature*, #10, 1961.

Lough, J., *English Theatre Audiences in the 17th and 18th Centuries*, London, 1957.

Lukacs, G., *Literatur-Soziologie*, Neuwied, 1961.

Monnet, P., *Monographie de l'Edition*, Paris, 1956.

Pichois, C., "Vers une sociologie historique des faits littéraires," *Revue d'Histoire littéraire de la France*, 1961, #1.

Pottinger, D. T., *The French Book Trade in the Ancient Regime*, Harvard, 1958.

Schücking, L.L., *Die Soziologie der literarischen Geschmäcksbildung*, Leipzig, 1931.

Wellek, R., and Warren, A., *Theory of Literature*, New York, 1949.

"Littérature et grand public," *Informations sociales*, 1957, #1.
"Etudes sur la lecture et le livre en France," *Syndicat national des Editeurs*, Paris, 1960.

The Sociology of Literature: Some Stages in Its History
Jacques Leenhardt

from

International Social Science Journal, vol. XIX, no. 4.

The sociology of literature:
some stages in its history

Jacques Leenhardt

The expression 'sociology of literature' covers two very different types of research, bearing respectively on literature as a consumer product and literature as an integral part of social reality, or, considered from another angle, bearing on society as the place of literary consumption and society as the subject of literary creation.

Even these distinctions, however, are not sufficiently precise; on the one hand, literary consumption, the final phase of the process, entails production with a view to consumption and then the distribution of the works produced through channels which, owing to their respective character-istics, lead to discrimination between the different literatures disseminated and which must therefore be defined in each case: bookshop, lending library, etc.; on the other hand, we shall see that the writers considered in this article do not perhaps throw sufficient light on the relationship be-tween a society and its literature.

It is necessary, however, to establish *a priori* this fundamental distinction, which will explain the choice of the works and trends of thought to be dealt with here and which will therefore also justify the exclusion of an entire part of contemporary sociological research on literature. Thus, the present article will contain no information about literary consumption and its conditions.

Let us begin with a historical definition of the subject under consideration. The idea of a sociology of literature may be said to be already completely contained in the title of Madame de Staël's *De la Littérature considérée dans ses Rapports avec les Institutions Sociales* (1810). With the help of the sociological concepts of her own time and of Montesquieu's time, Madame de Staël undertook to show the original characteristics of the ancient and modern literatures of the north and of the south. For us, she is a precursor possessing great insight but not sufficiently versed in sociology to be able to realize her aim completely. The desire to carry out a 'positive' study of literature should, however, be recognized as the first requirement of all sociological research aimed at 'excluding . . . the ideas which circulate around us and which are only, so to speak, the metaphysical representation of certain personal interests'.[1]

The ideological character which literary criticism tends to assume could not be more firmly denounced, and it is easy to understand Madame de Staël's taste for German literature, which she regarded as 'perhaps the only literature which began with criticism',[2] while she considered that, in France, 'the domination of an aristocratic class . . . explains why art has been essentially respect for good form'.[3]

If Madame de Staël's example can help us to classify present-day research in the field of the sociology of literature, it is because she inaugurated a sociological tradition which never precisely defined the relationship between society and literature, or between society and the writer, although it affirmed the existence of such a relationship. It might be said that, for the exponents of this tradition, this relationship is determined by the entire range of co-variations, but that, unfortunately, there is no theory of these co-variations, whereas, if this relationship is considered in terms of functionality, the Marxian theory of consciousness offers a fundamental instrument on the theoretical level. In this connexion, a cautious approach is necessary for the Marxian theory of consciousness has put forward several and frequently contradictory points of view. (It should be recalled that Marx was the first to declare that he was not a 'Marxist'.) Leaving these quarrels aside we shall take as our starting-point a simple and a very general axiom: human thought and, consequently, its products are closely bound up with man's actions, particularly his actions in regard to the world about him.

Even more than a theory of consciousness, which, at least at the level on which we consider it, is almost a truism, it was method which the precursors of the sociology of literature lacked most. They could not pursue their ideas right to the point of a scrupulous reading of texts: thus the comparisons which their 'intuition' suggested to them remained distant or artificial. It is true that their lack of a clearly defined method did not prevent their studies from yielding positive and often abundant results, but the field of variation of their explanations, from the vaguest to the most ingeniously arbitrary, cannot hide this fundamental shortcoming.

This article will be concerned mainly with the situation in the United States of America, the Federal Republic of Germany and France. We have been obliged to make this arbitrary choice owing to the usual difficulties: problem of languages (Eastern European countries), inadequate information (South America) and, lastly, the impossibility of dealing exhaustively with our subject in a few pages.

Sociological literary criticism in the United States of America has evolved, perhaps more than anywhere else, in accordance with the social

---

1. Madame de Staël, *De la Littérature considérée dans ses Rapports avec les Institutions Sociales*, Éditions Droz, 195, p. 295.
2. Madame de Staël, *De l'Allemagne*, Paris, Flammarion, Vol. 1, Chapter IV, p. 147.
3. ibid., pp. 216-17.

situation. After the First World War great interest was taken in novelists of the realistic school (Dos Passos, Steinbeck) and there was a great surge of enthusiasm for community ideals. At the same time, the purpose of criticism was considered to be the active participation in history rather than a real attempt at criticism.[1] It was in this spirit that the *Partisan Review*—which was to survive on this political basis only until 1936—was founded in 1934.[2]

V. F. Calverton, whose book *The Newer Spirit* is typical of this first generation of American 'sociological' criticism declared: 'The genesis or environment of a piece of art is indispensable to an understanding of its effects upon its observers.'[3]

Thirty years later, Roy Harvey Pearce, in 'Historicism Once More', sought to re-establish 'a kind of criticism which is, by definition, a form of historical understanding'.[4] After the formalism of the 'new critics', he again felt the need to study literary forms from the standpoint of their historical and social importance.

Thus, this tradition, based at the start on complete ideological and critical confusion, made its reappearance, but after a rather long eclipse.[5] However, it was not until 1957, when L. Löwenthal's *Literature and the Image of Man* and I. Watt's *The Rise of the Novel* were published, that American criticism began to ascribe real importance to the sociological approach to literature.

In *The Rise of the Novel*, Ian Watt studies eighteenth-century English literature, particularly Defoe, Richardson and Fielding. He notes that these first three English novelists were of the same generation; this was not a mere coincidence; moreover their genius could not have created a new literary form (the novel) unless there had been particularly favourable literary and social conditions. To ascertain these conditions, the specific nature of the novels in question must be defined. They have always been noted for their 'realism', it being stressed that 'Moll Flanders is a thief,

---

1. It is significant that the best bibliography relating to the subject under consideration, namely the bibliography published by H. D. Duncan in *Language, Literature and Society*, Chicago, Ill., University of Chicago Press, 1953, gives, under the heading 'General treatments of the nature of literary perspective', forty-eight titles distributed by decades as follows: before 1900, 2; 1900-9, 4; 1910-19, 1; 1920-9, 12; 1930-40, 22; 1940-9, 6; after 1950, 1.
2. This review had the following programme: 'Working toward the abolition of the system that breeds "imperialist war, fascism, national and social oppression".' It reappeared in 1937 with a declaration of political neutrality.
3. V. F. Calverton, *The Newer Spirit*, New York, 1925, p. 61; see also *The Liberation of American Literature*. Mention must be made here of J. Cabau's very instructive book: *La Prairie Perdue. Histoire du Roman Américain*, Le Seuil, 1966, in which the author attempts to trace American novelists' eternal quest for the 'prairie', which symbolizes the golden age of the North American continent.
4. R. H. Pearce, 'Historicism Once More', *Kenyon Review*, 1958.
5. In his book entitled *The Liberal Imagination. Essays on Literature and Society*, London, Secker & Warburg, 1951, L. Trilling tries to show the relationship between the instability of society and that of the characters he studies. 'The predicament of the characters in *A Midsummer Night's Dream* and of Christopher Sly seems to imply that the meeting of social extremes and the establishment of a person of low class always suggested to Shakespeare's mind some radical instability of the senses and the reason' (p. 210).

Pamela a hypocrite, and Tom Jones a fornicator'.[1] Watt, on the contrary, emphasizes another and, in his view, more essential aspect: 'the novel's realism does not reside in the kind of life it presents, but in the way it presents it'.[1] It is on the basis of this definition that he is able to compare the English eighteenth-century novel and French philosophical realism; he adopts a dispassionate attitude and is more concerned with 'scientific' truth than his predecessors and with the sociological conditions of the period.

Although all of Watt's concrete analyses are aimed at showing the 'realistic attitude' which characterizes these novels, he emphasizes that their success is due solely to the link which exists between this new literary *genre* and a new public. The period concerned saw an increase in the size of the reading public which, until then, had been extremely limited owing to the lack of public instruction and the exorbitant price of books (a copy of *Tom Jones* cost more than a farm worker's weekly wage). Numerous factors played a part in this development (libraries, suppression of patronage by booksellers, instruction given in charity schools and the fall in the price of books, especially of novels). However, for Watt, the essential point is to show that the three novelists concerned found themselves ideologically situated at the very centre of the preoccupations of this new public, this middle class: 'As middle-class London tradesmen they had only to consult their own standards of form and content to be sure that what they wrote would appeal to a large audience . . . not so much that Defoe and Richardson responded to the new needs of their audience, but that they were able to express those needs from the inside. . . .'[2]

'In so doing, Defoe initiated an important new tendency in fiction: his total subordination of the plot to the pattern of the autobiographical memoir is as defiant an assertion of the primacy of the individual experience in the novel as Descarte's *Cogito ergo sum* was in philosophy.'[3]

It will no doubt be objected that this is essentially a 'literary' study. In our view, this in no way means that it may not approach the subject from a sociological angle; moreover it must be admitted that if literary experts had not themselves profited by what sociology has to offer them it is unlikely that sociologists would have seriously interested themselves in literature for some considerable time to come.

In this connexion, we cannot but share L. Löwenthal's astonishment when, in 1961, in *Literatur und Gesellschaft*, he sadly notes that: 'It is symptomatic that (in the U.S.A.) there is still no complete and up-to-date bibliography relating to the sociology of literature and art.'[4]

The enormous American production of sociological works obviously

---

1. I. Watt, *The Rise of the Novel*, Berkeley, Calif., University of California Press, 1957, p. 11.
2. ibid., p. 59.
3. ibid., p. 15.
4. 'Es ist symptomatisch, dass es (in den USA) keine bis auf heutigen Tag fortgeführte, umfassende Bibliographie zur Literatur- und Kunstsoziologie gibt.' L. Löwenthal, *Literatur und Gesellschaft*, Neuwied, Luchterhand, 1964, p. 244. (American edition: *Literature, Popular Culture and Society*, Prentice-Hall, 1961.)

comprises numerous 'notes' on literature but these notes do not at all compensate for the general dearth which is so obvious in this field. Many theoretical summaries by 'literary critics' must also be mentioned, particularly the *Theory of Literature* by René Wellek and Austin Warren; in Chapter IX, entitled 'Literature and Society', the authors make a brief critical study of Taine and certain Soviet mechanist Marxists[1] such as Grib and Smirnov, in particular, but unfortunately without taking into account other trends of sociological criticism and without getting to the heart of the problems involved or providing the theoretical tools for a real sociology of literature. Thus, we are nearly always reduced to generalities, which although correct, are of little practical value; however, they seem to satisfy many authors. The following may be quoted as an example: 'The sociology of knowledge also aids intellectual history by indicating in what way literature can affect society. As has been pointed out, this system does not claim that all thought is socially determined.'[2]

Thus, these studies seem too often to be fragmentary; in any case, they do not replace solid and concrete studies such as L. Löwenthal's *Literature and the Image of Man*, which is extremely rare of its kind. It must be noted, however, that Löwenthal is a writer in the German sociological tradition and that, since 1926, he has worked in Frankfurt with Th. W. Adorno and M. Horkheimer, to whom, incidentally, his study is dedicated.[3] The chapters on Cervantes, Shakespeare and Molière are particularly interesting. Speaking about Molière, Löwenthal points out the great similarity between the ideas of the dramatist and those of the philosopher Gassendi, and he states: 'With the exception of the Misanthrope, there is not a single person in Molière's plays who claims the right and the responsibility to create the world in the image of his own reason as did the figures of Shakespeare and Cervantes. A completely new tone is evident. Except for a light touch of ritualized deference, no major figure in Molière feels in any way motivated by affairs and ideologies of the State and, except for the Misanthrope, no person goes into mourning and despair as a result of alienation from the established mores of society.' Further on, Löwenthal adds: 'Middle-class society is entering a period of common sense and adjustment.'[4]

Fairly remote from the preoccupations and methods of Watt and Löwenthal, but closer to a certain formalism with which he has combined a

1. R. Wellek and A. Warren, *Theory of Literature*, New York, Harcourt Brace & Co., 1942. It is significant that the critics nearly always attack the most mechanistic authors in order to refute every attempt at a sociological approach, Grib and Smirnov rather than Gramsci or Lukács. This is another example of the too frequent practice of oversimplified classifications.
2. Alex Kern, 'The Sociology of Knowledge in the Study of Literature', *The Sewanee Review*, Vol. 50, 1942, p. 513.
3. It should also be noted that I. Watt, like G. Thomson, is not of American but of English background (Cambridge). See Thomson's publications: *Marxism and Poetry*, New York, 1946, and *Aeschylus and Athens. A Study in the Social Origin of Drama*, London, 1941.
4. L. Löwenthal, *Literature and the Image of Man. Sociological Studies of the European Drama and Novel*, 1600-1900, Boston, Mass., The Boston Press, 1957, p. 125.

personal philosophy, K. Burke proposes to undertake a study of literary language in the widest sense of the term, i.e., in the form given to it in everyday life: 'In so far as situations are typical and recurrent in a given social structure, people develop names for them and strategies for handling them.'[1]

The same is true of proverbs, which are the most sophisticated form of literary art, the product of complex civilizations, for use in rhetorical contexts. Unfortunately, Burke's theory suffers from a systematic dramatization of human relationships through which he wishes to explain language as the strategy of communication: 'What would such sociological categories be like? They would consider works of art, I think as strategies for selecting enemies and allies, for socializing losses, for warding off the evil eye, for purification, propriation. Art forms like "tragedy" or "comedy" or "satire" would be treated as equipments for living, that size up situations in various ways and in keeping with correspondingly various attitudes.'[2]

This constant tendency to philosophize is very detrimental to Burke's work, which reflects very great insight.

We have often distinguished the situation of sociological criticism in Germany from that in other countries. What exactly is this situation?[3] In Germany we find a philosophical and sociological tradition which is directed to a much greater extent towards the sociology of literature. In this country, the heritage of Hegel and Marx has lasted for generations, and it would be impossible to name all those who have been influenced by it. Certain Marxian writers, like F. Mehring, may be mentioned in this connexion. Mehring defines his conception of the relationships between social structures and literary works as follows: 'The ideological heritage also exercises an influence, which has never been denied by historical materialism; but its effect is simply like that of the sun, the rain and the wind on a tree which is rooted in the rough soil of material conditions, modes of economic production and social situation'.[4]

Taking this idea as his starting-point, Mehring in his major work, *Die Lessing Legende*, tries to destroy the 'legend' according to which Lessing was truly attached to the kingdom of Frederick II of Prussia. In his analysis, he stresses Lessing's opposition to the Prussian Court and interprets the 'legend' as an unconscious falsification, an ideological superstructure of an economic and political development: the alliance of the German middle

---

1. Quoted by H. D. Duncan, *Language, Literature and Society*, op. cit., p. 84.
2. K. Burke, *The Philosophy of Literature Form: Studies in Symbolic Action*, Baton Rouge, La., Louisiana State University Press, 1941, p. 293. Quoted by H. D. Duncan, *Language, Literature and Society*, op. cit., p. 266. See also K. Burke, *A Grammar of Motives*, New York, Prentice-Hall Book Co., 1945.
3. Although 'the father of Russian Marxism', G. V. Plekhanov had a certain influence throughout the whole of Europe; his work on literature, *Dramatic Literature and Painting in Eighteenth-century France considered from the Sociological Standpoint*, 1905, is unfortunately harmed by a rather narrow sociological outlook which considerably diminishes its importance. See also *L'Art et la Vie Sociale*, Éditions Sociales, 1949.
4. F. Mehring, 'Ästhetische Streichzüge', Neue Zeit XVII, I 1898-1899, *Zur Literaturgeschichte*, Vol. II, pp. 254-5.

classes with the Prussian State during the nineteenth century and the desire to 'reconcile its actual present with its idealized past by making the era of classical culture an era of Frederick the Great'.[1]

This approach to a sociological study of literature is not the only one. Since Dilthey and through the Kantian tradition, another approach has revealed itself: the use of the concept of form as applied to society and its cultural productions.

G. Lukács adopts an intermediate approach: his work, Kantian at the start, then Hegelian and Marxian, represents the corpus of the most complete sociology of literature yet produced by a single author. We shall mention only two typical works belonging to the first period of his abundant production: *The Soul and Forms* and the *Theory of the Novel*.[2] It is in these works that Lukács seems to use the most flexible method, even if now and again, especially in the first part of the *Theory of the Novel*, he is rather prone to adopt a definitely philosophical attitude. The important point, however, as far as the sociology of literature is concerned, is that Lukács had, even at this stage, defined the concept of 'forms', of 'significant structure'. These 'forms' represent for him the privileged modes of meeting between the human soul and the absolute. They are non-temporal forms, 'essences' such as, for example, the tragic outlook which he regarded at that time as the only true and authentic one.

In his view the tragic outlook is an attempt to live in accordance with the principle of all or nothing. Tragic characters are unaware of the fact that there is no complete correspondence between thought and action; they are conscious of their will-power and of its limits. If their actions did not coincide with their words, they would seem ridiculous.

Ever in quest of a new world outlook, Lukács studied a literary *genre*: the essay. He wonders how far this form, intermediate between literature and philosophy, corresponds to a particular world outlook. Like philosophy, the essay studies the problem of the absolute, the whole, values in general, independently of phenomena. On the other hand, like literature, the essay deals with specific cases, in respect of which it seems tempted to offer an explanation. What, then, is the nature of the essay, situated as it is between the general and the particular? Lukács shows that the essay, always written 'on the occasion of', represents essentially a problematic form, by means of which the author seeks answers to the major problems of life, but always in connexion with specific cases.

In the *Theory of the Novel*, Lukács quits the domain of pure forms in order to relate them to the world. He abandons his Kantian attitude and adopts a Hegelian approach. He regards the novel as the characteristic literary form of a world in which man never feels entirely a part (as he did in the Middle Ages and in Ancient Greece, which Lukács wrongly considers

1. F. Mehring, *Die Lessing Legende*, Stuttgart, Dietz, 1893. Quoted by M. Löwy in the Dietz edition, Berlin, 1926, p. 8.
2. G. Lukács, *Die Seele und die Formen*, Berlin, Fleischel, 1911; *La Théorie du Roman*, Paris, Gonthier, 1963.

a kind of golden age of the community) nor entirely a stranger. There is a community in the novel, as in all epics, but unlike the *epopee*, the novel also takes into account the radical opposition between man and the world, between the individual and society.

Karl Mannheim, whose original ideas are very similar to those of Lukács, from whose friendship he derived great profit, is perhaps the writer whose name is most closely linked in the public mind with the sociology of knowledge. For many years he directed a collection, 'The International Library of Sociology and Social Reconstruction', of which he was the founder and in which he published his own *Essays on Sociology of Knowledge*[1] as well as works by S. Ossowski, G. Misch, H. A. Hodges, A. Belgame, etc.; but he is known mainly for his chief work, *Ideologie und Utopie*.[2] In this now classic study, Mannheim draws an interesting distinction between the progressist form of false consciousness, Utopia, and its conservative form, ideology. He goes on to distinguish the liberal Utopias—those of the eighteenth-century enlightenment, for example,—from chiliasm, these Utopias usually being peculiar to the *Lumpenproletariat*. As opposed to these two progressist forms, the conservative ideology emphasizes the real, in so far as it is, as compared with what ought to be.

However, with regard to literature proper, Mannheim cannot be credited with concrete research comparable to that carried out by Lukács.

Following Lukács' return to Hungary after a long stay in the U.S.S.R. and Mannheim's emigration to England, it is mainly around the Frankfurt school that the sociology of literature developed in the Federal Republic of Germany after the Second World War.

The writings of Th. W. Adorno and M. Horkheimer influenced the first generation of research workers who found in the Marxian-Hegelian method a flexible and efficient instrument for their research. Special mention must be made of their joint work, *Dialektik der Aufklärung*, which was published in the Netherlands in 1947 and in which they analyse the process of auto-destruction of the ideals of the enlightenment up to the establishment of the fascist régime: 'For us there is no doubt—therein resides our *petitio principii*—that freedom inside the community is inseparable from enlightened thinking. However, we feel we have just as clearly perceived that the concept of this enlightened thinking, no less than the concrete historical forms—the social institutions—in which it is embodied, already contains the seeds of the regression which is taking place everywhere today.'[3]

1. K. Mannheim, *Essays on Sociology of Knowledge*, London, 1952. (The International Library of Sociology and Social Reconstruction.)
2. K. Mannheim, *Ideology and Utopia: An Introduction to the Sociology of Knowledge*, New York and London, 1936.
3. 'Wir hegen keinen Zweifel—und darin liegt unsere *petitio principii*—dass die Freiheit in der Gesellschaft von aufklärenden Denken unabtrennbar ist. Jedoch glauben wir genau so deutlich erkannt zu haben, dass der Begriff eben dieses Denkens, nicht weniger als die konkreten historischen Formen, die Institutionen der Gesellschaft, in die es verflochten ist, schon den Keim zu jenem Rückschritt enthalten, der heute überall sich ereignet.' Th. W. Adorno and M. Horkheimer, *Dialektik der Aufklärung*, Amsterdam, Querido, 1947, p. 7.

The part of Th. W. Adorno's work which deals with the sociology of literature largely comprises numerous short essays published mainly in the three volumes of *Noten zur Literatur* and in *Prismen: Kulturkritik und Gesellschaft*.[1] His essay 'Aldous Huxley und die Utopie' is in the second of these works. Dealing with the Utopian ideas of *Brave New World*, Adorno writes: '(Huxley's) attitude is in spite of itself akin to an upper-middle-class attitude which loudly proclaims that its support of a profit economy owes nothing to self-interest but is based on love of mankind.'[2]

For Adorno, men are not yet ready for socialism, being unable to make use of the liberty to be accorded them. In his view, however, such truths are compromised, not so much by the use that may be made of them, but because they are empty truths inasmuch as they deify what they call 'man', treating him as a 'datum', hypostatizing moreover the person who sets out to observe him: 'This coldness lies at the very roots of Huxley's system.'[3]

At the basis of Huxley's attitude, in spite of his indignation against evil, there is a construct of history which has time. Huxley's novel lays the guilt for the present upon that which does not yet exist. His upper-middle-class ideology has time and makes the present endure through a fictional future.

Close to Adorno in thought, if not in style, W. Benjamin, in spite of a literary career tragically interrupted by the war, wrote a certain amount of historical, social and aesthetic criticism, including *Das Kunstwerk im Zeitalter seiner technischen Reproduzierbarkeit*, in which he puts forward some original ideas on the changes undergone by art since it became subject to mechanical reproduction. What was once a unique object has ended by becoming standardized: 'Thus is affirmed, in the domain of intuition, a phenomenon analogous to that represented on the theoretical plane by the importance of statistics. The alignment of reality with the masses and the related alignment of the masses with reality constitute a process with infinite bearings as much upon thought as upon intuition.'[4]

So the sociological problem expands to allow room to the material conditions in which works of culture develop and reach their public in so far as these conditions themselves modify creators' modes of thought.

But to pursue this further would be to pass beyond the strict limits of this article to a study of the public, public tastes and the forms of cultural circulation such as has been undertaken in the Federal Republic of Germany notably by L. Schücking in *Die Soziologie der literarischen Geschmackbildung*[5]

1. Th. W. Adorno, *Noten zur Literatur*, Frankfurt, Suhrkamp, 3 vols., 1958-65; *Prismen: Kulturkritik und Gesellschaft*, Munich, D.T.V. GmbH Co. K.G., 1963.
2. 'Die Haltung (Huxley's) bleibt unwillentlich jener grossbürgerlichen verwandt, die souverän versichert, keineswegs aus eigenem Interesse den Fortbestand der Profitwirtschaft zu befürworten, sondern um der Menschen willen.' Th. W. Adorno, *Prismen: Kulturkritik und Gesellschaft*, op. cit., p. 116.
3. 'Solche Kälte wohnt im Innersten von Huxley's Gefüge.'
4. W. Benjamin, *Das Kunstwerk im Zeitalter seiner technischen Reproduzierbarkeit*, Frankfurt, Suhrkamp, 1963.
5. L. Schücking, *Die Soziologie der Literarischen Geschmackbildung*, Leipzig, Teubner, 1931.

or E. Auerbach in *Das französische Publikum des 17. Jahrhunderts*.[1] Auerbach does not, however, keep to this aspect of 'sociological' analysis. In his major work *Mimesis*,[2] he paints a huge fresco of realism in Western literature from Homer to Virginia Woolf, and more especially in French literature. He endeavours to trace the law of evolution operating here and brings a rich harvest of new ideas to an already classic project. His work, however, goes further than this in that he puts forward a very detailed critical analysis showing how the transformations of social reality and of the ways of thinking and feeling that go with them have repercussions not only upon the content of literary works, but also upon their style and even syntax. In so doing, Auerbach has cleared the way for research into the problem of forms in all their social manifestations—research which will be a future project of the sociology of literature.

The more recent and more strictly sociological and deductive studies of E. Köhler, assembled in part in his book *Trobadorlyrik und höfischer Roman*, consider in detail French literature of the Middle Ages. A constant exchange can be noted between literature and society in the twelfth century, the one throwing light on the other, which latter serves, however, as its foundation. It was an age of upheaval, with society in search of a new order—the courtly ideal, an age which saw the last of the *chanson de geste*, 'whose conception of life is still homogeneous and in which truth, one and immutable, has always an obligatory character'.[3]

The *chanson de geste* had had a meaning for the people of the Middle Ages, united as they were in the bosom of the Church and in consequence seeing everything in terms of salvation. Towards 1160 the court romance novel makes its appearance with the legend of King Arthur, thus giving the feudal society the 'historical' justification of its existence. But to guarantee its stability, the new society needed a common ideal, one, however, that concealed the factual cleavage between the upper and the lower aristocracy, a cleavage based essentially upon wealth. This conjuncture, which was to ensure a certain cohesion between hierarchically separated elements, finds expression, according to Köhler, in the poetic paradox of the 'renunciation of full realization' in courtly love, a renunciation to be understood as 'the sublimated projection of the lower nobility's lack of possessions and of a consequent lack of concrete social and economic relationships'.[4]

To conclude with a summary of the sociology of literature in the Federal Republic of Germany, we can therefore say that it progressed far more

1. E. Auerbach, *Das französische Publikum des 17. Jahrhunderts*, Munich, 1933. (Münchener Romanistische Arbeiten, No. 3).
2. E. Auerbach, *Mimesis. Dargestellte Wirklichkeit in der abendländischen Literatur*, Berne, Francke, 1946.
3. 'Dessen Lebensverständnis noch homogen und für welches noch ein und dieselbe Wahrheit verbindlich ist.' E. Köhler, *Trobadorlyrik und höfischer Roman*, Berlin, Rütten & Loening, 1962, p. 9.
4. 'Die sublimierte Projektion der Besitzlosigkeit des Kleinadels, also konkreter gesellschaftlich-ökonomischer Verhältnisse.' ibid, p. 7. See also M. Waltz, *Rolandslied, Wilhelmslied-Alexiuslied. Zur Struktur und geschichtlichen Bedeutung*, Heidelberg, C. Winter, 1965.

quickly and especially that it opened up far wider perspectives, armed as it was for its task with the concepts of a native philosophical tradition.

The French sociological tradition took a very different turn under the influence of Comte and Durkheim. It has, however, a precursor whom the sociology of literature could well rescue from the oblivion that has overtaken him, J. M. Guyau. Guyau's so-called aesthetico-ethical doctrine has been rightly condemned, but the methodological interest of some of the chapters preceding his concrete analyses in *L'Art du Point de Vue Sociologique* have gone unnoticed. Guyau found himself faced by two opposed theoretical standpoints, the historicist naturalism of Taine and romantic idealism.

Choosing an original approach he avoids the Tainian impasse, which consists of relating each fragment of a work to a historical fact presumed to be its cause. He proposes on the contrary to consider the work as a whole, as a system, and to 'discover the significant facts expressive of a law, those which, among the confused mass of phenomena, constitute points of reference and form a link, a pattern, a figure, a system'.[1]

Having thus affirmed since 1889 the structuralist nature of criticism, Guyau indicates cautiously to the sociologist that his work is itself partly creative of its object, because it makes an arbitrary selection related to his system of values. The famous *Wertfreiheit*, which caused so much ink to flow at the beginning of the century, could not be more openly challenged. But this fundamental statement implies another, more directly concerned with the sociology of literature.

If, in fact, the intellectual process of criticism is always linked to a system of values, then *a fortiori* so is that of the writer. The problem of values therefore leads of necessity to that of action and Guyau defines very precisely what links the two: 'The genius of art and the genius of contemplation have the same role (as that of action), for what is called contemplation is only action reduced to its first stage, maintained in the domain of thought and imagination.'[2]

Genius is therefore defined by its capacity to anticipate this action, to offer the reader 'a sort of inner vision of possible forms of life'.[3] It follows naturally from this conception of the work that it is not outside it that the means of understanding it must be sought but within itself inasmuch as it expresses this possible life by a system; here Guyau is very evidently criticizing the lack of nuances in Taine's explanation by means of the 'environment' as well as the psychology of it. For him society is important before everything, but inasmuch as it appears in the structure of the work, as a system of points of reference: 'Taine postulates the earlier environment as producing individual genius; one must therefore suppose that individual genius produces a new environment or a modification of the environment. These two doctrines are two essential parts of the truth; but Taine's doctrine is more applicable to mere talent than to genius, that is to say to

1. J. M. Guyau. *L'Art du Point de Vue Sociologique*, 7th ed., F. Alcan, 1906, p. 65.
2. ibid., p. 44.
3. ibid., p. xiii.

initiative. Once again we do not mean by these words an absolute initiative or invention, an invention which would be a creation out of nothing; but a new synthesis of pre-existing elements, like the combination of images in a kaleidoscope.'[1]

This does not alter the fact that Guyau was completely incapable of applying his theory to a concrete critical investigation. His studies of Hugo and Lamartine are based far more on his personal philosophy than on sociological criticism, which explains of course the oblivion into which he has fallen. However, it is not uninteresting to examine the theoretical approach of a sociologist of literature, and within these limits Guyau's theory can still be of value.

Far removed from Guyau's theories, which unfortunately bore no fruit, an analysis was drawn up in the early part of the century which was to revolutionize the historical study of mediaeval literature, J. Bédier's *Les Légendes Épiques*.[2] Bédier set out to uproot a firmly held prejudice according to which the French *chansons de geste* dated from the seventh, eighth, ninth and tenth centuries, being written therefore at the same time as the events they describe. In opposition to Grimm's arbitrary constructs, Bédier showed that the *chansons de geste* date from the eleventh century, the date of the oldest manuscripts in our possession, that they emanated from sanctuaries, places of pilgrimage and fairs and that finally, so far as they are legends having a historical basis, they imply the participation of scholars. Thanks to concordant geographical references, he showed that the descriptions of scenery were based on the pilgrim routes and that, apart from these very specific routes, the countries traversed remained unknown. But pilgrims, clerks and *jongleurs* do not suffice to explain the *chansons de geste*; it is in the time of the Crusades, in eleventh-century Spain, in the Holy Land and in the outpouring of ideas and sentiments which formed the framework of feudal and chivalrous society that the artisans of epic poetry have their place—pilgrims, scholars, *jongleurs*, knights, villeins and poets.

Bédier also shows brilliantly the progress that can be made if, instead of its customary rather abstract approach to literature, literary history studies the actual conditions in which these works saw the light.

G. Lanson is far removed from Bédier in thought and approach, and it may cause surprise to find him mentioned among the forerunners of the sociology of literature. It must not be forgotten, however, that he not only gave theoretical pledges of his interest in sociology and its use in literary criticism, but also formed some useful hypotheses which have not yet been fully explored. In an article on 'History and Sociology' he wrote: 'The ego of the poet is the ego of a group, a wider ego when it is Musset who sings, more restricted in the case of Vigny, a religious group when it is d'Aubigné, a political group when it is the Victor Hugo of *Les Châtiments*.'[3]

1. ibid., p. 42.
2. J. Bédier, *Les Légendes Épiques. Recherche sur la Formation des Chansons de Geste*, 2nd ed., H. Champion, 1917.
3. G. Lanson in *Revue de Métaphysique et de Morale*, 1904, pp. 627-8.

Fully aware of the relationships between creative work and groups, Lanson even outlines a sociology of literary criticism: 'At the basis of Boileau's judgements on Homer or Ronsard, what do we find but the picture of Homer or Ronsard in the collective mind, in the consciousness of a French seventeenth-century group? Dogmatism can in fact escape the charge of universalizing its individual impressions only provided it has socialized its thought.'[1]

Here it is important to see how Lanson by implication justifies the method he in fact practised, basing it in the last resort on sociological knowledge. If his quest was biography, he was to find, though biography, relationships of participation in a collective consciousness: 'We have reduced this personality to being—partially (so as not to let our affirmation go beyond our knowledge)—a focal point for rays emanating from the collective life around it.'[2]

With L. Febvre, we again leave the literary specialists and find literature at the heart of the preoccupations of a historian who more than any other wanted 'to pose, with regard to a man of singular vitality, the problem of the relationship of the individual to the collectivity, of personal initiative and social necessity which is perhaps the chief problem of history'.[3]

Such is Febvre's plan as stated in the preface to *Un Destin: Martin Luther*, even if there remains a certain gap between the plan and its realization, at least on the strictly sociological plane.

The case of *Autour de l'Heptaméron* is a little different. Here L. Febvre still purposes to go beyond the false evidence accumulated by critics against Marguerite de Navarre with their use of epithets as hasty as they are superficial, such as 'hypocrite'—a term more suggestive of 'the mentality of a second-rate newspaper' than of historical analysis.[4] He sets out to show that the incompatibility between the broadly Gallic and the profoundly Christian aspects of the *Heptaméron* cannot be explained either by an alleged internal dialectic of the work or by the ambivalent personality of Marguerite de Navarre, but by the difficulties of coexistence between the Christian religion and court morality under François I.

The key to the question of the *Heptaméron* must therefore be sought in the 'relationship of religious beliefs to the ideas, institutions and morals of a period; a problem outside the field of literary history'.[5] One cannot but subscribe to this comment, even if the analysis itself does not fully qualify as sociological, L. Febvre being primarily an historian.

The same applies to *Le Problème de l'Incroyance au XVIᵉ Siècle. La Religion de Rabelais*,[6] Febvre's most famous work, which we only mention

1. ibid., p. 269.
2. ibid., pp. 630-1.
3. L. Febvre, *Un Destin: Martin Luther*, Rieder, 1928, p. 7.
4. L. Febvre, *Autour de l'Heptaméron. Amour Sacré, Amour Profane*, 3rd ed., Gallimard. 1944, p. 223.
5. ibid., p. 14.
6. L. Febvre, *Le Problème de l'Incroyance au XVIᵉ Siècle. La Religion de Rabelais*, Albin Michel, 1962.

here, although it, too, is of direct interest to the sociologist of literature.

Nevertheless there has not been, since Taine, any major research in France into the sociology of literature. Many men of letters have put forward interesting ideas on the subject but have not followed this through thoroughly in their work. As for the sociologists, one is tempted to mention Halbwachs, so fitted did he seem to be to produce a sociological study of literature, but the subject remained outside the field of his actual preoccupations. So it is once again Germany which produced the writer B. Groethuysen, who in the 1920s brought out in French the first work written in the sociological spirit. This was not exactly a study of literature but of the *esprit bourgeois*.[1] Groethuysen promptly established a relationship between this type of mentality and that historical monument, the *Encyclopédie*. What could be more suggestive, in this context, than the few pages of *Mythes et Portraits*? By the term *l'avoir scientifique*, B. Groethuysen very accurately labelled the advent of the appropriation of knowledge at the turning point between the Renaissance and modern times: 'It is the spirit of possession which essentially distinguishes the "Encyclopédie" from the Orbis pictus in which the Renaissance travellers used to note the curious and interesting things they had seen on their journeys. "Renaissance Man" had remained an adventurer, a wanderer without property. Thus he was not yet able to say "the knowledge we have . . .". With the arrival of the *bourgeois*, and the establishment of his predominance in the domains of law and science, a change was brought about. He began by making a careful distinction "with a comparison of opinions at all levels", and "weighing up his reasons" between what he knew and what he did not know, counting only as really possessed that which he was sure he knew and which he could situate in "the order and train of human knowledge".[2]

P. Bénichou's *Morales du Grand Siècle* must not be underestimated. The author set out first of all to show the links between morality in the spirit of Corneille and court nobility under Louis XIV. This morality, he tells us, did not demand the suppression of nature before all else; it must rather be understood in the context of the *tradition noble* inherited from feudalism. The only duty is to be worthy of oneself, to expel self-doubt, to become conscious of one's own identity. But such heroism implies recognition by someone else. Yet the people of Rome and Bithynia, who might have been possible witnesses, do not appear on the stage. So it is in the audience that the hero finds his necessary interrogator and witness. Bénichou, in an analysis breaking with long tradition, shows that Descartes, in his *Traité des Passions*, does not look for the means of crushing desire by voluntary effort, but seeks far more the conditions of a harmony between the impulse and what

1. B. Groethuysen, *Les Origines de l'Esprit Bourgeois en France*. I: *L'Église et la Bourgeoisie*, Gallimard, 1927. 7th ed., 1956.
2. B. Groethuysen, *Mythes et Portraits*, 3rd ed., Gallimard, 1947, pp. 91-3.

is good. The harmony is attained at the level of that nature which transcends nature, known as *l'homme généreux*.[1]

With Racine, the position is different. The depreciated legacy of chivalry imposed upon him limits within which his genius could find expression. The age of aristocratic rebellion was over, the triumph of absolutism having rendered it obsolete. So in Racine's work the proud and voluble heroine gives way to the heroine who bewails her lot in secret. The aristocratic ideal still fascinates him, but it is too late to give it embodiment. The whole of Racine's genius developed within the context of this contradiction.

In Molière's *Dom Juan*, Bénichou sees the divorce of the 'noble' mentality from religion. Moral libertinage, cynical disavowal of the old idea of *noblesse oblige*, vainly and persistently opposed to Dom Juan by his father, has the effect of placing its adepts outside any tenable social position and, consequently, outside all solid and effective sovereignty. Dom Juan, *grand seigneur*, is at the same time a fallen being, in his right place in this period of the ultimate political decay of the nobility. Rodrigue and Nicomède are valid human models, Dom Juan is not. From the *importants* to the *roués*, this type of scandalous gentleman bestrides the centuries of monarchy, great because of his scorn for the cringing stupidity of men, and because of his ability to put pleasure before interest. Dom Juan is a revolutionary, although he embodies values that are past.

Finally, the sociology of literature, as considered in this article, has found its most coherent expression in L. Goldmann, that is to say, once again in a mind trained in traditions different from ours. This repeated finding of ours should have its issue in a sociology of French sociological epistemology, but the question lies outside our present subject.

For Goldmann, the sociology of literature has in view the understanding of the meaning of a work. To him this means clarifying the total network of meanings which internal analysis of a work reveals by an explanation, by the insertion of this network in a whole of wider significance: the social group. *Le Dieu Caché* is based on this approach.[2] We shall not give an analysis of this work here, elements of which are dealt with by the author in the present number of the *Journal*.

In *Pour une Sociologie du Roman*, Goldmann develops the problem of a sociological study of the novel at two levels. At the most general level he

1. P. Bénichou, *Morales du Grand Siècle*, Gallimard, 1948, p. 25.

   See also S. Doubrovsky, *Corneille et la Dialectique du Héros*, Gallimard, 1963, a work in which the author adopts a more differentiated position by showing the transition of a purely aristocratic hero (Le Cid) to a 'mercantilist' attitude: 'emulation is transformed into bargaining, thus itself becoming merchandise' (p. 191). This is what Doubrovsky calls the 'passage from aristocratic ontology (autonomy of the monads) to monarchic ontology (being, by participation with the one)' (p. 208).

   On this evolution towards 'mercantilism' in human relations in Corneille's plays, see also J. Ehrmann's article 'Les Structures de l'Échange dans Cinna', *Les Temps Modernes*, No. 246, 1965, pp. 929-60.

2. L. Goldmann, *Le Dieu Caché. Étude de la Vision Tragique dans* Les Pensées de Pascal *et les tragédies de Racine*, Gallimard, 1956. English translation by P. Thody, London, Routledge & Kegan Paul, 1964.

affirms that 'the problem of the novel is therefore to make that which in the mind of the writer is abstract and ethical (the values) the essence of a work in which this reality could not exist except in the form of a thematized absence . . . or, which is the same thing, a depreciated presence'.[1]

This book also contains a long study of the novels of Malraux. The study is in two parts: first, a concrete analysis which brings to light the very coherent structure of Malraux's novelistic universe; second, an analysis of a historical and sociological type showing the transformations that Western society and particularly Western capitalism underwent before 1912 and 1945, as well as—and this is a major event after the continual succession of crises—the appearance of mechanisms of intervention and of State regulation within Western capitalism. These profound changes have had, according to Goldmann, particular importance for Western society as a whole and particularly for the ideological evolution of Malraux, who to a large extent personified them in the field of the novel. Goldmann characterizes these changes as follows: 'Fading of revolutionary hopes and prospects: birth of a world in which all important acts are reserved for a specialist *élite*; reduction of the majority of men to mere instruments of the acts of this *élite*, having no real function in cultural creation or in social economic and political decisions; the difficulty of pursuing imaginative creation in a world in which it can refer to no universal human values—all these being problems which bear as obviously upon the last stage of Malraux's work as upon the developing evolution of our societies.'[2]

At the end of this rapid survey of the history of the sociology of literature, we are again faced with the initial question, Madame de Staël's question: what are the relationships of literature to society?

It will have been observed that, throughout our survey, we have not been able to make good the initial theoretical lack to which we have drawn attention. To try to bind the scattered fragments together would be beyond the scope of this article, for it would more or less amount to constructing an entire theory.[3] But we could, on the other hand, loosen a few threads, and, by way of conclusion, propose the beginnings of a programme of study.

By what they say, and still more by what they do not say, the books we have mentioned seem to indicate two directions for research. The first consists of a microsociological study of groups which comprise a world vision. An example is given in this number of the *Journal* in connexion with Stendhal. The essential aim of this empirical and strictly sociological research must be the study of the actual conditions operating between creative groups and individuals. These mediations obviously have two aspects, sociological and psychological. They derive therefore, at a certain level, from a genetic psychology which alone permits an escape from the

1. L. Goldmann, *Pour une Sociologie du Roman*, Gallimard, 1964, p. 22.
2. ibid., pp. 179-80.
3. We refrain only because L. Goldmann develops the elements of such a theory elsewhere in this issue of the *Journal*.

dichotomies of the social and the psychological. Probably the studies of J. Piaget would supply the point of departure for this building up of theory which is so gravely lacking at present.

The second direction that research should take would lead to a more scrupulous reading of texts. Until now, with the exception of Auerbach, analysis has dealt only with the over-all meaning of a work. An attempt might be made to show the possibilities of adopting the technique perfected by the symptomatologists of literature and upon what bases it would be possible to enter into a fruitful critical dialogue with them.

When these two fundamental aspects of research into the sociology of literature have been sufficiently illustrated by precise study, we will have attained a satisfactory measure of strictures, to the extent that the hypothesis represented by the first reading of a text will be verified, on the one hand, by its insertion in a larger reality (the group and its mental structures or visions of the world) and, on the other hand, by the possibility of including, in that reading, the symptomatological structures of the text.

[*Translated from the French.*]

The Sociology of Literature: Status and Problems of Method
Lucien Goldmann

from

Internation Social Science Journal, vol. XIX, no. 4.

The sociology of literature: status and problems of method

Lucien Goldmann

The genetic structural sociology of culture has given rise to a number of works which are characterized, in particular, by the fact that, in seeking to establish an operational method for the positive study of human facts—and, more especially, of cultural creation—their authors have been obliged to fall back on a type of philosophical reflection that might, in a somewhat general way, be described as dialectic.

The result is that this attitude may be presented either as an effort of positive research incorporating a mass of reflections of a philosophical character or as a philosophical attitude directed, in the first place, towards positive research and, in the end, constituting the methodological basis of a whole series of specific research activities.

Having, on more than one occasion, chosen the former of these methods of exposition, we shall endeavour to adopt the second. In doing so, however, it is important to stress from the very outset—but without much hope as to the effectiveness of this warning, for prejudices die hard—that the few remarks of a general and philosophical nature which follow are not prompted by any speculative intention and are put forward only in so far as they are essential to positive research.

The first general observation on which genetic structuralist thought is based is that all reflection on the human sciences is made not from without but from within society, that it is a part—varying in importance, of course, according to circumstances—of the intellectual life of that society and, through it, of social life as a whole. Furthermore, to the selfsame extent to which thought is a part of social life, its very development transforms that social life itself more or less, according to its importance and effectiveness.

In the human sciences, the subject of thought is thus seen to form part, at least to some extent and with a certain number of mediations, of the object to which it is directed. On the other hand, this thought does not constitute an absolute beginning and it is, in a very large measure, shaped by the categories of the society which it studies, or of a society deriving therefrom.

Thus the object studied is one of the constituent elements—and even one of the most important—of the structure of the thought of the research worker or workers.

Hegel summed all this up in a concise and brilliant formula—'the identity of the subject and object of thought'. We have merely attenuated the radical character of this formula—the result of Hegelian idealism, for which all reality is spirit—by substituting for it another, more in conformity with our dialectic materialist position according to which thought is an important aspect, but only an aspect, of reality: we speak of the partial identity of the subject and the object of research, that identity being valid, not for all knowledge, but only for the human sciences.

Whatever view is taken of the difference between the two formulas, however, they both affirm implicitly that the human sciences cannot have as objective a character as the natural sciences and that the intervention of values peculiar to certain social groups in the structure of theoretical thought is, at the present time, both general and inevitable in them.

This does not in any way, moreover, mean that these sciences cannot, in principle, attain a rigour similar to that of the sciences of nature; that rigour will merely be different and it will have to allow for the intervention of valorizations that cannot possibly be eliminated.

The second basic idea of any dialectic and genetic sociology is that human facts are the responses of an individual or collective subject, constituting an attempt to modify a given situation in a sense favourable to the aspirations of that subject. This implies that all behaviour—and consequently every human fact—has a significant character, which is not always evident but which the research worker must, by his work, bring to light.

The same idea can be expressed in several different ways—by saying, for instance, that all human behaviour (and, probably, even all animal behaviour) tends to modify a situation felt by the subject to be a disequilibrium so as to establish an equilibrium or, again, that all human behaviour (and, probably, all animal behaviour) can be translated by the research worker in terms of the existence of a practical problem and of an attempt to solve that problem.

Starting from these principles, the structuralist and genetic conception, the creator of which is unquestionably George Lukàcs, favours a radical transformation of the methods of the sociology of literature. All the earlier works—and most of the university works undertaken subsequently to the appearance of this conception—were concerned and still are concerned, in this discipline, with the content of literary works and the relationship between that content and the collective consciousness, that is to say, the ways in which men think and behave in daily life. This being the standpoint adopted, they naturally arrive at the result that the relationships between these two contents are all the more numerous, and literary sociology is all the more efficacious, according as the author of the writings studied has given proof of less creative imagination and has contented himself with relating his experiences whilst transposing them as little as possible. Furthermore, this type of study must, by its actual method, break up the unity of the work by directing its attention above all to whatever in the work is merely the reproduction of empirical reality and of daily life. In short, this sociology proves to be all the more fertile the more the works studied are mediocre. Moreover, what it seeks in these works is more documentary than literary in character.

It is not at all surprising, in these circumstances, that the great majority of those who are concerned with literature consider this kind of research as being, in the best of cases, only of very relative value and sometimes reject it altogether. Genetic structuralist sociology starts from premises that are not merely different but even quite opposite; we should like to mention here five of the most important of them:

1. The essential relationship between the life of society and literary creation is not concerned with the content of these two sectors of human reality, but only with the mental structures, with what might be called the categories which shape both the empirical consciousness of a certain social group and the imaginary universe created by the writer.

2. The experience of a single individual is much too brief and too limited to be able to create such a mental structure; this can only be the result of the conjoint activity of a large number of individuals who find themselves in a similar situation, that is to say, who constitute a privileged social group, these individuals having, for a lengthy period and in an intensive way, lived through a series of problems and having endeavoured to find a significant solution for them. This means that mental structures or, to use a more abstract term, significant categorial structures, are not individual phenomena, but social phenomena.

3. The relationship already mentioned between the structure of the consciousness of a social group and that of the universe of the work constitutes, in those cases which are most favourable for the research worker, an homology which is more or less rigorous but often also a simple significant relationship; it may therefore happen, in these circumstances—and it does indeed happen in most cases—that completely heterogeneous contents and even opposite contents, are structurally homologous, or else are found to be in a comprehensive relationship at the level of categorial structures. An imaginary universe, apparently completely removed from any specific experience—that of a fairy tale, for instance—may, in its structure, be strictly homologous with the experience of a particular social group or, at the very least, linked, in a significant manner, with that experience. There is therefore no longer any contradiction between, on the one hand, the existence of a close relationship between literary creation and social and historical reality and, on the other hand, the most powerful creative imagination.

4. From this point of view, the very peaks of literary creation may not only be studied quite as well as average works, but are even found to be particularly suitable for positive research. Moreover, the categorial structures with which this kind of literary sociology is concerned are precisely

what gives the work its unity, that is to say, one of the two fundamental elements of its specifically aesthetic character and, in the case we are interested in, its truly literary quality.

5. The categorial structures, which govern the collective consciousness and which are transposed into the imaginary universe created by the artist, are neither conscious nor unconscious in the Freudian sense of the word, which presupposes a repression; they are non-conscious processes which, in certain respects, are akin to those which govern the functioning of the muscular or nervous structures and determine the particular character of our movements and our gestures. That is why, in most cases, the bringing to light of these structures and, implicitly, the comprehension of the work, can be achieved neither by immanent literary study nor by study directed towards the conscious intentions of the writer or towards the psychology of the unconscious, but only by research of the structuralist and sociological type.

But these findings have important methodological consequences. They imply that, in the human sciences, all positive study must always begin with an effort to dissect the object studied, so that the object is seen as a complex of significant reactions, the structure of which can account for most of the partial empirical aspects they present to the research worker.

In the case of the sociology of literature, this means that, in order to understand the work he is studying, the research worker must in the very first place seek to discover a structure which accounts for practically the whole of the text and must, for that purpose, observe one fundamental rule—which, unfortunately, the specialists of literature respect only very rarely—namely, that the research worker must account for the whole of the text and must add nothing to it. This means, too, that he must explain the genesis of that text by trying to show how and in what measure the building up of the structure which he has brought to light in the work has a functional character, that is to say, to what extent it constitutes an instance of significant behaviour for an individual or collective subject in a given situation.

This way of posing the problem entails numerous consequences, which modify profoundly the traditional methods of study of social facts and, in particular, of literary facts. Let us mention a few of the more important of these, taking first the fact of not attaching special importance, in the comprehension of the work, to the conscious intentions of individuals and, in the case of literary works, to the conscious intentions of their authors.

Consciousness, indeed, is only a partial element of human behaviour and, most frequently, has a content which is not adequate to the objective nature of that behaviour. Contrary to the views of a certain number of philosophers, such as Descartes or Sartre, significance does not appear with consciousness and is not to be identified with it. A cat which is chasing a mouse behaves in a perfectly significant manner, without there being necessarily, or even probably, any consciousness, even of a rudimentary character;[1] of course, when man and, with him, symbolic function and thought appear in the biological scale, behaviour becomes incomparably more complex; the sources of problems, conflicts and difficulties, and also the possibilities of resolving them, become more numerous and more involved, but there is nothing to indicate that consciousness often—or even occasionally—covers the whole of the objective significance of behaviour. In the case of the writer, this same idea may be expressed in a much simpler fashion: it very frequently happens that his desire for aesthetic unity makes him write a work of which the over-all structure, translated by the critic into conceptual language, constitutes a vision that is different from and even the opposite of his thought and his convictions and the intentions which prompted him when he composed the work.

That is why the sociologist of literature—and, in general, the critic—must treat the conscious intentions of the author as one indication among many others, as a sort of reflection on the work, from which he gathers suggestions, in the same way as any other critical work, but on which he must form his judgement in the light of the text, without according it any favour.

Next we have the fact of not over-estimating the importance of the individual in the explanation, which is above all the search for the subject, whether individual or collective, for which the mental structure which governs the work has a functional and significant character. The work has almost always, of course, an individual significant function for its author, but, most frequently, as we shall see, this individual function is not, or is only very slightly, connected with the mental structure which governs the truly literary character of the work, and, in any case, it does not in any way create it. The fact of writing plays—and, more precisely, the plays he really wrote—doubtless had significance for the individual Racine, in the light of his youth passed in Port-Royal, his relations later with people of the theatre and with the Court, his relations with the Jansenist group and its ideas, and also many events in his life with which we are more or less familiar. But the existence of the tragic vision was already a constituent element of the situations forming the starting-point from which Racine was led on to write his plays, whereas the building up of that vision, under the influence of the ideologists of the Jansenist group of Port-Royal and Saint-Cyran, was the functional and significant response of the *noblesse de robe* to a given historical situation. And it is with reference to that group and to its more or less developed ideology that the individual Racine had later to face a certain number of practical and moral problems which resulted ultimately in the creation of a work shaped by a tragic vision pursued to an extremely advanced degree of coherence. That is why it would be impossible to explain the genesis of that work and its significance merely by relating it to Racine's biography and psychology.

---

1. Descartes is thus obliged to reduce the cat to a machine, that is to say, to eliminate it as a specific reality, and Sartre leaves no place for it in *l'Être et le Néant*, which recognizes only the inert *En-soi* and the conscious *Pour-soi*.

Thirdly, we have the fact that what are commonly called 'influences' have no explanatory value and, at the very most, constitute a factor and a problem which the research worker must explain. There are at every moment a considerable number of influences which may have their effect on a writer; what has to be explained is the reason why only a small number of them, or even only a single one, has really had any effect, and also why the works which have exerted this influence were received with a certain number of distortions—and precisely with those particular distortions—in the mind of the person they influenced. But these are questions to which the answer must be sought in the work of the author studied and not, as is usually thought, in the work which is supposed to have influenced it.

In short, comprehension is a problem of the internal coherence of the text, which presupposes that the text, the whole of the text and nothing but the text is taken literally and that, within it, one seeks an over-all significant structure. Explanation is a problem of seeking the individual or collective subject (in the case of a cultural work, we think, for the reasons we have given above,[1] that it is always a collective subject that is involved), in relation to which the mental structure which governs the work has a functional character and, for that very reason, a significant character. Let us add that, so far as the respective places of explanation and interpretation are concerned, two things which seem to us to be important have been brought to light by the works of structuralist sociology and by their confrontation with psycho-analytical works.

The first is the fact that the status of these two processes of research is not the same from two standpoints.

When libido is involved, it is impossible to separate interpretation from explanation, not only during, but also after, the period of research, whereas, at the end of that period, the separation can be effected in sociological analysis. There is no immanent interpretation of a dream or of the delirium of a madman,[2] probably for the simple reason that consciousness has not even any relative autonomy on the plane of the libido, that is to say on the plane of the behaviour of an individual subject aiming directly at the possession of an object. Inversely, when the subject is transindividual, consciousness assumes much greater importance (there is no division of labour and, consequently, no action possible without conscious communication between the individuals who make up the subject) and tends to constitute a significant structure.

---

1. See Lucien Goldmann; *Le Dieu Caché.* Gallimard, 1956; *Sciences Humaines et Philosophie,* Gonthier, 1966; *Recherches Dialectiques,* Gallimard, 1959; *Le Sujet de la Création Culturelle* (communication to the second Colloque International de Sociologie de la Littérature, 1965).
2. This, moreover, is why in France, where Freud's celebrated book *Traumdeutung* was published under the title *Explication des Rêves,* it was only after many years that certain psycho-analysts perceived that 'Deutung' means interpretation and not explanation. In actual fact, if, for a long time, this title did not give rise to any problems, this was above all because it was as valid as the original title. It is, in fact, impossible, in the Freudian analyses, to separate interpretation from explanation, as they both appeal to the unconscious.

Genetic sociology and psycho-analysis have at least three elements in common, namely: (a) the assertion that all human behaviour forms part of at least one significant structure; (b) the fact that to understand such behaviour it must be incorporated in that structure—which the research worker must bring to light; (c) the assertion that structure is really comprehensible only if it is grasped at its genesis, individual or historical, as the case may be. In short, just like the sociology which we favour, psycho-analysis is a genetic structuralism.

Their opposite character resides, above all, in one point: psycho-analysis attempts to reduce all human behaviour to one individual subject and to one form, whether manifest or sublimated, of desire for the object. Genetic sociology separates libidinal behaviour, which is studied by psycho-analysis, from behaviour of an historical character (of which all cultural creation forms part) which has a transindividual subject and which can be directed towards the object only through the mediation of an aspiration after coherence. It follows that, even if all human behaviour is incorporated both in a libidinal structure and in an historical structure, it has not the same significance in the two cases, and the dissection of the object must not be identical either. Certain elements of art or of a literary composition —but not the work or the composition in their entirety—may be incorporated in a libidinal structure, and this will enable the psycho-analysts to understand them and to explain them by relating them to the individual's subconscious. The significances revealed will, however, in this case, have a status of the same order as that of any drawing or any written composition of any madman; furthermore, these same literary or artistic works, incorporated in an historical structure, will constitute relative structures which are practically coherent and unitary, possessing very great relative autonomy; this is one of the constituent elements of their truly literary or truly artistic value.

All human behaviour and all human manifestations are, indeed, to a varying degree, mixtures of significances of both kinds. However, depending on whether the libidinal satisfaction predominates to the point of destroying the autonomous coherence almost completely, or whether, inversely, it is incorporated in the latter, whilst leaving it almost intact, we shall have before us either the product of a madman or a masterpiece (it being understood that most human manifestations lie somewhere between these two extremes).

The second is the fact that, despite the ample university discussions that have taken place, more particularly in the German universities, with regard to comprehension and explanation, these two processes of research are by no means opposed to one another and are not even different from one another.

On this point, we must, in the first place, eliminate all the romantic literature devoted to the sympathy, 'empathy' or identification necessary to understand a work. To us, comprehension seems to be a strictly intellectual process; it consists of the description as precisely as possible, of a significant structure. It is, of course, true that as in the case of any intellectual process, it is favoured by the immediate interest the research worker takes in his subject—that is to say, by the sympathy or antipathy or indifference which the object of research inspires in him; but, on the one hand, antipathy is a factor which is just as favourable to comprehension as is sympathy (Jansenism has never been better understood or better defined than by its persecutors when they formulated the famous 'Five Propositions', which are a rigorous definition of the tragic vision) and, on the other hand, many other factors may be favourable or unfavourable to research, for instance, a good psychic disposition, good health or, inversely, a state of depression or an attack of toothache; but all this has nothing to do with logic or epistemology.

It is necessary to go further, however. Comprehension and explanation are not two different intellectual processes, but one and the same process, related to different co-ordinates. We have said above that comprehension is the bringing to light of a significant structure immanent in the object studied (in the case with which we are concerned, in this or that literary work). Explanation is nothing other than the incorporation of this structure, as a constituent element, in an immediately embracing structure, which the research worker does not explore in any detailed manner but only in so far as such exploration is necessary in order to render intelligible the genesis of the work which he is studying. All that is necessary is to take the surrounding structure as an object of study and then what was explanation becomes comprehension and the explanatory research must be related to a new and even vaster structure.

Let us take an example. To understand *Les Pensées* of Pascal or the tragedies of Racine is to bring to light the tragic vision which constitutes the significant structure governing the whole of each of these works; but to understand the structure of extremist Jansenism is to explain the genesis of *Les Pensées* and of the tragedies of Racine. Similarly, to understand Jansenism is to explain the genesis of extremist Jansenism; to understand the history of the *noblesse de robe* in the seventeenth century is to explain the genesis of Jansenism; to understand class relations in French society of the seventeenth century is to explain the evolution of the *noblesse de robe*, etc.

It follows that all positive research in the human sciences must necessarily be conducted on two different levels—that of the object studied and that of the immediately surrounding structure, the difference between these levels of research residing above all in the degree to which the investigation is carried on each of these planes. The study of an object—a text, a social reality, etc.—cannot indeed be considered sufficient except when it has revealed a structure which accounts adequately for a considerable number of empirical facts, especially those which seem to present particular importance[1] so that it becomes, if not inconceivable, at least improbable,

---

1. We have already said that in the case of literary texts the problem is simpler for, owing to the advanced structuration of the objects which are the subject of the research and the limited number of data (the whole text and nothing but the text), it is in most cases

that another analysis could put forward another structure leading to the same or to better results.

The situation is different in regard to the surrounding structure. The research worker is concerned with this only in respect of its explanatory function in relation to the object of his study. It is, moreover, the possibility of bringing such a structure to light that will determine the choice of that particular one among the more or less considerable number of surrounding structures which appear to be possible when the research is first embarked upon. The research worker will therefore halt his study when he has sufficiently revealed the relationship between the structure studied and the surrounding structure to account for the genesis of the former as a function of the latter. He can also, however, of course, carry his research much further; but, in that case, the object of the study changes at a certain moment and what was, for instance, a study on Pascal may become a study on Jansenism, or on the *noblesse de robe*, etc.

This being so, although it is true that in the practice of research, immanent interpretation and explanation through the surrounding structure are inseparable, and no progress can be made in either of these fields, except through a continual oscillation from one to the other, it is none the less important to make a rigorous distinction between interpretation and explanation in their nature and in the presentation of the results. Similarly, it is essential always to bear in mind not only the fact that the interpretation is always immanent in the texts studied (whereas the explanation is always external to them), but also the fact that everything which is placed in the relationship of the text with the facts which are external to it—whether it is a question of the social group, of the psychology of the author or of sunspots—has an explanatory character and must be judged from that standpoint.[1]

possible, if not in theory, at all events in practice, to replace this qualitative criterion by a quantitative criterion, namely a sufficiently large portion of the text.

1. We stress this point because, in discussions with specialists in literature, we have very often found them claiming that they refuse explanation and content themselves with interpretation whereas, in reality, their ideas were quite as explicative as our own. What they were refusing was sociological explanation in favour of psychological explanation which traditionally accepted, had become almost implicit.

In fact—and this is a particularly important principle—the interpretation of a work must comprise the whole of the text at the literal level and its validity is to be judged solely and exclusively in relation to the proportion of the part of the text which it succeeds in integrating. Explanation must account for the genesis of the same text, and its validity is to be judged solely and exclusively in accordance with the possibility of establishing at least a rigorous correlation—and as far as possible a significant and functional relationship—between, on the one hand, the development of a vision of the world and the genesis of a text originating from it, and, on the other hand, certain phenomena external to the latter.

The two prejudices which are the most widespread and the most dangerous for research consist, on the one hand, in thinking that a text must be 'sensible'—that is to say, acceptable to the thought of the critic—and, on the other hand, in demanding an explanation in conformity with the general ideas either of the critic himself or of the group to which he belongs and whose ideas he embodies. In both cases, what is demanded is that the facts should be in conformity with the research worker's own ideas, whereas what should be done is to seek out the difficulties and the surprising facts which apparently contradict accepted ideas.

Now, though this principle seems easy to respect, deep-rooted prejudices cause it to be constantly transgressed in practice, and our contacts with specialists of literary studies have shown us how difficult it is to get them to adopt, with regard to the text they are studying, an attitude which, if not identical with, is at least similar to that of the physicist or the chemist who is recording the results of an experiment. To mention only a few examples taken haphazard, it was a specialist of literary history who explained to us one day that Hector cannot speak in *Andromaque* since he is dead, and that what occurs is therefore the illusion of a woman whom an extraordinary and quite hopeless situation has driven to the extreme limits of exasperation. Unfortunately there is nothing at all like that in Racine's text, from which we learn only, on two occasions, that Hector— the dead Hector—has spoken.

Again, another historian of literature explained to us that Dom Juan cannot be married every month because, even in the seventeenth century, that was in practice impossible, and that consequently it was necessary to take that affirmation in Molière's play in an ironical and figurative sense. It is hardly necessary to say that if this principle is accepted, it is very easy to make a text say anything one likes—even the exact opposite of what it explicitly states.[1]

What would be said of a physicist who denied the results of an experiment and substituted for them others which pleased him better, for the sole reason that the former appeared to him to be unlikely.

Again, in a discussion at the Royaumont symposium (1965) it was extremely difficult to get the supporters of psycho-analytical interpretations to admit the elementary fact that—whatever opinion one may hold of the value of this kind of explanation, and even if it is given a preponderant value—one cannot speak of the subconscious of Orestes or of a desire of Oedipus to marry his mother, since Orestes and Oedipus are not living men but texts and one has no right to add anything whatsoever to a text which makes no mention of the subconscious or of incestuous desire.

The explanatory principle, even for any serious psycho-analytical explanation, can reside only in the subconscious of Sophocles or Aeschylus, but never in the subconscious of a literary character who exists only through what is explicitly affirmed about him. In the field of explanation, it is to be noted that literary specialists have a regrettable tendency to give pride of place to psychological explanation, regardless of its efficacity and its results, simply because it seems to them the most plausible, whereas quite obviously the only truly scientific attitude consists in examining, in as impartial a manner as possible, all the explanations that are put forward, even those which are apparently the most absurd (that is why we men-

---

1. Similarly, in a fairly well-known dissertation on Pascal, the author quoting the latter's affirmation to the effect that 'things are true or false according to the point of view from which one looks at them', added, as a good Cartesian, that Pascal had of course expressed himself badly and that what he meant was that things *appear* to be true or false according to the point of view from which one looks at them.

tioned sunspots just now, although no one has seriously thought of finding an explanation in them), making a choice solely and exclusively in accordance with the results to which they lead and in accordance with the more or less considerable proportion of the text which they make it possible to account for.

Starting from a text which for him represents a mass of empirical data similar to those by which any other sociologist who undertakes a piece of research is faced, the sociologist of literature must first tackle the problem of ascertaining how far those data constitute a significant object, a structure on which positive research can be carried out with fruitful results.

We may add that, when faced by this problem, the sociologist of literature and art finds himself in a privileged situation as compared with research workers operating in other fields, for it can be admitted that in most cases the works which have survived the generation in which they were born constitute just such a significant structure,[1] whereas it is by no means probable that the analyses of the daily consciousness, or even current sociological theories, coincide in those other fields with significant objects. It is by no means certain for instance that objects of study such as 'scandal', 'dictatorship', 'culinary behaviour', etc., constitute such objects.

However that may be, the sociologist of literature must—like any other sociologist—verify this fact and not admit straightaway that such and such a work or such and such a group of works which he is studying constitutes a unitary structure.

In this respect, the process of investigation is the same throughout the whole field of the sciences of man. The research worker must secure a pattern, a model composed of a limited number of elements and relationships, starting from which he must be able to account for the great majority of the empirical data of which the object studied is thought to be composed.

It may be added that, having regard to the privileged situation of cultural creations as an object of study, the requirements of the sociologist of literature may be much greater than those of his fellow sociologists. It is by no means excessive to require a model to account for three-quarters or four-fifths of the text and there are already in existence a certain number of studies which appear to satisfy this requirement. We use the term 'appear' because, simply as a result of the insufficiency of material means, we have never been able to carry out a check of any work paragraph by paragraph, or speech by speech, although from the methodological standpoint, such a check obviously presents no difficulty.[2]

It is obvious that, most frequently in general sociology and very frequently in the sociology of literature, when research is concerned with several

1. This fact itself constituting the epistemological and psycho-sociological condition of such survival.
2. It may be added, in this connexion, that in a first attempt which we undertook in Brussels, and which was concerned with Jean Genêt's Les Nègres, it was possible, for the first pages, to account not only for the initial hypothesis regarding the structure of the universe of the work but also for a whole series of formal elements of the text.

works, the research worker will be led to eliminate a whole series of empirical data which appeared at the outset to form part of the proposed object of study, and on the other hand, to add other data of which he had not thought in the first place.

We shall give just one example. When we started a sociologicial study on the works of Pascal, we were very quickly led to separate *Les Provinciales* from *Les Pensées* as corresponding to two different visions of the world, and therefore to two different epistemological models, with different sociological bases—centrist and semi-Cartesian Jansenism, the best known representatives of which were Arnauld and Nicole, and extremist Jansenism, which was unknown up to that time and which we had to seek and find in the person of its chief theologian, Barcos, the abbé of Saint-Cyran, not far removed from whom were, amongst others, Singlin, Pascal's director, Lancelot, one of Racine's masters, and above all, Mother Angélique.[1] The bringing to light of the tragic structure which characterized the thoughts of Barcos and Pascal led us, moreover, to include in our research four of the chief plays of Racine, namely, *Andromaque, Britannicus, Bérénice* and *Phèdre*—a result which was all the more surprising because, up to that time, misled by superficial manifestations, the historians of literature who were trying to discover relationships between Port-Royal, and Racine's works sought them on the plane of content and directed their attention above all to the Christian plays (*Esther* and *Athalie*) and not to the pagan plays, the structural categories of which nevertheless corresponded strictly to the structure of thought of the extremist Jansenist group.

Theoretically, the sucess of this first stage of the research and the validity

---

1. The major difficulty presented by most studies on Pascal arises, moreover, from the fact that the authors of the works in question, starting from a psychological explanation, whether explicit or implicit, did not even imagine that Pascal could, in a few months, and perhaps even in a few weeks, have passed from one philosophical position to another, strictly opposite, which he was the first among the thinkers of Western Europe to formulate with extreme rigour. They admitted as being self-evident the existence of a kinship between *Les Provinciales* and *Les Pensées*.

Now, as the two texts did not—and do not—lend themselves to a unitary interpretation, they were obliged to invoke all sorts of reasons (stylistic exaggerations, texts written for libertines, texts expressing the thought of libertines and not Pascal's thought, etc.) to explain that Pascal meant to say—or at least thought—something quite different from what he had in fact written. We took the opposite course, starting by taking note of the rigorously coherent character of each of the two works and of the fact that they were almost entirely the opposite of each other, and only after that posing the question of how it was possible for any individual—however great a genius he might be—to pass so quickly from one position to another, quite different and even opposed, and it was this that led us to the discovery of Barcos and of extremist Jansenism, which suddenly threw a light on the whole problem.

In fact, while he was writing *Les Provinciales*, Pascal had to face an elaborate theological and moral school of thought, which enjoyed great prestige in Jansenist circles and which criticized him and rejected the views which he maintained. He had therefore, for a period of more than a year, to ponder the question whether it was he or his extremist critics who were right. The decision in favour of a change of position thus came to maturity slowly in him, and there is nothing surprising in the fact that a thinker of Pascal's stature after a prolonged period of meditation on a position which finally led to its adoption, should have been able subsequently to formulate it in a more radical and more coherent fashion than had been done by the chief theorists who had defended that position before he did.

of a model of coherence are shown, of course, by the fact that the model accounts for practically the whole of the text. In practice, there is however another criterion—of the nature not of law but of fact—which indicates with sufficient certainty that one is on the right path. This is the fact that certain details of the text, which had not in any way attracted the research worker's attention up to that point, suddenly appear to be both important and significant.

Let us once more give three examples in this connexion.

At a time when verisimilitude constitutes a rule that is almost unanimously accepted, Racine, in *Andromaque*, makes a dead man speak. How can such an apparent incongruity be accounted for? It is sufficient to have found the pattern of the vision which governs the thought of extremist Jansenism to note that, for that thought, the silence of God and the fact that he is simply a spectator have as their corollary the fact that there exists no intramundane issue which makes it possible to safeguard fidelity to values, no possibility of living validly in the world, and that any attempt in this direction is blocked by unrealizable—and moreover in practice unknown—requirements of divinity (requirements which most frequently present themselves in a contradictory form). The profane transposition of this conception in Racine's plays results in the existence of two mute characters, or of two mute forces, which incarnate contradictory requirements: Hector, who demands the fidelity, and Astyanax, who demands the protection of Andromaque; Junie's love for Britannicus, which demands that she should protect him, and her purity which demands that she should accept no compromise with Néron; the Roman people and love, for Bérénice; later, the Sun and Venus, in Phèdre.

Although, however, the mutism of these forces or of these beings in the plays which incarnate absolute requirements is bound up with the absence of any intramundane solution, it is obvious that at the moment when Andromaque finds a solution by which it seems to her to be possible for her to marry Pyrrhus in order to protect Astyanax and to commit suicide before becoming his wife, in order to safeguard her fidelity, the mutism of Hector and Astyanax no longer corresponds to the structure of the play and aesthetic requirements, stronger than any external rule, result in the extreme improbability of the dead man who speaks and indicates a possibility of overcoming the contradiction.

We take as our second example the famous scene of the appeal to magic in Goethe's *Faust*, in which Faust addresses himself to the Spirits of the Macrocosm and of the Earth, which correspond to the philosophies of Spinoza and Hegel. The reply of the second Spirit sums up the very essence of the play and, even more, of the first part of it—the opposition between, on the one hand, the philosophy of enlightenment, whose ideal was knowledge and comprehension, and, on the other hand, dialectical philosophy, centred on action. The reply of the Spirit of the Earth—'You resemble the Spirit you understand, and not me'—is not merely a refusal; it is also its justification. Faust is still at the level of 'understanding', that is to to say, at the level of the Spirit of the Macrocosm, which is precisely what he wanted to outdistance. He will not be able to meet the Spirit of the Earth until the moment when he finds the true translation of the Gospel according to Saint John ('In the beginning was action') and when he accepts the pact with Mephistopheles.

Similarly, in Sartre's *La Nausée*, if the self-taught character—who also represents the Spirit of Enlightenment—reads the books in the library in the order of the catalogue, this is because the author has, consciously or unconsciously, aimed his satire at one of the most important features of the thought of enlightenment—the idea that knowledge can be conveyed with the help of dictionaries in which the subjects are arranged in alphabetical order (it is only necessary to think of Bayle's *Dictionnaire*, Voltaire's *Dictionnaire philosophique* and, above all, the *Encyclopédie*).

Once the research worker has advanced as far as possible in the search for the internal coherence of the work and its structural model, he must direct himself towards explanation.

Having reached this point, we must interpolate a digression concerning a subject which we have already touched upon. There is, indeed—as we have already said—a radical difference between the relationship of interpretation to explanation in the course of the research and the way in which that relationship presents itself at the end of the research. In the course of research, indeed, explanation and comprehension strengthen each other mutually, so that the research worker is led to revert continually from one to the other whereas, at the time when he halts his research, in order to present the results of it, he can, and indeed must, separate his interpretative hypotheses immanent to the work fairly sharply from his explanatory hypotheses which transcend it.

As it is our intention to stress the distinction between the two processes, we shall develop the present statement on the imaginary supposition of an interpretation that has been carried to an extremely advanced point by means of immanent analysis and which is only subsequently directed towards explanation.

To look for an explanation means to look for a reality external to the work which presents a relationship to the structure of the work which is either one of concomitant variation (and this is extremely rare in the case of the sociology of literature) or, as is most frequently the case, a relationship of homology or a merely functional relationship, that is to say, a structure fulfilling a function (in the sense which these words bear in the sciences of life or the sciences of man).

It is impossible to say *a priori* which are the realities external to a work which are capable of fulfilling such an explanatory function with reference to its specifically literary features. It is, however, an actual fact that, up to the present time, in so far as historians of literature and the critics have concerned themselves with explanation, they have based themselves mainly on the individual psychology of the author and sometimes—less frequently and, above all, only fairly recently—on the structure of thought of certain social groups. It is therefore, for the moment, unnecessary to consider any other explanatory hypotheses, although one has certainly no right to eliminate them *a priori*.

Against the psychological explanations, however, several overwhelming objections present themselves as soon as one reflects on them a little more seriously. The first—and the least important—of these is that we have very little knowledge of the psychology of a writer whom we have not known and who, in most cases, has been dead for years. The majority of these so-called psychological explanations are therefore simply more or less intelligent and fanciful constructions of an imaginary psychology, built up, in most cases, on the basis of written evidence and in particular on that of the work itself. This is not merely going round in a circle but going round in a vicious circle, for the so-called 'explanatory' psychology is nothing other than a paraphrase of the work it is supposed to explain.

Another argument—a much more serious one—which may be brought against psychological explanations is the fact that, so far as we are aware, they have never succeeded in accounting for any notable portion of the text, but merely for a few partial elements or a few extremely general features. Now, as we have already said, any explanation which accounts for only 50 to 60 per cent of the text offers no major scientific interest, since it is always possible to construct several others which explain an equal portion of the text, although naturally not the same portion. If results of this kind are accepted as satisfactory, it is possible at any moment to fabricate a mystic, Cartesian or Thomist Pascal, a Cornelian Racine, an existentialist Molière, etc. The criterion for the choice between several interpretations then becomes the brilliance of mind or the intelligence of such and such a critic as compared with another—and this, of course, has nothing whatsoever to do with science.

Lastly, the third—and perhaps the most important—objection that can be brought against psychological explanations is the fact that although they undoubtedly do account for certain aspects and certain characteristic features of the work, these are always aspects and characteristic features which in the case of literature are not literary, in the case of a work of art are not aesthetic, in the case of a philosophical work are not philosophical, etc. Even the best and most successful psycho-analytical explanation of a work will never succeed in telling us in what respect that work differs from a piece of writing or a drawing by a madman, which psycho-analysis can explain to the same degree, and perhaps better, with the aid of similar processes.

This situation derives, we think, in the first place from the fact that although the work is the expression both of an individual structure and of a collective structure, it presents itself as an individual expression, especially as: (a) the sublimated satisfaction of a desire for the possession of an object (see the Freudian analyses of Freudian inspiration); (b) the product of a certain number of individual psychic 'montages', which can find expression in certain special features of the writing; (c) the more or less faithful or more or less distorted reproduction of a certain number of facts acquired or experiences lived through.

But in all this there is nothing that constitutes any literary, aesthetic or philosophical significance—in short, any cultural significance.

To remain in the realm of literature, the significance of a work does not lie in this or that story—the events related in the *Orestes* of Aeschylus, the *Electra* of Giraudoux and *Les Mouches* of Sartre are the same, yet these three works quite obviously have no essential element in common—nor does it lie in the psychology of this or that character, nor even in any stylistic peculiarity which recurs more or less frequently. The significance of the work, in so far as it is a literary work, is always of the same character, namely, a coherent universe within which the events occur and the psychology of the characters is situated and within the coherent expression of which the stylistic automatisms of the author are incorporated. Now, what distinguishes a work of art from the writing of a madman is precisely the fact that the latter speaks only of his desires and not of a universe with its laws and the problems which arise in it.

Conversely, it is true that the sociological explanations of the Lukàcsian school—however few as yet in number—do precisely pose the problem of the work as a unitary structure of the laws which govern its universe and of the link between that structured universe and the form in which it is expressed. It is also true that these analyses—when they are successful—account for a much greater portion of the text, frequently approaching the whole. It is true, lastly, that they not only bring out, in many cases, the importance and significance of elements that had completely escaped the critics by making it possible to establish links between those elements and the rest of the text, but they also bring to light important and hitherto unperceived relationships between the facts studied and many other phenomena of which neither the critics nor the historians had thought until then. Here again we shall content ourselves with a few examples.

It had always been known that, at the end of his life, Pascal had reverted to science and to the world, since he even organized a public competition on the problem of roulette, and also the first public conveyances (five-sous coaches). Yet no one had established any relationship between this individual behaviour and the writing of *Les Pensées* and, in particular, the central fragment of that work relating to the *Pari*. It is only in our interpretation, when we connected the silence of God and the certainty of his existence, in Jansenist thought, with the special situation of the *noblesse de robe* in France, after the wars of religion, and with the impossibility of finding a satisfactory intramundane solution to the problems by which it was faced, that we became aware of the link between the most definitely extremist form of that thought, which carries uncertainty to the point of its most radical expression by extending it from the divine will to the very existence of the divinity, and the fact of situating the refusal of the world not in solitude, external to it, but within it by giving it an intramundane character.[1]

Similarly, once we had established a relationship between the genesis of Jansenism among the *gens de robe* and the change in monarchical policy and the birth of absolute monarchy, it became possible to show that the conversion of the Huguenot aristocracy to Catholicism was nothing other than the reverse of the same medal and constituted one and the same process.

One last example, which goes as far as the problem of literary form. It suffices to read Molière's *Dom Juan* to see that it has a different structure from the other great plays of the same author. Indeed, although Orgon, Alceste, Arnolphe and Harpagon are confronted by a whole world of interhuman relations, a society and, in the case of the first three of them, a character who expresses worldly good sense and the values which govern the universe of the play (Cléante, Philinte and Chrysale), there is nothing of that sort in *Dom Juan*. Sganarelle has only the servile wisdom of the people which we find in nearly all the valets and servants of the other plays of Molière; so that the dialogues in *Dom Juan* are in reality only monologues in which different characters (Elvire, the Père, the Spectre), who are in no way related to one another, criticize Dom Juan's behaviour and tell him that he will end up by provoking the divine wrath, without his defending himself in any way. Furthermore, the play contains one absolute impossibility, namely, the affirmation that Dom Juan gets married every month, which, quite obviously, was out of the question in the real life of the period. Now, the sociological explanation easily accounts for all these peculiarities. Molière's plays are written from the standpoint of the *noblesse de cour*, and the great character plays are neither abstract descriptions nor psychological analyses, but satires of real social groups, the picture of which is concentrated in a single psychological trait or special peculiarity of character; they are aimed at the *bourgeois*, who loves money and does not think that it is made above all to be spent, who wishes to exert his authority in the family, who wants to become a gentleman; the religious bigot and the member of the Compagnie du Saint-Sacrement, who interfere with the life of others and combat the libertine morality of the Court; the Jansenist—worthy of respect, of course, but too strict and refusing the slightest compromise.

Against all these social types, Molière can bring social reality, as he sees it, and his own moral attitude—libertine and epicurean—the liberty of woman, readiness to compromise, a sense of proportion in all things. In the case of *Dom Juan*, on the contrary, there is no question of a different social group, but of individuals who, within the very group depicted by the work of Molière, exaggerate and display no sense of proportion. That is why it is impossible to set in opposition to Dom Juan any moral attitude different from his own. All that can be said to him is that he is right to do

---

1. This return to the sciences, which was a strictly logical piece of behaviour, of course shocked the other Jansenists who, being certain of the existence of God, did not admit the *Pari*; whence the childish legend of the fit of toothache which led to the discovery of roulette.

what he does, but not to exaggerate or go as far as the absurd. Moreover, in the only sphere in which the moral attitude of the Court, at all events in theory, approves the fact of going to the extreme limit and does not find any exaggeration—that of courage and daring—Dom Juan becomes an entirely positive character. Apart from this, he is right to give alms to the beggar, but not to do so in a blaspheming manner; it is not absolutely necessary that he should pay his debts, but he must not make too much of a fool of Monsieur Dimanche (again, in this matter, Dom Juan's attitude is not really antipathetic). Finally, the chief subject of controversy in the matter of the moral attitude of the libertine being, of course, the problem of relations with women, Molière had to make it understood that Dom Juan is right to do what he does, but that, in this also, he goes beyond the limit. Now, apart from the fact, which is clearly indicated, that he goes too far in assaulting even peasant women and in not keeping up his rank, this limit could not be defined with any degree of precision. Molière could not say that Dom Juan was wrong in seducing a woman every month, whereas he should be satisfied to seduce one every two or every six months; whence the solution which expresses exactly what had to be said—Dom Juan gets married—and there is nothing reprehensible about that; it is even a very good thing to do—but, unfortunately, he gets married every month; which is really going too far!

Having spoken especially, in this article, of the differences between the structuralist sociology of literature, on the one hand, and the traditional explanation offered by psycho-analysis or literary history, on the other hand, we should now like also to devote a few paragraphs to the supplementary difficulties by which genetic structuralism is separated from formalistic structuralism, on the one hand, and from empirical and non-sociological history, on the other hand.

For genetic structuralism, the whole range of human behaviour (we employ this term in its widest possible sense embracing also psychical behaviour, thought, imagination, etc.) has a structural character. At the opposite extreme therefore from formalistic structuralism, which sees in structures the essential sector, but only a sector, of over-all human behaviour, and which leaves aside what is too closely connected with a given historical situation or a precise stage of a biography, thus leading up to a sort of separation between the formal structures and the particular content of that behaviour, genetic structuralism lays down as a principle the hypothesis that structural analysis must go much further in the sense of the historical and the individual and must one day, when it is much more advanced, constitute the very essence of the positive method in history.

But it is then that, finding himself faced by the historian, who attaches prime importance to the individual fact, in its immediate character, the sociologist who is a supporter of genetic structuralism encounters a difficulty which is the opposite of the one which separated him from the formalist for, notwithstanding the opposition which exists between them, the historian and the formalist both admit one essential point, namely, the incompatibility between structural analysis and concrete history.

Now it is evident that immediate facts do not have a structural character. They are what in scientific parlance might be called a mixture of a considerable number of processes of structuration and destructuration, which no man of science could study as they are, in the form in which they are immediately given. It is a well-known fact that the noteworthy progress of the exact sciences is precisely due, *inter alia*, to the possibility of creating experimentally, in the laboratory, situations which replace the mixture, the interplay of active factors constituted by the realities of daily life, by what might be called pure situations—for instance, the situation in which all the factors are made constant with the exception of one which can be made to vary and of which the action can be studied. In history, such a situation is, unfortunately, impossible to achieve; it is none the less true, however, that here, as in all other fields of research, what is immediately apparent does not coincide with the essence of phenomena (otherwise, as Marx once said, science would be useless), so that the chief methodological problem of the social and historical sciences is precisely that of working out the techniques by means of which it is possible to bring to light the principal elements the mixture and interplay of which constitute empirical reality. All the important concepts of historical research (Renaissance, Capitalism, Feudalism, and also Jansenism, Christianity, Marxism, etc.) have a methodological status of this nature, and it is very easy to show that they have never coincided in any strict fashion with any particular empirical reality. It is none the less true that genetic structuralist methods have made it possible nowadays to establish concepts which are already very close to less comprehensive realities but which continue, of course, to retain a methodological status of the same nature. Although we cannot here dwell at length on the fundamental concept of the possible conscious,[1] let us at least say that, in its orientation towards the concrete, structuralist research can never go as far as the individual mixture and must stop short at the coherent structures which constitute the elements of it.

This is perhaps also the place to state that, as reality is never static, the very hypothesis that it is entirely constituted of processes of structuration implies the conclusion that each of these processes is, at the same time, a process of the destructuration of a certain number of earlier structures, at the expense of which it is in course of coming into being. The transition, in empirical reality, from the predominance of the former structures to the predominance of the new structure is precisely what dialectical thought designates as 'the transition from quantity to quality'.

It would therefore be more correct to say that, at any given moment, social and historical reality always presents itself as an extremely complex mixture, not of structures, but of processes of structuration and destructuration, the study of which will not have a scientific character until the

---

1. See Lucien Goldmann, *Conscience Réelle et Conscience Possible* (communication to the fourth World Sociology Congress, 1959) and *Sciences Humaines et Philosophie*, Gonthier, 1966.

day when the chief processes have been made clear with a sufficient degree of rigour.

Now, it is precisely on this point that the sociological study of the master-pieces of cultural creation acquires special value for general sociology. We have already emphasized that, in the whole range of social and historical facts, the characteristic feature and the privilege of the great cultural creations reside in their extremely advanced structuration and in the weakness and fewness of heterogeneous elements incorporated in them. This means that these works are much more readily accessible to structuralist study than is the historical reality which gave birth to them and of which they form part. It means also that, when these cultural creations are brought into relationship with certain social and historical realities, they constitute valuable pointers in regard to the elements of which these realities are constituted.

This shows how very important it is to incorporate the study of them in the field of sociological research and in general sociology.[1]

Another problem which is of importance to research is that of verification. In dealing with it, we should like to mention a project which we have had in mind for some time but which we have so far not been able to carry out. It is a question of passing from individual and artisanal research to a form of research which is more methodical and, above all, is of a collective character. The idea was suggested to us by work for the analysis of literary texts on punched cards which, in most cases, is of an analytical character and starts from constituent elements in the hope of arriving at a general comprehensive study—which, to us, has always seemed to be problematical, to say the least.

The discussion has gone on for a long time; in modern times, it has continued since the days of Pascal and Descartes. It is the argument between dialectic and positivism. If the whole, the structure, the organism, the social group, the relative totality, are greater than the sum of the parts, it is illusory to think that it is possible to understand them by starting from the study of their constituent elements, whatever the technique employed in the research. Inversely, it is obvious that one cannot content oneself with the study of the whole either, since the whole exists only as the sum of the parts that make it up and of the relationships by which they are linked.

In fact, our research always took the form of a continual oscillation

---

1. In so far as the great literary works are directed towards what is essential in the human reality of a period, the study of them may also furnish valuable indications regarding the psycho-sociological structure of events. It is thus that Molière might, it seems to us, have seized on and described an essential aspect of historical reality when, in the cabal of the bigots, he distinguishes the effort to group the *bourgeoisie* in the resistance to the recent social changes and the new morality to which they have given birth, more particularly at the Court, from the few rallying-points of the great lords. For Tartuffe, Orgon's attempted seduction is essential. For Dom Juan, the decision to pretend hypocritically to be a good man and a bigot is only one among many exaggerations and lies on the same plane as, for instance, his libertinage and his provocative and outrageous attitude in the scene with the beggar.

between the whole and the parts, by means of which the research worker attempted to build up a model, which he compared with the elements, and then reverted to the whole and made it precise, after which he came back once more to the elements, and so on, until the time came when he considered both that the result was sufficiently substantial to be worth publishing and that any continuation of the same work on the same object called for an effort that would be disproportionate as compared with the additional results he might hope to obtain from it. It is in this sequence of research that we have thought it might be possible to introduce—not at the beginning, but at some intermediate stage—a process that would be more systematic and above all collective. It has seemed to us, indeed, that when the research worker has built up a model which appears to him to present a certain degree of probability, he might, with the help of a team of collaborators, check it by comparing it with the whole of the work studied, paragraph by paragraph, in the case of a text in prose; line by line, in the case of a poem; speech by speech in the case of a play, by determining: (a) to what extent each unit analysed is incorporated in the over-all hypothesis; (b) the list of new elements and new relationships not provided for in the initial model; (c) the frequency, within the work, of the elements and relationships provided for in this model.

Such a check should enable the research worker subsequently (a) to correct his outline, so as to account for the whole of the text; (b) to give his results a third dimension—that of the frequency, in the work in question, of different elements and relationships making up the over-all pattern.

Never having been able to carry out a piece of research of this kind on a sufficiently vast scale, we decided recently to undertake one, so to speak experimentally, as a sort of prototype, with our collaborators in Brussels, on Genêt's *Les Nègres*, a work concerning which we had already sketched out a fairly advanced hypothesis.[1] Progress is, of course, extremely slow and the study of a single text like *Les Nègres* will take more than an academic year. But the results of the analysis of the first ten pages were surprising, inasmuch as, over and above the mere verification, they have enabled us to take the first steps with our method in the field of form, in the narrowest sense of the word, whereas we had thought hitherto that that field was reserved for specialists whose absence from our working groups we had always greatly regretted.

Lastly, to conclude this introductory article, we should like to mention a possibility of extending research, which we have not yet explored but which we have been contemplating for some time, by taking as a starting-point Julia Kristeva's study on Bakhtin.[2]

Although we have not said so explicitly in the present article, it is

1. See Lucien Goldmann, *Le Théâtre de Genêt: Essai d'Étude Sociologique*, Cahiers Renaud-Barrault, November 1966.
2. Published in *Critique*, No. 239. We should make it clear that we are not entirely in agreement with Kristeva's positions and that the considerations we have presented here have merely been developed after reading her study, without strictly coinciding with hers.

obvious that, in the background of all our research, there is a precise concept of aesthetic value in general and of literary value in particular. This is the idea developed in German classical aesthetics, passing from Kant, through Hegel and Marx to the early works of Lukács, who defines this value as a tension overcome between, on the one hand, sensible multiplicity and richness and, on the other hand, the unity which organizes this multiplicity into a coherent whole. From this point of view, a literary work is seen to be all the more valuable and more important according as this tension is both stronger and more effectively overcome, that is to say, according as the sensible richness and multiplicity of its universe are greater and as that universe is more rigorously organized, and constitutes a structural unity.

Having said this, it is no less obvious that, in almost all our work, as in that of all research workers who are inspired by the early writings of Lukács, the research centres round one single element of this tension—unity, which, in empirical reality, takes the form of a significant and coherent historical structure, the foundation of which is to be found in the behaviour of certain privileged social groups. All the research of this school in the field of the sociology of literature had hitherto been directed, in the very first place, towards bringing to light coherent and unitary structures governing the all-embracing universe which, in our view, constitutes the significance of every important literary work. This is because, as we said earlier, it is only quite recently that this research has taken its very first steps in the direction of the structural link between the universe and the form which expresses it. In all this field of research, the other pole of tension—the multiplicity and richness—was admitted merely as one item of the data concerning which it could at most be said that, in the case of a literary work, it was made up of a multiplicity of individual and living beings who found themselves in particular situations, or else of individual images—making it possible to differentiate between literature and philosophy, which expresses the same visions of the world on the plane of general concepts. (There is no 'Death' in *Phèdre* and no 'Evil' in Goethe's *Faust*, but only Phèdre dying and the strictly individualized character of Mephistopheles. On the other hand, there are no individual characters either in Pascal or in Hegel, but only 'Evil' and 'Death'.)

In pursuing our research in the sociology of literature, we have however always acted as if the existence of Phèdre or of Mephistopheles was a fact on which that science had no hold, and as if the more or less living, concrete and rich personality of those characters was a purely individual aspect of creation connected, in the first place, with the talent and psychology of the writer.

Bakhtin's ideas, as expounded by Kristeva, and the probably more radical form which she gives them when she develops her own conceptions,[1]

---

1. To the division of literary works into monological and dialogical, Kristeva adds the fact that even the literary works which Bakhtin describes as monological contain, if they are valid as literature, a dialogical and critical element.

seemed to us to open up a whole new and supplementary field for sociological investigation applied to literary creation.

Just as, in our concrete studies, we emphasized almost exclusively the vision of the world, the coherence and unity of the literary work, so Kristeva,[1] in her study programme, rightly characterizing this dimension of the mental structure as being connected with doing, with collective action and—at the extreme limit—with dogmatism and repression, stresses above all what is open to question, what is opposed to unity and what, in her view (and we think she is right on this point also), has a non-conformist and critical dimension. Now, it seems to us that all the aspects of literary work brought to light by Bakhtin and Kristeva correspond quite simply to the pole of richness and multiplicity in the classical conception of aesthetic value.

This means, in our view, that Kristeva adopts a unilateral position when she sees in cultural creation, in the first place, although not exclusively, the function of opposition and multiplicity (of 'dialogue' as opposed to 'monologue', to use her terminology) but that what she has described nevertheless represents a real dimension of every truly important literary work. Moreover, by stressing the link which exists between the vision of the world, coherent conceptual thought and dogmatism, Kristeva has implicitly drawn attention to the sociological character not only of these elements, but also of what they refuse, deny and condemn.

By incorporating these reflections in the considerations that we have developed so far, we are led on to the idea that almost all great literary works have a function that is partially critical in so far as, by creating a rich and multiple universe of individual characters and particular situations —a universe that is organized by the coherence of a structure and of a vision of the world—they are led to incarnate also the positions which they condemn and, in order to make the characters which incarnate them concrete and living, to express all that can be humanly formulated in favour of their attitude and their behaviour.

This means that these works, even if they express a particular vision of the world, are led, for literary and aesthetic reasons, to formulate also the limits of this vision and the human values that must be sacrificed in its defence.

It follows that, on the plane of literary analysis, it would, of course, be possible to go much further than we have done hitherto, by bringing to light all the antagonistic elements of the work which the structured vision must overcome and organize. Some of these elements are of an ontological nature, especially death, which constitutes an important difficulty for any vision of the world as an attempt aimed at giving a sense to life. Others are of a biological nature, especially eroticism, with all the problems of

---

1. Not knowing Russian, and not having been able to read Bakhtin's works, it would be difficult for us to distinguish clearly between Bakhtin's own ideas and their development by Kristeva. For that reason we refer in the present article to the whole of the positions of Bakhtin and Kristeva whilst attributing them to the latter.

suppression studied by psycho-analysis. But there are also a certain number, by no means negligible, of elements of a social and historical nature. This is why sociology can, on this point, make an important contribution by showing why the writer, in a particular historical situation, chooses, among the great number of possible incarnations of antagonistic positions and attitudes which he condemns, precisely the few which he feels to be particularly important.

The vision of the tragedies of Racine condemns in radical fashion what we have called *les fauves* dominated by passion and *les pantins* who continually make mistakes about reality. But it is hardly necessary to recall to what point the reality and human value of Oreste, Hermione, Agrippine, or of Néron, Britannicus, Antiochus, Hippolyte or Thésée are incarnated in Racine's tragedy and to what a point Racine's text expresses in comprehensive fashion the aspirations and sufferings of these characters.

All this should be the object of detailed literary analyses. We consider it probable, however, that if passion and the struggle for political power find a much stronger and more powerful literary expression in Racine's works than virtue which is passive and incapable of understanding reality, this difference of intensity in literary expression has its foundation in the social, psychical and intellectual realities of the society in which Racine lived and in the reality of the social forces to which the Jansenist group was opposed.

We have already indicated the reality of the social groups to which, in Molière, Harpagon, Georges Dandin, Tartuffe, Alceste and Dom Juan corresponded (the *bourgeoisie*, the Compagnie du Saint-Sacrement and the cabal of the bigots, the Jansenists, the aristocracy of the Court given to exaggeration) or, in Goethe's *Faust*, Wagner (the thought of enlightenment).

We halt our study at this point. It is obvious that this final part has, for the moment, only the value of a programme, the realization of which will depend on the course taken by the future development of sociological research relating to cultural creation.

[*Translated from the French.*]

Lucien Goldmann is director of studies at the École Pratique des Hautes Études, Paris, and director of the Centre for the Sociology of Literature of the Free University of Brussels. His best-known work is Le Dieu Caché *(1956) (English translation:* The Hidden God, *1964), a study of the tragic vision in Pascal's* Les Pensées *and Racine's plays. Amongst his other works are* Sciences Humaines et Philosophie, Recherches Dialectiques *and* Pour une Sociologie du Roman *(1964).*

The Interaction between 'Reality – Work of Art – Society'
Vladimir Karbusicky

from

International Social Science Journal, vol. XX, no. 4.

The interaction between 'reality - work of art - society'

Vladimír Karbusicky

No one can deny that a work of art stems from reality and that it has an influence on society. There will be less agreement on the actual nature of the interrelations between reality, a work of art, and society and on the place and possible influence therein of social and cultural institutions and communication media.

Many attempts have recently been made to provide theoretical answers to these questions through the application of information theory. This is, in fact, such a common approach that, before we start analysing the various aspects of these interrelations, we have to make clear why we are so 'out of date' as to be unwilling to adopt the language and methods of information theory. We do not, of course, wish to play down the usefulness of information theory but, for historical reasons, its application is, for the time being, limited. What interests us here is what this method offers today, although we do not wish to cast doubt on the possibility that, in future, the experimental models which are at present incompatible with contemporary practice may lead to theoretical formulations on a higher level of thinking in the context of information theory. It must also be mentioned that, in formulating theoretical models in aesthetics and the sociology of art, the mere fact of using the terminology of information theory has a noetic significance. For example, a convincing model of the extent of 'understanding of serious music' in relation to the degree of education, i.e., the acquired perception capacity of the individual (a correlation which has been empirically established in the sociology of music) can be constructed by using the concepts and terminology of information theory. But these are, at present, special cases, not valid for music or art as a whole. There are, for the time being, two main difficulties in the general application of the theory of information.

Firstly, the mathematical and statistical methods used to determine the amount of information and redundancy best express regular systems and structures with high probabilities, whilst art is naturally inclined to violate 'rules', and the very principle of aesthetics often lies in the artist's 'rebellion'.

For this reason, tedious mathematical analyses usually result, in the end, in a poor, abstract 'vocabulary' of recurring phenomena. So far as music is concerned, for instance, this might be likened to reducing the language of Kafka's *The Trial* to basic English, used to describe where Mr. K. went and what he did, so as to measure the 'information content' of Kafka's novel. Secondly, the influence of living art can scarcely be expressed through the classic pattern of the transmission of information. There are forms of art, such as music, which seemingly conform to such transmission: the score is the code, the performer is the transmitter, the medium of transmission is the channel, listening is the reception of the message, understanding is the decoding of information, etc. But what about other forms of art? Where does transmission of information enter into architecture, non-representational art, the dance, etc.? And, as we shall see, things are not quite so simple as they may seem even in the case of music and certainly not in the case of poetry or drama. Is the obtaining of 'information' from the 'messages', which the artist 'encodes' for us, really the final effect and meaning of art? This question must be asked even when 'information' is very broadly interpreted.

The over-simplified application to art of 'information transmission' schemes is mainly due to failure to understand the multifunctional character of art. Most of those applying these schemes completely forget that the communication function is only one of many functions of art. They make abstractions regardless of what they are abstracting from, so that they are liable to overlook other functions (which they regard as 'inessential') which may sometimes be the very essence of a given work or genre.

Let us consider, for example, what is the difference, in a 'communication' model of art, between the gnoseological, and the hedonistic and recreational functions. The more original a work of art, the less stereotyped, and therefore the less susceptible of treatment by information theory, the more it has to teach us. The fewer stereotyped, 'alphabetical', stylized elements it comprises, the less will it be 'comprehensible' in only one way. The wider the 'range of information', the greater the gnoseological significance. Conversely, a system of probabilities based on stereotyped forms, with the redundancy required for optimum 'transmission of information', may show a very high value from the point of view of information content even though the value from the point of view of knowledge is almost nil. Nevertheless, it will be extremely functional from the hedonistic and recreational point of view: perception of such structures follows the regular paths of neurons without encountering any real resistance. The final effect is not the decoding of information but simply stimulation of the 'receiving apparatus'. A typical example is listening to a background of light music on the radio, where the half-conscious perception of well-known tunes produces a sense of relaxation and pleasure.

Another instance of the relations between a work of art and society in which the communication function—paradoxical as it may seem—has scarcely any place, is the so-called 'sociogenic' effect of art, which may take various forms. It may, for example, be a subsidiary, adventitious effect of a genre associated with a quality akin to 'aesthetic enjoyment', which is influenced by a given environment (sculpture and painting, music and singing in church, etc.). Or it may be the function of art as a 'signal' for the introduction of social and psychological factors (cf. conventional, symbolic elements in national anthems, where the 'primary information', hidden in the anachronistic text, representing a 'petrification' of the nation's history, no longer matters and where, in most cases, people do not even remember the words at all). A sociogenic effect may also be produced, however, when, for example, a group refuses to accept a certain type of art. An instance is a group of people who dislike modern art, representing a group of 'receivers' which will not 'decode the message transmitted'. This paradoxical situation where 'the social effect of art is inoperative' would provide material for a humorist.

Art itself, in any case, resists the pressure of communication requirements. Certain trends in art, regarded by society as 'extreme', in fact represent non-communication or the absolutely 'non-obligatory' character of information. Aesthetically effective structures may be produced which merely provide an impulse, representing a visual or auditory 'happening' (Stockhausen's *Ereignis*). They stimulate the consciousness of the percipient but suggest only: 'choose what you like, think what you like, react as you like'. This can be explained in several ways. It may be a non-institutional reaction by the individual against the totalitarian demands of industrial society—or an appeal to the individual to become a co-creator instead of being a purely passive receiver. But it may also be a reaction against the teaching still found in schools and institutes about the direct relations between reality, works of art and society.

Most modern writings on art teaching and interpretation suggest that the models described above, applying the theory of information in more or less popular form, provide the institutional and pragmatic conception of the meaning of art. The model may be expressed roughly as in Figure 1. Thus, what was put into the work of art and encoded (that is, in explanatory terms, 'what the poet wanted to say') radiates from the work to the destination. The idea embodied in a work of art is simply released to act on the recipient and thus influence society. There is no textbook which can resist quoting, as proof of this, the cases of suicide among readers of *The Sorrows of Werther*. The same argument is also used by those who believe in the necessity of institutional and State censorship: may not a work of art lead to an undesirable movement in society (especially where youth is concerned)? There has probably never been a cultural Inquisition in the world which has not justified its action by reference to the interests of the young whose brilliant future that inquisition is in duty bound to protect with holy zeal.

As this model shows, the role of social and cultural institutions is, in general, very simple: it consists, firstly, in making a suitable 'choice' of educationally desirable works of art and, secondly, in directing them to the consumer in such a way as to promote perception of the 'content'. The

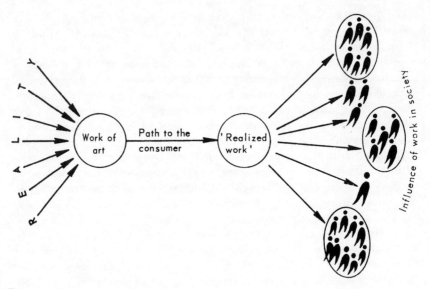

FIG. 1.

important thing is that the work is made available and appropriately 'presented' institutionally.

From this position it is logically only a step to simple intervention when the model does not operate, when the consumer does not 'understand' the work: as there cannot possibly be anything wrong with the institutional channels through which the work reaches the receiver, the fault must lie in the work itself, or in the artist whose creations are 'incomprehensible'. It is not fortuitous that in our century, when the pressure of the economic systems of industrial society is bringing totalitarianism to more and more spheres of human activity, we find the strongest tendencies towards control in art that history has ever seen.

The main target of the aggressivity of society (and sometimes of the State) are those elements which are incompatible with the pragmatic, educational conception of art, which are 'good for nothing', art for art's sake, evidence of the 'irresponsibility' of the artist. In the nineteenth century, it was chiefly the subjective element in expression which infuriated respectable society; in the twentieth century, it is principally the essentially meaningless 'aesthetic play of materials' (colours, words, tones and sounds, shapes, movements, etc.), which is branded as undesirable, heretical 'formalism'. The way in which this sort of 'formalism' has been attacked on ideological grounds in our century will remain one of the most grotesque phenomena in the history of art: the Nazis called it 'cultural bolshevism', the Stalinists, a 'product of the rotting decay of imperialism'—in both instances with the consent of the mass of consumers who mistrust such art on principle, because of its 'incomprehensibility'. Nor can it be said that the various ideologies have even yet quite given up hurling the accusation of formalism at one another; it would be truer to say that it is now done in more subtle ways.

On the other hand, there is a tendency to give greater prominence to elements which are capable of more definite meaning, and therefore of practical, ideological use: symbolic and figurative elements. By 'figurative', we mean showing direct correlations between the structure of the work and reality as it is familiar to the average consumer—descriptions in literary works, likeness of shape and colour in the visual arts, pleasant melodies which are easily remembered in music, spectacular film sets, etc. These totalitarian tendencies—whether apparent in the all-powerful 'consumer art' industry or in the support afforded by the Establishment—are directly counter to real art or, in other words, to the natural dispersion of ideas. There is a perpetual psychological struggle against the normal human intentionality of perception, preventing the consumer from perceiving a work as he should and could. The mass consumer is not entitled to choice: he will either react precisely as intended (take, for example, the well-ordered sequences of excitement and emotion in the film *War and Peace*, with their expurgated, reduced content) or else he will not react at all—sitting in an armchair, eating his sandwiches, he will watch on the television screen, one after the other, the effects of the napalm bomb, a scooter race, a helicopter crash, the birth of quintuplets, and the havoc caused by an earthquake, without being required, or indeed able, to react sympathetically—to be afraid at what is frightening, to weep with those who weep, to laugh with those who are happy.

Whenever new art emerges, institutions have to decide what to do with it, how desirable it is, how useful it may be. I shall quote one example from my own country. In 1955, Czechoslovakia heard for the first time about the existence of electronic and concrete music.[1] Two main institutions were to be expected to take a stand on the matter, being directly concerned: the monopoly institution, the Union of Composers, which might be expected to have a typical defence reaction against the unknown; and the institutions making up the cultural industry, which were in a position to make practical use of the theory and might therefore be expected to show interest. The Union of Composers indeed reacted in accordance with the ideological tone of those days and denounced this music as an 'invention of decadent bourgeois society'. The strong institutional resistance was maintained until about 1961. In spite of this ideological condemnation and denunciation electronic and concrete music was introduced into films and heard on the radio. The first film with electronic music, *Invention of Destruction*, based on a novel by Jules Verne, came out in 1958, and was followed by a whole series of science-fiction films and sound-montage programmes on the radio. In 1965 a survey of response to musical forms was made by playing to selected audiences a whole range of recorded music, from folk music to electronic. Only a small percentage confessed to liking electronic music (3-12 per

1. J. Matejcek, 'Poznámky o elektronické a konkrétní hudbe' (Some notes on electronic and concrete music), *Hudební rozhledy (Musical review)*, No. 6, Prague, 1965.

cent) but a relatively high percentage (40-70 per cent) had already heard electronic music.[1] The institutional influence of the cultural industry had thus marked up a considerable success in the space of five to eight years. The context in which electronic and concrete music had been used had obviously had a strong influence on the trend of listeners' imagination.

To the question 'What images does this music evoke' the majority of replies mentioned: things connected with outer space (space flight, unknown galaxies, space, infinity, the twinkling of stars in the universe, meteors, other planets, a Martian landscape, great distances, emptiness, something ethereal, eternal silence) or terror and catastrophe (fear, cruelty, despair, anxiety, chaos, explosion of atomic bomb, destruction of the world, death, approach of evil, foreboding, a tragic end, an accident) or phantasy and movement (supernatural, abstract, harmony of spheres, transparency, excursion into the future, the twenty-second century, Utopia, metamorphoses, beginning of movement, unfolding of shapes, wandering) or mystery (the unknown, the fabulous, supernatural beings, life after death, prehistoric creatures, heaven, shadows, darkness, haunted castles, darkness of the forest), etc. All these show a strong conventional influence, but there were also unconventional images (sunrise, sheep in the mountains, the underwater world, etc.) This is not the place for a full examination of the psychological problems involved in such a survey (e.g., the semantic influence of the word *predstava*[2] used in the questionnaire; the association of the impulse imparted by this word with the impulse from the sound of the music, its structure; the influence of its concrete meaning on the listener's response to the question; the influence of the listener's own tendencies in observation, assimilation, etc.). We simply wish to point out that these statistics confirm a notion already familiar in experimental aesthetics: that the images evoked by music (and by other 'semantically free' forms of art) are varying, and that it is only when a number of associated conditions of perception are satisfied that the images suggested are sometimes identical or similar. This percentage of similarity (e.g., the conventional image of the universe) is the only foundation of common 'comprehensibility' and similar representation, i.e., 'communicability' and therefore also the basis for possible use of a 'transmission of information' model. This is, however, not a special case; a typical, natural case, involves a whole range of images. For example, an excerpt from the composition of H. Eimert, 'Epitaf für Aikichi Kuboyama', evoked the following contradictory images and recollections:

'I thought of the beautiful composition of Paul Klee and Piet Mondrian' (a student of architecture, age 25).

'It's like a circular saw outdoors in January and the man operating it has frozen hands and the belt is slipping' (a driver, age 24).

'This is not music. It reminds me of the mediaeval Inquisition and the burning of witches. Or some pictures of Picasso' (an office-worker, age 50).

1. *Vyzkum soucasné hudebnosti (Survey on contemporary musicality)*. New and enlarged edition, Prague, 1968.
2. *Predstava* may mean either 'image' or 'idea' (translator's note).

'A feeling of whirling movement, spirals in the air, an abstract impression of rhythm and movement, multitudes of colours' (a scientist, age 32). Here we must again leave aside the problem of experimental aesthetics which consists of determining whether it is possible to deduce from the reactions of the consumers any opinion on the inherent 'content' of the work. We have here what is called an aesthetic experience, without any decoding of information. When A. Silbermann began using the word *Erlebnis* (experience) in the sociology of art,[1] he was criticized for introducing terminology from psychology. Experimental surveys (especially when, as in Czechoslovakia, we have available thousands of replies which can be used for statistical purposes and not merely samples of a few dozen, as has usually been the case in experimental aesthetics) rather confirm that, methodologically, *experience*, as the final effect on the consumer, is a valid approach. A further advantage is that recent developments in phenomenology have revealed other aspects of this concept and given it a subtler noetic significance. What concerns us here is that experiment has really furnished evidence of the intentionality of perception which conditions the extreme qualitative dispersion of experiences, their 'content', the 'meanings' and emotions they call forth. The quality of an aesthetic experience may be influenced by social and psychological factors and by institutional pressures, but it is none the less the basis of the percipient's intellectual reaction.

Aesthetic experience may thus be defined as a state of stimulation of the consciousness caused by the perception of the work of art at a given time and evoking from the 'traces' left by previous experiences (either artistic or outside art) varying reflexes involving emotion, imagination and meaning. A work of art conceived in this way (and this conception is not speculative but experimentally deduced) becomes an impulse setting off an individual intellectual process rather than a codification of 'information'. It may not be impossible to devise a mathematical model to cover this within the framework of information theory but it will not be the same model of interactions that we have been presented with up to now.

In our experimental model we naturally come up against the basic ontological problems of art. We are aware of the fact that the series of interrelations 'reality - artist - work - institution - consumer - society' is extremely complex and that it varies not only from case to case but according to the form of art. In some arts, the work can serve only as a 'means of realization' (musical scores, plays, novels, poems); in others, the work is a finished creation, once and for all (a statue, painting, electronic music on tape, film). Some works of art are realized in privacy by a great number of scattered individual creations (reading a novel); others involve the effects of mass psychology (theatrical performances, concerts, films), etc.

Another series of problems arises in connexion with the inspiration of the work, and here we are faced with a basic theoretical question in the sociology of art: is the social reality (membership of a group, group relations and

1. A. Silbermann, *Wovon lebt die Musik*, chapter 3, 'Das Musikerlebnis und sein Sozial-Bestimmendes', Regensburg, 1957.

pressures, influence of institutions and of the State ideology on the creative process, pressure of historical events, prestige, ethics, etc.) only one of the realities to which the artist reacts (the others being natural, biological, psychological, intellectual realities together with existing art, the properties of the material the artist is working with the aesthetic standards and values of the given time and conditions), or is it the common denominator of all these realities, on which their organization and interpretation depend? Is the social reality one of many factors contributing to the creation of a work or does it determine all the other factors to such a degree that it can be regarded as the main structural factor?

We cannot, of course, deny the social character of human consciousness, nor that sociability is essential in man's ontogenesis—a real Mowgli would be an animal in a human body. One cannot live in a society without being dependent on it. However, at a certain cultural level, it is possible to extricate oneself from this dependency. Science is the most obvious means for such liberation, as can be seen in the dialectic relation between science and ideology: an ideology can be made scientific, but science cannot be made into an ideology without ceasing to be science. The sentence 'We cannot live in society without being dependent on it' means something quite different, depending on whether a psychologist or a politician is speaking. Institutions, and the élite of the ruling classes, will always tend to emphasize this dependence, whilst a scientist, a philosopher or an artist will seek emancipation from it. Science is the typical instrument of the critical attitude towards the sociability that evolution imposes, but art can also play the same role. It is, indeed, usually art which first succeeds—and more effectively than science—in opposing the dependence required by the Establishment. There are important gnoseological elements in such an active attitude: a work deriving from opposition can offer society much food for reflection and self-discovery.

As this is a problem which has not yet been studied experimentally but has been more or less deduced from the needs of certain ideologies, we are for the moment free to choose our way of formulating the model to show the relation between the social and other realities. Let us therefore consider the co-ordinated influence of realities dialectically as a thesis to be disputed. The spheres of reality affecting both the creation of the work and its perception ('consumption') may be set out as in Figure 2.

We scarcely need to point out that this is a model corresponding to the present historical stage of development. The case would be different, for example, in a primitive society where 'art' is still at the syncretic stage (combined effect of words, dramatic and visual elements, dancing and music in ritual), where the aesthetic function is not yet isolated and where the utilitarian (mainly magical) functions predominate. In the subjective awareness of such a society (our model is also, of course, the product of a subjective awareness of our civilization), the pre-artistic creations are not regarded as the results of a creation to reality but, on the contrary, as a special means whereby the subject influences reality, which is then

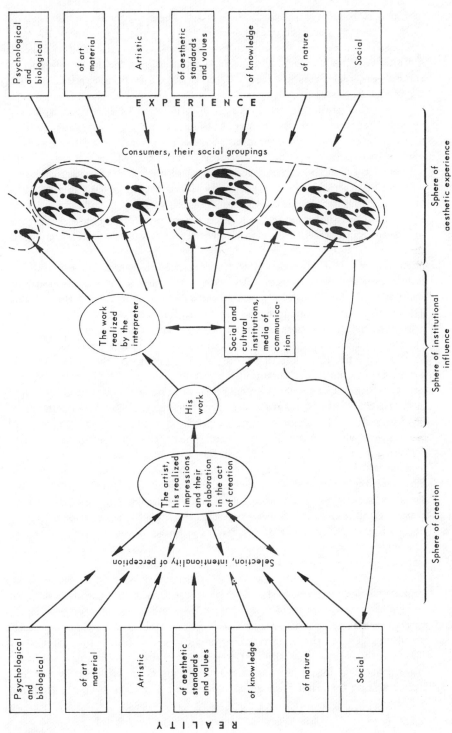

Fig. 2.

'compelled' to adapt itself as ritual requires. The conception of art in various types of society, considered as a whole, varies between models of the sort described above and the operation of 'pre-art' in pre-feudal society. Primitive utilitarian tendencies in art—art used as a means of influencing reality—are to be found, of course, even in relatively advanced societies organized as States.

In scientific studies, it is always necessary to begin by artificially isolating certain phenomena in order to analyse them. In the same way, the sociology of art isolates from the autonomous series of interrelations 'reality - artist - work - institution - consumer - society' everything which belongs to the sphere of its own experimental and theoretical interest in society: social and cultural institutions, social relationships, ideology, the artist's membership of social groupings, social consumption of art, social and ecological factors influencing the quality of aesthetic experience, etc. Very often, however, we forget to reintegrate the isolated element afterwards. This is liable to give rise to 'pan-sociological' theories which explain the whole process, from the moment of creation to the experience, purely as the natural outcome of the social process. Psychology and aesthetics are disregarded; sociology solves everything. 'Short circuits' between society and the work of art are then typical phenomena. We could, for example, instance a monograph on Purcell in which the victory of monody over counterpoint around 1600 is explained as reflecting the victory of absolutism over the balance of classes in the Elizabethan realm[1]—or the argument that Goya's work simply represents the maturing of the Spanish revolution. Wagner's music, again, reflects 'The power [violence] of imperialism and the foreboding of catastrophe in a class which sees nothing before it but the ineluctable need for expansion', as we read in a work by a well-known sociologist and philosopher who was not able to avoid the snares of pan-sociologism.[2]

Some popular writers on Hegel have appropriated his noetic term 'reflection' (*Widerspiegelung*) and begun to spread a definition which would make art 'the reflection of reality' but, in their eyes, the only reality is the social reality of class, group and institution. The ancient dualism God - man, matter - soul, external world - subject, is thus mechanically transferred to the relations 'society - work of art'. No attention at all is paid to the question of whether the structure of a work of art does not also derive from the inner forces of the artist, his psyche, his instincts ('hereditary codes of behaviour') the struggle of creative intent with material (colours, sounds, words charged with semantics, harmonics, stone, screen projection, etc.) or from biological factors (eroticism, youth, old age, etc.). The mere fact of saying 'reflects reality' instead of 'reacts to reality' reduces the artist to the role of a passive executant, just as the manipulating institutions would wish him to be.

It is thus obvious that the first step for integrating sociological analysis into the series of interactions we are considering is to include known social factors among the other realities to which the artist reacts. We can then no

1. R. Sietz, *Henry Purcell. Zeit, Leben, Werk*, Leipzig, 1955.
2. Th. W. Adorno, *Dissonanzen*, 3rd ed., 1963.

longer maintain that social reality is always and everywhere the 'ultimate determining principle' of artistic creation. Then, too, institutional intervention and its influence is seen to be much more modest than would often be liked. At the moment of creation, the influence of biological reality on a work of art may well outweigh that of social reality (the artist's age may represent a stronger impulse in the creation of a work than a revolution occurring at that point in time). Again, whilst the reality of knowledge (substance of matter, nature of the universe, historical events, etc.) is derived from socially neutral science, the reality of aesthetic standards is more largely subordinated to ideology. The influence of social reality clearly varies from case to case, and consequently the value of a work for the purposes of social reflection also varies.

Should we then cease to ask as Th. W. Adorno does, that the sociology of art should be concerned with the 'social decoding of a work',[1] when we know, in any case, that analysis of the social determining factors cannot make a real contribution to the full analysis of the whole complex structure?

It would, of course, be creditable to sociology if it could meet this requirement, provided that it bears in mind that its own particular mode of analysis is only one of the possible approaches likely to lead to an explanation of a work of art, and that only the reintegration of its results and their comparison with those of historical, aesthetic, psychological and other analyses can provide a fuller picture.

We must also consider, however, what are the methods—apart from the more or less 'intuitive short-circuits' to which we have referred—that the sociology of art, in its present state, can offer for the analysis of a work's genesis. Its approach is piecemeal and unsystematic, adapting itself to the difficulties of its subject-matter (it is for this reason that the sociology of literature has so far been mainly a speculative 'sociology of literary creation' and not at all a sociology of consumption, which is extremely difficult to pin down, owing to the fact that literary works are 'realized' in countless different places by individual reading); all we have are statistical figures for the taste of various consumers, but very little else. Thousands of works of art are created daily and the empirical sociology of art still cannot suggest a single methodologically sound standardized experimental method for analysing the social conditions and environmental circumstances of their creation. It has not yet even occurred to the sociologists of art to take a look at the social processes associated with the entirely new phenomena which are revolutionizing the structure of art's field of action, such as the electronic and concrete music referred to above.

Vainglorious patrons, social and cultural institutions and the enlightened bureaucrats of the State machinery are thus constantly able to pass themselves off as the support and inspiration of art, without having to show how they contribute to the construction of the work for which they arrogate credit to themselves. They can safely claim 'their part' in a work even when the artist's intentions in creating it are diametrically opposed. The institu-

1. Th. W. Adorno, *Einleitung in die Musiksoziologie*, 1962.

tions concerned with the propagation of art are often ignorant of their own position in the series of interrelations between reality, works of art and society; they are not even aware of the possibilities they command with regard to the different forms of art and its morphology (we have only to think of the incessant struggle to overcome the difficulties arising in presenting authentic art through the media of mass communication, which are better suited for dealing with stereotyped forms—in short, 'consumer' art—whereas art drawing on the unique character of aesthetic experience is not generally amenable to the present forms of presentation, although those working in the mass media are not aware of this).

We have tried, above, to see what is the true position of social and cultural institutions and the mass media in the chain of interrelations between 'reality, work of art and society'. We are well aware that this statement will not be enough to enable those institutions deliberately to take up the position which, in our opinion, should be theirs. To oblige them to do so, convincing analyses of the sociology of art and culture are needed. Until we have proper methods of analysis and convincing results of the empirical study of their effects, of course, we shall have to rely instead on efforts made in the ideological field, including in all probability those designed to ridicule neronic complexes or awkward attempts to 'guide' or 'direct' artistic creation, to decide whether a movement in art is 'desirable' or not, to curtail artistic freedom by political and 'moral' censorship, and to enlist the 'indignation' of good citizens against the temerity of those who flaunt accepted standards.

[*Translated from Czech*]

Note. The author has made use of the findings of certain of his previous studies, listed below.

(The conception and aesthetics of 'light music'.) *Hudební veda*, Prague, 1967, no. 1-3. (German summary.)

Zur empirisch-soziologischen Musikforschung. *Beiträge zur Musikwissenschaft*, 1966, no. 3-4.

(Survey of response to music.) (In collaboration with J. Kasan.) Prague, 1964; new and enlarged edition, Prague, 1968. (Summaries in German, French, Russian and English.)

(Social factors in aesthetic perception. Contribution to the relations between sociological and aesthetic experiment.) *Estetika*, Prague, 1967, no. 3. (German Summary.)

(Experiment in musical sociology. Methods of empirical and sociological research in art.) Two contributions to the collection: *Problems in the sociology of music*. Prague, 1967. (Summaries in Russian, French, English and German.)

(Realism. Content analysis of musical publications 1948-65.) Partially published in *Hudební rozhledy*, 1966, no. 18.

The Sociological Approach to Literature
W. Witte

from

Modern Language Review, vol. 36, no. 1, 1941.

Reprinted by permission of the author and the Editors
of *Modern Language Review*.

THE SOCIOLOGICAL APPROACH TO LITERATURE

IT is widely admitted that the literature of any given period on the one hand and the social, economic, and political forces of that period on the other are in some important way interconnected, although critics are often reluctant to define the precise nature of this connexion. Professor Bruford may be held to command general assent when he writes:

Social and political factors exercise at all times a pervasive influence on culture in general, an influence which is none the less important for being difficult to trace with any final certainty.[1]

Some scholars, indeed, confidently believe that they can trace these elusive connexions; as witness, in the field of German studies, such well-known works as Kuno Francke's *History of German Literature as determined by Social Forces*[2] and Alfred Kleinberg's *Die deutsche Dichtung in ihren sozialen, zeit- und geistesgeschichtlichen Bedingungen*.[3] The very titles of these books proclaim that their authors have committed themselves uncompromisingly to the sociological approach.

Not many critics go quite so far. Yet most of them admit, if only tacitly and by implication, that the sociological approach is legitimate and that it may be illuminating. Evidence of this is not far to seek, and a few random examples will suffice to illustrate the point.

Critics who write on Chaucer will usually relate *Troilus* to certain features in the structure and development of contemporary society. They will point out that certain conventions of medieval chivalry (for instance those concerning the relations of the sexes, summed up in the formula of Courtly Love) were still widely known and understood, still felt to be an element in the social life of the time, although they were no longer taken quite so seriously as they used to be. The critics will then proceed to show how this social change pervades the very fabric of *Troilus*, and how some features of the poem (to say nothing of its general spirit) cannot be properly appreciated unless the social evolution behind it is understood—an evolution which finds its living embodiment in the superbly ambiguous figure of Pandarus.[4]

Shakespeare will provide another example. The characteristically vigorous, buccaneering spirit of Elizabethan literature is often related to the widening of political horizons and the fierce and strenuous living in

[1] W. H. Bruford, *Germany in the Eighteenth Century* (Cambridge, 1935), p. 291.
[2] London, 1901.   [3] Berlin, 1927.
[4] The art of Neidhart von Reuental might be mentioned as a parallel case; cf. A. Hübner's introduction to the anthology *Frühe deutsche Lyrik* (Berlin, 1935), pp. 20–1.

that period of English history. Dr Caroline Spurgeon points out[1] that one of the two main recurrent sets of images predominating in *Othello* is the imagery of the sea; and one is at once tempted to ask whether the specific emotion in *Othello* would have tended to clothe itself in this particular kind of imagery, had the poet not lived at a time when the hearts of Englishmen were stirred by the exploits of their fellow-countrymen on distant seas and when their imagination was following these adventurers to 'the very sea-mark of their utmost sail'.

Or—to turn to German literature for a third illustration—are critics not agreed that in Grimmelshausen's *Simplicissimus* we have (if it be permitted to adapt Goethe's famous dictum) 'die wahrste Ausgeburt des Dreissigjährigen Krieges'?

There is no need to multiply instances in order to show that the sociological approach to literature is widely accepted and practised, even by critics who do not explicitly advocate it. What then are the arguments in favour of this mode of approach?

Using the terms 'Communication' and 'Significance' in the sense which Professor L. Abercrombie attaches to them in his *Principles of Literary Criticism*,[2] one may say that literature communicates significant experience. Now experience, of whatever order it may be, does not take place in a social vacuum. The life of the individual who has the experience is not a separate, self-sufficient entity; it is one particular thread in the larger fabric of the society in which he happens to live. It does not matter whether the individual's attitude towards that society is one of acquiescence or approval, or whether it is that of a rebel: as weft or warp, he remains part of the pattern. The society to which he belongs, even when he rebels against it, surrounds him and colours his view of the world. It provides him with a framework of thought and beliefs which may be said to bear some resemblance (on a non-metaphysical plane) to Kant's Categories, in that it limits the conditions under which experience is possible at all, and thereby enters into the experience itself. This framework is very complex; no exhaustive analysis of it is possible. In an inventory of its more important components, the following, amongst others, would have to be catalogued. Firstly, a set of social conventions and taboos regarding the relations between the sexes, between parents and children, as well as people's behaviour in the company of their fellow-men. Secondly, a set of commonly, or at any rate widely, accepted ethical standards. Thirdly, a set of religious and philosophical beliefs, or more

---

[1] *Leading Motives in the Imagery of Shakespeare's Tragedies.* Reprinted in *Shakespeare Criticism*, 1919–35 (World's Classics, no. 436). Cf. pp. 45–7.

[2] Reprinted in *An Outline of Modern Knowledge*, 3rd impression (London, 1932).

often a miscellany of such beliefs, concerning the position and role of man in the universe. Fourthly, a given type of economic organization, with a greater or lesser emphasis on the importance of material possessions. Lastly, the political structure of a given community, embodying certain conceptions of government, of the individual's position in the state, and of international relations.

All these elements, together with many others, furnish the individual with a technique of living that varies from one age to another. They do not merely form the outward setting, the background of his experience; rather they may be pictured as the mould in which that experience is cast, and which determines its shape. In more abstract language, they may be said to constitute the system in terms of which the individual lives his life and views the world. Being thus of the very essence of experience, they enter into and condition any communication of it that may be attempted in literature. In the words of Mme de Staël:

Mais comment résister à l'influence de son temps, et quel est l'homme dont le génie même n'est pas à beaucoup d'égards l'ouvrage de son siècle?[1]

Taine and Marx unflinchingly followed this argument to its logical conclusion. Taine's famous theory, set forth with all the lucidity and persuasive grace which Marx so sadly lacks, leads him to the conclusion that literary developments are rigidly determined, that the problems which literature presents are problems of 'psychological mechanics', that literary works are, in fact, 'resultants' produced by the interplay of certain forces: Race, Environment, and what he calls 'Moment', i.e. the cumulative influence of past events in any given situation. These three underlying causes determine the precise character of any work of literature, just as the structure of a rock is determined by the lie of the geological stratum to which it belongs.

As for Marx, it is a well-known fact that there is no unanimity amongst the commentators and critics who have striven to elucidate the writings of the master. However, as far as the bearing of his theories on literature is concerned, a few ideas emerge fairly clearly. In his *Introduction to the Critique of Political Economy*, Marx asks the rhetorical question:

Is the view of nature and of social relations which shaped Greek imagination and Greek art possible in the age of automatic machinery, and railways, and locomotives, and electric telegraphs?[2]

The belief which inspires this question and predetermines the negative answer forms one of the cornerstones of the Marxian doctrine. It is the

[1] *De l'Allemagne*, ch. 11.
[2] K. Marx, *A Contribution to the Critique of Political Economy*, translated from the 2nd German ed. by N. I. Stone, Chicago, 1904. The passage quoted occurs in the fragmentary *Introduction to the Critique of Political Economy* given in the Appendix.

belief that, in the last resort, the economic structure of society determines
the things of the mind. Religion, political and ethical creeds, laws, art
and literature are, in the celebrated phrase of the Marxists, a 'superstructure' erected on the foundation of economic conditions and economic
organization. That superstructure may be so impressive as to make people
forget the foundation on which it rests; in other words, people may be
tempted to invest the things of the mind with an illusory independence.[1]
We should do well to remember, however, that 'even the autonomous
creation of the mind, the flights of fancy by which men often think they
transcend the limits of space and time—art, religion, and philosophy—
obey an order, in addition to their own, which is imposed upon them
from without'.[2]

It follows that any cultural activity, such as literature, cannot be
fruitfully studied apart from the economic, social, and political organization of the society that produced it. From the Marxian point of view the
sociological approach to literature would thus seem to be the only
proper one.

What arguments can be advanced against this position? Critics who
deprecate the sociological approach do not, as a rule, attempt to deny the
existence of relations between literature on the one hand and social,
economic, and political factors on the other. They assert, however, that
those factors are not of essential importance, that in any case they cannot
be isolated, and that the study of them therefore affords no help when it
comes to the analysis and appreciation of any specific work of literature.

These critics would argue that in order to understand any given
phenomenon—such as a work of literature—one must obviously have
some idea of what is relevant to it and what is not. A great many things
may be involved in it and related to it in various ways; but that does not
mean that they are all equally relevant. In fact, according to the
so-called Axiom of Internal Relations every single thing in the universe
is related to everything else, so that if one thing is affected in any way, all
other things are affected at the same time, however slightly. Most people
would probably agree that such a theory, while not without a certain
academic interest, does not help at all when one is trying to understand
and interpret any specific phenomenon, since it is obviously impossible to
include in one's account a network of relations which ramify all through
the universe. In other words, a total explanation of anything is beyond

---

[1] Cf., e.g., N. J. Bukharin, *Marx's Teaching and its Historical Importance*; in *Marxism and Modern Thought* (London, 1935), p. 38.
[2] Sidney Hook, *Towards the Understanding of Karl Marx* (London, 1933), p. 109.

the bounds of possibility. For practical purposes, one has to content oneself with relations which can be clearly traced and which, for that reason, appear particularly relevant.

The opponents of the sociological approach would apply this argument to the problem of the influence of social, economic, and political factors on any given work of literature. They would conclude that the sociological approach does not greatly help the literary critic to grasp and interpret the things that interest him primarily: the individual achievement and the particular personality behind it.

It is along these lines that Lanson criticizes Taine.[1] He admits that it may be possible to explain, with the aid of Taine's theory, why certain literary currents have been followed, how certain literary forms have come into favour; it may be possible to account for the general trend of feeling and interest, the prevalent modes of thought in a given period. But he points out, on the other hand, that there are things—and they are not the least important ones—that do not fit in with Taine's rigid determinism, such as genius, intensity of vision, energy and originality of artistic expression. The appearance of the great man and the great work is not explicable in terms of Taine's theory.

Nor, for that matter, can their non-appearance be explained. Saintsbury affirms this when he writes:

The best explanation why there is no poet in English who is the equal of Chaucer, between Chaucer himself and Surrey, is that, as a matter of fact, no such poet appeared.[2]

The arguments which are brought against Taine apply with equal force to Marx. Marx's views on literature being only an offshoot of his whole philosophical and economic doctrine, his critics usually prefer to strike at the root of the doctrine by questioning that fundamental materialism which represents the things of the mind, such as literature, as mere by-products of an economic process.

Rejecting the sociological approach for the reasons stated, many critics favour either one or the other of two different methods which may be respectively described as the historical-biographical method and the method of pure aesthetics.

The exponents of the former seek to trace the genesis of a literary work by collating such drafts and variants as may be extant and by investigating the record of the poet's life (often in very minute detail) in order to relate a given work to the inner experiences that gave rise to it.

[1] Gustave Lanson, *Histoire de la Littérature française*, 19th ed. (reprint of 11th and 12th eds., Paris, 1909–12), pp. 1045–6.
[2] G. Saintsbury, *A Short History of English Literature*, 8th ed. (London, 1925), p. 154.

The followers of the method of pure aesthetics contend that the proper object of the study of literature is the actual works, not things that lie outside or behind them, such as the social conventions they reflect, or the personal experiences that stimulated their authors. All that really matters, the quintessence of what a poet or a writer had to give, is in the works themselves, and there is no need to look for it elsewhere. Two quotations from French critics of note may serve to characterize this view:

C'est par elle-même que vaut une œuvre littéraire, non par la réalité dont elle est significative.[1]

On ne voit pas très bien comment la connaissance de l'homme est nécessaire pour juger l'œuvre, pour en apprécier le mérite intrinsèque.[2]

These statements are supplemented by one from the pen of a popular contemporary philosopher:

...the source of the work of particular artists, the schools to which they belong, their influence upon their successors are irrelevant to aesthetic appreciation, and it is not necessary to know how, when, or by whom a work of art was created in order that the vision of the reality which it imperfectly reveals may be enjoyed.[3]

Explicitly or implicitly, these critics claim to study literature *sub specie aeternitatis*, in that they seek to define and to emphasize what they conceive to be the universally and enduringly significant features of a work. In order to judge what those features are, they obviously need criteria that are similarly immutable. To discover these is a notoriously difficult task. Dr I. A. Richards suggests that the required criterion is to be found in the emotional equilibrium brought about by the contemplation of a work, a state of mind and feeling in which all one's impulses are harmonized and none is frustrated ('synaesthesis'). S. Alexander, less subjectively inclined, lays stress on the property of the work rather than the mental state induced by it.[4] Professor L. Abercrombie finds the significance of a work of literature in its (formal and objective) unity, the perfectly articulate interrelationship of all its parts and the complete coherence of the whole, whereby experience in literature transcends ordinary experience. Professor Joad postulates an intangible (Platonic) Form of Beauty, and (intuitively) judges a work according to the degree of its participation in that Form. Others prefer to think and judge in terms of general human significance—a criterion manifestly derived from the idea of fundamental elements in human nature which remain constant

[1] René Doumic, *Hommes et Idées du XIXe Siècle* (Paris, 1903), p. 153.
[2] G. Pellissier, *Le XIXe Siècle par les Textes* (Paris, n.d.), p. 395, footnote 4.
[3] C. E. M. Joad, *Guide to Philosophy* (London, 1936), p. 353.
[4] S. Alexander, *Beauty and other Forms of Value* (London, 1933), p. 50.

everywhere and at all times, and calling to mind the concept of 'l'homme universel' as it appears in French classical literature.

Whatever may be one's opinion of all these theories, it must be observed that the sociological approach does not conflict with them. Admittedly, it tends towards a different emphasis by insisting on the element of change in literature and literary criticism, as in all other human activities. But that does not mean that it is incompatible with Gautier's belief that

>...les Vers souverains
>Demeurent
>Plus forts que les airains

—the belief in the existence of universal values and significances that endure while all else changes. On the contrary, if there be such things, then the sociological approach would help to reveal and define them. Either it would enable the critic to detach those elements in a work of literature which are merely of the time and, in that sense, accidental; or it would help to show how human experience, though limited and localized in time and space, may be universalized and made permanent in literature. In either case, the sociological approach to literature would have proved its worth.

Its critics, however, would object (as was pointed out above) that it does not help to study the relation of literature to social, economic, and political factors because that relation cannot be clearly traced in any specific case and its relevance, therefore, cannot be assessed.

Is this true?—It is not very hard to think of cases where the argument does not hold good. One such case is the kind of literature that falls into a definite social pattern. Chaucer's *Troilus* was mentioned earlier on; another instance that comes to mind is the efflorescence of M.H.G. *Minnesang*, where the particular influence of the whole tenor of courtly society, with its characteristic ideals, its rules of conduct, and its make-believe, can be plainly seen. The old popular ballads, in England and Scotland as well as in Germany, afford another example; it has often been pointed out how this kind of folk poetry was affected by the events of the time as well as by the prevailing technique of living.[1]

Again, the argument manifestly does not apply when social and economic conditions or political events actually form the theme of literary works. To illustrate the point, one might instance those sonnets and odes of Wordsworth's which are gathered together under the general heading of *Poems dedicated to National Independence and Liberty*; Gerhart Hauptmann's *Die Weber*; Richard Dehmel's poem *Der Arbeitsmann*, with its

[1] Cf. e.g., A. Quiller-Couch, *Studies in Literature*, 1st Series (Cambridge, 1927), pp. 22 et seq.

atmosphere of threatening thunder, or the bitter revulsion of Gordon Bottomley's *To Iron-Founders and Others* and Paul Zech's *Fabrikstrasse tags.* (The message of these poems is echoed by some contemporary critics who regard the present type of large-town machine civilization as essentially hostile to Poetry.[1]) Even Rilke, who refuses to concede lasting importance to the engrossing innovations of modern industrialism, feels moved to define his attitude towards them ('O das Neue, Freunde, ist nicht dies'). Further illustrations are to be found in Georges Duhamel's recent novel *Le Combat contre les Ombres*, or in the intimate literary portraits of various trades which Pierre Hamp has painted in such works as *Le Rail, Vin de Champagne, Le Lin.*

Yet another fact that militates against the argument in question is the influence on the author of his potential public's expectations and demands.[2] Do we not find that a strong and homogeneous society may impose its demands on a poet whose natural inclinations might otherwise have directed his art into different channels? Consider the example of William Collins: the poet whose delicately romantic genius flashes out now and then, in such poems as the *Ode to Evening* or *How Sleep the Brave*, conforms in most of his work to the prevailing fashion and uses the accepted clichés.

In all these cases the influence of social, economic, and political factors on specific works of literature is manifest. But even where the connexion is not so obvious, it does not by any means follow that it is irrelevant. If a connexion is hard to disentangle from a whole skein of other connexions, the critic is not therefore entitled to dismiss it as unimportant. The factors referred to may operate in a way not immediately observable on the surface of the finished work, just as personal experiences often undergo all sorts of transmutations before they appear in literature. The influence of either element is none the less real for being thus obscured. National aspirations, for instance, reacting against foreign models and influences, may create an emotional climate that can be felt even in works not at all political in character, and we shall appreciate such works better if we are aware of this element in them. Thus, in poems on themes of nature and friendship by Klopstock and his admirers of the Hainbund one discerns the spirit of high-minded patriotic endeavour that informed these poets, fostering their emotionalism and causing them to contrast their own

---

[1] Cf. F. Strich, *Dichtung und Zivilisation* (Munich, 1928); G. Steinhausen, *Deutsche Geistes- und Kulturgeschichte von 1870 bis zur Gegenwart* (Halle, 1931); Pierre Hamp, *La Littérature, image de la Société* (Encyclopédie Française, vol. XVI).

[2] Cf. in this connection Levin L. Schücking, *Die Soziologie der literarischen Geschmacksbildung* (Leipzig and Berlin, 1931), especially chapter V.

ideals of simple virtue with the sophisticated ways of those who, like Wieland, walked in the counsel of the ungodly.

It may be objected that an observation of this kind lacks precision, and we have seen the arguments with which critics have attacked the theory of Taine. While admitting that his theory helps to account for general currents of thought and feeling in a given period (and we may add in passing that this is in itself no mean achievement!), they point out that it can never explain the appearance of the great man and the great work.

The force of this criticism would appear to depend on the meaning one attaches to the word 'explain'. Obviously, the creation of a great work of literature cannot be 'explained' with the kind of precision that is possible in the analysis of a mathematical problem. There is little doubt that Taine's critics are right in finding fault with him for trying to treat a living process as if it were a problem of mechanics; and Taine himself did not persist in maintaining his theory in its most rigid form.[1] But if those who favour the sociological approach cannot claim to 'explain' the genesis of a great work in precise terms of cause and effect, neither can anybody else, whatever his method. The scholar who adopts the historical-biographical method may be able to describe in intimate detail the experience reflected in a poem; the adept in the method of pure aesthetics may quicken our appreciation of its inner harmonies: and nobody would wish to deny that both modes of approach can be delightful and illuminating. But at the same time, it is evident that by relating a poem to an experience behind it (even if that can be done with exactness), or by analysing its aesthetic qualities, we do not 'explain' the poem itself; we do not explain why and how a particular poet bodied forth a particular aspect of his experience in a particular form. That process defies explanation; and the irreverent critic who would pluck out the heart of the poet's mystery may find himself in the position of Guildenstern to whom Hamlet administers his annihilating rebuff: 'Why, look you now, how unworthy a thing you make of me....'

Since the sociological approach to literature does not imply 'explanation' of literary works in a mechanistic, materialistic sense, those who practise it are not affected by the arguments with which critics have assailed the Marxian position. Many of the things which throughout this discussion have been labelled 'social, economic, and political factors' are not material entities, and it is quite possible to believe in the sociological approach without subscribing to the Marxian doctrine.

W. WITTE.

ABERDEEN.

[1] Cf. R. Doumic, loc. cit., p. 176.

Literature and the Study of Society
L.C. Knights

Inaugural lecture as Professor of English Literature,
Sheffield University, 1947. Published by Sheffield
University 1948.

LITERATURE AND
THE STUDY OF SOCIETY

Inaugural Lecture: 28th May, 1947.

AN inaugural lecture has this distinction: there is necessarily one person who benefits from it. I refer, of course, to the lecturer, who is forced to clear up his mind concerning some aspect of his special subject so that he can present it as lucidly as possible to an audience largely composed of specialists in very different fields from his own; an audience, moreover, who, being free from the compulsions causing a certain deference in the usual lecture-room, will only give their attention if they are interested, and their assent so far as they see reason. It is partly because of this—that we meet here not simply as specialists but as members of a university with an intellectual life in common—that I have chosen to speak to-day not of the scope and functions of an English School—its internal economy—but of those rather neglected aspects of literary studies where these join hands with history and sociology and the study of politics. I wish to define the kind of contribution that a disciplined interest in literature can make to the study of society as a whole. And although I shall confine myself to the past—to the relations of literature and social history—I need not hide my conviction that the kind of enquiry I have in mind has an intimate bearing on our present unavoidable preoccupations with the social forms of to-day and to-morrow.

A second reason, related to the first, has also determined my choice of theme. In recent years a good deal has been said about the dangers of excessive specialization, about the need to broaden the scope of university studies, about the need for our universities to produce not merely specialists, but genuinely educated men and women who are alive to the intellectual trends of the present and equipped to take their bearings in the contemporary world. I, personally, am in whole-hearted sympathy with the spirit prompting these demands. But I also think that unless we give some very hard thought to the educational problems involved there is a danger lest in our anxiety to open windows and give our pupils more air we only create some uncomfortable draughts. In other words, a mere addition of courses —no matter how exciting they sound: outlines of modern literature for the scientist, outlines of biology, psychology and post-Marxian economics for the Arts man—will not in itself meet our needs. Living interests are organized interests; what we need to discover is how one interest, one field of enquiry, opens into another by a natural progression from a given centre of attention, so that the university "subject" —the specially chosen field—is not abandoned but further illuminated as its necessary relations with other "subjects" are explored. To discover how far the curriculum can be planned to foster such exploration without losing its way in the soft soil of half-knowledge calls for experiment and co-operation.[2] The first step in co-operation is for the specialist to expose himself and to say honestly, even naïvely, where he thinks the points of contact may be made, and what he regards as the contribution of his own studies to a better understanding of common problems. That is my second reason for speaking to-day not of the problems of literary criticism or literary scholarship, but of the relations between literature and social history.

My first task, I suppose, is to say what I mean by social history and where I think its main interest lies. Clearly it will not do to say, as a very distinguished historian has said recently, that "Social history might be defined negatively as the history of a people with the politics left out".[3] Such a conception is likely to result, in practice, in a rather fragmentary collection of more or less interesting pieces of information about the everyday life of the past: it certainly will not make of social history a significant study. The social historian is not concerned with what is left over when other historians have staked their claims; he is concerned with the bases of a people's culture.

Modern anthropology has made us familiar with the idea of a culture as a complex of functionally interrelated institutions and social habits, to which there corresponds a generally accepted pattern of motives, beliefs and attitudes. Civilized societies cannot be described as simply as Professor Malinowski's Trobriand Islanders; and my use of "culture" is different from the anthropologist's. But when all allowance has been made for greater complexity, I think it is true to say that the idea of a *pattern* of culture in any given phase of civilization has become a commonplace of our thinking about the structure and functioning of societies. It is a pattern determined by the predominant needs, interests and abilities of a certain people at a certain time. To reveal that interlocking pattern in the complexities of everyday living, to define the dominant energies of a society as these express themselves in economic enterprise, in social and cultural institutions, in domestic arrangements—this is an essential part of the task of the social historian. But only a part. As well as a description of these things we need an attempt at evaluation. What, we want to know, was the human significance of this or that particular social set-up? We are therefore confronted with a further problem. At what point do value judgments enter into a description of society? How do they enter? What standards can we apply in framing our own conclusions concerning the *quality* of living in different types of

2 Some practical suggestions will be found in F. R. Leavis's *Education and the University, a Sketch for an English School*—the most valuable contribution that I know of towards the solution of the problems touched on in this paragraph.

3 G. M. Trevelyan, *English Social History*, p. vii.

society? I am not so simple as to suppose that we can label some
societies "good" and others "bad"; and I know that the study of
society, whether by the sociologist or the historian, often demands the
application of a method as rigorously scientific and free from ethical
implications as possible. Yet it is obvious that any given set of social
and cultural forms encourages some activities and interests, and dis-
courages others; that it makes possible a wider or narrower play of
man's inherent energies; that, in short, it fosters certain *values,* which
in turn are built into the social life of the community. It is here, it
seems to me, that the central interest of social history lies. And it is
in attempting to grasp the qualitative aspect of the social life of the
past that our thinking about the present problems of society is
fertilized and quickened.

My contention is that if social history and the study of society
need facts—facts of the kind that are the special province of the
economic historian or the historian of institutions—they have also,
of necessity, an evaluative aspect.[4] How, then, can we define our
standards, sharpen our tools of analysis, and make our judgments more
substantial than the expression of personal prejudice? One answer is,
by coming to undertand the social significance of a people's art forms,
above all—because words are so intimate a part of daily living—of
their literature. The social historian *needs* literature, not to supply
bits of local colour but as a basis from which to start. He needs, as
an essential qualification, the sensitiveness and powers of discriminating judgment of the literary critic.

In advocating an approach to history through literature I may
seem merely to be echoing the doctrines of Taine, as set forth in his
well-known Introduction. Literature, he claimed, like all man's
cultural achievements, is the product of a particular set of circumstances, which in turn are determined by the three great factors of
la race, le milieu et le moment. It is the business of the literary
historian to reveal the laws by which the final product, the work of
art, has emerged from the complex interplay of these primary factors.
But the procedure I have in mind is entirely free from the scientific
pretensions that mark Taine's exposition of his method; writing at a
time when the natural sciences claimed to set the standard of
intellectual respectability, he was only too eager to align his researches
with those of botany or physiology.[5] It is plain from his practice

4 Lord Beveridge has recently reaffirmed his conviction that we should regard the
social sciences "as sciences and not as a branch of the humanities". (*The
Universities Quarterly,* Vol. I, No. 3, p. 237.) Professor Maurice Ginsberg some
years ago expressed a different opinion: "I agree (he said) that economics and
sociology in general should be kept distinct from ethics, but would urge that they
should also be brought into definite relation. Confusion is likely to arise if their
distinctness is not recognized, but also if they never meet at all. The effective
handling of social problems involves a synthesis, but not a fusion, of social
science and social philosophy". (*The Sociological Review,* October, 1937.)
5 "*Ce sont ces règles de la vegetation humaine que l'histoire à present doit
chercher*". Of Stendhal he said, admiringly, "*il importait dans l'histoire du
cœur les procédés scientifiques, l'art de chiffrer, de décomposer et de déduire
. . . il traitait des sentiments comme on doit en traiter, c'est-à-dire en naturaliste
et en physicien, en faisant des classifications et en pesant des forces*".

that Taine was in fact a critic; but the bias of his approach is towards classification and the discovery of "laws". The "literary documents" are to be handled, as it were, objectively. Of these literary documents he says, "they are instructive because they are beautiful : their utility grows with their perfection". But what do they teach, and what is their use? We find the answer a few sentences later :—"It is chiefly by the study of literature that one may construct a moral history, and advance towards the knowledge of psychological laws, from which events spring". What, if we accept this view, we are in danger of forgetting, is that the *primary* importance of literature is that it embodies values; and embodied value is not something we inspect like a monument, but something to which we respond. Whatever "use" we may make of literature is entirely dependent on our remembering that.

A similar, though even stronger, objection may be made to a more recent school of social thought which also claims a scientific objectivity in tracing the laws of historical development. Marxist historians have shown a lively sense of the inter-connexion of the various factors in a given historical situation, of something similar to what Taine called "the law of mutual dependence". The dependence that they trace is, of course, that of social, political and cultural forms on "the prevailing method of economic production and exchange". I have recorded elsewhere[6] my sense of the inadequacy of this kind of analysis : the Marxist use of the word "economic" begs far too many questions. What I wish to emphasize here is that this approach empties the past of all living significance. The standard by which the Marxist judges the past is the classless society that will be brought into being by the laws of the historical process : all that contributes towards this process is good or "progressive"; all that is at variance with it is bad or "reactionary". Measured by this standard, the past can only appear a dim preparation for something still to come : it is left with no *intrinsic* value. Now it cannot be too firmly insisted that the man who reveals the significance of the past *for us* is the man who has grasped the significance of the past *for itself,* as it was lived. True, we are the heirs of the past, and there are very urgent reasons for trying to understand what the past has contributed to our own here and now. But the very condition of this contributing is that each phase should have had its own possibilities of fulfilment and that values should have flowered in lives and works. It is these intrinsic values —with which, as soon as we recognize them as intrinsic, we can enter into relation—that are surely our main concern.

We can now, I think, begin to see more clearly why literature is of such fundamental importance for the social historian's task. And I mean literature considered as literature, that matters for what it is, not simply for what it says or offers as evidence. Consider what you

6 In *Drama and Society in the Age of Jonson.*

do when confronted with a poem. You may analyse its obvious form, its rhyme-scheme and metrical pattern; you may extract its "content" and relate it to events in the poet's biography; you may classify it in relation to works of the same literary *genre*. But the poem remains dead. It only comes alive when it is read with full responsiveness to its structure of meaning; and reading of this kind—the kind that all poetry, all literature, demands—is, as I. A. Richards says, "a constructive . . . free creative process; a process of conception through which a new being is growing in the mind".[7] It is in this active *realizing* process, in which the poem ceases to be an object from the vast museum of the past and becomes living and actual, that the value of the poem is disclosed.

In art a piece of the past is always waiting to become present and to reveal the values that it embodies. But now one more question remains. How, you may say, does art reveal anything of the past except itself? In order to answer that question we must consider briefly some of the ways in which a work of literature is related to the general life. First, and most obviously, there is what by a convenient metaphor we are accustomed to call the intellectual climate—the ideas and intellectual modes current within a given social group. These ideas—which the creative writer will use or reject, but is in any case unable to ignore—form part of a tradition which is constantly enriched, changed or modified by new discoveries; as in the age of Shakespeare and Bacon the Christian tradition of the Middle Ages had been modified by the Reformation, the rediscovery of the Classics, and the economic expansion, and was in process of being modified by the new science. The study of the prevailing intellectual currents, as in Professor Willey's *Seventeenth-Century Background,* or of the prevailing moral currents, as in R. H. Tawney's *Religion and the Rise of Capitalism,* has a direct bearing on the appreciation of literature on the one hand, and on the understanding of society on the other. Since the work of the creative writer is inevitably shaped by the intellectual climate—whether by conscious or unconscious assimilation, or by conscious attempts to modify or reject; and since the intellectual currents do not flow in a void but need visible channels in the day-to-day organization of society, the social historian will be concerned both with the ideas themselves and with the actual working of the agencies of cultural transmission and diffusion.[8]

But little as we can afford to neglect the intellectual climate in our attempt to discover how a work of art embodies more than the immediate personal experience of its author, to define the ideas that helped to shape a given work and to trace their sources is only a beginning. In this connexion the very phrases that we find ourselves

7 "The Interaction of Words", in *The Language of Poetry,* edited by Allen Tate.
8 Leslie Stephen's brilliant essay, *Literature and Society in the Eighteenth Century,* is an example of this kind of social history that could only have been written by a man whose interests were centred in literature.

using are sometimes of a misleading simplicity. "Intellectual background" is not just background; and it is part of something much
larger than itself. As for "climate of opinion", even if some more
comprehensive word could be substituted for "opinion", "climate"
would still need to be supplemented by some such metaphor as "soil",
from which things grow. The truth is that the tone and temper of
an age is made up not only of shared thoughts and intellectual and
moral assumption, of "beliefs", but of sentiments, modes of perception
and attitudes pervasive in the general life—of something roughly
corresponding to sensibility in the individual. In any period there
is a tendency not only to accept without much question certain
assumptions and to think along certain lines, but also to be sensitive
and responsive to certain elements of experience rather than to others,
and to be responsive in particular ways. These habitual and implicit
modes of consciousness are sometimes made explicit as intellectual
concepts and "ideas", and as such they may be built into systems of
thought that will in turn contribute to the wider stream : just as the
sense of neighbourliness in medieval life was built into social theory
which, in turn, fostered a sense of the individual's obligations to the
community. But as *ideas* they tend to lose relation with the living
pattern of interests, perceptions and attitudes in which alone they
have their full meaning. It is on these shared modes of being, which
shape a people's language and which can be traced to the interests
habits and aptitudes of daily life, that the culture of an age is built.
So pervasive as to be taken for granted at the time by all but the
exceptionally conscious, when the "climate" has changed they are
accessible in their *active* state only in works of art. For just as it is
the artist's function to bring into consciousness what is taken for
granted, or dimly perceived, and to test its implications, so we in turn
—in a kind of spiritual ecology—may use the work of art to explore
the conditions of cultural health or decay. But only if we are literary
critics—sensitive, that is, along the widest possible range—not simply
abstracters of ideas. In short, as I have said, the very condition of our
using literature in this way is that we shall first have responded to it :
if we treat it simply as evidence, as material, it will certainly not
answer any of the more interesting questions, for we shall not have
asked them.

II.

Since what I am advocating is not a system to be applied, but
only the cultivation of certain kinds of insight in our study of the past,
I need not apologize for the random nature of the examples with
which I must now try to illustrate my theme. If I confine myself
to the great age of English literature in the seventeenth century this
will be partly because it is a great age, a crucial one for our under
standing of the present, partly because of all the periods of the past

it is the one in which I find myself most at home. To guard myself against a possible charge of narrowness I may fittingly invoke here the name of my predecessor in this Chair, Professor Geoffrey Bullough. You know, even better than I, that in his case at least a special devotion to the seventeenth century was in no way incompatible with a lively interest that extended through all the fields of literature and beyond, to other arts.

There is in the first place the question of language; and by language I mean not only the words into which the fluid forms of discourse may be split up, but idioms and turns of phrase and all the varied elements of expression that in an individual writer make up his "style". And just as style (as we often say) is the man, so what may be called the common style of a social group is intimately revealing. Language is an index of deep-seated habits of perceiving, thinking, and registering experience. It is a social product, moulded by the needs and interests of those who use it. For my present purpose Miss Mildred Campbell, in her excellent scholarly book on *The English Yeoman under Elizabeth and the Early Stuarts,* offers a useful starting-point. Of the yeoman's speech—"the homely robust speech of Chaucer's pilgrims enriched by two centuries of growth"—she says:

> "Words and phrases filled with imagery occupied a large place in everyday conversation. Yeomen of the north country scorned to speak of the 'decease' of a relative or friend, or of his 'dying', but clung rather to the older and more imaginative word, 'forth-farren'. A burial was frequently spoken of; but as often they called it the 'homebringen', or told how one was 'brought home handsomely'. The word 'dusk' is of early English origin, but many countryfolk found more picturesque ways of referring to that part of the day. In the north they drove their sheep home 'betwixt sunsett and day going'; and to Devon and other west country yeomen it was the time 'between the lights'.
>
> "Idiom, proverbs, and figures of speech . . . flavoured their talk at every turn. The wife of a Cheshire yeoman said of one of her neighbouring gossips that 'she could take a tale out of the ground to shame or undo anyone'. A north country yeoman expressed his feeling about a neighbourhood matter by declaring that he 'wold never sturr his foot in his shoe about the business further'. Robert Furse advised his children not to trouble themselves about the affairs of others but to 'lett everye man shutt his own bowe'."[9]

My only quarrel with Miss Campbell's account concerns the use of the word "picturesque", which in its modern connotation suggests something either quaint or consciously cultivated. The yeoman's speech was not picturesque in this sense: it was spontaneously vivid,

9 *Op. cit.,* pp. 362-363.

vigorous and forthright, so that one feels the impact of direct experience in the words. Westmorland yeomen, Miss Campbell tells us, engaged in a dispute over their tenant-rights, declared that their landlords intended "to pull the skin over their ears and bray their bones in a mortar . . . and when our ancient liberties are gone theill puke and poole and peele us to the bare bone".[10] Similarly, in a year of dearth (1630) preachers denounced horders of corn "who pinched the guts of the poore to fill and extend their own purses".[11] These are random but representative examples. Readers of Elizabethan pamphlet literature will know how even a humdrum writer will suddenly make a scene vividly present, or sum up a personal or moral quality in a telling phrase. If, then, the very language of the people testifies to an alertness of the senses and a directness of moral judgment, some very interesting questions present themselves. To what extent were these qualities fostered by direct contact with nature and the natural processes, by the common forms of work and skill, by religion and tradition? These, I think, are questions that admit of answers that can be grounded on something more solid than sentimental fantasy about the past. When Bunyan makes By-Ends say, "I am become a gentleman, thought to tell the truth my grandfather was but a waterman, looking one way and rowing the other", I think it is plain that he writes as a member of a community that had a pretty shrewd eye for personal characteristics, and a pithy idiom at command to describe them.[12] The vigorous popular language of the sixteenth and seventeenth centuries was certainly not produced by a people that went through life in a haze. By contrast, there are elements in the modern idiom whose sole function seems to be to blur the feelings and confuse thought. "Corporal infliction", said Cobbett indignantly of the Mutiny Act of 1811, "*Corporal infliction*"—that is to say flogging. Why do you mince the matter? Why not name the thing?" What Cobbett would have said to the modern use of such words and phrases as "progressive", "reactionary", "bourgeois", "democratic and peace-loving states", let alone of "the liquidation of adverse elements", I do not know. And when we compare the idiom represented here with the common speech of the seventeenth century that seems unable to mince the matter, we are forced to ask ourselves some searching questions about the comparative value of different kinds of environment and about the meaning of "progress".

Here, then, is a field of great interest for the historian of culture who is sensitive to words and who has some insight into the relation between language and consciousness. He is also likely to find it significant that the common idiom, though mingled with learned or courtly elements, is strongly represented in the poetry of writers so

---

10 *Op. cit.*, p. 152. "Puke and poole"; *sc.*, pook and poll, or pluck and clip.
11 *Op. cit.*, p. 188.
12 The point is made by F. R. Leavis in an essay on "Literature and Society", in *Scrutiny*, Vol. XII, No. 1.

different as Shakespeare, Ben Jonson and George Herbert. Now when the common language is used by a deliberate artist the qualities inherent in the language are more sharply defined: attitudes and modes of judgment that may be taken for granted by contemporaries are realized and tested by being brought into relation with the writer's most intimate feelings for values in specific situations. Shakespeare is a storehouse of material. Consider, for example, the significance of the metaphors drawn from natural life and organic processes by means of which he so often defines his most important judgments of personal qualities and human relations.

> She that herself will sliver and disbranch
> From her material sap, perforce must wither
> And come to deadly use.

> For his bounty,
> There was no winter in it, an autumn 'twas
> That grew the more by reaping.

There is no question of his idealizing the natural at the expense of the specifically human, and there is certainly no appeal to "natural impulse" as an unquestioned standard: in the plays from which I have quoted essential values are defined by the interplay of very varied kinds of awareness, of which the "organic" metaphors represent only one. But it is equally certain that for the author of *The Winter's Tale* the relation of the highest human values to natural and instinctive life—of "grace" to "the red blood"—was a central preoccupation. The condition of his marvellous, life-long exploration of that relationship was an intimate inbred knowledge of the matrix of "nature" within which human life has developed. If that knowledge was fostered—as there seems no doubt it was—by the conditions of life in Elizabethan England, the plays themselves put us in possession of data of the greatest importance for an understanding of the relations of civilization and civilized values to the natural bases of society.

This question is too complex to be pursued further here. A simpler but no less instructive line of enquiry would start from Shakespeare's handling of social and political themes. What is notable here is the resolute refusal to reduce political personages to a category or social situations to a formula: what might appear as generalized issues are invariably presented in terms of the personal and specific. Indeed, in the early history plays, from *Richard III* and *King John* to *Henry V*, much of the humour and irony springs from the juxtaposition of the conventional, public view of affairs and the human actuality. We may note further that although rusticity and provincialism are often shown as ignorant and in need of correction, some of the most penetrating social criticism is made when representatives of the "local" world are brought into direct relation with high policy. In *Coriolanus,* the greatest of the "political" plays, which is also one of the great tragedies, the political is intimately related to the personal within the setting of a community that is vividly present in its concrete day-to-day activity. The rich complexity of attitude that the play embodies, springing as it does from a refusal to ignore any aspect of the actual in the interest of an "idea", makes the play a perpetual source of refreshment when we are in danger of thinking too consistently in terms of "politics" as a closed category. And implicit in the presentation of conflict, deepening the tragedy, is the reconciling conception of the state as an organic society, an extension of the natural bonds of human relationship.

Now Shakespeare's realist approach to politics, his sane grasp of the *ends* of public activity, were not simply the result of individual enquiry and intellectual speculation. Clarified, organized and given substance by his own genius, the social insight that his plays embody was itself a social product. In the townships and small rural communities of Elizabethan England there was none of the imper-sonality that characterizes the working of the modern state. Not only was economic dealing much more personal and direct, a large part of local government (both in its legal and more general sense) was in the hands of well-known members of the community : the individual was not yet submerged in the official.[13] In these small social units, therefore, "human problems can be truly perceived, which in larger social structures must more or less necessarily be sacrificed".[14] The intensely local life of Elizabethan England, by its very nature, prompted a constant reference of public activity to the sphere "beyond politics." So, too, the obvious need for mutual aid, if the life of the community was to be maintained, was at the foundation of the idea so pervasive in Shakespeare (and closely related to traditional social theory) that health within the state, the body politic, is a matter of the integration of different parts, different functions, different rights, into an organic whole. I suggest that to make our own the insights embodied in Shakespeare's plays is radically to improve our equipment for understanding the quality of the social life of his period and the bearing of this on some of our own social problems.

In these matters, let me repeat, there is not one single line of enquiry to be pursued, nor one single method to be applied. In the example I have just given, Shakespeare's plays will obviously not tell us all we need to know about the life of the Elizabethan community : they can only prompt new insights into the facts that may be revealed by the patient investigation of the historian. Literature, however, is also directly revealing of the social life from which it

13 Miss Campbell reminds us of how many of the services that are to-day profes-sionalized were in the older village community performed by neighbours for each other. *Op. cit.* pp. 382 ff.

14 Eli Heckscher, *Mercantilism,* Vol. I, p. 42. (Surely the last word of the quotation should be "distorted?")

springs. We may instance the Metaphysical poetry of the first half of the seventeenth century. Here the observation to start from is that Metaphysical poetry touches life at many points. I am not referring to subject-matter (though that is varied), but to the range of interest and awareness that is brought to bear on any "subject". We come from the poetry with a renewed awareness of the multiple nature of man, of the possibility—actualized in the best of the poems —of living simultaneously at many levels. In Donne's love poetry, for example, man—the actual experiencing individual—is felt as intimately enmeshed in the world of sense and instinct; and sense and passion are vividly expressed in their fresh immediacy. But in Donne there is always present the need to become *fully* aware of the immediate emotion, and the effort to apprehend—to grasp and realize—leads inevitably to the quickening of faculties so often only dimly present in the expression of sensation and feeling. In the best of his love poems there is active not only passion or affection, but a ranging and enquiring mind. Conversely, the most ecstatic experience is felt in terms "which sense may reach and apprehend". This is only another way of saying that in Donne thought, feeling and bodily sensation are intimately blended. And with this dimension of depth is a dimension of breadth : "the most heterogeneous ideas" are brought to a focus. The range of Donne's intellectual and worldly interests is a commonplace of criticism and it is because these interests are so vividly *there*—whether introduced directly or by way of simile and metaphor—that the greater poems of passion seem so solidly grounded.

Without overlooking the important differences from Donne, we can say something similar of George Herbert. Whereas Donne illuminates passion by play of mind, Herbert brings to the expression of his religious experience the familiar word of everyday things. But his homely imagery is not simply a form of expression; it is an index of habitual modes of thought and feeling in which the different aspects and different levels of his personal experience are brought into intimate relation to each other. An additional observation is that the stream of his personal experience—more clearly than Donne's—is fed from sources apparently remote in the social topography of the period. His poetry, with its intellectual cast and its tone of courtesy, is plainly the work of one who moves easily in the cultivated circles of his time; and the contemporary learning that he assimilates takes its place in a solid traditional education that respects, without being overawed by, the new science. But if Herbert is courtly and Metaphysical, he is also popular. He has an instinctive feeling for common speech— pithy, sententious and shrewd, summing up character in a concrete image :

> Then came brave Glory puffing by
> In silks that whistled, who but he?

And, as with Donne, his interests and the modes of his sensibility are integrated in a uniquely personal idiom.

What I am trying to do is to put into terms more immediately useful for my purpose the familiar conception of the Metaphysicals as possessing "a mechanism of sensibility that could devour any kind of experience". The later generation of these poets, apart from Marvell, had not the force of Donne or Herbert, but almost all the poets represented in Sir Herbert Grierson's well-known anthology express a vivid play of various interests that are felt as having an intimate bearing on each other. That is why the greater poems make such a disturbing, reverberating impact on the mind of the reader, and even some of the poems that appear slight on a first reading are found to have behind them a range and weight of experience: there is "the recognition, implicit in the expression of every experience, of other kinds of experience that are possible".

Now it seems to me that a positive distinctive quality common to half a dozen good poets and a number of competent and interesting ones, all writing within the same half-century, is not likely to be the result of a purely literary relationship to the founder of the "school", whose individual genius can be regarded as the sole source of his followers' idiom. It is much more likely that the distinctive note of Metaphysical poetry—the implicit recognition of the many-sidedness of man's nature—is in some ways socially supported; that—to borrow some phrases from a suggestive passage in Yeats's criticism—"unity of being" has some relation to a certain "unity of culture". Professor Grierson remarks, "It was only the force of Donne's personality that could achieve even an approximate harmony of elements so divergent as are united in his love-verses".[15] When we recognize the truth in this, as we must, we need to keep in mind also the complementary truth tersely expressed by Ben Jonson—"Rare poems ask rare friends".[16]

The tag from Jonson suggests where, as social historians, we should begin our enquiries. We need to know who the Metaphysical poets expected to be interested in their verses, who they met and at what levels, what were the functions, interests and traditions of those who composed their immediate circle. All these questions represent work still to be done. We can say in a general way, however, that the social milieu of the Metaphysical poets was aristocratic in tone, connecting in one direction (partly, but certainly not exclusively, through patronage) with the inner circles of the Court, in another with the universities and with the middle and upper ranks of the ecclesiastical, administrative and legal hierarchies, and in yet another with the prosperous merchant class represented by Izaak Walton and the Ferrars. Partly through local attachments and partly through the

15 *The Poems of John Donne,* Vol. II, Introduction, p. xlvii.
16 *To Lucy, Countess of Bedford, with M. Donne's Satires.*

country houses of the gentry, its members were moreover in touch with the life of rural England. Thus the most varied interests, the most varied functions in the national life, were brought into relation. Within this social group the poet was not simply a poet, the politician was not simply a politician. Sir Henry Wotton may be taken as a representative figure, and Wotton (as he is admirably presented in the *Life* by Mr. Logan Pearsall Smith) was a diplomat, courtier and scholar, an amateur of the new science, a minor poet and a friend of poets. When we consider together the literary and the historical evidence we are, I think, justified in concluding that the social milieu of the Metaphysical poets was one in which there was an *active* culture : there was "a current of ideas in the highest degree animating and nourishing to the creative power". Through this milieu the poets whose work brings so much of "the whole soul of man into activity" touched life at many points, for tradition and the actual social organization alike fostered a range of contacts with contemporary life that is, to say the least, rare in the later history of English literature. It is by a direct development from our interest in the poetry—and only *as* a development of that interest—that we find ourselves contemplating issues of this kind, which are, I think, in the highest degree relevant to the purposes of the social historian.

My last example will be brief and my deductions tentative, for I am painfully aware that I have not yet done the work that might allow me to speak with authority. I have recently been reading in the histories of two revolutions, written by men who took an active part in many of the events that they describe—Trotsky's *History of the Russian Revolution* and Clarendon's *History of the Rebellion in England*—and it occurs to me that the difference of method and approach in these two books is highly revealing and instructive, in ways not consciously intended by their authors. I am not concerned with the reliability of either Clarendon or Trotsky as historians, but with the interests and assumptions that underlie their methods of presenting their material. Trotsky is clearly the product of a civilization keenly conscious of scientific law. His vigorous intellect works in terms of masses and social forces, and the slightest fluctuation in the main course of events is caught and pinned into place as a logically necessary exception. Clarendon is weak where Trotsky is strong—in the diagnosis of the more impersonal movements of history : by the side of the more scientific historian he sometimes appears as naïve. What distinguishes his work is the vivid power with which he characterizes his main actors. Many of his character sketches display a skill in analysis analogous to that of a very good novelist. Even when we regard the two men simply as chroniclers of events it is plain that the balance of advantage does not lie entirely with the possessor of the more up-to-date equipment. If Clarendon sometimes mistakenly attributes representative acts to purely personal motives, in reading Trotsky we are constantly aware of the absence of the irrational, or non-rational, motives that certainly played a part in the actions he describes.[17] But it is when we consider the two men as representatives, or portents, that the differences become most revealing. Trotsky is the exponent of political will that masquerades as destiny or impersonal law. It is only because he can ignore so many of the varying impulses determining conduct that he can subsume all phenomena under certain abstract laws. As with some other revolutionaries, this partial blindness is connected with an autocratic habit of mind: you assert that the situation is simpler than it is, and then you try to make people conform to the decreed pattern. In other words, the inhuman characteristics of the new political type that Mr. Koestler has analysed in *Darkness at Noon* are already latent in the workings of Trotsky's mind. Clarendon, of course, was a "reactionary": at all events he was on the losing side. But what is shown by his firm grasp of the personal factor in history and his shrewd and subtle appraisal of character, is that he was the product of a society within which there was a highly developed sense of the person, a society for which personal and moral issues mattered, and which possessed a language in which these issues could be intelligently discussed. Clarendon's most intimate friend in youth was Falkland; and the circle that Falkland gathered about him at Great Tew—that "university in a purer air"—was of men notable for the humanity that informed their extensive learning.[18] It is to the especial significance of this circle that the *History of the Rebellion* —regarded not simply as a history, but as a document of the moral sensibility of the age—may direct our attention. When we are told by a Marxist historian that Clarendon "is hardly an impartial witness. . . . Of course he wanted to boost the old régime", we reply that this is a gross over-simplification; for it entirely ignores the qualities, inherent in Clarendon's handling of his material, that were to contribute to the more lasting achievements of civilization long after the political cause that he supported was lost.

With this I must put away my samples, protesting, like Ben Jonson's mountebank, that "I have nothing to sell, little or nothing to sell". All I wish to recommend is a certain way of looking at things, an approach to social history and the study of society that starts from and keeps constantly in mind the values embodied in literature. This approach is infinitely flexible, and (let me repeat) if it demands literary tact and taste, the active exercise of the sensibility, it also demands the co-operation of other and different disciplines. That is

17 As an analyst of crowd behaviour he could have learnt something from the author of *I Promessi Sposi*.

18 It included Sheldon, Earle, Hales and Chillingworth. Matthew Arnold's essay on Falkland (in *Mixed Essays*) is a valuable commentary on Falkland and his circle. See also J. A. R. Marriott's *The Life and Times of Lucius Cary, Viscount Falkland*.

why it seems to me of especial importance that it should be cultivated within a university; for here, if anywhere, is an opportunity for different kinds of understanding to meet in fruitful intercourse. Each kind of understanding has necessarily its own discipline, and no one would wish to see weakened any of the hard-won special methods by which men arrive at different aspects of the truth. But a discipline that remains always, as it were, self-enclosed, that loses its connexions with the wider human field in which we try to find an answer to the question, "Knowledge for what?"—such a discipline become ultimately sterile. If there is one truth more than another that has forced itself on me in my own ponderings of these matters it is that civilization is essentially co-operative. A university is, or should be, a civilization in microcosm; and it is in the mutual interplay of different disciplined interests that "the idea of a university" is realized.

On the Eve
Edward Shils

from

Twentieth Century, vol. 167, no. 999, 1960.

On the Eve

Edward Shils

I

IT was bound to come, sooner or later. Once Britain was impelled, reluctantly and slowly, to move forward from being the model of Edwardian modernity to being a lively up-to-date country, contemporary in every respect, sociology was bound to find first a foothold, then a niche and now a whole platform. It is not that Britain did not know about sociology. In a sense, sociology got started in Britain – as is often emphasized in circles where such claims constitute the main activity of sociologists – but like modern industrial technology it had to be taken elsewhere to be improved and developed. The sober attempts of a small group of dourly noble reformers and administrators in the nineteenth century to find out the real 'condition of England' were the first of their kind in history. For the first time men sought to arrive at a judgement on their own society through the disciplined and direct study of their fellow citizens, by observing them, and by speaking with them and by the systematic recording of these observations and conversations. Sociology has certainly grown since the Poor Law Commissioners, Henry Mayhew and Charles Booth, but their mode of learning about their own society is still essential to sociology. Contemporary sociology might be more knowledgeable, more imaginative, more ingenious than they were, but it would not be what it is without them. After this great surge which ran over two-thirds of a century, British sociological powers seemed to exhaust themselves. In France and Germany, powerful and learned minds thought about the nature of society and tried to envisage modern society within the species of all the societies known to history. In America, sociologists busied themselves in villages and in the city streets, carrying on the work of Booth, finding illustrations of the ideas of Simmel, Tönnies, and Durkheim and developing a few of their own. In Britain, however, for nearly fifty years, while anthropology and economics flourished as in no other country, sociology gathered the soft dust of libraries, bathed in the dim light of ancestral idolatry and produced only the grit of resentment. Here and there during these socio-logically sterile decades, there was a momentary pulse of life but it never spread and the air of death soon reasserted itself. Graham Wallas on politics, Tawney on the culture of class, Hogben and Ginsberg on social selection gave off some sparks which no one ever nurtured into even a small flame. Outside the London School of Economics, sociology was scarcely even allowed to touch the handle of the university door. In the half-world of journalism and politics, an odd little series called *Fact* and a wild gypsy crusade called Mass Observation lived briefly and passed away unnoticed and unmourned.

Now sociology is returning. It has become an O K thing. Since the Second World War, it has become established in more than half of the modern universities. Oxford, rolling with the attack, at the end of the 'forties created a lectureship, which, with skill bred of long practice, was then cramped in cold inhospitality. Cambridge is yielding to the pressure of external opinion, to an internal movement of young and middle-aged Turks and to the enthusiasm of undergraduates, who, inspired by their own liveliness and some American paper-backs, have been carrying on a sociological *guerilla*. The popular press publishes the results of sociological enquiries and would publish more if there were more. *The Times* offers the lofty patronage of its leader columns and its news pages. *The Guardian* makes its turnover available to sociologists. *The Spectator* reviews their work with kindness and *The New Left Review* regards the 'right kind' of sociology as its charge. So the times are changing, and, in the madness of this age, sociologists in a small way join the ranks of the beneficiaries of change, like women, Negroes, working-men, young people and the other outcasts of more spacious times.

II

Why did sociology fail to establish itself in Britain during the first half of the present century except in the furtive, half-starved way which we know? The simplest answer would be to say that sociology was not good enough to fare better. If the world were a scene of justice, that answer would be acceptable. It is not, however, a scene of justice and to accept that answer is to take, as true, the wall-eyed beliefs of those who defend much that is equally nonsensical and less important. It would be to share the dreary and well-polished complacency of Oxford and Cambridge and to exonerate them from their responsibility for its intellectual backwardness and its institutional feebleness. It is Oxford and Cambridge who have hidden themselves in the wood pile. The smugness of Oxford and Cambridge, their near-monopoly of the cleverest and liveliest young people, and their intellectual tyranny must bear primary responsibility for the retrograde condition of sociology in Great Britain. How could sociologists come into existence in Britain when in Oxford and Cambridge, sociologists were looked upon as pariahs, as no better than Americans or Germans? How could sociology establish itself as a subject worthy of a free-born Englishman when it was a product of German abstruseness and American indiscriminateness, when its practitioners in England were often awkward foreigners or restive lower-class boys and when its chief representative was the London School of Economics.

Why were Oxford and Cambridge so obstinate? To some extent, they were right in their assertion that sociology is no science, and that its works are often painfully inelegant in presentation. But that is not anywhere near the whole story, nor at all close to the root of the matter. The central fact is that the highest type of British intellectual – the Oxford and Cambridge intellectual of the first half of this century – is a man of acute intelligence and fastidious standards exercised within the constraints of a narrow imagination and an undeveloped heart. Sociology is a study which has for its ultimate object the ramification of the logic of the heart. The narrow imagination and the undeveloped heart cannot cope with the logic of the heart as it beats in daily life and in times of crisis.

Sociology is not at present and is not likely to become in the near future a subject for intellectual sharpshooters. Too many points can be scored off sociology by those who regard intellectual activity not as discovery but a game in which the prizes go for rigour and elegance of proof, and for proving the other fellow wrong. Discoveries are not made in this way, least of all self-discoveries and the discoveries of the self in one's fellow-man. The tutorial system with its emphasis on concise argument and its suppression of the sympathetic understanding of overtones has been a bulwark against the emergence of the sociological way of groping towards the light. The progress of the pure sciences in Oxford and Cambridge in the present century, of economic theory and latterly of analytic and ordinary language philosophy with their rigorous procedures, subtle and precise distinctions and their utter aridity of mind were also uncongenial to the fumbling and inchoate ways of sociology and its frequent loss of itself in winding side-tracks or in the empyrean.

The real difficulty lay, however, in the undeveloped heart, the inability to embrace the condition and state of mind of one's fellow man through contact and imagination. Sometimes this inability justified itself through respect for the other man's privacy, sometimes it took the forms of sheer indifference or political zeal. Whatever its manifestation, it expressed a narrow range of imagination, a desiccated capacity for empathy with the dispositions of other human beings in one's own society. It was all right, from this point of view, for an Englishman to go to study the Africans in the bush or the natives of the Pacific islands – but even there the chief of those British scholars who did so were from the Antipodes, from Poland and from the Russian Pale via South Africa. (The most distinguished English anthropologist of his time lived in one variety of exile or another for most of his career.) Englishmen did study the natives of the Empire but few of them did it as much or with the penetration of the 'foreigners' like Malinowski, Gluckman, Fortes, Firth, Schapera, *et al.* To study the natives of Britain was another matter. It was almost unthinkable for an able-bodied and well-educated Englishman in his right mind to study the people of his own country. Mr Tom Harrison and Professor Charles Madge were thought to be madcaps for starting Mass Observation, and indeed they had to be to go so far from the boundaries of the academically permissible in the 1930s. (Only the Pole, Malinowski, extended a friendly hand to them.)

The cliché ordinarily adduced to explain the absence of British sociology is that the United Kingdom was until very recently a traditionally stable society which raised no fundamental problems, like Germany or France in the nineteenth century; it therefore did not require sociology to help it to ruminate on its problems. There might be a little truth in this cliché – but not much. It was not that the British social structure and its stability raised no questions; after all, there was a very lively public discussion of British institutions by politicians and journalists throughout the nineteenth and twentieth centuries. It was rather that once Oxford and Cambridge were established as intellectually respectable institutions, i.e. after the Royal Commissions on the Universities, the academic élite of Britain were resolute in their refusal to raise questions about the life of their fellow-countrymen. Adventurous travellers, colonial and Indian civil servants could be produced in plenty but not persons willing as amateurs to explore the lives of their own fellow countrymen. There have been, it is true, since late in the last century, a few university missionaries to the working classes, who were willing to live in 'settlements' in working class areas, and to offer instruction to members of the working classes. Even these worthy men have been put off by 'darkest England'. There was an inhibition about contact, a shyness, and at bottom, a plain deficiency of empathic capacity.

In the 'thirties of the present century, there was a slight animation of sociological interest, a few pieces of reportage of the life of the unemployed. The best of them – Bakkes's *The Unemployed Man* was, however, the work of an American, and Orwell's *The Road to Wigan Pier* was the work of an extraordinary personality who had contracted out of the British upper-middle class life and had never been to a university. At that time the London School of Economics was the only academic centre of sociological studies and it was no more a nursery of the power of sympathetic understanding than it is at present.

The late Karl Mannheim created a stir at the L S E in the 'thirties among churchmen, literary men of a Christian bent and publicists. The sociology which he promulgated did not involve contact with the lives of ordinary persons. It was a grandiose disquisition on epochal trends and the enthusiasm which it called forth among students sent very few of them into the field. (I do not recall that there was one native Briton among those who did a little field work under his sponsorship.)

There were many German refugees at the School of Economics who were attracted by sociology, but they were also in their special German fashion attracted by 'der englische Gentleman'; those who could, tried to pass as such, which meant that they became more British than the announcers on the B B C, they took to briar pipes and The Times and they would not be seen dead with sociology. The others whose appetites for sociology were stronger or more adventurous went to the United States; those who were left were the less successful, the W E A lecturers with their worn briefcases, who were scarcely good advertisements for the dignity of sociology.

When, after the war, the London School of Economics expanded, and sociology expanded with it, the offspring of foreigners, and those who had come to Britain as the children of refugees supplied a surprisingly large proportion of the students of sociology. They were timorous, even if often talkative outsiders; they lacked the self-confidence to do something which was not generally acknowledged and yet they clung to their subject with a touching affection. They were part of a larger group of recruits to sociology – in the second half of the 'forties – who came from the working and black-coated classes. These often gentle and sweet, sometimes felinely distrustful young people, for the most part felt themselves ill at ease, uncertain and unconfident of their ability to do something of which their elders and their examiners disapproved. They too felt themselves to be 'outsiders', and a natural shyness was accentuated by a sense of remoteness from the pillars of British society. Only very few of these were able to avoid the defiant suspicion which marks the descendants of Leonard Bast; some of those who succeeded are at present the best hopes of British sociology. The others fell by the wayside; insufficient prospects of employment, insufficient talents, insufficient encouragement from their elders, the indifference of a frightening environment overcame their perhaps too passive curiosity. Yet this generation was the first generation of a real British sociology. They deserve a loving if belated salute from one of their old teachers.

Bit by bit, in the decade and a half since the Second War the provinces have been populated. Professorships have been created and filled at Leeds, Nottingham, Birmingham; lectureships nearly everywhere. Liverpool had already had a substantial department of social science teaching and research under the direction of Professor Simey and it has continued to grow. The London School of Economics consolidated its cheerless imperium and exiled to the provinces its few graduates with genuine curiosity about British society and a warm-hearted willingness to make contact with living human beings. Yet, somehow, despite its expansion, academic sociology has not flourished in Britain. A number of modestly undertaken local surveys, some interesting work on educational selection, a judicious study of children and television, an austere review of social mobility in Britain, a study of the black-coated worker made, in the largest assemblage of black-coated workers in the world, without a single interview, a few suggestive surveys of university students, some solid studies of Negro immigrants and dock thefts in Liverpool, began to dot the map, but still the sociological study of British society has not caught on. (There are two sociological reviews in Great Britain, each issue filled with articles, but one is startled to see how few of them deal realistically, or even at all, with contemporary British society.) In general, therefore, the academic establishment of sociology in the modern universities had not succeeded in overcoming the handicaps to which we have referred.

The practice of sociology outside the universities has been no more successful. The Tavistock Institute of Human Relations began after the war with a staff of unusual brilliance and a remarkably diversified and rich experience in the Army, but it has never succeeded in exerting any influence in the world of academic sociology. At first, it was the object of awed inquisitiveness and malicious gossip; as it settled down to a comfortable career of consultation and research on industrial and administrative problems, it lost its charisma, and therewith its power to disturb. The Nuffield Foundation and other charitable trusts have sporadically supported social research, inside the universities and out, without dramatic consequences.

III

The present interest in sociology in Great Britain owes much of its stimulation to persons working outside the benefits of the system of British university sociology. We may mention in rapid order Michael Young and his staff, none of whom had academic sociological training and most of whose work is done without even the friendliness of academic sociology; Professor Richard Titmuss, who has had no formal academic training and who is officially the head of the department of social work at the London School of Economics; and Richard Hoggart and Raymond Williams, who probably had scarcely heard of sociology when they wrote the two books which have been so much discussed and so much drawn into the argument for the need for sociology.

Michael Young stands in the tradition of the bold amateur who does what impulse and imagination dictate, regardless of what the guardians of the official view require. He was the first of those Labourites who renounced the tired phrases of inherited socialist doctrine and sought contact with reality by other roads. Sociology was the road he chose to bring him into intimate relationship with contemporary society.

Professor Titmuss represents two unique British traditions, the private scholar, and the public servant who seeks to clarify, criticize and guide public policy in the light of systematic empirical study. In a way, he represents a sophisticated and deepened return to the tradition of the Webbs, the Poor Law Commissioners and the great Blue Books.

The preoccupation of the New Left with sociology has more resemblance to Michael Young's sociology than to Richard Titmuss's. They too are fed up with the clichés of socialist thought; but unlike Michael Young, the clichés they are struggling against are Marxian and not just Labourite. And they are, unlike Michael Young, a little more committed to a solution. Although they are critical of Marxism they also want to preserve as much as they can. For them, Professor C. Wright Mills is the man, and accordingly not much that is fruitful for the understanding of contemporary Britain can be expected from them. But there are others in 'the New Left' who are not so much interested in saving their mind's face and who really want to understand what intrigues and disturbs them. They still have their strong political interests but they are open enough, honest enough, and humane enough to be curious. It is among them that some of the omens of good fortune for British sociology should be sought.

The reception in intellectual circles, of the books of the Institute of Community Studies, of Hoggart's *The Uses of Literacy*, and of the other works which make up the sociological renaissance of the past few years has no single explanation. In part and perhaps fundamentally it is a product of the fact that, if Britain is not becoming truly democratic socially, its intellectuals are at least beginning to develop some deeper sense of affinity with the sectors of society which exist outside Oxford, Cambridge, the Civil Service, the Church of England

and the House of Commons. This extension of awareness has, to some extent, arisen from the increased numbers of offspring of the working and lower middle classes, who, having passed through universities, and entered the civil service and the learned professions, have carried with them some memories of life in the outer zones of British society. The achievement of a more widely shared affluence has made for greater visibility of the lower classes; their way of life and their pleasures have simply become more noticeable to the educated. They themselves appear more often in districts of the large towns into which lower-class persons did not previously enter, their shops attract the eye by their brightness and their fullness. Then too, television has made the intellectuals much more sensitive to the existence of the lower classes. As in the United States, the pleasures, the tastes and the outlook of the previously excluded classes force themselves into the field of attention of the educated. More important than any of this is the growth of the sense of affinity, of the extension of the capacity for empathy.

IV

Now what are the prospects that these present whispers will turn into voices and that the voices will gain coherence and articulation? It might seem ridiculous in view of the present sterility of much of British academic sociology to say that it depends on what happens in the universities. Still, it is probably true.

The progress of sociology in Britain rests on its effective establishment in the two ancient universities. This does not just appear ridiculous; it is also unpleasant to acknowledge the strategic importance of these institutions which have not, by their conduct with regard to sociology, deserved to enjoy such a crucial position. The fact, none the less, remains. The older universities still get the cleverest and most imaginatively daring students and they confer self-confidence on them, even if they did not quite have it when they came up. The modern universities still get the sweet, shy, blanched children, the awkward, the angular, deferential, resentful, hard working, intelligent and often very gifted. They are frequently a bit uneasy and their uneasiness is not relieved by the sense that they are members of great and highly respected universities – which they often are. Indeed their teachers' inclination to look on them as the visible evidence of their own exile from the golden triangle of Oxford, Cambridge, and London, only reinforces the students' vague sense of being cave-dwelling outcastes. With this state of mind, little genuinely fruitful sociology can be carried on. Truthful sociology cannot be done effectively by those who feel alien to their own society, who feel themselves cast out by it and who also feel that the subject they are studying is looked down upon. It will take some time for this attitude to die out because it is deeply engrained.

In the meantime, sociology will have to seek its recruits among persons who are not so cripplingly afflicted. The students who come up to the ancient universities seem not to be so afflicted by this lack of self-esteem. Self-esteem is not, however, the sole requirement for doing sociology, it is just one of them. The imaginative feeling for patterns of life and outlook other than one's own is also a necessity and this frequently is not nurtured by the tone of intelligent complacency which the ancient universities foster in their pupils. None the less, the superior intellectual quality of the undergraduates of Oxford and Cambridge gives these two universities a great asset, were they to take seriously the cultivation of sociological studies.

Sociology does not require for its progress a whole social class, or an entirely new breed of men. It only needs a few hundred people at a time, perhaps only a thousand in a quarter of a century. Even in a land of frozen and contracted hearts, it certainly should be possible for several thousand to be found.

Sociology requires not only curiosity, openness of imagination and high intelligence, it also requires decent institutional sponsorship and patronage. The modern universities have, thus far, done practically nothing to provide this. Oxford, having grudgingly created the lectureship more than a decade ago, then, as if by design prevented it from becoming effective. Sociology failed at Oxford on its early trials, not because Oxford has such wonderfully high standards to which sociology as it stands at present could not attain. It failed because Oxford was not interested in its success. The subject made no progress in the syllabus. Oxford now has the chance to start again and it remains to be seen what it will do. Cambridge too has launched itself upon the sea of sociology, but at present it has neither vessels nor crew. Its earnestness of intention is still to be tried. The conditions of its launching do, however, seem considerably more propitious than they were at Oxford a decade ago.

For sociology to establish itself at the older universities it will have to cope with the prejudices of the custodians of the longer-settled subjects and their competition for the students' time and attention. Students have to take examinations and they cannot afford to spend very much time on subjects in which they will not be examined. And to get the subject accepted on the degree syllabus will require that its representatives not only be able teachers and investigators but that they also be skilful academic politicians with the good connections which politicians need in any sphere of life, not least in universities. It is indispensable, therefore, that the sociologists be completely *persona grata*. They must be Fellows of esteemed colleges. They should be British. The sociologist who is a graduate of the university, where he is teaching and conducting his research, will enjoy additional political advantages in the representation of his subject. They should also be *sociologists*, as good as the present state of the subject allows.

The recent triumphs of sociology at Cambridge are not necessarily enduring triumphs. The friends of sociology at Cambridge should remember that most triumphs leave behind aggrieved feelings and hopes of revenge, and that it is quite possible that they do so at Cambridge too.

A victory on paper is only the beginning and it would be a mistake to think the matter can rest there. The Visiting Professorship of Social Theory at Cambridge, which at first seemed to be the opening of the door to sociology, turned out in the end to resemble a victory for the patient wisdom of its enemies. Could not the present situation be of a piece with its predecessor?

When we ponder the proximate academic future of British sociology, we must never omit the economists from our reflections. The heirs and the constructors of a great intellectual tradition, they do not, with a few exceptions, find sociology to their taste. Their experience of the Marshall lectures given by Professor Talcott Parsons did not cause them to reconsider their original views. Quite to the contrary! Its sloppiness and vagueness in comparison with the elegance and precision of their own subject, and its un-Britishness, all make for a distrustful or contemptuous attitude towards sociology. Then, too, sociologists are competitors with economics for what is going. The economists already showed their skill in snaffling any loose money when they made off with the funds provided by the Treasury on the recommendation of the Report of the Clapham Committee on Social and Economic Research. Is there any reason to think that their eyes or hands have lost their cunning since then? Their current amiability towards sociology might well be genuine; if it is, then sociology will certainly benefit from close association with a subject of such high standards in research and analysis.

The resistances of Oxford and Cambridge are strengthened by the bearing of official British sociology in the modern universities. The contempt and condescension of those external to sociology in the academic world are equalled by the rancour and rivalry of some of the sociologists and their satellites. Some of them, quite apart from their own intellectual powers – which are in a few cases quite outstanding – are as great enemies of the development of their subject as those who are more avowedly on guard against it. A subject validates itself in part by its representatives. What can be thought of a field in which, as in the case of British sociology, each man's hand is raised against each other man, and in which it is raised especially maliciously against those who do not fit an uncertain 'party line'. Of course, boorishness and cliqueishness are not necessarily incompatible with intellectual creativity – witness, for example, the professors of the German universities in their greatest age. Creativity is not, however, the accompaniment of these qualities in contemporary British sociology. The prejudice which it does to British sociology is not offset by the general insistence on the creation of more chairs in other universities and the allocation of more funds for sociological research.

v

The present impetus towards sociology derives from the enthusiasm of some exceptional young students and the congeniality of educated public opinion. Are they strong enough to overcome the prejudices of the older academic generation? The vagueness and vastness of the expectations of the well-wishers of sociology contain seeds of instability. Their expectations are of a nature which lays them open to easy disappointment. They have been nurtured on William H. Whyte's *The Organization Man*, David Riesman's *The Lonely Crowd*, C. Wright Mills's *White Collar* and *The Power Elite*, Michael Young's and Peter Willmotts's *Family and Kinship in East London*, Peter Townsend's *The Family Life of Old People*, and

Richard Hoggart's *The Uses of Literacy*. These, in their various ways, are interesting books presenting material or putting forward attractive interpretations of contemporary American and British societies. They are only a tiny fragment of what makes up sociology to-day and it is entirely possible that once students and general readers learn about the rest of the unwieldy mass of sociology, their interest will moderate. There is much that is technical in sociology, much that is crude and much that is trivial. It will take expert guidance for the novice to make his way among the scattered oases of sociological literature.

One wonders whether the present favour of educated public opinion will continue to shine on sociology. That favour is largely a phenomenon of the weeklies and the superior Sunday papers. The enthusiasms of these organs are notoriously labile; they wax and wane from issue to issue, from month to month. Journalists must not bore their readers and they do not wish to bore themselves. They like mild and fresh sensations, their minds wander.

Fortunately for sociology, however, the congeniality of educated opinion is not solely a function of editorial policies. It is also a product of a genuine turn of the imaginative tide of British intellectual life. The novel of 'exquisite sensibility' as we know it from Virginia Woolf, E. M. Forster, Elizabeth Jane Howard, Rosamond Lehmann, L. P. Hartley, Denton Welch and numerous others has moved over to make space for a more adventurous, more widely ranging imagination, no less sensitive and deeper in its sympathies. The novels of Colin MacInnes, Malcolm Bradbury, Alan Sillitoe, Robert Kee, Philip Callow, Kingsley Amis, John Wain, *et al.*, and the plays of John Osborne, Arnold Wesker, Bernard Kops and their like express an opening of the British intellectual imagination which had been lacking for some decades. The incorporation into English literature of writers from the periphery, Dan Jacobson, Doris Lessing, Samuel Selvon, V. S. Naipaul, Victor Anant – and they are not alone – bring evidence that the Welfare State and the worldwide growth of a more inclusive social sensitivity have not left British intellectual life untouched. It is in the growth of this new sensitivity, this greater openness to the previously hidden experiences of fellow men, that the possible foundations for a relatively enduring establishment of the sociological outlook may be perceived.

VI

The fate of sociology in Britain depends however, as much on sociology itself and on the sociologists themselves, as it does on the more external events of academic machinery and the state of educated public opinion. The question is whether sociology can deliver the goods and what kinds of goods it can deliver? The best thing about sociology is its marvellously interesting subject-matter. Thus far, sociology has not lived at the level of its subject-matter.

To-day, seen from a distance, sociology is almost as exciting intellectually as Marxism was twenty-five years ago. Its ancient subject matter has the fascination of novelty. Its technique and its theory are capable of offering an intellectual challenge – not in their present state as demanding or as rewarding as the problems of physics or economic theory or linguistics, but the experience of contact with the subject-matter compensates for their shortcomings.

The first task of British sociology is to study British society, not just its Negroes or widows or its juvenile delinquents, although these are very worthwhile topics. It has to study how people live in every class and generation, in representative occupations, in towns and villages, in offices, workshops, churches, parties, pubs, and clubs. There is no substitute for direct contact through intimate interviewing and first-hand and prolonged observation. Obviously, other sources have to be drawn upon – historical writings, public records, personal documents, officially gathered statistics. Large-scale surveys using questionnaires and semi-skilled interviewers – such as are used by public opinion polling organizations – will some-times be in order, but nothing can replace intimate fieldwork as a means of training sociologists and of obtaining realistic knowledge. A new régime of British sociology which does not give primacy to intimate and intensive interviewing might just as well spare itself the pains of birth. Of course, sociology should not be confined to such work – it should reach back into history and far out past the boundaries of Britain. The sensibility which reaches beyond contemporary Britain will be enormously enriched by the disciplined, first-hand study of British society. The general sociological theory which guides historical, comparative and macrosociological studies will be much better for being tested and tempered by empirical studies in contemporary Britain.

In its self-improvement, British sociology will do well to outgrow its preoccupation with America and American sociology. British sociology to-day suffers excessive intellectual dependence, coupled with writhing discomfort. Hence the eagerness to applaud every bit of derogatory nonsense which is purveyed about America and American sociology. This dependence will end when British sociologists have become sufficiently interested in their own society to be drawn to and guided by its problems, and this they will do when they really feel at home in it.

The qualities which make a good sociologist are moral and psychological as well as intellectual. Good training will make a naturally inclined sociologist better. It can make a person who is not a sociologist by natural inclination into a more useful hewer of wood and drawer of water. British sociology cannot afford that luxury. Hence, selection will be as important as training. Whether an aspirant to a sociological career feels at home the length and breadth of his country and in every class is as important a criterion for a selection committee to bear in mind, as his erudition, his critical powers and his speed of response.

The problem posed by our discussion of the future of sociology in Britain is really a problem of the development of British society. There is a circle in British society which is created and maintained by mirrors but which excludes and hurts those who think they are on the outside. Can that circle fade from consciousness, and from unconsciousness, and therewith from existence. Can the offspring of the poor and the middle classes cease to feel their exclusion from the mirage which through widespread belief is endowed with reality? Can the snobbery, of which the degrading, allegedly playful preoccupation a few years ago with 'U' and 'Non-U' was only one of many instances, dissolve so that Britain can become a society? Can it dissolve sufficiently and can the British heart develop sufficiently over the obstacles of condescension and fear, both masquerading as genuine dignity and privacy, for British sociologists to feel that they are one with their society? Can they cease to be timorous, startled, captious, carping, overwhelmed outsiders and come to feel that their society is open to them and that they can accordingly study it through sympathy? The slow and tentative movement of British sensibility in this direction is the best hope of British sociology, and without it, chairs, departments, syllabi and grants will be useless.

Literature and Sociology: In Memory of Lucien Goldmann
Raymond Williams

from

New Left Review, 67, 1971.

Reprinted by permission of the author and *New Left Review*.

Raymond Williams

Literature and Sociology:

in memory of Lucien Goldmann

Last spring Lucien Goldmann came to Cambridge and gave two lectures. It was an opportunity for many of us to hear a man whose work we had welcomed and respected. And he said that he liked Cambridge: to have trees and fields this near to lecture-rooms. I invited him and he agreed to come back again this year. More particularly we agreed to exchange our current work directly, for we were both aware of the irony that the short physical distance between England and France converts, too often, to a great cultural distance, and especially at the level of detail. And then, in the autumn, he died, at the age of 57. The beginning of a project had to revert to print, as must perhaps always finally happen. But first I want to remember him directly, as an act of respect and as an active acknowledgment of what I believe is now necessary: a bringing together and a discussion of work and ideas occurring in very different traditions but nevertheless sharing many common positions and concerns. My regret, of course, is that he cannot be here to take part in the dialogue*. For the manner of his lectures in Cambridge was precisely dialogue: in a sense to my surprise, having read only his published writings, which are marked by a certain defining and systematic rigour.

I think many people have now noticed the long-term effects of the specific social situation of British intellectuals: a situation which is changing but with certain continuing effects. In humane studies, at least, and with mixed results, British thinkers and writers are continually pulled back towards ordinary language: not only in certain rhythms and in choices of words, but also in a manner of exposition which can be called unsystematic but which also represents an unusual consciousness of an immediate audience: a sharing and equal-standing community, to which it is equally possible to defer or to reach out. I believe that there are many positive aspects of this habitual manner, but I am just as sure that the negative aspects are serious: a willingness to share, or at least not too explicitly to challenge, the consciousness of the group of which the thinker and writer—his description as intellectual raises the precise point—is willingly or unwillingly but still practically a member. And while this group, for so long, and of course especially in places like Cambridge, was in effect and detail a privileged and at times a ruling class, this pull towards ordinary language was often, is often, a pull towards current consciousness: a framing of ideas within certain polite but definite limits.

It is not at all surprising to me, having observed this process, to see so many students, since the early 'sixties, choosing to go instead to intellectuals of a different kind. In sociology, where we have been very backward—indeed in many respects an undeveloped country—there are, of course, other reasons. But the same thing has happened in literary studies, where for half a century, and in Cambridge more clearly than anywhere, there has been notable and powerful work. A sense of certain absolute restrictions in English thought, restrictions which seemed to link very closely with certain restrictions and deadlocks in the larger society, made the search for alternative traditions, alternative methods, imperative. Of course all the time there was American work: in what appeared the same language but outside this particular English consensus. Theory, or at least system, seemed attractively available. And most American intellectuals, for good or ill, seemed not to have shared this particular integration with a non-intellectual class. Complaints that a man explaining his life's work, in as precise a way as he could, was not instantly comprehensible, in a clubbable way, to someone who had just happened to drop in from his labour or leisure elsewhere, seemed less often to arise.

And it was then noticeable that in certain kinds of study the alternative manner became attractive and was imitated: at times substantially, in the long reach for theory; at times more superficially, in certain habits of procedural abstraction: the numbered heads and sub-heads of an argument; definitions attaining the sudden extra precision of italics; the highly specialised and internal vocabulary. Everybody except the

*Text of a lecture given at the Lady Mitchell Hall, Cambridge, on 26 April 1971.

English, it suddenly seemed, thought or at least wrote in this way. To rely on other kinds of order and emphasis was a provincial foible. A break with the English bourgeoisie, in particular, seemed to demand these alternative procedures and styles, as one of the few practical affiliations that could be made at once and by an act of will.

But really the situation was more complicated. It needed Chomsky, in his specialist work a very rigorous thinker, to remind us how easily the abstract methods and vocabulary of a particular social science could be used to achieve another kind of consensus, with a fundamentally abstract ruling class and administration. As in one of his examples, the bombing of refugee peasants in Vietnam could be described, in a show of procedure, as accelerated urbanization. Very aware of this danger, which does not have to be called but can be called dehumanising and mystifying, English thinkers could easily, too easily, fall back on their older habits, professing not to understand abstractions like a power structure though they could traditionally understand a microcosm, or not to understand reification though they could understand the objective correlative, or not to know mediation although they knew catharsis. Certain received habits of mind, a very particular and operative selection of traditional and pre-democratic concepts and adjustments, acquired, by what one has to call alchemy, the status of concrete, or of minute particulars. Yet the more clearly one saw this happening, the more clearly one had also to see the genuinely mixed results of a social situation in which intellectuals had little choice but to define themselves as a separate profession: able then to see more clearly into the society which would appoint but not embrace them, acquiring a separate and self-defining language and manner which at least was not limited by the more immediate prejudices and encouragements, but was nevertheless a language and a manner of the monograph and the rostrum: a blackboard numbering, a dictated emphasis, a pedagogic insistence on repeatable definitions: habits which interacted strangely with the genuine rigour of new and bold inquiries and terms.

Problems of Theory

Lucien Goldmann, a thinker trained in this major continental tradition, born in Bucharest and moving to Vienna, to Geneva, to Brussels, to Paris, had at once this separated mobility and this impersonality: very clearly in the style of his work. But it was very interesting to me, having read his work presented in those familiar ways, to hear the voice of a different mind: mobility in that other sense—the quick emotional flexibility, the varying stares at his audience, the pacing up and down of this smiling man in his open-necked shirt, more concerned with a cigarette than with notes but concerned above all with the challenge of his argument, a challenge that evidently included himself. There was a sense of paradox: of amused but absolute seriousness, of provisional but passionate conviction; a kind of self-deprecating and self-asserting boldness. Perhaps the paradox was Goldmann in Cambridge, but it may be more.

For I think we cannot doubt that in sociology and in literary studies we are living through a paradox, and this presents itself to us in many different ways but most evidently as a problem of style. The basic form of the paradox is this: that we need theory, but that certain limits of existence and consciousness prevent us from getting it, or at least making certain of it; and yet the need for theory keeps pressing on our minds and half-persuading us to accept kinds of pseudo-theory which as a matter of fact not only fail to satisfy us but often encourage us to go on looking in the wrong place and in the wrong way. An idea of theory suggests laws and methods, indeed a methodology. But the most available concept of laws, and from it the most available organized methods, come in fact, as Goldmann reminded us, from studies that are wholly different in kind: from the physical sciences, where the matter to be studied can be held to be objective, where value-free observations can then be held to be possible, as a foundation for disinterested research, and so where the practice of hard, rigorous, factual disciplines can seem—indeed can impressively be—feasible.

And then I think it is clear that the existence, in works of literature, of material so laden with values that if we do not deal directly with them we have literally nothing to deal with, leads to an obvious crisis in the whole context of a university which defines itself, more and more, in terms of rigorous, specialist, disinterested disciplines. It is hardly surprising that in England it has been literary critics, and above all Leavis, who have led the opposition to what Goldmann calls 'scientism'. The record in sociology has been less clear and, I would say, less honourable. For of course it is possible in social studies, by acts of delimitation, isolation, definition, to produce or project certain kinds of objective material which can be held to be value-free because none of the connections to the rest of experience or to other kinds of relationship are made. Even values themselves can be studied in this way, as in a more or less sophisticated opinion polling: that while a percentage believes this another percentage believes that, and this result, until the next time, is the end of the research. And I wouldn't want to say that the results of these kinds of work mightn't contribute, very valuably, to the central business of social studies, which because it must deal with men in social relationships and in history must, whether it knows it or not, deal with active values and with choices, including the values and choices of the observer. All I am saying is that in the end it is this centre that is absent, or is insufficiently present; and that from this very default, compounded by the historical failure to develop British social studies in any adequate way (and we remember the difficulty of getting them established in Cambridge at all), the claim began to be made that in literature, in English, where values and their discussion were explicit, a real centre, a humane centre, might be found.

But this is where the central problem of the relation between literature and social studies at once arises. We must not think, by the way, that in literary as in social studies the pursuit of the falsely objective wasn't undertaken. The classical languages, and by hasty derivation their literatures, could be studied by a rigorous internal methodology, which has had its effect on nearly all literary studies. The study of other languages in the same spirit, by isolated set texts and the like, has similarly been inserted into the process of literary study, often explicitly as a way of providing at least some rigorous discipline. In our own studies of the very rich and important English medieval literature, such internal methodologies, and a relative isolation from active questions of value and of history, have made considerable headway. Everything is again justifiable, in its own immediate terms; it is the connection of those terms to the central inquiry that has become problematic or, more graciously, ultimate.

The outstanding difference between physical and humane studies is not only a matter of inevitable questions of expressed and active values. It is also a matter of the fact of change: that societies and literatures have active histories, which are always inseparable from active values. But in literary as in some social, historical and anthropological studies these facts of change can be projected into an apparent totality which has the advantage of containing them and thus of making them at last, like the rocks, stand still. In literature the most common of these false totalities is tradition, which is seen not as it is, an active and continuous selection and reselection, which even at its latest point in time is always a specific choice, but now more conveniently as an object, a projected reality, with which we have to come to terms on its terms, even though those terms are always and must be the valuations, the selections and omissions, of other men. The idea of a fixed syllabus is the most ordinary methodological product of just this assumption. And of course, given this kind of totality, the facts of change can then be admitted, but in particular ways. We can be positively invited to study the history of literature: only now not as change but as variation, a series of variations within a static totality: the characteristics of this period and the characteristics of that other; just as in empirical history we come to know this period and that, but the 'and' is not stressed, or is in any case understood as temporal variation rather than as qualitative change.

Similar false totalities have been very widely projected in economics, in political theory, in anthropology and even in contemporary sociology, where variation is seen as a fact but as only a fact, which does not necessarily involve us with the disturbing process of active values and choices. Certainly, as is so often said, we cannot do without the facts, and it is a hard, long effort to get them. But this persuasive empiricism is founded, from the beginning, on the assumption that the facts can be made to stand still, and to be, as we are, disinterested. Theory, we are told, can come later, but the important point is that it is there, tacitly, from the beginning, in the methodological assumption of a static, passive and therefore empirically available totality. The most obvious example, from literary studies, is the methodology of the study of 'kinds' or 'genres'. There, making all the empirical work possible, is the prior assumption of the existence, within the 'body' of literature, of such 'permanent forms' as epic, tragedy, or romance, and then all our active study is of variations within them, variations that may be admitted to have proximate causes, even a social history, but that in their essential features are taken in practice as autonomous, with internal laws: an *a priori* and idealist assumption which prevents us not only from seeing the important history of the generation of such forms, which whatever might be said are never in fact timeless, but also from seeing those radical and qualitative changes, within the nominal continuity of the forms, which are often of surpassing importance in themselves and which indeed, at times, make a quite different method of study, a method not depending on that kind of general classification, imperative.

The Limits of 'Practical Criticism'

Yet it is on none of these methods, with their apparent objectivity, that the claim of literature to be the central human study has rested. It has been on 'practical criticism', which deserves attention in itself and because it is from this, paradoxically, that much of the English work in literary sociology has come. I know Goldmann would have been surprised—every visitor is surprised—to meet the full intensity, the extraordinary human commitment, of this particular and local allegiance. In his attack on 'scientism' he might for a moment have assumed that there were Cambridge allies, who had attacked the same thing in the same word. But this wouldn't have lasted long. Goldmann's attack on scientism—the uncritical transfer of method from the physical to the human sciences—was above all in the name of a critical sociology; whereas that word 'sociology' has only to be mentioned, in practical-critical circles, to provoke the last sad look at the voluntarily damned. And I would give it about fifteen minutes, as Goldmann began to describe his own methodology, for that crushing quotation to be brought out from Lawrence:

'We judge a work of art by its effect on our sincere and vital emotion, and nothing else. All the critical twiddle-twaddle about style and form, all this pseudo-scientific classifying and analysing of books in an imitation-botanical fashion, is mere impertinence and mostly dull jargon.'

So no methodology here, thank you; only sincere and vital emotion. But who decides the sincerity and vitality? If you need to ask that you couldn't begin to understand the answer. People decide it, in themselves and in an active and collaborative critical process.

But which people, in what social relationships, with each other and with others? That, at whatever risk of damnation, is the necessary question of the sociologist. Practical criticism is vulnerable at several points: in its hardening into an apparently objective method which is based, even defiantly, on subjective principles; in its isolation of texts from contexts; in its contemplative aspects, which have often made it hostile to new literary work. But all these weaknesses are most apparent, we say, when it is badly done: well or badly being again an internal criterion. In fact, however, all these weaknesses, or potential weaknesses, follow from the specific social situation of its practitioners. The real answer to that question—which people, in what social relationships?—was, as we all know, precise and even principled: the informed critical minority. What began as the most general kind of claim, a visibly human process centred on the apparently absolute qualities of sincerity and vitality, ended, under real pressures, as a self-defining group. But then, because the critical activity was real, very different social relations—a sense of isolation from the main currents of a civilisation in which sincerity and vitality were being limited or destroyed, an implacable opposition to all the agents of this limitation or destruction —emerged and forced a generalization of the original position. English literary sociology began, in effect, from this need of a radical critical group to locate and to justify its own activity and identity: the practical distinction of good literature from the mediocre and the bad extending to studies of the cultural conditions underlying these differences of value—a critical history of literature and of culture; and then further extending, from its starting-point in critical activity, to one major element of these conditions, the nature of the reading-public. The particular interpretation then given was of course one of cultural decline; the radical isolation of the critical minority was in that sense both starting-point and conclusion. But any theory of cultural decline, or to put it more neutrally, of cultural crisis—and the practical critics had little difficulty in establishing *that*—acquires, inevitably, wider social explanations: in this case the destruction of an organic society by industrialism and by mass civilization.

In the 1930's this kind of diagnosis overlapped, or seemed to overlap, with other radical interpretations, and especially, perhaps, with the Marxist interpretation of the effects of capitalism. Yet almost at once there was a fundamental hostility between these two groups: a critical engagement between *Scrutiny* and the English Marxists, which we can have little doubt, looking back, *Scrutiny* won.

But why was this so? That the *Scrutiny* critics were much closer to literature, were not just fitting it in, rather hastily, to a theory conceived from other kinds, mainly economic kinds, of evidence? I believe this was so, but the real reason was more fundamental. Marxism, as then commonly understood, was weak in just the decisive area where practical criticism was strong: in its capacity to give precise and detailed and reasonably adequate accounts of actual consciousness: not just a scheme or a generalization but actual works, full of rich and significant and specific experience. And the reason for the corresponding weakness in Marxism is not difficult to find: it lay in the received formula of base and superstructure, which in ordinary hands converted very quickly to an interpretation of superstructure as simple reflection, representation, ideological expression—simplicities which just will not survive any prolonged experience of actual works. It was the theory and practice of reductionism—the specific human experiences and acts of creation converted so quickly and mechanically into classifications which always found their ultimate reality and significance elsewhere— which in practice left the field open to anybody who could give an account of art which in its closeness and intensity at all corresponded to the real human dimension in which art works are made and valued.

I have said there was a victory, and it was indeed so crushing that in England, for a generation, even the original questions could hardly be raised. People already knew, or thought they knew, the answers. Still today, I have no doubt, the work of Lukács or of Goldmann can be quickly referred to that abandoned battlefield. What have they got, after all, but a slightly updated vocabulary and a new political lease of life?

I think they have more, much more, but I am sure we must remember that decisive engagement, for certain real things were learned in it, which make the specifically English contribution to the continuing inquiry still relevant, still active, however much any of us might want to join in the run from the English consensus to a quite other conscious-ness and vocabulary.

It was above all, as I have said, the received formula of base and super-structure which made Marxist accounts of literature and thought so often weak in practice. Yet to many people, still, this formula is near the centre of Marxism, and indicates its appropriate methodology for cultural history and criticism, and then of course for the relation be-tween social and cultural studies. The economic base determines the social relations which determine consciousness which determines actual ideas and works. There can be endless debate about each of these terms, but unless something very like that is believed, Marxism appears to have lost its most specific and challenging position.

The Social Totality

Now for my own part I have always opposed the formula of base and superstructure: not primarily because of its methodological weaknesses but because of its rigid, abstract and static character. Further, from my work on the nineteenth century, I came to view it as essentially a bourgeois formula; more specifically, a central position of utilitarian thought. I did not want to give up my sense of the commanding im-portance of economic activity and history. My inquiry in *Culture and Society* had begun from just that sense of a transforming change. But in theory and practice I came to believe that I had to give up, or at least to leave aside, what I knew as the Marxist tradition: to attempt to develop a theory of social totality; to see the study of culture as the study of relations between elements in a whole way of life; to find ways of studying structure, in particular works and periods, which could stay in touch with and illuminate particular art works and forms, but also forms and relations of more general social life; to replace the formula of base and superstructure with the more active idea of a field of mutually if also unevenly determining forces. That was the project of *The Long Revolution*, and it seems to me extraordinary, looking back, that I did not then know the work of Lukács or of Goldmann, which would have been highly relevant to it, and especially as they were working within a more conscious tradition and in less radical an isolation. I did not even then know, or had forgotten, Marx's analysis of the theory of utility, in *The German Ideology*, in which—as I now find often happens in reading and re-reading Marx—what I had felt about the reductionism now embodied in the base-superstructure formula was given a very precise historical and analytic focus.

This being so, it is easy to imagine my feelings when I discovered an active and developed Marxist theory, in the work of Lukács and Gold-mann, which was exploring many of the same areas with many of the same concepts, but also with others in a quite different range. The fact that I learned simultaneously that it had been denounced as heretical, that it was a return to Left Hegelianism, left-bourgeois idealism, and so on, did not, I am afraid, detain me. If you're not in a church you're not worried about heresies; the only real interest is actual theory and practice.

What both Lukács and Goldmann had to say about reification seemed to me the real advance. For here the dominance of economic activity over all other forms of human activity, the dominance of its values over all other values, was given a precise historical explanation: that this dominance, this deformation, was the specific characteristic of capitalist society, and that in modern organized capitalism this dominance—as indeed one can observe—was increasing, so that this reification, this false objectivity, was more thoroughly penetrating every other kind of life and consciousness. The idea of totality was then a critical weapon against this precise deformation; indeed, against capitalism itself. And yet this was not idealism: as assertion of the primacy of other values. On the contrary, just as the deformation could be understood, at its roots, only by economic analysis, so the attempt to overcome and surpass it lay not in isolated witness or in separated activity but in practical work to find, to assert and to establish more human social ends in more human political means.

At the most practical level it was easy to agree. But the whole point of thinking in terms of a totality is the realization that we are part of it; that our own consciousness, our work, our methods, are then critically at stake. And in the particular field of literary analysis there was this obvious difficulty: that most of the work we had to look at was the product of just this epoch of reified consciousness, so that what looked like the theoretical breakthrough might become, quite quickly, the methodological trap. I cannot yet say this finally about Lukács, since I still don't have access to all his work; but in some of it, at least, the major insights of *History and Class-Consciousness*, which he has now partly disavowed, do not get translated into critical practice, and certain cruder operations—essentially still those of base and super-structure—keep reappearing. And I still read Goldmann collaboratively and critically asking the same question, for I am sure the practice of totality is still for any of us, at any time, profoundly and even obviously difficult.

Yet advances have been made, and I want to acknowledge them. In particular Goldmann's concepts of structure, and his distinctions of kinds of consciousness—often based on but developed from Lukács— seem to me very important. And they are important above all for the relation between literary and social studies. At a simpler level, many points of contact between literature and sociology can be worked on: studies of the reading public, for example, where literary analysis of the works being read and sociological analysis of the real formations of the public have hardly yet at all been combined. Or the actual history of writers, as a changing historical group, in any full critical relation to the substance of their work. Or the social history of literary forms, in their full particularity and variety but also in the complex of their relation with other formations. I attempted each of these kinds of analysis in a preliminary way in *The Long Revolution*, but I felt then and have felt ever since a crucial absence of collaborators, and especially of people who did not say or have to say, as we approached the most difficult central problems, that there, unfortunately, was the limit of their field.

Goldmann, of course, did not accept these limits. He spoke now as sociologist, now as critic, now as cultural historian; but also, in his own intellectual tradition, a philosophy and a sociology were there from the beginning; the patient literary studies began from that fact. Thus, when he spoke of structures, he was consciously applying a term and a method which did not so much cross as underlie the apparently separate disciplines. It is a term and a method of consciousness, and so the relation between literature and sociology is not a relation between, on the one hand, various individual works and on the other hand various empirical facts. The real relation is within a totality of consciousness: a relation that is assumed and then revealed rather than apprehended and then expounded. Much that has to be proved, in our own tradition—and especially the very existence of significant primary relations between literature and society—can there be surpassed, in an active general position. The methodology can be formulated, in general philosophical and sociological terms, before the particular analyses begin. Looking at our work it could be said that we lacked a centre, in any developed philosophy or sociology. Looking at his work—and for all his differences he was representative of that whole other tradition—it could be said that he had a received centre, at the level of reasoning, before the full contact with substance began.

Structures of Feeling

I think the subsequent argument, if it can be developed, has this necessary tension and even contradiction of method. I will give a central example. I found in my own work that I had to develop the idea of a structure of feeling. This was to indicate certain common characteristics in a group of writers but also of others, in a particular historical situation. I will come back to its precise application later. But then I found Goldmann beginning, very interestingly, from a concept of structure which contained, in itself, a relation between social and literary facts. This relation, he insisted, was not a matter of content, but of mental structures: 'the categories which simultaneously organize the empirical consciousness of a particular social group and the imaginative world created by the writer'. By definition, these structures are not individually but collectively created. Again, in an almost untranslatable term, this was a genetic structuralism, necessarily concerned not only with the analysis of structures but with their historical formation and process: the ways in which they change as well as the ways in which they are constituted. The foundation of this approach is the belief that all human activity is an attempt to make a significant response to a particular objective situation. Who makes this response? According to Goldmann, neither the individual nor any abstract group, but individuals in real and collective social relations. The significant response is a particular view of the world: an organizing view. And it is just this element of organization that is, in literature, the significant social fact. A correspondence of content between a writer and his world is less significant than this correspondence of organization, of structure. A relation of content may be mere reflection, but a relation of structure, often occurring where there is no apparent relation of content, can show us the organizing principle by which a particular view of the world, and from that the coherence of the social group which maintains it, really operates in consciousness.

To make this more critical, Goldmann, following Lukács, distinguishes between actual consciousness and possible consciousness: the actual, with its rich multiplicity; the possible, with its degree of maximum adequacy and coherence. A social group is ordinarily limited to its actual consciousness, and this will include many kinds of misunderstanding and illusion: elements of false consciousness which will often, of course, be used and reflected in ordinary literature. But there is also a maximum of possible consciousness: that view of the world raised to its highest and most coherent level, limited only by the fact that to go further would mean that the group would have to surpass itself, to change into or be replaced by a new social group.

Most sociology of literature, Goldmann then argues, is concerned with the relatively apparent relations between ordinary literature and actual consciousness: relations which show themselves at the level of content, or in conventional elaboration of its common illusions. The new sociology of literature—that of genetic structuralism—will be concerned with the more fundamental relations of possible consciousness, for it is at the centre of his case that the greatest literary works are precisely those which realize a world-view at its most coherent and most adequate, its highest possible level. We should not then mainly study peripheral relations: correspondences of content and background; overt social relations between writers and readers. We should study, in the greatest literature, the organizing categories, the essential structures, which give such works their unity, their specific aesthetic character, their strictly literary quality; and which at the same time reveal to us the maximum possible consciousness of the social group—in real terms, the social class—which finally created them, in and through their individual authors.

Now this is, I believe, a powerful argument, and I make my observations on it within that sense. The idea of a world-view, a particular and organized way of seeing the world, is of course familiar to us in our own studies. Indeed I myself had to spend many years getting away from it, in the ordinary form in which I found it presented. The Elizabethan world-picture, I came to believe, was a thing fascinating in itself, but then it was often more of a hindrance than a help in seeing the full substance of Elizabethan drama. Again, I learned the Greek world-picture and was then baffled by Greek drama; the Victorian world-picture and found the English nineteenth-century novel amazing. I think Goldmann's distinction might help us here. He would say that what we were being given was actual consciousness, in a summary form, whereas what we found in the literature was the often very different possible consciousness. I have no doubt this is often true, but it is as often the case that we need to reconsider the idea of consciousness itself. What is ordinarily extracted as a world-view is, in practice, a summary of doctrines: more organized, more coherent, than most men of the time would have been able to make them. And then I am not sure that I can in practice always distinguish this from the kind of evidence Goldmann himself adduces as possible consciousness, when he is engaged in an analysis. Moreover I think either version is often some distance away from the real structures and processes of the literature. I developed my own idea of structures of feeling in response to just this sense of a distance. There were real social and natural relationships, and there were relatively organized, relatively coherent formations of these relationships, in contemporary institutions and beliefs. But what seemed to me to happen, in the greatest literature, was a simultaneous realization of and response to these underlying and formative structures. Indeed, that constituted, for me, the specific literary phenomenon: the dramatization of a process, the making of a fiction, in which the constituting elements, of real social life and beliefs, were simultaneously actualized and in an important way differently experienced, the difference residing in the imaginative act, the imaginative method, the specific and genuinely unprecedented imaginative organization.

We can feel the effect, in all this, of major individual talents, and indeed I believe that there are discoverable specific reasons, of a social kind, in the immediate histories of writers, why this imaginative alternative was sought. But I am also sure that these creative acts compose, within a historical period, a specific community: a community visible in the structure of feeling and demonstrable, above all, in fundamental changes of form. I have tried to show this in actual cases, in the late-nineteenth and twentieth-century European drama, and in the development and crisis of the nineteenth and twentieth-century English novel. And what seems to me especially important in these changing structures of feeling is that they normally precede those more recognizable changes of formal idea and belief which make up the ordinary history of consciousness, and that while they correspond very closely to a real social history, of men living in actual and changing social relations, they again normally precede the more recognizable changes of formal institution and relationship, which are the more accessible, indeed the more normal, history. This is what I mean by saying that art is one of the primary human activities, and that it can succeed in articulating not just the imposed or constitutive social or intellectual system, but at once this and an experience of it, its lived consequence, in ways very close to many other kinds of active response, in new social activity and in what we know as personal life, but of course often more accessibly, just because it is specifically formed and because when it is made it is in its own way complete, even autonomous, and being the kind of work it is can be transmitted and communicated beyond its original situation and circumstances.

Now if this is so it is easy to see why we must reject those versions of consciousness which relate it directly, or with mere lags and complications, to a determining base. The stress on an active consciousness, made by Lukács and Goldmann, gives us a real way beyond that. And it might be possible to say that the relation I have tried to describe—between formal consciousness and new creative practice—might be better, more precisely, described in the terms of Lukács and Goldmann: actual consciousness and possible consciousness. Indeed I hope it may be so, but I see one major difficulty. This relation, though subtle, is still in some ways static. Possible consciousness is the objective limit that can be reached by a class before it turns into another class, or is replaced. But I think this leads, rather evidently, to a kind of macro-history: in many ways adequate but in relation to actual literature, with its continuity of change, often too large in its categories to come very close, except at certain significant points when there is a radical and fundamental moment of replacement of one class by another. As I read Goldmann, I find him very conscious of just this difficulty, but then I am not sure that it is accidental that he is much more convincing on Racine and Pascal, at a point of evident crisis between a feudal and a bourgeois world, than he is on the nineteenth and indeed twentieth-century novel, where apparently small but no less significant changes within a bourgeois society have to be given what can be called micro-structural analysis. To say, following Lukács, that the novel is the form in which, in a degraded society, a man tries and fails to surpass an objectively limited society and destiny—the novel, that is to say, of the problematic hero—is at once illuminating and partial; indeed, the evidence presented for it is so extremely selective that we are almost at once on our guard. No English novels are considered at all: the other side of that enclosure of which we are usually, on our side of the channel, so conscious. But while one can offer, willingly, *Great Expectations, Born in Exile, Jude the Obscure*, and in a more complicated but still relevant way *Middlemarch*, one is left to face a different phenomenon in, for example, *Little Dorrit*. And I think this is not only an argument about particular cases. The most exciting experience for me, in reading Lukács and Goldmann, was the stress on forms. I had become con-vinced in my own work that the most penetrating analysis would always be of forms, specifically literary forms, where changes of view-point, changes of known and knowable relationships, changes of possible and actual resolutions, could be directly demonstrated, as forms of literary organization, and then, just because they involved more than individual solutions, could be reasonably related to a real social history, itself considered analytically in terms of basic relation-ships and failures and limits of relationship. This is what I attempted, for example, in *Modern Tragedy,* and I then have to say that I have since learned a good deal, theoretically, from the developed sociology of Lukács and Goldmann and others, in just this respect. But much of the necessary analysis of forms seems to me barely to have begun, and this is not only, I think, a matter of time for development.

Perhaps I can put the reason most sharply by saying that form, in Lukács and Goldmann, translates too often as genre or as kind; that we stay, too often, within a received academic and ultimately idealist tradition in which 'epic' and 'drama', 'novel' and 'tragedy', have in-herent and permanent properties, from which the analysis begins and to which selected examples are related. I am very willing to agree that certain general correlations of this kind, between a form and a world-view, can be shown. But we have then to face the fact, above all in the last hundred years, that tragedy and the novel, for example, exist, in-extricably, within the same culture, and are used by identical or very similar social groups. Or the fact that within modern tragedy, and even more within the novel, there are radically significant changes of form in which many of the changes in literature and society—changes at the pace of a life, an experience, rather than of a whole historical epoch—can be most directly apprehended. Certainly this is recognized in practice. Goldmann has an interesting contrast between the traditional bourgeois novel and the new novel, of Sarraute or Robbe-Grillet, which he relates to a more completely reified world. Lukács makes similar distinctions, from Balzac through Mann and Kafka to Solzhenitsyn. But the full theoretical issue, of what is meant by form, is still in my view confused, and perhaps especially by the fact that there is this undiscarded ballast of form in a more abstract, more supra-historical sense. Thus even a Goldmann can say, as if he were an ordinary idealist and academic critic, that Sophocles is the only one of the Greek dramatists who can be called tragic 'in the now accepted sense of the word'. The prepotence of inherited categories is then striking and saddening.

Past Victories, Present Penalties

But then limitations of this kind are organically related to the strengths of this alternative tradition. The habitual and as it were inevitable relation of structure to doctrine, or the application of formal categories, is a characteristic of the developed philosophical position which in most other respects is a source of real strength. That is why it is so important, now, to go beyond the kind of argument which developed in England in the 'thirties, for while particular refutations of this or that reading, this or that method, have an immediate significance, in our whole situation they can hide the fact that behind our local English practicalities is a set of unexamined general ideas, which then suddenly materialize on quite another plane as a sort of social theory: from the critical minority to minority culture and education; or from the richness of past literature to a use of the past against the present, as if the past, and never the future, the sense of a future, were the only source of values. The local victory of the 'thirties was bought at a price we have all since paid: that the more active relations between literary and social studies, and the more fundamental and continuing relations between literature and real societies, including present society, have in effect been pushed away from attention, because in theory and in practice any critical examination of them would disturb, often radically, our existing social relations and the division of interests and specialisms which both expresses and protects them.

I want to end by emphasising two concepts, used by Goldmann, which we ought to try to clarify, theoretically, and which we ought to be trying, collaboratively, to test in practice. The first is the idea of the 'collective subject': obviously a difficult idea, but one of great potential importance. Literary studies in fact use a related idea again and again. We say not only 'the Jacobean dramatists' 'the Romantic poets' and 'the early Victorian novelists', but also we often use these descriptions in a quite singular sense, to indicate a way of looking at the world, a literary method, a particular use of language, and so on. In practice we are often concerned with breaking down these generalizations, and that is right: to know the difference between Jonson and Webster, or Blake and Coleridge, or Dickens and Emily Brontë, is in that real sense necessary. Yet beyond this we do come to see certain real communities, when we have taken all the individual differences into account. To see only the differences between Blake and Coleridge, but not also the differences between a Romantic poem and a Jacobean play and an early Victorian novel, is to be quite wilfully limited and indeed quite unpractical. And then to be able to give an account of this precise community, a community of form which is also a specific general way of seeing other men and nature, is to approach the problem of social groups in a quite new way: for it is not the reduction of individuals to a group, by some process of averaging; it is a way of seeing a group in and through individual differences: that specificity of individuals, and of their individual creations, which does not so much deny as affirm real social identities, in language, in conventions, in certain characteristic situations, experiences, interpretations, ideas. Indeed the importance for social studies may well be this: that we can find ways of describing significant groups which include, in a fundamental way, those personal realities which will otherwise be relegated to a quite separate area. To have a sociology concerned only with abstract groups, and a literary criticism concerned only with abstract individuals and works, is more than a division of labour; it is a way of avoiding the reality of the interpenetration, in a final sense the unity, of the most individual and the most social forms of actual life.

The problem is always one of method, and this is where the second idea, of the structures of the genesis of consciousness, must be taken very seriously. We are weakest, in social studies, in just this area: in what is called the sociology of knowledge but is always much more than that, for it is not only knowledge we are concerned with but all the active processes of learning, imagination, creation, performance. And there is very rich material, within a discipline we already have, for the detailed description of just these processes, in so many individual works. To find ways of extending this, not simply to a background of social history or of the history of ideas, but to other active processes through which social groups form and define themselves, will be very difficult but is now centrally necessary. For relating literary process to the social product, or the social process to the literary product—which is what now we mostly do—in the end breaks down, and people retire, though not for long, to their tents. But if in every case we can try, by varying forms of analysis, to go beyond the particular product to its real process—its most active and specific formation—I believe we will find points of connection that will answer, as our separated studies so often do not, to our closest sense of our own living process.

On each of these points—the idea of the collective subject, and the idea of the structures of the genesis of consciousness—Lucien Goldmann's contribution, though unfinished, was significant. Locked as he was in much immediate controversy, he seems often to have been limited to restating his most general positions; yet even here, in ways that in summary I have not been able to indicate, he produced refinements and further definitions, in so complex a field, from which we can all learn. We can dissent, as I often do, from particular formulations and applications, and still recognize the emphasis, the exceptionally valuable emphasis, which he gave, theoretically and practically, to the development of literary and social studies. And this is more than a professional concern. Beyond the arguments, as listening to him last Spring in Cambridge it was not difficult to see, there is a social crisis and a human crisis in which, in just these ways, we are ourselves involved: for the achievement of clarity and significance, in these most human studies, is directly connected with the struggle for human means and ends in a world that will permit no reserved areas, no safe subjects, no neutral activities. Now and here, in respecting his memory, I take the sense he gave: of a continuing inquiry, a continuing argument, a continuing concern; of a man who made, in our time, a significant response, and with whom we can find, as I think he would have said, a significant community, a way of seeing and being and acting in the world.

An Objective Approach to the Relationship
between Fiction and Society
Ruth A. Inglis

from

American Sociological Review, vol. 3, no. 4, 1938.

AN OBJECTIVE APPROACH TO THE RELATIONSHIP BETWEEN FICTION AND SOCIETY

RUTH A. INGLIS

Bryn Mawr College

THE relationship between literature and society[1] has been the subject of considerable discussion.[2] It is generally agreed that both literary standards and society are variables. Beyond that lies an area of marked controversy from which, for the sake of clarity, have been abstracted two general points of view which I call the "reflection theory" and the "social control theory." Succinctly, the reflection theory holds that literature *reflects* society; the control theory, that it *shapes* society.

In "Literary Indices of Social Disorganization," Elliott and Merrill assume the characteristic reflection-theory position by examining post-War literature in order to "read the social barometer."[3] Anthropologists and others frequently use the literature of a people as a source of clues to the nature of their culture. Even the words and form in which ideas are couched throw light upon the ideas, customs, and beliefs extant in a group. Since an author usually writes for readers having membership in his own society, the presumption is that literature will reflect what they have in common. This inferential approach to the unknown via the qualities of a related known is like examining a well worn glove to find out the shape of the owner's hand. If it works, such an approach is extremely useful. The question is, in the case of literature and society, does it work? Does literature reflect society? And if so, is the reflection a true or a distorted one? What aspects of society are reflected?

Unlike the reflection theory, the social control theory vests in literature an active role of leadership. Proverbially, the pen is mightier than the sword, and certain problem novels and plays such as Ibsen's *Doll House*, Harriet Beecher Stowe's *Uncle Tom's Cabin*, and most of Dickens' works are claimed to have had tremendous social influence. The basic assumptions of the social control theory as related to literature are a passive suggestibility in readers and a dynamic power inherent in words. However, the proponents of censorship, those who lean most heavily upon this theory, have never adequately explained the process involved nor can they predict the social effect of a given piece of writing. Nevertheless, the fact that dictators

---

[1] According to *Webster's Dictionary*, literature is "The total of preserved writings belonging to a given language or people" including both the *belles lettres* and journalistic or other ephemeral writing. *Society* means the pattern of social relationships characteristic of a group of people at a given time and place.

[2] See A. Guérard, *Literature and Society*, New York, 1935, and R. P. Utter and G. B. Needham, *Pamela's Daughters*, New York, 1936.

[3] M. A. Elliott and F. E. Merrill, *Social Disorganization*, 45, New York, 1934.

and others use literary forms of propaganda and censorship with such apparent effectiveness prevents our dismissing this theory, with all its theoretical shortcomings, before submitting it to objective test.

Although the two theories differ markedly, both may be partially correct. A particular essay or novel may reflect one aspect of society while suggesting a change in another sphere. A sympathetic portrayal of the *status quo* undoubtedly acts as a stimulus for its preservation. Logically, there is room for a good deal of variation in the different types of literature. Everyone knows that fairy tales are not supposed to be true whereas biographies are, and the aims and purposes of authors cover a wide range from instruction or amusement to acknowledged propaganda. At present, therefore, it is impossible to offer any more generalized conclusions than that literature sometimes reflects and sometimes controls society. The questions herein raised must be applied to a specific kind of writing as related to a particular society.

The method, in brief, was to compare social change with changes in fiction. Heroines of fiction were made the pivotal point for two main reasons. First, the heroine is statistically a simple, tangible unit of measurement which is comparable to the members of the feminine population at large. Feminine attributes have been a focal point in social change of late. Socially, politically, and economically women have entered new fields of activity. Increasingly large numbers of women have left their homes to work in offices or factories. Meanwhile, what was happening to the heroines of fiction? What percentage of them was gainfully employed? If there was an increase since 1900, did it *precede* or *follow* the actual increase in employed women? An increase in the number of women gainfully occupied followed by an increased number of employed heroines would constitute substantial evidence for the reflection theory. If the order of events were reversed, it would support the control theory, even admitting there were other factors than literature involved in the actual social change.

The second important reason for centering attention upon the heroine is that she constitutes a useful "symbolic model," a make-believe character whose traits may be emulated. The concept of imitation is important to both theories. The reflection theory holds that the heroine is modeled *from* actual women whereas the social control theory maintains that she is a model *for* them. The criterion for determining whether heroines or real women are the models is priority of change. Obviously, the "model" must change before its "imitation" can change. It is, of course, entirely possible that a particular author may model a heroine after a working girl friend of his and that his story may influence some other girl to seek a job in an office. This sort of interaction undoubtedly occurs, and, if it could be done, a study of enough such cases might be enlightening. However, we are concerned only with the larger cumulative aspects of the two processes.

The Saturday Evening Post was chosen as a source of American fiction because of its large circulation and apparent uniformity over the years. From January, 1901, to December, 1935, the first romantic short story of the month was chosen for analysis, a total of 420 stories over the thirty-five year period. Throughout this time, Mr. George H. Lorimer was the Editor, and aside from his growth in years and experience, there were no marked internal changes of policy or personnel. For present purposes, *The Post* is a constant while fiction and society are two variables.

The Post, a mass magazine with neither overly intellectual nor notably "low-brow" tendencies, would seem to be the ideal literary common denominator, the perfect *mirror* or *modifier* of the times, if there is any. At any rate, it has frequently been called both. According to an adviser to hopeful short story authors, "Its fiction deals with American subjects and the people of today accurately,"[4] but Vernon Louis Parrington stated, "*The Saturday Evening Post* is fast regimenting the American mind."[5]

The selection of stories within *The Post* and of heroines within the stories was made as objective as possible. Romantic stories are those mainly concerned with the love interest; not the comic, the character, the animal, the dialect, or the purely historical story. Obviously, there had to be a heroine. If there was more than one important woman in the plot, the criterion for deciding the identity of the heroine was the amount of space devoted to her. For present purposes, the heroines are simply the women in the stories whose persons and activities were the most fully described.

Although the heroines were analyzed in terms of such physical and social characteristics as hair and eye coloring, stature and weight, age, marital status, and attractiveness, only on an economic or occupational level was direct comparison with societal change possible. The United States Census was the best available source of employment statistics for women since there are no reliable annual data. The heroines were divided into those (1) gainfully and (2) not gainfully occupied, like the Census classification.

The use of Census material involves certain methodological difficulties. The data are not strictly comparable from decade to decade because of changes in methods of collecting and classifying them. As an example, Joseph Hill states, "The decrease in the percentage of women reported in the Census as gainfull employed—from 25.5 in 1910 to 24.0 in 1920—cannot be accepted as indicating an actual decline in the tendency of women to engage in gainful occupations. It is accounted for in part by the change in the date of the Census and in the instructions to enumerators in regard to returning women as farm laborers and in part by a decrease in the proportion of young women in the total adult female population."[6] By careful

---

[4] W. B. McCourtie, "Where and How to Sell Manuscripts," *The Writers' Digest* (*A Directory for Writers*), 27, 1931.

[5] *Main Currents in American Thought*, vol. III, 327, New York, 1930.

[6] J. A. Hill, *Women in Gainful Occupations, 1870 to 1920*, Census Monograph IX, 27, Washington, 1929.

statistical analysis, however, Hurlin and Givens have attempted to iron out the above differences,[7] and their "presumptive trends" are preferable to the raw Census data.

Since the employed heroines were all over sixteen years of age and almost entirely native white Americans, further correction of the Census data was necessary in order to eliminate extraneous trends in the foreign born and Negro female population. My method is shown in Table 1 below. It is based on the assumption that there is a consistent proportional relationship existing between the native white and the *total* gainfully occupied women sixteen years of age and over and those ten years of age and over, *i.e.*, that (a) the percentage of *native white* females *ten* years of age and over gainfully occupied is to (b) the percentage of *all* females *ten* years of age and over gainfully occupied as (x) the percentage of *native white* females *sixteen* years of age and over gainfully occupied is to (d) the percentage of *all* females *sixteen* years of age and over gainfully occupied (a:b::x:d).

TABLE 1. DERIVATION OF THE PERCENTAGE OF NATIVE WHITE FEMALES 16 YEARS
OF AGE AND OVER GAINFULLY OCCUPIED

Classification Group	1890	1900	1910	1920	1930
(a) Percentage of native white females 10 years of age and over gainfully occupied	13.1[1]	15.3[1]	19.2[2]	19.3[2]	20.7[2]
(b) Percentage of all females 10 years of age and over gainfully occupied[3]	17.4	18.8	21.9	21.1	22.0
(x) **Percentage of native white females 16 years of age and over gainfully occupied**	14.5	16.8	21.2	22.0	23.8
(d) Percentage of all females 16 years of age and over gainfully occupied[3]	19.0	20.6	24.3	24.0	25.3

[1] From *Twelfth Census of the U. S. —1900, Occupations*, lxxxiii, table entitled "Percent which the number of persons engaged in gainful occupations forms of the total number 10 years of age and over in each element of the population, for both sexes and each sex separately," Washington, 1904.

[2] From *Fifteenth Census of the U. S.—1930*, vol. 5, 74, Table 1, Washington, 1933. Since the 1910 and 1920 figures include Mexicans, they were also added to the 1930 figures, an increase amounting to only two-tenths of one percent. It would have been desirable to have used Hurlin-Givens' figures throughout the derivation, but they were not available for this classification group. However, the nature of their corrections are not especially applicable to the native white female group, and it is not believed that this materially affects the final figures.

[3] R. G. Hurlin and M. B. Givens, *loc. cit.*, 274, Table 2.

The heroine and the Census groups having been equated for age, nationality, and race, a comparison of the employment trends of both is shown in Table 2 below. The fact that the total heroine population has been artificially limited to twelve each year whereas the actual population has increased during the past thirty-five years has been controlled by the use of percentages rather than actual figures.

[7] R. G. Hurlin and M. B. Givens, *Recent Social Trends in the United States*, chap. 6, 270–271, footnote 5, New York, 1933.

TABLE 2. PERCENTAGE OF HEROINES AND OF NATIVE WHITE FEMALES
16 YEARS OF AGE AND OVER GAINFULLY OCCUPIED

Dates	Females[1]	Heroines
1890	14.5	
1900	16.8	
1910	21.2	
1900–10[2]		30.0[3]
1920	22.0	
1910–20[2]		34.2
1930	23.8	
1920–30[2]		34.2

[1] See Table 1.

[2] The heroine figures represent cumulative totals over the ten-year periods, and therefore are not strictly comparable to the Census figures.

[3] Part of the higher percentage of employed heroines than employed women may be due to the greater proportion of young women in the heroine group.

The above table shows a notable relationship beteeen the changes in the percentage of fictional and actual working women. From 1900 to 1910, there was a rise of 4.4 percent in the percentage of employed women, a sudden increase in comparison with the other decades. This was followed by a very slight increase in 1920. On the other hand, the percentage of employed heroines increased from 30 percent during the decade from 1900 to 1910 to 34.2 percent during the 1910–1920 period and then remained constant. In both cases there is a marked rise followed by a plateau, but the fictional trend lags about a decade behind the actual trend. At this point, *Saturday Evening Post* stories "reflect" reality.

Of course, the fact must not be overlooked that data for the beginning of the women's movement is lacking. If the figures could be extended back to 1900, or even to 1850, they might show that the earliest and perhaps the largest increase in employed heroines preceded the first great influx of women into economic occupations. At present, there is no way of knowing, since *The Saturday Evening Post* was very different before 1897 and the earlier Censuses are too crude to be used without correction. Here is a study for a historical sociologist who is familiar with nineteenth century sources of reliable female occupational statistics and fiction. As yet, the evidence in Table 2, although it clearly supports the reflection theory, is incomplete.

Furthermore, the reflection theory did not operate consistently throughout all the comparisons made in the present study. For instance, according to the U. S. Census reports, the average age of the female population is becoming higher whereas the heroines are not only disproportionately young but were becoming more youthful. Nowhere in the stories does the problem of female child labor exist, although it has been especially acute in America during the past thirty-five years.

The economic status of the heroines was analyzed, and on the basis of an arbitrary standard of economic well-being or their condition relative to that of other characters in the stories they were divided into three categories, the affluent, the poor, and those of unknown economic status.[8] Obviously, this classification was designed to fit the heroine group rather than the actual population. The large middle class is conspicuous by its absence, although part of it and most, but not all, of the employed heroines are counted as "poor." Membership in this class does not necessarily mean dire need but is rather an indication of the need to spend carefully and live economically on a limited income. The "affluent," on the other hand, are subject to no such limitations. The wealthy class constitute 42 percent, the poor, 33 percent, and those of unknown economic status, 25 percent of the total heroine population, evidently a very unrealistic weighting in view of economic conditions in society. The trend also showed little connection with actual conditions. Effects of the War, the postwar expansion, nor the depression, were not reflected in the economic status of the heroines.

The employed heroines were engaged in a wide variety of occupations, including office and factory workers of all kinds, nurses, teachers, waitresses, artists, models, newspaper reporters, two professional criminals and one spy. Almost half of the heroines were engaged in some form of entertainment or office work. The rest were scattered too widely to permit any trend analysis or comparison with Census data. It is significant that whereas the proportion of heroines working in offices was similar to that reported in the Census, the entertainers were disproportionately represented. More than one-fourth of all employed heroines were entertainers. The explanation probably lies in the fact that moving-picture actresses and radio performers receive a disproportionate amount of public attention.

The above examples indicate that although the stories do not consistently reflect actual conditions in American life, they do mirror certain typical American attitudes and ideals, such as the tendency to take prosperity for granted, the lack of class consciousness and belief in the freedom of opportunity for everyone, the glorification of wealth and of youth and of those who entertain us. In these respects, the American pattern of values is reflected more clearly than the actual facts of American life.

There is no indication that the social control theory was operating in the present investigation. No fictional changes were found which preceded actual changes. It is important to remember, however, that although the stories are not true in the historical or logical sense, nearly all of them are decidedly within the realm of actual or possible experience. The heroines are idealistic—as might be expected from romantic stories. Their motives and manners are capable of being emulated because they conform to popular standards and ideals in American life. The short stories probably tend to

---

[8] Provision must be made for "unknowns" because short story authors frequently leave much to the readers' imagination. For example, economic status in irrelevant and hence not divulged in many stories with hospital, high school, or sport settings.

reenforce these standards because the hero and heroine are almost always rewarded for their virtue, and the happy ending is very typical. In this way, the stories undoubtedly encourage the preservation of the *status quo* as far as moral and social attitudes are concerned. Only in this restricted sense has the social control theory been substantiated by the present study.

On the basis of the above data, it is possible to draw two rather different sets of tentative conclusions. First, both the reflection and the social control theories have been partially justified, and second, both theories have been discredited since neither operated consistently. The latter conclusion leads to an hypothesis of the relationship between literature and society which is similar to that claimed by Will Hays for the movies, namely, that their only purpose is to amuse. This would hold that since the sole function of literature is to entertain its readers, neither are specific social trends reflected in detail or with accuracy nor is any direct control exerted by the literature. However, in order to serve the purpose of amusement, literature must remain in the same universe of discourse as its public and thus reflect the prevailing customs and mores in a general way, and the successfully amusing story must control the reader at least to the extent of commanding attention. The problems of the kind and extent of reflection and control which take place still remain.

However, the present study is recognized as being more suggestive in method than conclusive in results, and the reader is warned against drawing unwarranted conclusions about literature in general. *Saturday Evening Post* romantic short stories are one kind of popular and ephemeral literature. It is hoped that the method herein developed will be applied to other kinds of fiction. Factual studies might reveal whether the reflection or social control purpose is a measure of the "goodness" of good literature. Possibly the distinction between "best sellers" and other modern novels is that the former reflect current society whereas the latter try to change it.

There is no reason to believe that the authors of *The Post* stories were consciously trying either to reflect or to control the attitudes or behavior of their readers, but some authors do have such ulterior motives. A fascinating study could be made of literature with a definitely propagandistic aim. Chamberlain in *Farewell to Reform* cites *The Jungle* by Upton Sinclair as "one pamphlet of the decade of muck which led to a direct, tangible, immediate reform,"[9] but, as Chamberlain says, it offered no solution to the stockyards situation; the technique was to reflect actual conditions in such a way as to constitute a call to action to remove those conditions. Is this typical of the problem novel? What determines its success? How distorted is the reflection?

Another very different kind of "control" literature is found in Sunday School papers, and an analysis of Sunday School stories intended for high school students and young adults might prove very fruitful. How realistic

---

[9] J. Chamberlain, *Farewell to Reform*, 185, New York, 1933.

are the characters and the situations? How subtle are the morals? How effective are they? Such a study might well include an attitudinal and behavioral analysis of a selected group of regular readers.

Not only is the effect of literature upon its readers of interest but also the limitations which a specific reader-audience imposes upon authors. From this point of view, of course, the whole field of fiction for children is a fertile area for investigation. The specialized magazines also offer possibilities for study. What proportion of stories in *The Country Gentleman* is about city people? Are city people disparaged? Has the "city slicker" stereotype been perpetuated? Have stories about farm homes with electric lights and appliances preceded or followed the electrification of the rural areas? It should be interesting also to determine if there are any differences between the fiction of general mass magazines read by both men and women and those prepared especially for women, such as *Good Housekeeping* and *The Ladies Home Journal*. Further comparisons might be made with élite magazines like *The Atlantic Monthly* and *Harpers* intended for intellectuals and such sophisticated magazines as *The New Yorker*.

Regional fiction is said to be "an undeniable asset for the sociological student,"[10] but, so far as I know, there has been no attempt to determine the accuracy with which such authors have depicted the social conditions of the culture areas in which they have laid their scenes.

The literature of minority racial and national groups in the United States could be studied profitably to determine the relationship of the literature of the group to its adjustment in this country. Is most Negro and Jewish fiction of the reflection or the social control type? Are stories in the foreign language press concerned with conditions in the old country or in America? Are the characters recent immigrants, naturalized citizens, or people of old native "American" stock? Do the heroes and heroines cling to the old or assume the new culture traits?

The method used in studying *The Saturday Evening Post* heroines might be called "longitudinal" since it concentrates upon one homogeneous type of fiction in a single medium. By analyzing a larger number of heroines from a wide variety of sources, a "cross-sectional" method might be developed. Such data would, in one sense, be more comparable to Census statistics. The problem could be attacked from the standpoint of changes in morality, increasing divorce, changes in styles of clothing and behavior such as are involved in the popularization of the Gibson Girl and the rapid rise of athleticism, as well as from economic, political, and ideological trends.

At any rate, here is an attempt to make objective a problem which has long been stated only in speculative and impressionistic terms.

---

[10] M. J. Vincent, "Regionalism and Fiction," *Social Forces*, March, 1936, 14:340.

Literature as Equipment for Living
Kenneth Burke

from

The Philosophy of Literary Form by Kenneth Burke. Louisiana
State University Press, Baton Rouge, 1941.

LITERATURE AS
EQUIPMENT FOR LIVING

HERE I shall put down, as briefly as possible, a statement in behalf of what might be catalogued, with a fair degree of accuracy, as a *sociological* criticism of literature. Sociological criticism in itself is certainly not new. I shall here try to suggest what partially new elements or emphasis I think should be added to this old approach. And to make the "way in" as easy as possible, I shall begin with a discussion of proverbs.

I.

Examine random specimens in *The Oxford Dictionary of English Proverbs*. You will note, I think, that there is no "pure" literature here. Everything is "medicine." Proverbs are designed for consolation or vengeance, for admonition or exhortation, for foretelling.

Or they name typical, recurrent situations. That is, people find a certain social relationship recurring so frequently that they must "have a word for it." The Eskimos have special names for many different kinds of snow (fifteen, if I remember rightly) because variations in the quality of snow greatly affect their living. Hence, they must "size up" snow much more accurately than we do. And the same is true of social phenomena. Social structures give rise to "type" situations, subtle subdivisions of the relationships involved in competitive and coöperative acts. Many proverbs seek to chart, in more or less homey and picturesque ways, these "type" situations. I submit that such naming is done, not for the sheer glory of the thing, but because of its bearing upon human welfare. A different name for snow implies a different kind of hunt. Some names for snow imply that one should not hunt at all. And similarly, the names for typical, recurrent social situations are not developed out of "disinterested curiosity," but because the names imply a command (what to expect, what to look out for).

To illustrate with a few representative examples:

Proverbs designed for consolation: "The sun does not shine on both sides of the hedge at once." "Think of ease, but work on." "Little troubles the eye, but far less the soul." "The worst luck now, the better another time." "The wind in one's face makes one wise." "He that hath lands hath quarrels." "He knows how to carry the dead cock home." "He is not poor that hath little, but he that desireth much."

For vengeance: "At length the fox is brought to the furrier." "Shod in the cradle, barefoot in the stubble." "Sue a beggar and get a louse." "The higher the ape goes, the more he shows his tail." "The moon does not heed the barking of dogs." "He measures another's corn by his own bushel." "He shuns the man who knows him well." "Fools tie knots and wise men loose them."

Proverbs that have to do with foretelling (the most obvious are those to do with the weather): "Sow peas and beans in the wane of the moon, Who soweth them sooner, he soweth too soon." "When the wind's in the north, the skilful fisher goes not forth." "When the sloe tree is as white as a sheet, sow your barley whether it be dry or wet." "When the sun sets bright and clear, An easterly wind you need not fear. When the sun sets in a bank, A westerly wind we shall not want."

In short: "Keep your weather eye open": be realistic about sizing up today's weather, because your accuracy has bearing upon tomorrow's weather. And forecast not only the meteorological weather, but also the social weather: "When the moon's in the full, then wit's in the wane." "Straws show which way the wind blows." "When the fish is caught, the net is laid aside." "Remove an old tree, and it will wither to death." "The wolf may lose his teeth, but never his nature." "He that bites on every weed must needs light on poison." "Whether the pitcher strikes the stone, or the stone the pitcher, it is bad for the pitcher." "Eagles catch no flies." "The more laws, the more offenders."

In this foretelling category we might also include the recipes for wise living, sometimes moral, sometimes technical: "First thrive, and then wive." "Think with the wise but talk with the vulgar." "When the fox preacheth, then beware your geese." "Venture a small fish to catch a great one." "Respect a man, he will do the more."

In the class of "typical, recurrent situations" we might put such proverbs and proverbial expressions as: "Sweet appears sour when we pay." "The treason is loved but the traitor is hated." "The wine in the bottle does not quench thirst." "The sun is never the worse for shining on a dunghill." "The lion kicked by an ass." "The lion's share." "To catch one napping." "To smell a rat." "To cool one's heels."

By all means, I do not wish to suggest that this is the only way in which the proverbs could be classified. For instance, I have listed in the "foretelling" group the proverb, "When the fox preacheth, then beware your geese." But it could obviously be "taken over" for vindictive purposes. Or consider a proverb like, "Virtue flies from the heart of a mercenary man." A poor man might obviously use it either to console himself for being poor (the implication being, "Because I am poor in money I am rich in virtue") or to strike at another (the implication being, "When he got money, what else could you expect of him but deterioration?"). In fact, we could even say that such symbolic vengeance would itself be an aspect of solace. And a proverb like "The sun is never the worse for shining on a dunghill" (which I have listed under "typical recurrent situations") might as well be put in the vindictive category.

The point of issue is not to find categories that "place" the proverbs once and for all. What I want is categories that suggest their active nature. Here is no "realism for its own sake." Here is realism for promise, admonition, solace, vengeance, foretelling, instruction, charting, all for the direct bearing that such acts have upon matters of welfare.

2.

Step two: Why not extend such analysis of proverbs to encompass the whole field of literature? Could the most complex and sophisticated works of art legitimately be considered somewhat as "proverbs writ large"? Such leads, if held admissible, should help us to discover important facts about literary organization (thus satisfying the requirements of technical criticism). And the kind of observation from this perspective should apply beyond literature to life in general (thus helping to take literature out of its separate bin and give it a place in a general "sociological" picture).

The point of view might be phrased in this way: Proverbs are *strategies* for dealing with *situations*. In so far as situations are typical and recurrent in a given social structure, people develop names for them and strategies for handling them. Another name for strategies might be *attitudes*.

People have often commented on the fact that there are *contrary* proverbs. But I believe that the above approach to proverbs suggests a necessary modification of that comment. The apparent contradictions depend upon differences in *attitude*, involving a correspondingly different choice of *strategy*. Consider, for instance, the *apparently* opposite pair: "Repentance comes too late" and "Never too late to mend." The first is admonitory. It says in effect: "You'd better look out, or you'll get yourself too far into this business." The second is consolatory, saying in effect: "Buck up, old man, you can still pull out of this."

Some critics have quarreled with me about my selection of the word "strategy" as the name for this process. I have asked them to suggest an alternative term, so far without profit. The only one I can think of is "method." But if "strategy" errs in suggesting to some people an overly *conscious* procedure, "method" errs in suggesting an overly *"methodical"* one. Anyhow, let's look at the documents:

Concise Oxford Dictionary: "Strategy: Movement of an army or armies in a campaign, art of so moving or disposing troops or ships as to impose upon the enemy the place and time and conditions for fighting preferred by oneself" (from a Greek word that refers to the leading of an army).

New English Dictionary: "Strategy: The art of projecting and directing the larger military movements and operations of a campaign."

André Cheron, *Traité Complet d'Echecs:* "*On entend par stratégie les manoeuvres qui ont pour but la sortie et le bon arrangement des pièces.*"

Looking at these definitions, I gain courage. For surely, the most highly alembicated and sophisticated work of art, arising in complex civilizations, could be considered as designed to organize and command the army of one's thoughts and images, and to so organize them that one "imposes upon the enemy the time and place and conditions for fighting preferred by oneself." One seeks to "direct the larger movements and operations" in one's campaign of living. One "maneuvers," and the maneuvering is an "art."

Are not the final results one's "strategy"? One tries, as far as possible, to develop a strategy whereby one "can't lose." One tries to change the rules of the game until they fit his own necessities. Does the artist encounter disaster? He will "make capital" of it. If one is a victim of competition, for instance, if one is elbowed out, if one is willy-nilly more jockeyed against than jockeying, one can by the solace and vengeance of art convert this very "liability" into an "asset." One tries to fight on his own terms, developing a strategy for imposing the proper "time, place, and conditions."

But one must also, to develop a full strategy, be *realistic.* One must *size things up* properly. One cannot accurately know how things *will be*, what is promising and what is menacing, unless he accurately knows how things *are.* So the wise strategist will not be content with strategies of merely a self-gratifying sort. He will "keep his weather eye open." He will not too eagerly "read into" a scene an attitude that is irrelevant to it. He won't sit on the side of an active volcano and "see" it as a dormant plain.

Often, alas, he will. The great allurement in our present popular "inspirational literature," for instance, may be largely of this sort. It is a strategy for easy consolation. It "fills a need," since there is always a need for easy consolation—and in an era of confusion like our own the need is especially keen. So people are only too willing to "meet a man halfway" who will *play down* the realistic naming of our situation and *play up* such strategies as make solace cheap. However, I should propose a reservation here. We usually take it for granted that people who consume our current output of books on "How to Buy Friends and Bamboozle Oneself and Other People" are reading as *students* who will attempt applying the recipes given. Nothing of the sort. *The reading of a book on the attaining of success is in itself the symbolic attaining of that success.* It is *while they read* that these readers are "succeeding." I'll wager that, in by far the great majority of cases, such readers make no serious attempt to apply the book's recipes. The lure of the book resides in the fact that the reader, while reading it, is then living in the aura of success. What he wants is *easy* success; and he gets it in symbolic form by the mere reading itself. To attempt applying such stuff in real life would be very difficult, full of many disillusioning problems.

Sometimes a different strategy may arise. The author may remain realistic, avoiding too easy a form of solace —yet he may get as far off the track in his own way. Forgetting that realism is an aspect for foretelling, he may take it as an end in itself. He is tempted to do this by two factors: (1) an *ill-digested* philosophy of science, leading him mistakenly to assume that "relentless" naturalistic "truthfulness" is a proper end in itself, and (2) a merely *competitive* desire to outstrip other writers by being "more realistic" than they. Works thus made "efficient" by tests of competition internal to the book trade are a kind of academicism not so named (the writer usually thinks of it as the *opposite* of academicism). Realism thus stepped up competitively might be distinguished from the proper sort by the name of "naturalism." As a way of "sizing things up," the naturalistic tradition tends to become as inaccurate as the "inspirational" strategy, though at the opposite extreme.

Anyhow, the main point is this: A work like *Madame Bovary* (or its homely American translation, *Babbitt*) is the strategic naming of a situation. It singles out a pattern of experience that is sufficiently representative of our social structure, that recurs sufficiently often *mutatis mutandis*, for people to "need a word for it" and to adopt an attitude towards it. Each work of art is the addition of a word to an informal dictionary (or, in the case of purely derivative artists, the addition of a subsidiary meaning to a word already given by some originating artist). As for *Madame Bovary*, the French critic Jules de Gaultier proposed to add it to our *formal* dictionary by coining the word "Bovarysme" and writing a whole book to say what he meant by it.

Mencken's book on *The American Language*, I hate to say, is splendid. I console myself with the reminder that Mencken didn't write it. Many millions of people wrote it, and Mencken was merely the amanuensis who took it down from their dictation. He found a true "vehicle" (that is, a book that could be greater than the author who wrote it). He gets the royalties, but the job was done by a collectivity. As you read that book, you see a people who were up against a new set of typical recurrent situations, situations typical of their business, their politics, their criminal organizations, their sports. Either there were no words for these in standard English, or people didn't know them, or they didn't "sound right." So a new vocabulary arose, to "give us a word for it." I see no reason for believing that Americans are unusually fertile in word-coinage. American slang was not developed out of some exceptional gift. It was developed out of the fact that new typical situations had arisen and people needed names for them. They had to "size things up." They had to console and strike, to promise and admonish. They had to describe for purposes of forecasting. And "slang" was the result. It is, by this analysis, simply *proverbs not so named*, a kind of "folk criticism."

3.

With what, then, would "sociological criticism" along these lines be concerned? It would seek to codify the various strategies which artists have developed with relation to the naming of situations. In a sense, much of it would even be "timeless," for many of the "typical, recurrent situations" are not peculiar to our own civilization at all. The situations and strategies framed in Aesop's Fables, for instance, apply to human relations now just as fully as they applied in ancient Greece. They are, like philosophy, sufficiently "generalized" to extend far beyond the particular combination of events named by them in any one instance. They name an "essence." Or, we could say that they are on a "high level of abstraction." One doesn't usually think of them as "abstract," since they are usually so concrete in their stylistic expression. But they invariably aim to discern the "general behind the particular" (which would suggest that they are good Goethe).

The attempt to treat literature from the standpoint of situations and strategies suggests a variant of Spengler's notion of the "contemporaneous." By "contemporaneity" he meant corresponding stages of different cultures. For instance, if modern New York is much like decadent Rome, then we are "contemporaneous" with decadent Rome, or with some corresponding decadent city among the Mayas, etc. It is in this sense that situations are "timeless," "non-historical," "contemporaneous." A given human relationship may be at one time named in terms of foxes and lions, if there are foxes and lions about; or it may now be named in terms of salesmanship, advertising, the tactics of politicians, etc. But beneath the change in particulars, we may often discern the naming of the one situation.

So sociological criticism, as here understood, would seek to assemble and codify this lore. It might occasionally lead us to outrage good taste, as we sometimes found exemplified in some great sermon or tragedy or abstruse work of philosophy the same strategy as we found exemplified in a dirty joke. At this point, we'd put the sermon and the dirty joke together, thus "grouping by situation" and showing the range of possible particularizations. In his exceptionally discerning essay, "A Critic's Job of Work," R. P. Blackmur says, "I think on the whole his (Burke's) method could be applied with equal fruitfulness to Shakespeare, Dashiell Hammett, or Marie Corelli." When I got through wincing, I had to admit that Blackmur was right. This article is an attempt to say for the method what can be said. As a matter of fact, I'll go a step further and maintain: You can't properly put Marie Corelli and Shakespeare apart until you have first put them together. First genus, then differentia. The strategy in common is the genus. The *range* or *scale* or *spectrum* of particularizations is the differentia.[1]

Anyhow, that's what I'm driving at. And that's why reviewers sometime find in my work "intuitive" leaps that are dubious as "science." They are not "leaps" at all. They are classifications, groupings, made on the basis of some strategic element common to the items grouped. They are neither more nor less "intuitive" than *any* grouping or classification of social events. Apples can be grouped with bananas as fruits, and they can be grouped with tennis balls as round. I am simply proposing, in the social sphere, a method of classification with reference to *strategies*.

The method has these things to be said in its favor: It gives definite insight into the organization of literary works; and it automatically breaks down the barriers erected about literature as a specialized pursuit. People can classify novels by reference to three kinds, eight kinds, seventeen kinds. It doesn't matter. Students patiently copy down the professor's classification and pass examinations on it, because the range of possible academic classifications is endless. Sociological classification, as herein suggested, would derive its relevance from the fact that it should apply both to works of art and to social situations outside of art.

[1] See footnote 1 (p. 225) of the essay, "Freud—and the Analysis of Poetry."

It would, I admit, violate current pieties, break down current categories, and thereby "outrage good taste." But "good taste" has become *inert*. The classifications I am proposing would be *active*. I think that what we need is active categories.

These categories will lie on the bias across the categories of modern specialization. The new alignment will outrage in particular those persons who take the division of faculties in our universities to be an exact replica of the way in which God himself divided up the universe. We have had the Philosophy of Being; and we have had the Philosophy of Becoming. In typical contemporary specialization, we have been getting the Philosophy of the Bin. Each of these mental localities has had its own peculiar way of life, its own values, even its own special idiom for seeing, thinking, and "proving." Among other things, a sociological approach should attempt to provide a reintegrative point of view, a broader empire of investigation encompassing the lot.

What would such sociological categories be like? They would consider works of art, I think, as strategies for selecting enemies and allies, for socializing losses, for warding off evil eye, for purification, propitiation, and desanctification, consolation and vengeance, admonition and exhortation, implicit commands or instructions of one sort or another. Art forms like "tragedy" or "comedy" or "satire" would be treated as *equipments for living*, that size up situations in various ways and in keeping with correspondingly various attitudes. The typical ingredients of such forms would be sought. Their relation to typical situations would be stressed. Their comparative values would be considered, with the intention of formulating a "strategy of strategies," the "over-all" strategy obtained by inspection of the lot.

The Literature of Extreme Situations
Albert Votaw

from

Horizon, 20, 1949.

ALBERT VOTAW

THE LITERATURE OF EXTREME SITUATIONS

In the Greek theatre scenes of violence took place off-stage. These sad and awful events were revealed to the audience only through the spoken words of the play's characters. Recently women fainted and riots broke out when in Sartre's play, *The Unburied Dead*, men were physically tortured on the stage.

The theme of pure violence has become central to literature today. Modern literature has come more and more to deal with lonely men in extreme situations—that is, in situations in which the use of power is so radically unbalanced that communication becomes virtually impossible. The relationships between master and slave, between torturer and victim, replace the collaboration of equals, which was the material of previous literatures. It seems that it is only by the blind violence of his reactions that the modern hero can somehow overcome his stupor and his despair, when confronted by the huge and hostile universe within which, abandoned by both friends and witnesses, he must make his way.

KAFKA AND MISS BLANDISH

It is not by accident that many of the literary ancestors of this literature of extreme situations are Americans. For the American imaginative writer, who was never 'kept' by an aristocracy and whose production was never highly regarded by the hustling American middle class, was the first to develop fully the themes of loneliness, violence, and despair which seem so close to reality to many contemporary readers. The violence and frustration of these 'American' writers, lost in the vast reaches of the New World, appeal to the modern European intellectual, who feels similarly abandoned in an historical process which, since no European country can be legitimately considered a great power, has ceased to be meaningful to him. Theirs is a particularly successful presentation of problems which many today, and with good reason, feel to be vital.

Like this 'American' genre, modern literature expresses the absurd necessity and the naked violence of man's solitary revolt against himself. And the literature of extreme situations has pushed these themes to an extreme in utilizing a development which pervades the whole literature of our times. For in a certain sense the literature-type for the generation which considers itself trapped between the Second and the Third World Wars is a symbiotic union of the modern detective story with the novels of Kafka.

The absurd universe of Franz Kafka awakened a response in the unhappy conscience of many an intellectual today. For them the world is only slightly more horrible than the nightmarish universe through which Kafka's heroes pass as if in a fourth dimension, without ever realizing any real contact. Kafka's anonymous heroes are condemned to a meaningless struggle with the minutiae of everyday existence while seemingly oblivious to the horrible absurdities of the world in which they are imprisoned; they must go through the motions of ordinary living whilst thrown into situations whose every aspect is a cruel mockery of normal life. In *The Castle*, K. arrives in a little village, to which he has been sent to exercise his trade. But he cannot begin to work until he is received at the castle, which dominates the village and from which all media of communication are systematically cut. Thus K. must continue his obstinate and inevitably fruitless attempts to gain entry to the castle without ever daring seriously to explore the possibilities of settling down *without* first passing by the castle. Likewise in *The Trial*, Joseph K. occupies his time with the inanities of daily existence while knowing all the time that he will one day be tried and convicted by a court whose function he ignores and under a law he does not know for a crime of which he is never accused.

It would be a mistake to regard Kafka's work exclusively from this angle. But in these two novels, as in his other works, one of the most important elements is certainly his picture of the hero, worried about the minor inconsistencies and problems of living while at the same time either unconscious of or resigned to the monstrous absurdities of the system within which he lives. Thus it would seem that the heroes of Kafka are not the genuine modern heroes. They are to a certain extent at one with their universe, as the heroes of the medieval farces and miracle plays were at one with their, to us, absurd universe of prayer, miracles and salvation. The salient mark of the modern hero is not simply that he is not at one with his universe, that he is estranged. *He is also in revolt.* Although his universe is Kafka's, his attitude is not.

If, ironically enough, it is to an intellectual that we owe the first full presentation of the absurd, this is not so with violence. The increasing emphasis on pure violence forms an integral part of the development of what we might call popular literature: the comics, the pulps, the detective stories, etc. The heavy-handed display of sexuality and violence in the comics today are a far cry from the innocent anti-social activities of the 'Thimble Theatre', 'The Captain and the Kids', or 'Krazy Kat'. Similarly remarkable is the shift from the cerebral exercise of Sherlock Holmes to the perverted brutality of the modern murder mystery.

There are two essential elements in the modern detective story which relate it to the literature of extreme situations. In the first place, the hero operates outside of the conventions of society. He is frequently a private detective, who, although formally dedicated to upholding law and order, can accomplish this only by violating certain of the laws of the society he is theoretically defending. His capabilities and achievements are sharply contrasted with the unimaginative and unproductive blunderings of the orthodox guardians of the peace. His activity is revolutionary in the sense that it ignores the legal framework of society. Like the political revolutionary, who justifies his destructive work by an appeal to the fundamental laws of society, he must violate the existing laws in the name of a higher good. And both figures, who stand alone, thrown back entirely on their own individual resources, must expiate their anti-social acts by the periodic submission to violence.

The other essential element of the modern detective story is, precisely, this presentation of violence. Violence is an integral part of the actions of those who, standing alone, violate custom in the name of some higher good. Literary tradition utilizes violence primarily as a means: it is the inevitable companion of those who deal regularly with the naked forces of power; it is also the expiatory mechanism by which the hero recognizes the superiority of society. But in the modern detective story a significant shift has occurred: violence becomes an end in itself. The description of gratuitous violence, frequently accompanied by marked sexual over-tones, has become more and more important. Especially in films or in the comics has the visual display of this gratuitous violence become primary. Aside from the subtle, perverted sexual gratification such scenes afford, the exercise of violence is a method by which the modern hero can purge himself of his guilty feelings of hatred against the stifling and hostile stupidity of the mediocrities who represent society, the crowd, the human race—all those ugly absurdities against which he is in revolt. Our time is, however, not a revolutionary time; thus the heroes of popular literature must always ultimately submit to the recognized authorities—moral or legal. It is only in the works of those writers who are in conscious revolt against society that this violence is permitted to remain in its unregenerate purity.

The development of this literature of extreme situations dates back into the last century. From Russia came the haunted cry of Dostoevski, presenting in his characters the passions of men who, fearing that God was dead, asked whether, now, everything was permitted. The adolescent Rimbaud poured out his hatred against God, society, and mankind; then denied his own poetic achievement to run guns in Abyssinia. The 'American' school highlighted these themes of estrangement and violence. For the first time, too, these themes were combined with the theme of social revolution, although it is significant that the heroes of even these writers remained isolated—like Robert Jordan, pressed on his belly in the sun, waiting for a violent and lonely death. So it is not surprising that today, after the death of so many illusions, these themes should reach their full development, not only in the writings of, for instance, the French existentialists (whom we consider to have most consciously exploited the possibilities of a literature of extreme situations) and of Camus, but also in the works of a host of other writers.

These themes—isolation, frustration, absurdity, violence—are entangled with a passionate assertion of human worth and dignity. Today's literature of extreme situations, although fully aware of the depravity of man, is not a literature of resignation or of conformity. In contrast with both Kafka and the detective story, then, it is a literature of conscious revolt. And its themes pervade almost the entirety of modern literature, so much so that in writers whose conclusions differ radically, there is a striking similarity, even to the extent of a near identity of language, in their presentation of certain key problems.

Ignazio Silone's recent play, *And He Hid Himself*, is a clear-cut call for a return to the primitive Christian ethic—hardly a Sartrian approach. Yet his characters, victimized by their own fear, can overcome their misery by the simple resolute decision (a familiar existentialist stand-by) to deny this fear. We have come to join the underground, say, in effect, the peasants at the end of Silone's play, because we want to exorcize the dishonour and fear which are rotting out our land. This is, as Jupiter tells Egistus in Sartre's *Flies*, the secret of the gods: 'Once liberty has exploded in the soul of a man, the gods can do nothing against that man.'[1] This is also the vulnerable spot of the Plague: ' . . . all that is necessary is for a man to surmount his fear and to revolt, and his (the Plague's) machine begins to break down.'[2] And the words of Silone's Fascist doctor, who states that he feels as if collaboration with the Fascist regime in Italy has somehow prevented him from living, are remarkably like those of Garcin (*No Exit*) or of Mathieu (*Age of Reason*), searching for *their* act, for the act which will give their life meaning, for the freedom without which their life has wasted away.

Equally striking, and much more frequently noted, are the similarities between Sartre and Malraux, whose essay, *Temptation of the Occident* (1925), Sartre has admitted, contains almost all of the themes of existentialist philosophy. (Malraux has also evoked the myth of Sisyphus, later to be developed by Camus.) For Malraux society is not evil or unreasonable: it is merely absurd—just that, no more and no less. Each man knows that he has chosen neither to be born nor to die; and what he resents more than anything else is the fact that the world is completely independent of him—of his very existence as well as of his desires. Man is, in fact, nothing but his acts. He is, therefore, isolated from his fellows, who are not his peers but those who judge him. (The theme of Sartre's *No Exit* is precisely that a man can be judged only by his acts, not at all by his ideals or hopes. And Sartre has pushed to an extreme this analysis of the Regard of another; it is this regard

[1] *Les Mouches*, from Sartre, *Theatre I*, Paris: Gallimard, 1947, p. 79. Here, as in all cases where reference is made to a French publication, the translation is the present writer's.

[2] Albert Camus, *État de Siège*, Paris: Gallimard, 1948, p. 178.

which, by destroying the personal universe which an individual carefully constructs about himself, immobilizes him and transforms him into some*thing* regarded, thus, in effect, judging him.) And, finally, Malraux's remark in *Man's Hope*, that death transforms life into destiny, thus fixing it in its ultimate absurdity and contingency, has been frankly utilized by Sartre in his own analysis of death in *Being and Nothingness*.

Similar themes, we have said, but different conclusions. For, unlike Silone, Sartre is frankly atheist, feeling that the concept of God is logically untenable and spiritually debilitating. And unlike Malraux, who is eternally in revolt and whose characters deny that any social transformation can ease the burden of their inmost alienation, Sartre seems definitely to feel that, although no social change can *in itself* improve man's condition, certain profound social changes are necessary before men can hope successfully to shake off their bad faith and spiritual misery.

EXISTENTIALISM AND THE ROMANTIC PROTEST

Much has been made of the similarities between existentialism and Romanticism. The unhappy conscience of the existential hero has been identified with the Romantic *mal de siècle* of the post-Napoleonic era. And to a certain extent this comparison is justified. Many of the existentialist philosophers utilized the currents of, especially, the English and German Romantics. (Heidegger, for example was especially fond of Hölderlin and Rilke.) Jean Wahl has categorically related the Romantic and existentialist periods since, in both, poetry and philosophy are combined and the strange is made familiar and the familiar strange (a feeling echoed by Rocquetin, hero of Sartre's first novel, *Nausea*).

But an even more important similarity is that in both cases the point of departure is a reaffirmation of the individual. This is a logical result of an age in which the basic values of a civilization are in question and when the old society is disintegrating. Unable to find comfort in the ideals of the society into which he was born, the intellectual is forced to look for them within himself—and within other individuals.

French classical philosophy and literature moved within certain prescribed and well-defined limits. Within these limits there was, of course, room for discussion and conflict. But, globally speaking, society and the universe were well ordered. Similarly in the late nineteenth century, although God was ignored or suppressed, the universe was clearly defined and Progress reigned benignly over the world. The formal structure and limited vocabulary of French classical literature were destroyed by the structural and linguistic effusion of Romanticism in the same fashion that the discoveries of modern physics have destroyed the mechanistic universe of nineteenth-century liberalism by demolishing its concepts of space, time, and causality. In the first case, the literary crisis became apparent immediate with the downfall of the Old Regime; in the second, it has taken the scientifically controlled atrocities of Auschwitz and of Hiroshima to sear on the literary consciousness that, if God does not exist, there is no reason for men to act as if He still did.

The parallel between the existentialist and Romantic protests becomes even more striking when one compares the political situation of France after the Napoleonic wars with the situation today. The French Romantic had grown up with his whole youth directed towards participation in the revolutionary conquests of Napoleon. With the defeat at Waterloo, the whole purpose was brutally torn from the lives of that generation, (e.g. Alfred de Musset, *Confessions d'un Enfant du Siècle*, and Alfred de Vigny, *Grandeurs et Servitudes Militaires*.) Similarly, many young French writers pinned their hopes on the Communist revolution and, subsequently, on the Liberation. Both were felt to be identical with socialism and with the realization of that type of society in which these writers felt they could lose their despair. But the French Communist Party, especially after the Nazi-Soviet Pact, has bitterly disappointed many French intellectuals; and the fond hopes which were entertained at the Liberation have, finally, been quietly murdered by the sordid realities of the Fourth Republic. Thus, as in 1815, a whole generation has suddenly been deprived of its ideal and its reason for existence.

This terrible isolation explains the popularity today of those writers whose situation was, precisely, marked by their lack of sympathy with the most dynamic social force of their time. The French Romantics were anti-bourgeois: whether monarchist, anti-political, or subsequent participants in the political battle for bourgeois democracy, they all despised and condemned the mediocrity, stupidity, and lack of aesthetic sensitivity of the middle class.[1] Camus and the French existentialists, in revolt against their society, are nevertheless, with the exception of Merleau-Ponty, equally anti-Stalinist. This stand, when one considers the vast influence of Stalinism among French intellectuals, can only accentuate the loneliness of these writers. And it is significant that Sartre's criticism of Stalinism—lack of good faith, anti-intellectualism, degeneration, etc.—parallels remarkably the Romantic attacks on the French bourgeoisie, both being almost exclusively literary in nature.

There are, then, two important ways in which the existentialists resemble the Romantics: both formulated an affirmation of individual worth as an antidote to the dissolution of society about them; both stood isolated from the new dynamic force of their time. In spite of these similarities, however, the existentialists differ from the Romantics in certain aspects so basic that the usual simple comparison between the two is misleading. In the first place, the military defeat of Napoleon, although reversing the revolutionary wave with which the young Romantics identified themselves, left them at least the Napoleonic legend and the dream of the Republic. Ideals are always easier to retain if the movements with which they are identified live on only in the imagination. On the contrary, those writers who once identified their ideas with the Soviet regime, have no such easy escape. They are constantly at grips with the Stalinist apparatus, the unburied, stinking corpse of their ideals. They cannot, therefore, look back nostalgically towards the revolutionary past, villainously and unfairly murdered by The Enemy. The comforting presence of an ideal, pure and undefiled by actuality, is denied these modern writers. Faced with an only too real movement, which claims to embody their ideals, they are thus more fully demoralized than were ever their Romantic predecessors.

More demoralized and infinitely more alone. The Romantics were, almost with out exception, both deeply religious and profoundly attached to nature. But even this solace is denied the modern intellectual. For many of them belief in God is impossible;

[1] Similarly, Dostoevski was opposed to the western ideas then infiltrating into Russia. Rimbaud rejected the entirety of bourgeois society, including its movements of protest; Kafka likewise, although in a less catagorical fashion. The 'Americans', isolated from American society, could never fully enter the Stalinist church.

they have retained this much, at least, of nineteenth-century liberalism. To resurrect God at this point—as has done, for instance, Silone—would be a denial of their entire past and a surrender to a force which has nothing in common with their own aspirations. Nature, too, is cold and disinterested in man's fate. Especially for those influenced by the existentialist emphasis on man's basic non-affinity with nature, the beauty and power of nature are no solace. No matter how loudly man in his anguish may cry out, the gods are unmoved and nature rests stony and silent. With no possible comfort available outside of his own tortured soul, the modern hero—and especially the existentialist hero—is more lonely than any man has ever been.

THE CONCENTRATION-CAMP UNIVERSE

If the modern hero is more lonely than the Romantic, he is not as alone. If the Romantic expressed his anguish in solitude, the modern hero is usually in—and against—the crowd. And, interestingly enough, this crowd is composed mainly of prisoners.

It is highly significant that the specific form which the literature of extreme situations most frequently takes is that of a literature of prisons, or, most recently, of concentration camps. This is not only true in a broadly metaphorical sense—in which one might say that the heroes of Kafka are imprisoned in the absurd universe about them, or that Faulkner's characters are imprisoned in a little village in Mississippi. The undertones of frustration and impotence, from which the modern hero can only emerge by pure violence, are being localized more and more in real prisons and prison camps. Prison is home for the characters of Malraux, Koestler, and Rousset. Camus's Stranger finishes his days in prison; and the characters of his second novel are imprisoned in a pestilential city. In Sartre's works, the themes of prison are even more emphasized: the heroes of *The Wall, No Exit,* and *The Unburied Dead,* are literally imprisoned; the characters of *Red Gloves* (as 'Dirty Hands' has been mis-translated) have imprisoned themselves in their flight from prison. Many of his other characters are enclosed within walls which, if not prison walls, serve as their equivalent. Marcelle, holed up in her room, faces the problems of freedom differently than does Mathieu, the drifter, the inauthentic, who is free to move from room to room (*Age of Reason*). The helpless invalids in *The Reprieve,* symbols of a decaying society, are glued in their beds, powerless even to respond to their bodily necessities without outside help. More and more the characters of modern fiction, whose actions are increasingly limited within the walls of the bedroom or the bar, are coming to reassemble the inhabitants of a vast prison camp.

To a certain extent this prison-camp literature is an extension of the flood of accounts which followed the collapse of Hitler's Reich. Deportees, internees, forced labourers, 'anti-social elements', prisoners-of-war—all of these categories had a story to tell. And, to the horror and initial incredulity of their audiences, their stories were remarkably similar. Almost without exception they told of how the concentration camp had, itself, become a society, cemented together by naked violence and terror and organized for certain absurd purposes which defy explanation by any classical liberal formulae. Almost all told of how it was the prisoners themselves, organized into veritable social classes, who administered the camps, fought among themselves for power, and were each others' torturers. Some of these accounts were written by men who needed to purge themselves in this way of an experience which, by its revelation of the infinite possibilities of man's inhumanity towards man, paralysed their will and infected their soul. Others were written by former members of the concentrationary upper class, justifications after the event for the atrocities they had to perpetuate in order to gain a few comforts for themselves and for some of their comrades. Still others are serious sociological studies, analyses, and warnings. But no matter what their nature, these accounts testify to the condition of men who have just escaped the concentration camp universe of the Nazis to discover the same system engulfing their country from the East; of men who have just passed through a period in which arrest or deportation had become the symbol of manhood.

But this is only a partial explanation. There are other, deeper reasons for the terrible actuality of the concentration camp literature. Certain themes which have been pointed up by this literature were already exploited generally in modern literature, and this well before the war. The historical fact that Nazi Germany imprisoned millions of persons, cannot account for the fact that modern literature, after first becoming a literature of extreme situations in general, is now becoming a literature of concentration camps in particular. Neither can it account for the marked similarity of treatment and theme between the existentialist and the concentrationary universe.

It would seem that in the concentration camp are realized more completely than ever before certain philosophic themes common to most existential thinkers but most fully developed by Sartre. For instance, the basic theme of man's existence is, philosophically, that he is thrown into a world without his willing it and with no place prepared for him. The situation, precisely, of those who, for no apparent reason—or, at least, not as the result of any 'criminal' act on their part—found themselves imprisoned; and this not in a prison, where their cell was prepared in advance, but in a camp, where they would have to wrest their bunk space from their fellow prisoners. The refusal on the part of certain prisoners to believe that they were really arrested and that some error had not been made; their compulsive faith that the laws of justice they were accustomed to would prevail even under the regime of terror (a feeling heightened in the Soviet camps by the practice of plastering the walls with revolutionary slogans)—these attitudes only increased the difficulties of adjustment. (In Sartre's philosophy these sterile tentatives, which follow man's refusal to recognize the absurdity of his situation, are called 'bad faith'.) The mental disintegration of newly arrived elements in the camps, as described by psychological observers, is paralleled by the feeling of abandonment and anguish of Kierkegaard or Sartre.

Even more striking than this general similarity are the near-identity of certain quite specific themes in both existentialism and the concentration camp literature. For the existentialists, one of the main problems of human existence is the flight from the crowd. The enervating anonymity which the mass engenders is one of the chief obstacles to a genuinely individual existence. In the concentration camp, the flight from the crowd takes on more urgency. For it is precisely the omnipresence of the crowd which completes the social disintegration of the prisoners. One is never alone: one eats in crowds, gulping down the food to prevent someone from stealing it; one walks and relaxes with a crowd; transportation is *en masse*; bodily functions must be performed hastily and amidst the jostling and smell of other bodies; and, ultimately, one sleeps with a crowd—not just in the presence of others, but twenty men on a shelf, for instance, packed so tightly together that one man cannot turn from one side to the other without forcing the whole group to do likewise. In such a situation it is easy to understand why 'Hell is the others', why there is no need for torturer or stake; the condemned serve themselves—cafeteria style.[1]

It is in precisely this aspect that the concentration camps differ from the prisons. In the latter, at least, the prisoner can retain his own dignity. When he is arrested, he is put into *his* cell. The prison administration looks to him: he is fed, interrogated, moved from cell to cell, etc. But all the while it is *he* who is the centre of a certain concern. Even under torture, it is still an individual's freedom and dignity which is in question: the one attacking, the other defending them. To be tortured means, for the victim, that he, as an individual, is considered as possessing something which the torturer desires. A man may or may not confess under torture. But he is never systematically degraded and demoralized, by accident as it were, as is the unfortunate inmate of a prison camp.

In such a situation it is easy to understand the prisoner's pre-occupation with his own body. As in Sartre's philosophy, it is by and through his own physical body—which at times he can regard as if he were regarding any other thing—that a man comes into relationship with the world about him. And this brute, physical thing is contingent and superfluous; it is *in excess*, with its pains, its sores, its smells, and its inadaptability. The prisoner becomes nauseated with his own body; if only he were not condemned to exist through this thing, how much less disgusting life would be. Certain accounts describe various prisoners regarding their diseased extremities with the almost ontological detachment of Sartre's analysis of the body in *Being and Nothingness*.

To escape from the terrible present, the prisoners exploited as fully as possible their dreams, reveries, and imagination. At night the prisoners frequently dreamed of vast spaces, of intricately finished works of art, of banquets, or of their hoped-for life after release—on the other side of the wall. During the day-time the occasional sight or memory of a beautiful scene or, above all, the constant reverie of his life which was and which was to be maintained the prisoner in a sort of never-never world, where past and future combined to make a present in which time had stopped. These dreams—these projects, if we may use the existentialist term—coloured the prisoners' existence. These dream-projects, especially those involving ultimate liberation, protected the

[1] Sartre, *Huis Clos*, in *Theatre I*, op. cit., pp. 133-4, 167.

prisoner from his surroundings; around them he organized his concentration-camp universe. The project and imagination, as in Sartre's psychology, became the primary mode of perception.

It is important that, in spite of the terror and in spite of the degradation, there was a certain area of free choice which, to a large extent, could determine a prisoner's chance of survival. We refer, of course, to the decision which almost every prisoner at one time had to make regarding the extent of his co-operation with the camp administration. This was in every sense of the word a free choice. Although this freedom can hardly be compared to the freedom of the British housewife to buy one of several brands of tooth-paste, it is infinitely more vital. Freedom, in this situation, is not a mere word; it is at the very heart of the prisoner's existence. That Sartre chose, then, to develop Hegel's discussion of the master and the slave in his own explication of liberty is only one more striking example of the appropriateness of his philosophy to the most important single experience of our times.

(This startling similarity extends even to certain minor points in the two literatures. In *Being and Nothingness*, for example, Sartre discusses the use of language, not as an instrument, but as one of the basic conducts of man, equal to love, desire, hate, etc. In the concentration camps, language was, likewise, a veritable conduct—the only free conduct, actually. For the one thing which the guards could not do in the Nazi camps was force the foreign prisoners to speak German. Recognizing this, these men revelled in the use of their native tongue, especially when in earshot of the guards. For the German prisoners their linguistic expression was in songs, some of which were sung with such vigour that they were eventually forbidden.)

The concentration camp is not, however, society. But the actuality of the literature of extreme situations is due ultimately to the fact that in the concentration camp is realized nothing more than the logical extension of certain aspects of modern society. This is obvious in the totalitarian states, where, as in the concentration camps, it is terror which holds the society together. But even in the more democratic states, social disintegration and irresponsibility, the forerunners of terror, are playing an increasing role. The subjugation of individual initiative to the enervating and unpredictable pressures of almost every aspect of a mass-production society is not unconnected with the naked brutality of a forced labour camp. The popularity of the concentration-camp literature is one indication of the unconscious fear that in these books is a prediction of man's fate.

The most obvious precursor of the forced labour camp is the assembly line. The intuitive discoveries of, for example, the Chaplin film, *Modern Times*, have been only recently studied systematically. It has been found that the monotony of work, the long trips to and from work, and the anonymous, mass existence of the factory worker in everything connected with his job result in widespread lack of initiative, demoralization, and an unhealthy complex of unexpressed resentment and guilt feelings. Like the prison camp inmate, the factory worker is, in many cases, nothing more than a number. Like the former, the factory worker is frequently shifted from job to job, forced to quit 'his' machine for another, for reasons unconnected with any of his immediate experiences—and hence, to him, arbitrary and absurd. And the system of relationships within the factory, including the one and only method of improving one's position—that, is by 'pull'—is mirrored in the concentration camp.

The most shocking aspect of the camps—and that it should be so shocking is itself significant—is the careful elaboration of the scientifically perfected methods of extermination. Nothing was wasted. The prisoners stripped themselves of all their clothing and then went into chambers in which their own body heat released the toxic gases. Afterwards, before burial, they were methodically stripped of hair, gold teeth, etc.—anything that might prove useful. The Nazi death camps, which, it should be remembered, were only *one* type of concentration camp, were a triumph of human ingenuity and science. The dream of the nineteenth century was the perfection of science to the point where man could control his environment. It was felt that this achievement could not but be good. The extermination camps, which were the technical realization of this ideal, have partly dispelled this illusion. As is the case outside the camps, the developments of science have created a nightmare world in which man, like the sorcerer's apprentice, can no longer control the forces he has unleashed. When a society stands on the threshold of a vast upheaval, technological changes develop a momentum of their own which, ever accelerating, upsets and deranges the entire structure of society. And we ordinary mortals, lacking the world-view of the well-paid preacher or engineer, instinctively react in self-defence against this force. In the technical achievements of the Nazi death camps, many persons saw a justification for their heretical fear of science.

This instinctive fear of science first was marked in popular literature. (Naturally. Since the intellectual, as a member of the middle class, is less defenceless against the ravages of technology than are the lower classes—especially the urban working class.) In both the comics and the films scientists and doctors have become villains. They are those who, by upsetting what was 'ordinary' and 'right', menaced the individual. The white coat of a doctor or of a laboratory worker has become, in many films and comic strips, the symbol of the unnatural and the horrible.

Finally, the concentration camp is the inevitable component of a society in which democratic procedures have been replaced by authoritarianism. This destruction of democracy is, unfortunately, not a simple matter of the triumph of evil men over good. It seems to be the almost inevitable outcome of a society which has become too big and too complicated. Factories and trade unions, private organizations and the state: all are heavily bureaucratized. These new behemoths, self-winding and self-regenerating, come more and more to dominate society as they destroy local initiative and responsibility. Thus democratic control becomes impossible: for how is the mass to control the specialist?

In a certain sense, the concentration-camp society is an answer to man's irresponsibility towards man—as in *The Castle* of Kafka no responsible individual interrelationships are possible: everything must be routed through the castle, through channels. Society has become so bureaucratized that no one knows any longer how to assess responsibilities, let alone to understand it fully. The only result can be the disappearance of small, self-governing bodies—what de Tocqueville over one hundred years ago called 'secondary powers'. With them disappear the training schools for democratic decision and control. Amorphous and enervated, the masses reach a point where only the concentration-camp state can control their actions and bring some sort of order—be it an absurd order—out of the chaos into which an overly bureaucratized society falls when it stubbornly clings to the ineffective machinery of liberal democracy.

The concentration camp is more than an experience. It is a portent and a warning. And modern literature, whose subject matter has become that of extreme situations and, specifically, of concentration camps, is a primitive reaction to this development. The French existentialists have then, in response to this situation, chosen merely to point up the themes of frustration, isolation, and futile violence, which pervade the whole of modern literature. They have not invented them.

The Writer and Social Strategy
Martin Turnell

from

Partisan Review, vol. 18, no. 2, 1951.

Reprinted by permission of the author.

Martin Turnell

THE WRITER AND SOCIAL STRATEGY

If we made a rough list of the principal European writers
of the last three hundred years, we should find that the vast majority
of them belonged to what are loosely called the middle classes. The
list would include a few aristocrats like the Duc de La Rochefoucauld
and the Duc de Saint-Simon and a few writers of proletarian origin
like John Bunyan or D. H. Lawrence; but they are exceptions and
represent only a tiny minority. Since this is so, it seems at first surprising that many writers should have spoken so ill of the class from which
they came, should have been so bitter in their denunciation of the
"bourgeois." Now the use of the expression "bourgeois" as a term of
abuse was not the invention of Karl Marx or of the nineteenth-century
anarchists. It is much older and, I feel tempted to add, much more
respectable. In 1666 the French novelist, Antoine Furetière, published
a work called *Le Roman bourgeois* which was a satirical picture of
middle-class manners in the seventeenth century. Three years later
Molière's comedy, *Le Bourgeois gentilhomme,* was played before
Louis XIV at the château of Chambord. Nor was this quite the beginning of the story. The bourgeois had been a stock figure of fun
in the old French and Italian farces and it was from this source that
Molière took his *bourgeois gentilhomme.*

Le Bourgeois gentilhomme is not of course among Molière's
supreme achievements. It was written for the purpose of light entertainment; and it is in his other works like *l'Ecole des femmes, Tartuffe*
and the *Misanthrope* that we must look for his most radical criticisms
of contemporary society. I shall suggest that the whole of his work
was an onslaught on the bourgeoisie, but before doing so I want to
look at the position of the middle classes in the seventeenth century.

They were, as their name suggests, a fluctuating body and we
can detect three main groups. There was an upper stratum which

tended to rise out of their class, to intermarry with the aristocracy or like the writers to move in court circles by virtue of their calling. At the other end of the scale were the provincials who were drifting toward the peasantry and who, living dim, ignorant and impoverished on their farms, were the constant butt of seventeenth-century wit. In between these two extremes came the bourgeoisie proper—the doctors, lawyers and merchants. They were prosperous, pious and respectable, and in spite of heavy attacks from the writers they were probably the most stable element in society.

Now though there are some grounds for identifying this middle stratum with the bourgeois of the novelists and playwrights, the identification cannot be absolute. The concept is not merely social; it is also moral. "When one has the good fortune to belong to a high rank," remarks a character in Molière's *Amphitryon,* "everything one does is fine and good." I think we can assume that the dramatist thoroughly endorsed this proposition. What he admired was *les grands,* was a certain aristocratic style of life. And the people whom he admired were not less great because they spent their lives at the Court instead of on the battlefield. Compared with *les grands,* the bourgeois represents (as a recent critic puts it) "a form of existence which is morally inferior and which is incapable of realizing *le beau caractère humain.*"[1] Looked at from this point of view, the whole of Molière's work is seen to be an attack on the middle-class way of life—particularly on its respectability. *L'Ecole des femmes* is an attack on the bourgeois conception of marriage; *Tartuffe* on its stuffy piety; *l'Avare* on a thriftiness which has turned into miserliness; the *Femmes savantes* on its intellectual pretensions. *Don Juan* certainly pillories the aristocratic free-thinkers of the day, but this does not prevent Molière from showing his bourgeois enemies in an excessively unfavorable light.

This attack on middle-class respectability, lack of adventurousness and, more important still, lack of real culture has led Molière's critics to describe his plays as subversive. There is certainly something in it. For we detect from time to time in his work a note of exasperation; and this exasperation probably led him to go further than he intended and developed into an apology not merely for the aristocratic style of life, but for a certain aristocratic licentiousness.

1. Paul Bénichou, *Morales du grand siècle,* Paris, 1948, p. 180.

So much for the writer's outlook. I want to turn next to his actual position in seventeenth-century society. In a short play called *La Critique de l'école des femmes,* which Molière wrote as a reply to his critics, the character who represents the dramatist himself uses these words:

The great test of all your comedies is the judgment of the Court. It is the taste of the Court that you must study if you want to discover the art of success. There is no place where opinions are so just; and without bringing in all the learned people who are there, through natural, simple good sense and mixing with the whole of the elegant world, there is created there an attitude of mind which, without comparison, judges things with more penetration than all the rusty learning of the pedants.

Now this was not idle flattery. There is no doubt that the Court of Louis XIV did represent an intellectual élite and that it did provide the writer with his audience. He lived by pleasing, and those whom he needed to please were first and foremost the people whom the King gathered round him.

How in fact did the writer live in the seventeenth century? The answer is that he lived by patronage. There were two forms of patronage—the private patron and the King.

The aristocrats were well pleased to have a few men of letters in their train and to pay for their services. When a dramatist published one of his plays it was generally prefaced by a fulsome eulogy addressed to one of the great; and the author was suitably recompensed. Some of the great were naturally more generous than others, and the writers soon found out who paid best for their dedications. One ingenious man made a practice of dedicating each edition of his books to a fresh patron simply by changing the name at the beginning of the dedication and drawing a further reward for his pains from the new patron.

I think that this suggests already the sort of relations which existed between what may be called the blood aristocracy and the intellectual aristocracy. The nobility paid the writer for his services, sometimes found a sinecure for him and for his literary friends in their households, but they also kept him strictly in his place. A writer who published a satire on a nobleman knew what to expect. A posse of the noble lord's servants would seek him out and administer a sound thrashing. Sometimes the victim would act himself. It is reported that one nobleman, who considered that he had been libeled by Molière, accosted the dramatist in a public place, caught hold of his head and rubbed his face violently against the metal buttons of his coat, repeating the gibes which had offended him in the play. The importance of the writer's function was fully recognized; he moved in high circles; but the division between him and the man of noble birth was absolute.

I turn now to what may be called state patronage. Handsome pensions had been given to men of letters under Louis XIII and during the Regency, but it was not until Louis XIV actually took possession of his throne in 1661 that an attempt was made to organize patronage on a substantial scale. Colbert at once enlisted the services of Chapelain, who was considered the greatest poet of the day, and invited him to prepare a suitable list of writers who were to be recommended for a pension. The list was duly prepared and the different writers endowed in accordance with their standing. They were expected to work for their money and one of Chapelain's most important duties—a duty which was zealously executed—was to go round and prod those authors whose stubborn muses failed to produce an ode of thanksgiving with sufficient promptness or who failed to commemorate royal births, deaths or convalescences. Those who still failed to deliver the goods or whose goods were not considered to be up to the necessary standard had the chagrin of discovering that their names were missing from the next year's list. On the other hand, those who like Racine grew in stature discovered—no doubt with gratitude—that the amount of their pensions kept pace with their literary progress. There were also other ways of rewarding the very great writers. Molière—always a favorite with Louis XIV—received a *gratification* every time one of his plays was performed before the King; and Racine and Boileau were made royal historiographers whose duty was to follow the armies and record the military victories of the Roi Soleil.

Unfortunately for the writers, the system of pensions was not quite as satisfactory in practice as it was in theory. There were delays in making payment and there were distressing discrepancies between the figures shown in the published list and the sums which they actually "touched." When the scheme was inaugurated, the pension was handed to the happy writer in a silk purse, but that did not last long.

Instructions were issued that the recipients must call and collect their pensions from the King's paymaster.

The system lasted from 1663—the year in which Chapelain's first list was made public—until 1690. It reached its peak in 1671. After that, the sums allocated to the purpose began to decline as Louis found other ways of spending his money—notably on the construction of the Palace of Versailles. In 1690 the whole scheme was jettisoned and deserving writers were privately rewarded.

What conclusions emerge? In the first place, the writers have already begun to form a class apart. They are decidedly hostile to that section of society into which they were born and like Molière do not hesitate to deliver violent attacks on it when the occasion arises. There is as yet nothing that can be called a genuine *déclassement*. The nobility refuse to admit for a moment that the writer or the artist is on the same social level as themselves; and though they find a place for him in their households, that place is essentially the position of a servant.

In the second place, the system of royal pensions can be said to consecrate the position of the writer in society, to stamp him as a useful and, indeed, an important member of the community. Now it must be emphasized that the system was in no sense charitable and that though Louis was a cultivated man, this alone would not have induced him to pay out substantial sums to writers. There was a solid business side to the transaction. The King and his ministers realized that the endowment of writers was very good publicity and contributed to the glory of the reign. Their function was perfectly clear. They were of course expected to introduce flattering references to His Majesty in their writings, and they did so; but—and this is the best side of the picture—they also performed this function simply by being very good writers, and the steadiness with which Racine's pension increased as his genius developed is highly creditable to everybody concerned.

In view of what I shall have to say about the nineteenth century, I want to emphasize particularly that in the main the writer was at one and not at odds with society. When, in the final scene of *Tartuffe*, Molière makes one of his characters say: *"Nous vivons sous un prince ennemi de la fraude,"* he meant what he said, and it seems to me that the whole of the play is behind this single line. Molière believed that in spite of abuses, which he did not hesitate to criticize, the order was in the main a sound one, and that the King was indeed the pivot of the whole grandiose and complicated structure. The abuses and scandals were seen in perspective and treated as flaws in an otherwise stable order. It is true that Racine had some stinging things to say about the dangers of absolute monarchy, that when we read him today we detect signs of the coming collapse and that La Bruyère had some pungent observations to make about the deplorable condition of the peasantry; but their criticisms were indirect and probably anything but obvious to contemporary audiences and readers. The prevailing impression is that the writer was a powerful support to the existing order. Nor should we forget that Saint-Simon's memoirs, with their devastating closing paragraph, did not see the light until the middle of the eighteenth century.

I do not propose to say more than a few words about the position of the writer in the eighteenth century. It was the century of the private rather than of the royal patron. It was also a good deal more democratic and egalitarian than the seventeenth century, and I think there is no doubt that the barriers between the nobility and the rest of society did tend to disappear. The private patron was less responsible than Louis XIV. He gave the tame writer plenty of license and rewarded him without much regard for the quality of his work, and he did not hesitate to administer a beating when the occasion arose.

II

The French Revolution and the destruction of the aristocracy created a completely new situation. We may think that the profession of literature had made considerable strides during the eighteenth century and that it was possible for the writer to rely to a much greater extent than before on the actual earnings from the sale of his works. That is true, but the gap between himself and his own class had also become wider, and when the aristocratic patron was swept away he found himself high and dry. This is how M. Jean-Paul Sartre describes the situation in his recent *Baudelaire*. In the eighteenth century, he says, the writer had been so to speak "aristocratized":

He belonged, however, by family ties, friendships and the mode of his daily life to a bourgeoisie which no longer had the means to justify him. The result was that he had come to feel that he was a person apart, in the air and rootless, a Ganymede who had been carried off in the claws of an eagle; and he had the continual feeling that he was superior to his milieu. But after the Revolution the bourgeoisie itself assumed power. It was this class which should logically have conferred on the writer a new status; but this could only have been done if the writer had consented to return to the bourgeois fold. Now there could be no question of that. In the first place, two hundred years of royal favors had taught the writer to despise the bourgeoisie; but, what was more important, he had been accustomed to regard himself as a clerk, cultivating pure thought and pure art. If he returned to his own class, he would undergo a radical change. If the bourgeoisie was, indeed, a class of oppressors, it was not parasitic; it despoiled the worker, but it worked with him. The creation of a work of art was equivalent to providing a service. The poet was expected to place his talent at the disposal of his class in the same way as an engineer. . . . In exchange, bourgeois society would invest the writer with a special aura. But he would lose on the deal. He would sacrifice his independence and his claim to superiority. He would, to be sure, be a member of an élite, but there was also an élite of doctors and an élite of solicitors. The hierarchy was constituted inside the class in accordance with its social utility; and the guild of artists would take a secondary position just above the teaching profession.

Such is M. Sartre's account of the situation which arose after the Revolution. Whatever its origins, the Revolution led to the emergence of a new and aggressive middle class—a middle class whose ethos was essentially bourgeois in the fullest sense of that term.

My first witness from among the writers of the time is Stendhal. I am going to quote three passages from his autobiography, *La Vie de Henri Brulard*:

My family were the most aristocratic people in the town. This meant that I became a fanatical republican on the spot.

All the elements which compose the life of Chrysale[2] have been replaced in my case by romance. I believe that this speck in my telescope has been useful to me as a novelist. There is a sort of *bassesse bourgeoise* to which my characters could never succumb.

I had, and still have, the most aristocratic of tastes. I would do everything in my power to ensure the happiness of the *peuple;* but I think that I would rather spend a fortnight of every month in prison than have to live with shopkeepers.

2. He was the bourgeois parent in Molière's *Femmes savantes.*

Stendhal like Baudelaire had personal reasons for revolting against the class into which he had been born, and we can see from the first of these three passages that his enthusiasm for political radicalism began as a protest against the attitude of his royalist family. We must, however, be clear about the implications of these pronouncements. Stendhal is not attacking merely the bourgeois like the majority of nineteenth-century writers. He is systematically rejecting the aristocracy, the bourgeoisie and the proletariat; and this makes his position a novel one. In the seventeenth and eighteenth centuries the writer had detached himself from one class, and if he did not succeed in becoming a member of a higher one, at least he achieved a clearly defined relation to it. In the nineteenth century he detached himself from the three main classes, but there was no other class or section of the community to which he could attach himself. This meant that ultimately he must form a new class of his own. With Stendhal the process did not go very far. He was constantly proclaiming his republicanism and his hatred of kings, but though he was officially a liberal republican, his fellow-republicans fare very ill in his novels. The principal character in *Lucien Leuwen*—the novel in which he attempts a direct criticism of the contemporary political scene—is continually deploring the dreary mediocrity of republicans and sighing for the return of a sort of silver age—very elegant, very aristocratic and, morally, decidedly lax. Although Stendhal was a great political novelist he took no active part in politics. He became like the heroes of his own novels an "outsider" and dedicated his books to "the happy few" who were scattered all over the world and who, he hoped, would enjoy them and sympathize with his opinions. But he made no attempt to organize his admirers. That was a task which was left to Baudelaire whose writings on the subject are really a development of the Stendhalian theory. His view of the writer's position is set out most clearly in his great essay on Constantin Guys:

Dandyism is an institution which though outside the law, has its own rigorous code to which all its adherents must strictly conform, however independent and free they may be by nature. . . . Dandyism appears chiefly in periods of transition when democracy is not yet all-powerful and aristocracy is only partly tottering and degraded. In the upheavals which belong to such periods, a handful of men . . . may conceive the plan of founding a new sort of aristocracy which will be all the more difficult to destroy because it will be based on the most precious and the most indestructible of faculties and on the divine gifts which work and money cannot confer.

Some of Baudelaire's sentences have a melodramatic ring and the word "dandy" has not worn well. It suggests something willfully freakish and "bohemian," something too local, too nineteenth century; but the reality for which it stands is not in doubt. It is a definition of the patrician attitude. I propose therefore to drop Baudelaire's term and re-name the "dandy" the patrician.

Baudelaire's essay is really the first attempt to create a writers' party. The writers must make common cause. Against the background of a society which is still fairly rigidly divided into three classes, we see the formation of what is in effect a new aristocracy based on the indestructible values which "work and money cannot confer," on the eternal values of intelligence and sensibility. Although the new aristocracy might be recruited from any social sphere, it soon developed its own peculiar characteristics and became in Baudelaire's words an exclusive "caste."

It is interesting to look at some of the political dicta which are to be found in Baudelaire's diaries and which have not had as much attention as they deserve:

There is no reasonable and certain form of government except an aristocratic one; monarchies or republics based on democracy are equally feeble and absurd.

Another entry has a prophetic note:

Politics. In short, in the eyes of history and of the French people, the great achievement of Napoleon III will have been to prove that the first comer who gains control of the telegraph and the national printing press can govern a great nation.

He penetrates to the heart of the matter when he observes in still another entry:

It is not particularly in political institutions that universal ruin or universal progress—for the name matters little—will manifest itself. It will be in the degradation of the human heart (*l'avilissement des coeurs*).

Although the issues were perceived more clearly in France and the statement of them by French writers was more radical, the movement was not confined to that country. Baudelaire's attack on the bourgeois and his plea for a patrician outlook had its parallel in

England in Arnold's attack on the "philistine" and his plea for "Hellenism":

"Our puritan middle classes," said Arnold, "present a defective type of religion, a narrow range of intellect and instruction, a stunted sense of beauty, a low standard of manners."

"If," wrote Baudelaire, "if a poet asked the State for permission to keep a few bourgeois in his stable, everyone would be greatly astonished; but if a bourgeois asked for some roast poet, it would be considered perfectly natural."

Baudelaire's violent tone may appear today to be somewhat exaggerated, but the conflict between the artist and the bourgeois was a real one and we need to see it in its historical setting.

In Stendhal's *Lucien Leuwen* one of the characters remarks to another:

M. Grandet is like myself at the head of the Bank, and since July[3] the Bank has been at the head of the State. The bourgeoisie has taken the place of the Faubourg Saint-Germain and the Bank is the nobility of the bourgeois class.

The Revolution had placed in power a middle class which was almost entirely devoted to money making. We know that the artist very properly refused to sell his pen to the bourgeois and their Bank, but this in itself is not sufficient to explain the violence of the opposition between the two. It seems at first as though there was nothing to prevent the artist from going on with his work without bothering about the banking activities of the bourgeois; but the conflict went much deeper than that. What the artist disliked was the bourgeois outlook, was Arnold's "narrow range of intellect and instruction, a stunted sense of beauty, a low standard of manners," because it was a threat to all that he stood for.

Now the conflict was sharpened because social and political changes had produced a change in the artist's vision. In the old unitary society the artist had been much more a "craftsman" than a "visionary." He might criticize abuses as Dante, Chaucer and Langland had criticized them, but there was no conflict between the artist and society. He not only expressed a communal as opposed to an individual experience; his work glorified an order in which he believed.

3. The advent of the July Monarchy.

Cracks began to appear in the social structure in the seventeenth and eighteenth centuries; but even in those centuries the writer was to a large extent the spokesman of an aristocratic élite. In the nineteenth century he was an "outsider" in an alien world. The old order had gone. There was no longer any external system to which his experience could be related. He therefore proclaimed that he was a "Seer" whose work was to discover a new order. He was engaged in his own way in a revision of values and, inevitably, he went into dangerous places where he made discoveries about human nature which were highly disturbing to his simpler minded contemporaries.

Nevertheless we sometimes have the impression that without willful provocation on the part of the artist there need have been no head-on collision, that the bourgeois were so immersed in the bank and the stock exchange that they would have been perfectly content to leave the artist to his own devices. That is not true. The modern artist is not merely a "Seer," he is also a revolutionary whose task is not to glorify the existing order but, as Rimbaud put it, to change it which means in practice to destroy it. Medieval art sprang from harmony between the artist and society, modern art springs from conflict between the two. It is of its essence subversive and the artist was right in doing his utmost to intensify the conflict.

The nineteenth-century preoccupation with money and material comfort and the desperation with which the commercial middle classes clung to *idées reçues* were the result of an immense sense of insecurity, an overwhelming need to find something solid and enduring in a world of dissolving values. Anything which threatened to aggravate their insecurity or to interfere with their operations on the stock exchange must be resisted at all costs. Given their premises, their instinct was obviously sound. For patrician art is necessarily individualist, sensitive, subtle, analytical, precarious and abstruse. Its very existence was unsettling, was a constant threat to security and business, as it was meant to be. The commercial middle classes retaliated by prosecuting Baudelaire and Flaubert on trumped-up charges of immorality and by breaking up exhibitions of paintings.[4] In doing so

4. "Trumped up" because their narrow preoccupation with sexual morality was evidently a rationalization, an attempt to suppress something far more disturbing which they sensed but could not define.

they made the artist a scapegoat whose sacrifice restored, or was intended to restore, their shattered complacency.

The active part taken by the nineteenth-century artist in politics seems at first perplexing. It is, perhaps, understandable that the youthful Rimbaud should have rebelled against his world and joined the Commune; but though the notes on politics which I have already quoted were almost certainly written after Baudelaire had severed his connection with the parties in 1851, it seems strange to meet him at the barricades in 1848 fighting on the side of the insurgents. His contemporaries thought so too. One of them has described him brandishing a gun which had obviously never been used, and declaring proudly: "I have just fired a shot." "Not for the Republic surely?" asked the observer incredulously. But Baudelaire simply shouted violently to his followers: "We must go and shoot General Aupick." "I had never been so painfully struck," concludes the observer, "by the lack of character in this nature which was in many ways so fine and so original."[5]

We know of course that Baudelaire like Stendhal suffered from an extreme mother-fixation and that for this reason hated his stepfather and his ideas as much as Stendhal hated his own father and his royalism. It seems to me that on this occasion, however, the reference to Aupick was a rationalization and that Baudelaire is a symbol of the bewildered artist at odds with society who really does not know whose side he is on or whom he should shoot. In later life he came to feel that his behavior had been inconsistent. "What was the nature of my intoxication in 1848?" he asked in his diary. He answered: "Thirst for revenge. Natural delight in destruction. A literary intoxication; the memories of books I had read." But there was a deeper reason. "I can understand a man forsaking one cause," he wrote, "in order to see what it feels like to support a different one."

At bottom the problem was psychological. The modern artist realized that he was an explorer trying to discover new realms of experience, that he was irrevocably committed to a policy of development and change. This meant that any form of conservatism, any

5. The observer was Buisson. The story is told in Crépet, *Charles Baudelaire,* pp. 78-9. On Baudelaire's political activities, see J. Mouquet & W. T. Bandy, *Baudelaire en 1848,* Paris, 1946.

policy which aimed at preserving a static order was felt to be inimical to his aspirations as an artist and must be opposed. Baudelaire himself spoke of the "dandy's" attitude of "opposition and revolt." It is difficult not to feel that his psychological need of perpetual change and an incomplete analysis of the political situation led him and others like him to make a major strategic error. In its initial stages, the conflict between the artist and the bourgeois was a middle-class crisis, was a struggle for supremacy inside a class to which both opponents belonged by birth. The correct strategy for the artist would have been to "contain" his opponents by becoming a permanent opposition and to limit the conflict which by spreading could only distract him from his proper work. Instead of that he made the mistake which is being repeated by the twentieth-century artist. He allowed himself to be carried away by the general atmosphere of violence—the "natural delight in destruction"—and he allowed his anxiety to destroy his *cultural* enemies to drive him into a *political* alliance with those elements whose triumph could only end in the destruction of the artist *and* the bourgeois. The artist can never subordinate his own interests to those of a particular class or a particular political party with impunity. The formation of the "exclusive caste" was the real solution of his problem, but by identifying himself with the revolutionary movements of his time he simply undid his own work. It was or should have been evident that they were trying to produce a world in which there was no place for the patrician or his art, that the last thing to be tolerated in a "classless society" is an "exclusive caste." The children of this world are wiser in their generation than the children of light. Revolutionaries always begin by wooing the artist because they are astute enough to see that he is the born "collaborator" who will do them service by undermining the moral and political foundations of the middle classes. They are ready enough, too, to make use of his pen for their propaganda, but once their political aims have been achieved they make short work of the artist and his like.

III

We can see, therefore, that though the conflict between the writer and the bourgeois was not the invention of the nineteenth century, the problem was completely transformed during that century by the identification of cultural and political aims. When we turn to our own age we find that the dilemma has become more acute. These are some characteristic pronouncements made by English writers between 1937 and 1947:

A writer who wishes to produce the best work that he is capable of producing must first of all become a socialist in his practical life, must go over to the progressive side of the class-conflict (Edward Upward).

The only thoroughly satisfying attitude for the writer today, the only way in which his life can become an integrated whole with the life around him, is by participation in political activity: yet such participation in political activity is likely to eliminate altogether his capacity to produce art (Julian Symons).

Either you go into politics or you stay out. . . . Literary values are human values: those who cherish literary values must associate themselves with political movements which set human values first: or they must reconcile themselves to being ineffectual bewailers of a dying civilization (Christopher Hill).

One of the oddest features of English literary life in the thirties was the tendency of young men who had had the most expensive sort of education to reverse the movement of their predecessors and to throw in their lot with what Stendhal contemptuously called "shop-keepers." It was not a very happy experiment in *déclassement*. They were in general despised by the party-member who did not hesitate to stigmatize them as "bourgeois," and political dogmatism ruined such small talent for verse-writing as they have possessed.

What is particularly disquieting about the three passages I have just quoted is the naive assumption that your only hope of writing well is to purchase the party ticket and the equally groundless assumption that politics should be preferred to art, that you must conform to the party line even if it means sacrificing yourself as a writer.

Although these assumptions must be rejected absolutely, the pronouncements of the three writers do draw attention to a genuine dilemma which cannot be shirked. It is of course the problem of the writer in politics which has become inseparable from the problem of the writer in society. The contemporary writer's obsession with politics is not accidental. It has been forced on him by the transformation of the political scene during the past hundred years. He has come to realize that he is a twofold being, that he has his duty as a writer and his duty as a citizen at the polling booth. When political parties in

England were divided over questions like Catholic Emancipation or the relative merits of protection and free trade, the writer could very well argue that his interests *as a writer* were not directly affected and that there was no need for him to vote at all. Now this attitude of political neutrality has become untenable. The writer cannot remain neutral in a world which is not only divided by irreconcilable philosophies, but by philosophies which touch life at almost every point and are therefore bound to affect his interests as a writer. This means that he is bound to take up a position toward the political conflicts of his time and that he must decide on the relation between his attitude as a writer and his attitude as a voter.

What then is he to do? Clearly his first obligation is to write well and to see that the writer in him is never sacrificed to the politician whatever his views. This means that he must remain true to the principle of non-attachment, that he must regard the words *déclassé et déraciné* as a factual description of his vocation. The social and political structure of a country is invariably rigid and is dictated by considerations which have very little to do with the aspirations of the writer. He may belong by birth to a particular class and he may regard one political party as less of a menace than another; but he can never give more than a limited support to any party because he is committed to standards which transcend their immediate aims and because there can never be absolute correspondence between his views as a writer and the policy of any one party. He simply has to make the best of a bad job. It is not a solution to imagine that we might one day have a center party which all men of good will might be able to support and which would effectively exclude the more disreputable elements of the present Right and Left. *"Entre autres idées enfantines, le prince prétend avoir un ministère moral."* This sentence from the *Chartreuse de Parme* explains very neatly the reasons for the collapse of liberal parties in all countries. In an age of violence and extremism there is no place for a *ministère moral,* and a party based on ethical principles is at a disadvantage in a world of political gangsters. Writers are always in a minority; they can never have sufficient influence in present conditions to change the political structure of a country, and a vote for a *ministère moral* merely increases the chances of the more dangerous of the other parties coming to power.

It cannot be too strongly emphasized therefore that a writer's responsibility as a writer is paramount. He cannot commit himself to party membership or, unreservedly, to any political program. His attitude must be completely opportunist. He cannot remain neutral, but it is not his business to work out political programs or to sell his pen to the propaganda machine of any of the parties. He should only take part in politics in so far as it is necessary to safeguard his interests as a writer. The nature and scope of his activities are dictated by the immediate political situation. In peaceful times he should give no more than a limited support to the party which is likely to do least damage to his interests as a writer. In times of political strife like the present he is bound to become more active. This necessarily makes the task of harmonizing his literary and his political views more difficult and brings me to my final point.

Baudelaire's general attitude remains valid, but the enemy is no longer the same. It would be sheer waste of time and energy to engage in sham fights against the bourgeois. We are faced with a far more serious threat to our independence and we should be clear about the nature of the enemy. It is doubtful whether the writer can today give even a limited support to any party; he must work and vote against the party which constitutes the greatest threat to his independence.

In a broadcast discussion on "The Artist and Society" in July 1948 Mr. V. S. Pritchett remarked: "Writers are saved by what can only be called the inherited professional instinct of party disloyalty." Mr. Graham Greene went one better: "And that is a genuine duty we owe society; to be a piece of grit in the State machinery."

As things are, there is virtually nothing to add to these statements of the writer's attitude. For the role of the patrician in the police State can only be that of saboteur and resistance leader.

Does Literature Reflect Common Values?
Milton C. Albrecht

from

American Sociological Review, vol. 21, no. 6, 1956.

Reprinted by permission of the author and the
American Sociological Association.

DOES LITERATURE REFLECT COMMON VALUES?

MILTON C. ALBRECHT

University of Buffalo

T HE relationship of literature and society has been variously conceived. Three general assumptions are that literature reflects society and culture, that it serves as a means of social control, and that it influences attitudes and behavior of people in ways considered in some respects desirable, in others undesirable.[1] For the present article, research was oriented to the reflection theory.

Like other arts, literature has in the past been assumed to reflect cultural norms and values, the ethos and the stresses of a society, the process of dialectical materialism, and the historical development of a society or culture.[2] Recently, divorce and prejudice in fiction have been studied, and some research has attempted to determine agreement between literary content and statistical data on occupations and population distribution in the United States.[3] The results have pointed to an emphasis on widespread American attitudes and ideals, reinforcing the idea that literature reflects common cultural values. It is this conception, also, which is logically consistent with the theory of social control.[4] The present research was focused, consequently, on the problem of literature reflecting cultural norms and values. It was limited, however, to the area of the American family and to short stories in large circulation magazines.

The principal hypothesis was that short stories read by large audiences, even though representing distinct reading levels, will express essentially the same basic values and ideals of the American family. It was anticipated, nevertheless, that variations in selection and emphasis of these values would occur among the several levels, derived probably from sub-cultural differences, but the precise nature of these variations was not predicted. This aspect of the study was regarded as exploratory.

The magazines should obviously represent as distinct cultural reading strata or social classes as possible. Warner's ranking of magazines according to their popularity in each of the six social classes was relied on chiefly.[5] His general results are strongly supported, for middle and lower levels especially, by Kass's technique of overlapping reading, which in turn has a high correlation with the ranking of cultural levels of magazines by the judgment of experts.[6] On the basis of these studies, *True Story* and *True Confessions* were selected for the lower level, the *American* and the *Saturday Evening Post* for the middle level, the *Atlantic* and the *New Yorker* for the upper level. Sampling was limited to issues for the year 1950 and included only "regular" short stories.[7]

[1] M. C. Albrecht, "The Relationship of Literature and Society," *American Journal of Sociology*, 59 (March, 1954), pp. 425–436.

[2] *Ibid.*, pp. 425–431.

[3] See J. H. Barnett and R. Gruen, "Recent American Divorce Novels, 1938–1945," *Social Forces*, 26 (March, 1948), pp. 332–337; B. Berelson and P. Salter, "Majority and Minority Americans: An Analysis of Magazine Fiction," *Public Opinion Quarterly*, 10 (Summer, 1946), pp. 168–190; R. Inglis, "An Objective Approach to the Relationship Between Fiction and Society," *American Sociological Review*, 3 (August, 1938), pp. 526–531.

[4] Albrecht, *op. cit.*, pp. 430–431.

[5] W. L. Warner and P. S. Lunt, *The Social Life of a Modern Community*, New York: Harcourt Brace and Company, 1941, pp. 386–406.

[6] B. Kass, "Overlapping Magazine Reading: A New Method of Determining the Cultural Levels," in P. Lazarsfeld and F. Stanton, *Communications Research, 1948–49*, New York, Harper and Brothers, 1949, pp. 130–151. See also W. L. Morgan and A. M. Leahy, "The Cultural Content of General Interest Magazines," *Journal of Educational Psychology*, 25 (October, 1934), pp. 530–536; W. A. Kerr and H. H. Remmers, "Cultural Value of 100 Representative Magazines," *School and Society*, 54 (November, 1941), pp. 476–480; J. H. Foster, "An Approach to Fiction Through the Characteristics of Its Readers," *Library Quarterly*, 6 (April, 1936), pp. 124–174.

[7] The year 1950 was selected for its avoidance of war influences and its closeness to recent research on cultural reading levels as well as on families. Omitted from the sample were "book-lengths," "short-shorts," serials, autobiographical reminiscences and informational pieces in the guise of fiction.

In order to avoid the fallacy of assuming that values found concentrated in fiction must inevitably be widespread in society, a framework derived from sources independent of literary materials was necessary. For this framework the "configurations" of Sirjamaki were chosen, although his list of eight was modified slightly and extended to ten moral ideas or values of the American family,[8] stated as follows:

1. Marriage is a dominating life goal, for men as well as for women.
2. Marriage should be based on personal affection and on individual choice.
3. The family should be a small independent unit, having a home of its own.
4. The exercise of sex should be contained within wedlock.
5. The criterion of successful marriage is personal happiness of husband and wife.
6. Marriage should be monogamous and permanent, but if mates are very unhappy, divorce is sanctioned.
7. The family roles of husband and wife should be based on a sexual division of labor, but with male status superior.
8. Individual values are esteemed in family living, though affection should be strong.
9. Children should be reared in a child's world and shielded from too early participation in adult woes and tribulations.
10. The best years of life are those of youth, and its qualities are the most desirable.

To prevent selective bias and to test as fully as possible for values other than those listed, two or more alternatives for each of the ten were formulated which modified and opposed the original statement. Alternatives

for marriage being a dominant goal, for example, are that marriage is less important than a successful career, that marriage should be rejected as too limiting emotionally and too restricting in terms of mobility, and that love should be a dominating goal, avoiding marriage.

Whenever possible, modifications were drawn from values known to occur among groups at one or another social level. An alternative to marriage being based on personal affection and individual choice is that marriage should be based primarily on parental preference and in-group solidarity— values fostered by upper-class families.[9] Or, instead of the exercise of sex being contained within wedlock, that the exercise of sex outside of wedlock should be permissible or condoned, that the exercise of sex before, if not after, marriage is expected. These alternatives were derived in part from Whyte's "A Slum Sex Code" and from other studies.[10] Alternatives for each of the ten original statements were formulated in the same way.

A schedule was devised of the original ten, together with the sets of alternatives. The sample totaled 189 stories, from which 36 were discarded as inappropriate in content or setting, leaving a final sample of 153 stories: 62 from the lower level, 59 from the middle, and 32 from the upper.

As the stories were read, direct or positive approval of values and goals were noted in authors' statements, in descriptions of characters' thoughts and behavior, and in the plot resolution. The approved values were recorded on a schedule card, whether for a listed value, for an alternative, or for any unlisted value. The principal value and theme were differentiated from subsidiary values and from certain implied or unquestioned values. The plot was also summarized, the main conflict described, and a selection made of statements representing the values strongly supported.

[8] J. Sirjamaki, "Culture Configurations in the American Family," *American Journal of Sociology*, 53 (May, 1948), pp. 464–471. His list is based on a variety of sources which show general agreement. The order of items was changed and numbers three and six added after consulting standard texts and specific studies: A. B. Hollingshead, *Elmtown's Youth*, New York: John Wiley and Sons, 1949; M. P. Redfield, "The American Family: Consensus and Freedom," *American Journal of Sociology*, 52 (November, 1946), pp. 175–183; M. Mead, "The Contemporary American Family as an Anthropologist Sees It," *American Journal of Sociology*, 53 (May, 1948), pp. 453–459; M. Mead, *Male and Female*, New York: William Morrow and Company, 1949; P. J. Campisi, "Ethnic Family Patterns: The Italian Family in the United States," *American Journal of Sociology*, 53 (May, 1948), pp. 443–449.

[9] Hollingshead, *op. cit.*, p. 85; A. Davis, B. Gardner and M. Gardner, *Deep South*, Chicago: University of Chicago Press, 1941, pp. 87–88, 95–99. See also C. Amory, *The Proper Bostonians*, New York: E. P. Dutton and Company, 1947; F. Lundberg, *America's 60 Families*, New York: The Citadel Press, 1946.

[10] W. F. Whyte, "A Slum Sex Code," *American Journal of Sociology*, 49 (July, 1943), pp. 24–31; Hollingshead, *op. cit.*, pp. 418–423.

TABLE 1. PERCENTAGE DISTRIBUTION OF FAMILY VALUES OCCURRING AS MAIN THEMES IN SHORT STORIES OF THREE CULTURAL READING LEVELS

Value Number	Lower Level		Middle Level		Upper Level		All Levels	
	N	Percentage	N	Percentage	N	Percentage	N	Percentage
1	8	11.26	10	16.13	0	0.00	18	11.11
2	26	36.62	33	53.22	3	10.33	62	38.27
3	2	2.81	0	0.00	0	0.00	2	1.24
4	3	4.23	0	0.00	2	6.90	5	3.09
5	15	21.12	4	6.45	7	24.14	26	16.05
6	1	1.41	0	0.00	1	3.45	2	1.24
7	3	4.23	3	4.84	1	3.45	7	4.32
8	9	12.68	6	9.68	6	20.69	21	12.96
9	1	1.41	0	0.00	2	6.90	3	1.85
10	0	0.00	3	4.84	0	0.00	3	1.85
Total Approved Values	68	95.77	59	95.16	22	75.86	149	91.98
Total Alternative Values	3	4.23	3	4.84	7	24.14	13	8.02
Totals	71*	100.00	62*	100.00	29†	100.00	162	100.00

* Total exceeds sample because of double themes in some stories.
† Total less than sample because themes of three stories not on family value.

The story, "A Place of Our Own,"[11] for instance, begins with a scene in which the embrace of husband and wife is interrupted by relatives passing through the front room to their quarters. This disturbs the wife so that she blurts out: "All right. You've got a job, and a wife and baby. When are we going to have a home?" This idea of a home of their own is repeated in varying forms more than twenty times, and obligations to the husband's mother and other relatives, the main opposing value, being stated seventeen times. Out of this conflict the plot is made, and it is resolved by husband and wife moving to their own home.

Thus the principal value of the family as a small independent unit in a home of their own (No. 3) is upheld by the plot resolution as well as by the sheer quantity of direct statements,[12] and indirectly by the repudiation of the opposing value. These conclusions

[11] *True Story*, December, 1950, p. 42 ff.

[12] As D. Jones observed about movies, the goals striven for by the chief characters are limited and are developed scene by scene so that they can easily be determined. This quantitative procedure was somewhat less applicable to stories from the *Atlantic* and the *New Yorker*, which involved fewer scenes for making their "point." See "Quantitative Analysis of Motion Picture Content," *Public Opinion Quarterly*, 6 (Fall, 1942), p. 419.

were recorded, together with marks or indices showing support for two subsidiary values: the necessity of happiness in marriage, and insistence on the dominant role of the husband. Tabulated also was the fact that marriage as an important goal in life was implied throughout the story.

The values in all the stories were identified and indices recorded in the same way. When all the evidence had been gathered, the values associated with main themes and story endings were examined first to determine the extent to which the ten listed values were approved as compared with alternatives. The results are presented in Table 1. Of 162 themes, 91.98 per cent upheld the basic values as stated, 8.02 per cent supported alternatives.

The detailed evidence of approval for basic and alternative values, apart from main themes, is shown in Table 2. Of 737 indices, 88.47 per cent were for the listed values, 11.53 per cent for alternative values. The overall quantitative evidence of our sample favors the conclusion that the cultural norms and values of the American family are strongly upheld in the short stories of wide-circulation magazines, even though they represent distinct cultural reading levels.

These summary results, however, tend to obscure somewhat the differences between levels. As shown in Table 1, the total percentage of themes supporting basic values is only 75.86 for the upper level as compared with 95.16 for the middle and 95.77 for the lower. (Both comparisons are significant at the 5 per cent level.) On the other hand, Table 2, a more complete tabulation of approval for basic and for alternative values, does not indicate these striking variations. In fact, the differences in total percentage of approval for basic values between the levels are not statistically significant. These results still support the hypothesis primarily, but to some extent they set apart the upper level in its treatment of themes.

The fluctuation in frequency of themes, however, apepars to be a special phenomenon common to all levels, as Table 1 indicates. The reflection theory (in its rather simplified state) seems to imply that cultural norms and values are expressed in literature about equally. From the variation in the occurrence of themes, it is obvious that basic values are not "reflected" directly and mechanically, as if they were of equal "weight." Certain values do not appear as main themes in stories at some levels, while others occur with a high degree of frequency. Although the intra-level difference— from zero to over 53 per cent—is highest for the middle level, the difference between extremes is statistically significant for all levels at the 1 per cent level of confidence.

Although these differences within levels are rather startling, the question most pertinent to our inquiry is whether the selective concentrations of themes are similar for each level. According to our hypothesis, a positive correlation should exist between the rank orders of frequency of each level. The coefficient of rank order correlation between the lower and the middle level is .76, between the lower and the upper is .65—both significant at the 5 per cent interval. The correlation between the middle and upper levels, however, is .32—not significant. If "expression" of basic values, therefore, is interpreted in terms of frequency of occurrence, there is positive correlation between levels except the middle and the upper. While largely supporting the main hypothesis, this

result again sets apart the upper level, but from the middle, not the lower level.

But why the concentration of frequencies on a relatively few themes? Combining all levels, four values occur with greatest frequency: marriage as a goal (No. 1), personal choice of marriage partner (No. 2), happiness in marriage (No. 5), and esteem for individuals along with strong affection (No. 8). Value No. 2 is overwhelmingly greatest in frequency, the percentage being more than twice that of its nearest rival, No. 5. In their historical study of "mass periodical fiction," Johns-Heine and Gerth also observe a typical clustering of themes. They think that such themes, once stabilized, "express national traditions and values tacitly supported by all." [13] This conclusion is probably true, but also highly inadequate in view of our results, since certain important family values are relatively neglected or omitted as themes in stories at some levels.

Clustering of themes, therefore, is probably a function of other variables besides widespread acceptance of the values represented—variables that must also account for the absence from each level of certain subjects. The broadly "romantic" character of our society is fairly appropriate to the dominant themes. The age of audiences may play a part, since younger readers presumably would be interested in marriage and the choice of marriage partner, and an older audience might account for the lack of themes on marriage at the upper level,[14] but these factors cannot also account for the absence of themes on the value of youth in the lower and on sex in the middle level. Taboos might explain the absence of themes on sex, but not on a family having a home of its own. The concern with happiness and with affectional problems in marriage may reflect certain stresses in modern families, but other strains—on older members, for example—are not equally developed. Leisure-time interests cannot adequately justify the concentrations, as Lowenthal thought accounted

---

[13] P. Johns-Heine and H. H. Gerth, "Values in Mass Periodical Fiction, 1921–1940," *Public Opinion Quarterly*, 13 (Spring, 1949), p. 105.

[14] See Johns-Heine and Gerth, *op. cit.*, footnote, p. 107; P. F. Lazarsfeld and R. Wyant, "Magazines in 90 Cities, Who Reads What?" *Public Opinion Quarterly*, 1 (October, 1937), pp. 35–37.

for the selection of heroes in popular biographies.[15] These varied suppositions show, in fact, little consistency and suggest that complex factors are at work for which no general explanation as yet exists.

The question of valid indices in stories to values that are widespread in society remains. If clustering of themes fails to indicate such values adequately, then one logical answer may be the general degree of approval of basic as compared with alternative values, as shown in Table 2. As mentioned

reveal the influence of sub-cultural differences, as well as the direction of non-conformity or of change. Together, the least accepted values may reveal the influence of sub-cultural differences, as well as the direction of non-conformity or of change. Together, the least accepted values are 4, 5, 6, 8, 9, 10. Of these, only 8 is common to all levels. Number 9 is strongly non-conformist at both the lower and the upper levels, number 6 at the lower and middle levels, and 4, 5, and 10 only at the upper level.

TABLE 2. PERCENTAGE DISTRIBUTION OF APPROVAL FOR BASIC AND FOR ALTERNATIVE VALUES, APART FROM MAIN THEMES, IN STORIES OF THREE READING LEVELS

Value Number	Lower Level		Middle Level		Upper Level		All Levels	
	Basic	Alternative	Basic	Alternative	Basic	Alternative	Basic	Alternative
1	96.30	3.70	97.83	2.17	82.61	17.39	94.31	5.69
2	100.00	0.00	100.00	0.00	86.36	13.64	96.15	3.85
3	94.82	5.18	95.74	4.26	96.00	4.00	95.38	4.62
4	94.87	5.13	100.00	0.00	69.23	30.77	90.00	10.00
5	96.88	3.12	96.43	3.57	75.00	25.00	92.12	7.88
6	73.33	26.67	80.95	19.05	83.33	16.67	78.26	21.74
7	93.10	6.90	95.45	4.55	85.71	14.29	92.31	7.69
8	57.14	42.86	76.47	23.53	69.23	30.77	65.62	34.48
9	60.00	40.00	100.00	0.00	50.00	50.00	64.28	35.72
10	86.67	13.33	90.00	10.00	60.00	40.00	86.00	14.00
Totals	88.13	11.87	93.52	6.48	81.05	18.95	88.47	11.53
Total Indices	297	40	231	16	124	29	652	85

earlier, there is no significant difference between the total percentages of any level, but the middle level conforms the most, followed by the lower, then the upper. In fact, only two of the basic values in the middle level receive approval less than 90 per cent, while the lower shows four and the upper, nine. If at least 80 per cent approval is selected as a standard, the middle level again shows only one or at most two values below this degree of support, while the lower has three and the upper, five. These results, for family values, may confirm in part the general observation that the dominant values in American society are derived from the middle class.

If the arbitrary standard of at least 80 per cent approval is used to indicate those values that are most widely accepted, then examination of the least accepted values may

As one might expect, a statistically significant difference exists in the proportion of support for values 4 and 5 between the upper level and both the lower and middle levels—at the 1 and 5 per cent interval respectively. For number 4 the modification given marked support (30.77 per cent) is that sex expression outside of wedlock is permissible or condoned. Although this alternative was expected primarily among lower-level stories, only one story supported this value, and then rather ambivalently. If the slum sex code operates in society at lower cultural levels, this fact is not reflected in lower-level stories. Whether the degree of non-conformity in stories of the upper level accurately reflects the attitude of upper-class families is uncertain. At any rate, the middle-level stories are the most consistent in showing no support for any modifications in this area, and in fact, for generally avoiding any direct references to the subject. As for number 5, the kind of alternative upheld to some degree

---

[15] L. Lowenthal, "Biographies in Popular Magazines," in P. Lazarsfeld and F. Stanton, *Radio Research, 1942–43*, New York: Harper and Brothers, 1944, pp. 517–518.

at the upper level, and insignificantly at the lower and middle levels, is an emphasis on duty in marriage and a concern for status. These modifications are consistent with values predominant in upper-class families.[16]

For value 10 the statistical significance is the same as for 4, though the small number of stories expressing this value at the upper level (only five) makes this result questionable. At any rate, the nature of the modification supported is the same at all levels: the recognition of the value of maturity as against that of youth. Sub-cultural differences, then, are not represented, except that middle-level stories are somewhat ambivalent in their support of maturity, continuing to give the strongest approval to youth.

Value 6 shows a considerable degree of support for alternatives, the lower and middle levels 26.67 and 19.05 per cent respectively, the upper, 16.67 per cent. As expected, there are no significant differences between levels, and the modification supported at all levels is the same: an insistence on marriage being permanent, a rejection of divorce. This high degree of agreement between levels suggests that the idea of divorce is not fully approved in society, which agrees with Goode's assertion that "there are many strong, if gradually weaker, moral prescriptions against it."[17] Perhaps the original statement should be somewhat modified. The data indicate also that the lower level is the most conservative in attitude, the middle more tolerant and the upper the most liberal of all. These differences, it should be noted, are a matter of verbal representation, and express perhaps greater "predisposition" toward acceptance of divorce among middle- and upper-level groups, but the actual incidence of divorce shows an inverse correlation with social classes.[18] Perhaps literary materials at the different levels operate as compensatory mechanisms to reality while still principally supporting basic values.

Values 8 and 9 are closely related, the one being concerned with affection in the family and esteem for individual values, the other with the shielding of children from adult problems. Statistically there is a significant difference at the 1 per cent interval between the middle and both the lower and the upper levels, for number 9. The middle level gives unquestioned support to this value, although only four evidences occur in nearly sixty stories. The subject appears as a main theme only in lower and upper-level stories. In both of these levels the type of modification supported is the same: that although children should be shielded, they should also be allowed full scope for emotional development. Stories portray the unfortunate consequences of overprotection, of parental neglect and dominance. These difficulties seem to derive primarily from patriarchial family systems, which are more characteristic of the lower and the upper than of the middle class.[19] But there is little or no overt approval of the idea that children should assume adult responsibilities as soon as possible, as one might expect from social conditions in the lower class, or that they should be extremely shielded, as seems to be true in the upper classes. In fact, the implication of the stories is that these families should be more individualistic, and this indirectly supports value 8, suggesting that the original statement of 9 should be revised.

Value 8, although among the highest in percentage occurring as main themes, ranks lowest in support of the basic value at both the lower and middle levels, though the proportion of non-conformity varies: lower, 42.86 per cent; middle, 23.53 per cent; upper, 30.77 per cent. Only the difference between the lower and the middle levels is statistically significant, at the 5 per cent interval. Nevertheless, the modification supported at all levels is that of subordinating individual values to family unity, with the lower level showing the greatest approval.

---

[16] Hollingshead, *op. cit.*, pp. 85, 88; Davis, Gardner and Gardner, *op. cit.*, pp. 90–91, 95 ff. See also original materials in R. Cavan, *American Family*, New York: Thomas Crowell Company, 1953, pp. 138–140.

[17] W. J. Goode, *After Divorce*, Glencoe, Illinois: The Free Press, 1956, p. 10.

[18] *Ibid.*, pp. 44–48, 66–68.

[19] See references in notes 9 and 16, above. Also, A. Davis and R. J. Havighurst, *Father of the Man*, Boston: Houghton Mifflin Company, 1947; A. Davis, "Child Rearing in the Class Structure of American Society," in *The Family in Democratic Society: Anniversary Papers of the Community Service Society of New York*, New York: Columbia University Press, 1949, pp. 56–69.

Since lower-class families are in fact the least stable,[20] the degree of emphasis in stories on sacrifices of parents and children to keep the family together may again, as for value 6, operate as a compensatory mechanism while reflecting the basic value of unity. In stories, as in life, individual values threaten family stability, not only at the lower but also at the upper level, and to a lesser extent even at the middle level. But insistence on unity, as in a patriarchal system, leads to frustration of children, as mentioned for value 9. The approval of modifications for both 8 and 9 shows inherent contradictions and conflicts, which apparently reflect general uncertainty of family roles and inadequately institutionalized family relationships.

Altogether, the support for alternative values does not seem to derive primarily from sub-cultural family values, except possibly for value 5. Although a number of statistically significant differences occur between levels, the direction of non-conformity is usually similar at all levels, and this similarity is especially marked for value 6, where no significant differences between levels exist. Though the alternative for value 9 apparently reflects the more patriarchal family systems of lower and upper classes, the emphasis tends to support indirectly value 8. These values that are most "deviant" at each level seem principally to point up areas of change, though neither the extent nor the direction can be determined without further research. They contrast with the relatively small proportion of non-conformity at any level for numbers 3 and 7, which show unquestioned support for nuclear families having homes of their own, and for males having some superior status, though the degree is occasionally in question. These areas contrast specifically with values 6 and 8, which, although generally upholding basic values, seem also to represent compensatory mechanisms to reality.

There is still the question of the upper level as a whole, which was set apart from other levels in its relatively smaller support of basic values as main themes and in its in-adequate correlation between rank order of frequencies of themes. Certain differences in specific values have also been mentioned. In addition, for values 1 and 2, a significant difference exists between the upper and the middle level, which is born out by stories which deal with deviant groups, such as hobos and homosexuals, who avoid marriage, and by stories that show some marriage choices being determined more by status considerations than by romantic attachment.

These distinctions deserve explanation. In respect to differences in frequency of themes, the crucial fact seems to be the range of subjects in stories, which is far greater for the upper than for the other levels. This greater range results in less concentration. For a single theme, as shown in Table 1, the highest percentage at the upper level is 24.14 per cent, while in the middle it is 53.22 per cent, which largely accounts for the lack of significant correlation between these levels. Incidentally, the wider range accounts also for the high rejection rate (43 per cent) and consequently for the relatively smaller sample of upper-level stories.[21] The greater range of subject matter is itself not a function of sub-cultural differences in *family* values, but probably of more education and wider perspective of readers. At any rate, family relationships in stories of the upper level are often placed in the context of a larger world, whereas the outlook in stories at the other levels—the lower particularly—is confined to the "world" of the family.[22]

The smaller percentage of support in upper-level stories for certain main themes, such as values 1 and 4, is probably determined by the way in which subjects are treated artistically. Deviant characters, including hobos and homosexuals, are usually presented in terms of their own values, with no plot resolution or conventional ending to indicate clearly the author's own value commitments or those of society. In other words, subjects are treated more objectively, cer-

[20] Hollingshead, *op. cit.*, p. 106, 117; A. B. Hollingshead, "Class Differences in Family Stability," *The Annals of the American Academy of Political and Social Science*, 272 (November, 1950), pp. 39–46.

[21] The discard from the middle level was only 20 per cent (for adventure stories) and none from the lower level.

[22] Similar differences in intellectual horizon were pointed out by W. L. Warner and W. E. Henry, "The Radio Daytime Serial: A Symbolic Analysis," *Genetic Psychological Monographs*, 37 (February, 1948), pp. 3–73.

tainly less moralistically, than at the other two levels. As Barnett says about "divorce" novels that are best in a literary sense, they are more "autonomous" than those that are written as popular fiction.[23] The stories are intended, apparently, to foster perspective and insight rather than a direct reinforcement of generally accepted values.

Except for the emphasis on status in respect to choice of mate (number 2) and in marriage situations (number 5), and possibly the greater familistic orientation, which is shared with the lower level, the upper-level stories do not seem to reflect subcultural family values. They express freedom in dealing with subjects that are socially taboo—a freedom that is often interpreted as license. Verbal or artistic non-conformity is commonly mistaken for the actual behavior of the upper class, as illustrated by the liberal attitude toward divorce, described earlier. It may be said, then, that in part at least, the larger percentage of non-conformity in stories of the upper level is determined by differences not in family values but in literary tradition.

In conclusion, our main hypothesis is largely upheld: short stories in wide-circulation magazines, though representing distinct reading levels, reflect cultural norms and values of the American family. In its simplified form, however, this concept of reflection

[23] J. H. Barnett, *Divorce and the American Divorce Novel, 1858–1937*, Philadelphia: (Privately printed) 1939, p. 139.

fails to account for significant differences in the frequency with which values occur as main themes. Frequency of themes is unreliable as a basis for determining widespread values, which seem to be indicated more certainly by detailed indices. These may provide a method of distinguishing the more firmly accepted from the more fluctuating and unsettled values. The evidence seems to indicate that the original statements for values 6 and 9 should be modified.

Competing ideas, however, were identified from analysis of stories, which in some respects distinguished the several levels. Familistic trends were found more marked in stories of the upper and lower levels, and concern for status was more emphasized at the upper and family unity at the lower level. But other expected variations from subcultural family differences failed to appear; the same type of non-conformity sometimes occurred at all levels. For some values the variations were in inverse ratio to reality, suggesting the operation of compensatory mechanisms in stories.

As a whole, the upper level differed most from the other levels, partly due to a few variations in family values, but considerably due to differences in general outlook and in literary tradition. The middle level, on the other hand, conformed the most closely with the basic values as originally formulated, which may in part confirm the general idea that the values most dominant in society are middle-class values.

The Impact of the Mass Media on Society
Samuel L. Becker

from

Educational Media: Theory into Practice, W.C.
Meierhenry and R.V. Winan (eds.). Charles E. Merrill,
Columbus, 1969.

The Impact of the Mass Media on Society

Samuel L. Becker

As far back as the development of printing, every major innovation in the mass media has been heralded by pronouncements in the popular and educational press that the savior of education has arrived and, conversely, pronouncements have been made that the executioner of culture and the other benefits of education is here.[1] This speculation

---

[1] One of the many examples of the latter is the assertion by J. B. Priestly, "We spend billions on education, only to have the good work—if it is good work—rapidly undone by the mass communication experts, waiting to pounce on the boys and girls as they come out of school." *New York Times,* October 4, 1953, Sec. 2, p. X15.

For an excellent history of the claims and counter-claims which have accompanied each media innovation since the beginnings of the silent film, see Robert Edward Davis, "Response to Innovation: A Study of Popular Argument about New Mass Media" (Unpublished Ph.D. dissertation, University of Iowa, 1965).

has been accompanied by surprisingly little research. Of course, most of the effects of the media are difficult to assess. Some of the long-range effects on attitudes, on culture, and on social structure may be assessable only through the methods of the social historian. Even with these methods, one cannot *pinpoint* causal relationships because media change develops slowly amidst a complex web of social change. It is only one of the threads. Some scholars say that it is not even meaningful to talk about the impact or effects of the mass media; that it is more meaningful to ask how various individuals and institutions *use* the media. This is the "functional" approach. However, an acceptance of this view is as misleading as a total acceptance of media as all-powerful change agents. A mass medium is both an index and agent of change; it is used by people, but it also affects those who use it—and perhaps even those who do not. A modern society is impossible without the mass media, and the mass media cannot operate except in a modern society.

To consider all of the effects of the media is beyond the scope of this paper. I shall concentrate, then, upon those effects which I believe are most relevant to the educator. The term "effects," as I am using it, should not be taken to indicate a causal relationship necessarily. In some cases, it will concern the ways in which the media are used and concomitant adjustments in the rest of our behavior; in other cases, the effects of content transmitted by the media will be considered, or the effects of the media themselves, independent of content. This last is an important distinction that too many persons overlook. In any of the cases to be considered, one must avoid equating the effect of the media with the direct effect of a serum administered with a hypodermic needle. All media effects are mediated by a myriad of factors such as the prior knowledge, habits, interests, and attitudes of the audience, and the social-cultural milieu in which the communication process occurs. The same film has different effects on different people, and the same medium has a different impact on two basically different cultures. The reader must keep this in mind in regard to the generalizations about media impact that follow.

EFFECTS OF NEW MEDIA ON THE OLD

The rise of each new medium of communication obviously results in some loss of power for the old. One of the latest examples of this is that, in spite of the fact that radio stations are making more money today than ever before, they have never regained the status they lost with the advent of television. One sees this reflected in the professional broadcasting associations, both commercial and educational. Though radio broadcasters far outnumber television broadcasters in these associations, they believe themselves to be poor country cousins. One also sees it reflected in the publicity which each gets in the print media. Though the Kennedy-Nixon "Great Debates" were on both radio and television, the discussion of the events in the press were centered on the telecasts, rather than on the radio broadcasts.

Old media are affected by the new when it is discovered that the new satisfy or serve some of the functions of the old better. For example, television cut deeply into the audience of movie houses. Radio saved itself only by serving needs which television could not, and by adapting the receiving apparatus so that it could literally follow one wherever he went—into the kitchen, the barn, the beach, or the automobile. In one sense, the educational film industry is doing the same thing by moving away from the type of subject matter which is being accepted by television, and toward the short, single-concept film in a cartridge which is much more flexible than educational television can possibly be. The Hollywood motion picture industry, however, has not yet found new functions to serve, other than prerecording television programs. Hollywood was completely dedicated to serving an entertainment function with light drama. Light drama is now provided by television without apparent cost to the audience and without the effort of "going out" to the movie house. A few film-makers seem to be attempting to find other functions to serve by dealing with more serious topics for a minority audience whom television does not adequately serve.

Broadcasting, both radio and television, has usurped much of the information-giving functions of the print media and even of face-to-face communication. The print media, as a result, have changed their emphasis in two ways: First, by an increasing attempt to cover stories which cannot be covered with microphone or camera and, second, and probably more important, by an effort to do more interpretation, trying to give order and meaning to the mass of complex facts with which the citizen is assailed. This second emphasis has probably always been a function of face-to-face communication, as individuals have turned to those whose opinions they respect for help in interpreting and ordering information, and, most important, deciding what to do about that information. Again, as first the print media and then, even more, the electronic media have taken the information-distribution function away from the opinion leaders, the leaders' organizing and guidance functions have probably increased in importance.

EFFECT OF THE AUDIENCE ON THE MEDIA

Before considering the impact of the media on their audiences, it should be noted that there is also an important influence in the other direction. Whenever one attempts to reach very large audiences (as most of the media in this country must), he becomes—in a very real sense—a captive of those audiences. The tastes and interests of selected audiences set limits within which a medium must operate to remain in business. The more expensive the production and distribution of a particular medium product is, the more attention must be paid to the "mass" audiences. And, as the costs of production and distribution rise, the producer must set his sights on larger and, by definition, less select audiences. The implication of this is that, in the United States and other countries in which the bulk of the media are not subsidized, they must serve an entertainment function in order to obtain the capital needed to support their other functions.

It is probably safe to say that more of the matter printed fifty to seventy-five years ago was intellectually challenging than is true today. The reason is that the literate audience was comparatively small and select and the total volume of printed matter was less. Today, with almost universal literacy in the United States, the market for mediocrity is much greater. Thus, the supply is greater. In absolute terms, there is more "good" material being printed now than fifty to seventy-five years ago, but it is less visible because of the flood of material for the literate but non-intellectual. In other words, the percentage of intellectuals does not rise in direct proportion to the growth in literacy.

The audience has another effect on the media which, though indirect, is probably much more important to an understanding of mass-communication processes. The personality traits of the audience members, their educational backgrounds, prior information, attitudes, interests, social positions, even areas of residence within a community or within the country create what we might call a set of screens. These screens differ for each individual in the population, so that different media products "get through" to each individual; those that get through are distorted in different ways for different individuals; and those that get through and are perceived similarly by different individuals, tend to be remembered in different ways. These are the phenomena which are generally labeled "selective exposure," "selective perception," and "selective retention." Evidence of the precise ways in which these screens operate is given in a study by Kaufman.[2] She discovered many

---

[2] Helen J. Kaufman, "The Appeal of Specific Daytime Serials," in Paul F. Lazarsfeld and Frank Stanton, eds., *Radio Research 1942–1943* (New York: Duell, Sloan and Pearce, 1944), pp. 86–107.

of the audience factors which determine the type of women exposed to the broadcasts of different daytime serials, and the way in which those exposed interpret what they hear.

THE MEDIA AND DIFFUSION OF INFORMATION

In 1920, *Colliers* magazine gave credit to the infant motion picture industry which, it said,

> . . . transformed insular creatures into cosmopolitans, putting a magic telescope to the vision of the farmer boy, townsman, and city hemmed-in folks. The movies have opened minds, and with them opened, people are forced to keep ahead of the intelligence thus awakened, and the imagination thus aroused.[3]

Similar claims have been made for radio and, more recently, for television. The evidence on this growth of knowledge, however, presents a far more complex picture.

It is clear that certain types of information are transmitted to more people more quickly than could possibly be the case without the mass media. Somewhat spectacular examples are:

1. The diffusion of information about the power failure and consequent blackout in the New York City area in 1965. The transistor radio is credited with a major role in averting disaster by bringing information to all who were, both literally and figuratively, in the dark.[4]

2. The almost instantaneous diffusion of information about the assassination of President John F. Kennedy to all parts of the world.[5]

3. The even more rapid diffusion in this country of information about the assassination of the President's assassin. Individuals in all parts of the country were eye-witnesses to the macabre drama as it was carried on television.

There are many more general examples which indicate the importance of the mass media to the diffusion of information. Consider that less than fifty years ago, seeing and hearing the President of the United States speak was an event which highlighted the lives of some of our

---

[3] *Colliers,* February 28, 1920, p. 16. Quoted in Davis, p. 63.

[4] *New York Times,* November 11, 1965, pp. 1, 40.

[5] Bradley S. Greenberg and Edwin S. Parker, eds., *The Kennedy Assassination and the American Public* (Stanford, Calif.: Stanford University Press, 1965). See especially pp. 89–146.

grandparents and great-grandparents. It was an experience that was shared by few of their fellow citizens. Rare is the citizen today who has not welcomed the President into his living room, courtesy of one of the television networks! Data from the polls in 1960 indicate that roughly eighty per cent of the population of the United States heard or saw at least one of the Kennedy-Nixon debates.[6]

For modern man, it is difficult to realize that, until recently, almost the sole source of information for the masses about the varieties of experience that lay beyond the limits of their personal lives was interpersonal communication. A major source of information for the elite was the book—in large part, the novel. Today, we take for granted the fact that adults obtain much of their information through the popular press and the electronic media. We tend not to be aware of the implications of this change.

Traditionally, the availability of information varied greatly among men. Thus, their pictures of the world to which they responded varied greatly. The mass media, and especially the electronic media which depend less on receiver skills, have made an increasing proportion of existing information available to all. Some traditional patterns of leadership have, in turn, been affected. (This will be considered further in the section on the effect of the media on social structure.) In a very real sense, space and time have been altered also. As one writer has noted, the new limits are not obvious, nor it is now clear what "authentic" experience is.

> Direct personal experience becomes indistinguishable from the vicarious, the compelling secondhand version, when the doings of the outer world are brought to us on television, as they happen. We know at the same moment as the astronaut whether his shot is successful. It is not only real life; it is real time.[7]

This is not to say that the media transmit events without distortion. There is bias in the selection of events to be covered, and distortion of those events which are selected. Most readers, listeners, and viewers accept as a truism that the media cover the events that they do because these events are news. "All the News That's Fit to Print" reads the masthead of the *New York Times*. Audience members fail to realize that such assertions are tautological; the events covered are news *solely*

---

[6] Elihu Katz and Jacob J. Feldman, "The Debates in the Light of Research: A Survey of Surveys," in Sidney Kraus, ed., *The Great Debates* (Bloomington: Indiana University Press, 1962), p. 190.

[7] Judith Wheeler, "The Electronic Age," *Saturday Review of Literature*, June 4, 1966, p. 22.

because they are printed in newspapers or broadcast on radio or television.

We have been conditioned by the media to accept as fact that bad news is news; good news is not news. The way in which individuals, especially individuals in other countries, perceive the "reality" of desegregation in the United States is an excellent illustration of this point. Media coverage tends to give the impression that trouble accompanies almost every effort at desegregation. The front pages and the headlines of newspapers do not accurately reflect the national, or even the southern situation where a large portion of the desegregation in schools and other civil rights advances are proceeding quietly. A striking, but far from isolated, example is seen in two reports concerning the effect of desegregation on the Washington, D. C. public schools. A report by a House of Representatives subcommittee stating that trouble resulted from this desegregation and recommending that segregation should be reinstated received front-page play in most newspapers. A contradictory report by the assistant superintendent of Washington schools, indicating that integration had gone well in the District, was buried on inside pages, if it was printed at all. Even the *New York Times* handled these two stories in this way.[8] This treatment of the news does not reflect racial prejudice on the part of newsmen; it reflects, rather, their definition of news, for we see them act in the same way for many types of stories.

This equating of news with conflict or, at times, with entertainment, is seen throughout the news media in coverage of all aspects of public affairs. Even when the Kennedy Foundation presented awards in December, 1962 to a group of scientists for their outstanding contributions to the prevention of certain types of mental retardation, the press gave better coverage to the jokes which Adlai Stevenson told at the dinner than to the important scientific news. Reading the account in many newspapers, it would be impossible to tell what the dinner was about; the awards were not even mentioned. The jokes were more "newsworthy" than the scientific research which had deep meaning to the fifteen or twenty million persons in the United States who live in families in which there is a mentally retarded individual and to the many more who will someday be in such a family.[9]

Not only does the audience get a distorted picture of reality because of the selectivity of the media in covering events, but also be-

---

[8] Walter Spearman, "Racial Stories in the News," in Walter Spearman and Sylvan Meyer, *Racial Crisis and the Press* (Atlanta, Ga.: The Southern Regional Council, 1960), pp. 12–15.

[9] Unpublished study in the files of the author.

cause the requirements of each medium result in a "shaping" of each event that is covered. Few newspaper stories are organized in an accurate time sequence. Newspaper stories tend rather to follow a pyramid arrangement, with the most spectacular part of the story first and the details on which the story is based last—where many readers never see them. In broadcasting, every event, no matter what its nature, must be constantly interesting so that the attention of the audience will be held. The result, to cite a trivial example, is that there never has been a dull baseball game on radio. An extended example of how television has distorted an important public event is the report of a study by Lang and Lang.[10] When General MacArthur was relieved of his Korean command by President Truman and returned to this country, the media gave ample coverage to his progress across the country. By the time he arrived for the MacArthur Day Parade in Chicago, audience members expected an exciting and unusual event. The Langs placed observers along the parade route. What they reported was compared with the images which were transmitted by television. Though observers on the scene found little excitement and relatively small crowds, the television viewer, because of the selection of pictures and the announcer's commentary, received the impression of wildly cheering and enthusiastic crowds. Thus, the often-heard statement that the mass media are "neutral"—that they are merely conveyor belts which transmit whatever one feeds onto them—is misleading. Clearly, each medium of communication imposes some of its own form upon that which it transmits.

> The barbecue-Chautauqua favored the oratorical elder statesmen and was especially susceptible to emotional and demagogic exploitation. Radio put a high premium on a pleasing voice and accent. Television . . . has created its own symbolic language: certain shorthand stereotypes which carry a maximum audio-visual message at a minimum cost.[11]

Though we think that we perceive some of these differences in symbolic language among the media, and though we act upon these perceptions, experimental verification of them to date is limited. One of the few experimental studies that I know about is more interesting for what it suggests than for what it proves. This is a study which a colleague and I did a number of years ago to study the interaction between type of political speaker and medium. We obtained film recordings

---

[10] Kurt Lang and Gladys Engel Lang, "The Unique Perspective of Television and Its Effect: A Pilot Study," *American Sociological Review*, XVIII (1953), pp. 3–12.
[11] Harvey Wheeler, "TV Technique," *Nation*, November 5, 1960, p. 343.

of three *Meet the Press* television programs: one with Senator Robert Taft, one with Governor Tom Dewey, and one with Senator Richard Russell. At the time of our study, all were possible Presidential candidates for 1952. We had nine groups of college students: one to *view* the program with each candidate, one to *listen* to the sound track of each program (as though it were a radio program), and one to *read* the script of each program. We found attitudes toward Senator Russell went up no matter which medium was used. In general, these Iowa students were unfamiliar with Russell prior to the experiment and so initial attitudes were unusually low. With Senator Taft, radio made little difference; attitudes went down for those who saw him on television, attitudes went up for those who read his statements in the script. For Governor Dewey, the opposite effect was found. Again radio made little difference; attitudes became more favorable for those who watched him on the program, attitudes became less favorable for those who read what he said. Interesting questions are raised about the symbolic language of each of these media which, apparently, works to the advantage or disadvantage of different speakers. Some of these differences are quite subtle, I believe. Others are more obvious, and fairly clear even from casual observation of the contemporary scene.

In addition to the media "shaping" the messages which they transmit, they are sometimes responsible for changing the event itself. Consider, for example, the changes which have occurred in public speaking as the means of transmission have changed.

Radio was hardly out of swaddling clothes before the need for some new type of political speaker was recognized. By 1928, the death knell had been sounded for "the spellbinder, gesticulating, pounding, striding up and down, stirred to frenzy by the applause of his audience" who, up to then, had been considered the great vote-getter. The *New York Times* had this to say of the 1928 campaign:

> Almost a funeral procession for the old-fashioned spellbinder, it is less important to sway crowds than to be able to send a voice quietly into a million or ten million homes and speak convincingly to men and women sitting by their own firesides.[12]

As radio continued to develop, the "conversational style" developed with it. How much of this was due to radio, and how much to an already existing trend is difficult to say. It is probable that radio's effect on the public acceptance of this new style of delivery was simply to accelerate and legitimize the trend. In any case, it clearly had an effect.

[12] *New York Times,* October 28, 1928, Sec. 10, p. 1.

Another event which the mass media are credited with changing is the national political convention. Radio, for example, was at least partially responsible for the smooth and apparently harmonious atmosphere of the 1928 Democratic national convention. In 1924, radio had allowed the nation to listen for the first time as the Democratic party leaders fought over condemnation of the Ku Klux Klan and over a Presidential nominee. The nation heard the fight between the Klan forces and their opposition. And for seventeen days, the nation listened to the monotonous drone of 103 successive ballots before a compromise candidate, J. P. Morgan's lawyer, John W. Davis, could be nominated. Four years later, it took only one ballot for the Democrats to nominate Al Smith.[13] Clearly, the Democratic party leaders were determined not to have their family squabbles overheard by the nation. Twenty-eight years later, history was repeated, with emphasis this time on the visual show rather than the aural. Walter Cronkite has said that the 1952 conventions were "the last to maintain the spontaneity of the normal manipulations of party politics in this country."[14] Some aspects of the 1952 convention broadcasts bored the audience, thus worrying network executives; other aspects showed the parties in a poor light, thus worrying party leaders. The result was a political face-lifting. "The National Committees of both parties started issuing guides to behavior for the delegates. They even established 'schools' that offered short dramatic courses on keeping one's eye—and mind—on the camera."[15] Anything that might have bored the audience or revealed too much political manipulation was swept out of view. The platform was packed with entertainers. The result is that, "instead of being candid eyewitnesses to this aspect of democracy, we have become spectators to a staged extravaganza."[16] Even as early as 1952, convention sites were selected with television coverage in mind. In that year, Convention Hall in Chicago was chosen by the parties, rather than the much larger Chicago Stadium, primarily because the former was more suitable for television. With this choice, party chieftains gave up roughly six thousand seats. One observer has noted that this surrendering of large blocks of tickets for a politician is roughly the equivalent of having to donate a goodly portion of blood.[17]

---

[13] Samuel L. Becker and Elmer W. Lower, "Broadcasting in Presidential Campaigns," in *The Great Debates*, pp. 29–30.

[14] Walter Cronkite, "Television and the News," in *The Eighth Art* (New York: Holt, Rinehart and Winston, Inc., 1962), p. 229.

[15] *Ibid.*, p. 230.

[16] *Ibid.*

[17] *New York Times*, June 15, 1952, Sec. 2, p. X9.

The existence of newspapers across the country led President Wood-row Wilson to hold the first White House news conference over fifty years ago, on March 15, 1913.[18] He saw these conferences as an oppor-tunity to express his points of view more clearly to the electorate through the newspapers. As other mass media developed and were brought into the news conference, its character changed. During Franklin D. Roosevelt's years, the conference remained an informal interchange between President and reporters, wherein the latter could ask any question and usually get a response. They could probe and discuss, and get a feel for the President and his ideas and he, in turn, could get a feel for them and their ideas. This now has changed. Per-haps it was inevitable as news from our nation's capitol became of greater interest throughout the world. However, the change seemed most evident as first film and then live television was introduced. The President is now on a stage and everyone has become an actor. The President has even resorted to planted questions at times.[19]

This changing of the event which broadcasters cover is not always a chance affair, nor are the changes manipulated only by politicians or others who want to appear in a favorable light. There are times when the broadcasters set about the change of such events very consciously; and this is not necessarily bad. It is important, however, that we be aware of these occurrences if we are to understand either mass com-munication or politics in this latter half of the twentieth century. One example of this conscious attempt to alter the political campaign scene is the series of Kennedy-Nixon debates of 1960 which, without ques-tion, would never have taken place if it had not been for broadcasting and the broadcasting leaders who promoted it. Without these debates, it is likely that Richard Nixon would have become President.

Thus, one of the effects of the mass media in effecting information diffusion is that the information diffused is biased in certain ways. The input to the media is selective in the events covered. Those that are covered are shaped to fit each particular medium. This, again, is a selective process in part, but also a distortion process. The existence of the media also change the event covered, as well as the message about the event, simply because they are there (somewhat like the "indeter-minacy" principle of quantum mechanics). Sometimes media presence leads to the event being changed because the persons involved in the event wish to project a different image over the media, and sometimes

[18] Ray Stannard Baker, *Woodrow Wilson, Life and Letters* (Garden City, New York: Doubleday, Doran and Co., 1931), IV, p. 229.

[19] *The Daily Iowan*, January 29, 1966, p. 2.

because media personnel become more than observers and transmitters; they become actual participants in the event.

In spite of the various kinds of information distortion, statistics on the exposure of people to information about public affairs, such as election campaigns, make it appear that the mass media have a strong and positive effect on both knowledge and interest in these matters. I mentioned earlier the eightly per cent of the population of the United States that heard or saw at least one of the Kennedy-Nixon debates in 1960. I am also reminded of the story which former Republican National Chairman Leonard Hall has told about the state of Maine. Maine was always a Republican state. People were born Republicans, so they went to the polls and voted Republican. Then, suddenly, they voted for some Democrats. Hall says that he asked an elderly Maine resident about what had happened. "Well," was the response, "we can't do anything with this television. Our children were brought up to think that Democrats had horns. Now they see them on television and realize some of them don't have horns a-tall."[20]

Though this story and the data from 1960 are impressive, they may be misleading if we assume that they indicate a *general* increase in knowledge and interest in public affairs brought about by broadcasting. It seems likely that interest and knowledge in national affairs, such as Presidential elections *have* increased, but at the expense of interest and knowledge of state and local affairs, such as congressional, state, and local elections. This is evident when one tries to get an audience for a senatorial candidate during an election campaign. It is very difficult. It is also evident in the decline of the political club, once the rallying point and training ground for local candidates, and a place where local issues could be hotly debated.[21] Two of the world's most imaginative and insightful sociologists, Paul Lazarsfeld and Robert Merton, have even hypothesized that the media sometimes contribute to political apathy and inertness, rather than to interest and action. This they call the "narcotizing dysfunction" of the media. They note that as an individual devotes more time to the media, he has less time to devote to organized social action. His involvement with politics, for example, becomes intellectualized, rather than action-oriented. As Lazarsfeld and Merton say:

> He comes to mistake *knowing* about problems of the day for *doing* something about them. His social conscience remains spotlessly clean. He *is* concerned. He *is* informed. And he has all sorts of ideas

---

[20] Leonard W. Hall, "How Politics is Changing," in J. M. Cannon, ed., *Politics U.S.A.* (Garden City, New York: Doubleday, 1960), pp. 107–108.

[21] *Ibid.*

as to what should be done. But after he has gotten through his dinner and after he has listened to his favored radio programs [or viewed his favorite television programs] and after he has read his second newspaper of the day, it is really time for bed.[22]

Considering our behavior from this viewpoint, one is bound to have second thoughts about the claims of the broadcasters that the electronic media are leading us to a social and political utopia. However, asserting that the media have a narcotizing dysfunction—even when it is done by such distinguished scholars as Lazarsfeld and Merton— does not make it so. Perhaps the hypothesis is sound; perhaps it is not. Without question, it is important and needs to be tested. The best evidence for this hypothesis so far comes from a study by Wiebe,[23] who explored public reactions to the televised Kefauver hearings on crime and corruption in New York City. The purpose of the hearings was to arouse public concern and to reduce apathy. Wiebe found that after the broadcasts more people said that they were concerned, but there was little evidence that apathy was reduced, for few respondents reported taking any actions to improve the situation.

Though the Wiebe study does not completely confirm the narcotizing dysfunction hypothesis, its findings are consistent with the hypothesis. I have not been able to find evidence that is contrary to the hypothesis. However, the Wiebe study shows only that the media do not lead to more action; it does not show that the media lead to *less* action. Therefore, we must conclude tentatively that the media do not increase participation in public affairs. On the other hand, there is no strong evidence that they have decreased overall participation in such affairs.

A major result of the faster and wider diffusion of information about events is that national or even international issues are made out of what were once local or regional issues. In this way, the media are contributing to the power of the central government and, particularly, of the chief executive. Prior to the development of the electronic media in particular, which, in turn, created what Woodrow Wilson called "national information" and "national opinion," Presidential powers in the United States tended to increase during periods of national crisis such as war or national depression, whereas Congressional powers increased relatively during other periods. Broadcasting has tended to

---

[22] Paul F. Lazarsfeld and Robert K. Merton, "Mass Communication, Popular Taste and Organized Social Action," in Wilbur Schramm, ed., *Mass Communications*, (Urbana: University of Illinois Press, 1960), p. 502.

[23] G. D. Wiebe, "Responses to the Televised Kefauver Hearings: Some Social Psychological Implications," *Public Opinion Quarterly*, XVI (1952), 179–200.

focus the attention of national audiences upon local or regional issues, literally making them into national crises. Examples are the problem of school integration in the South and unemployment in Michigan and Illinois. These problems are thrust upon the nation-wide scene by the mass media and, therefore, upon the President. In this indirect way, broadcasting has pushed the President further up the pole of political power, relative to the Congress,[24] and has contributed to the increasing power of the federal over the state and local governments (though it is far from the only force acting in this direction in either case).

The effect of this information which we get through the mass media is greatest when we have no direct experience with an object or event which the media cover. One study with first-grade children has shown that it is possible, through the mass media, to establish stereotyped images of social reality, for example of taxi drivers, where a child's normal experience has not previously provided contrary or conflicting information. But in areas of experience, where family and community experiences have already established strong image patterns in a child (for example, of the father, teacher, etc.), mass media apparently will not dislodge or destroy them.[25]

Most of us have had the experience of discovering that young children learn some things from the mass media—jingles from radio, commercials from television. At least they learn to identify brand names and brand packages. However, our evidence indicates that this learning is highly specific, with little transfer. That is to say, children who have viewed television regularly in the home do not appear to have acquired greater skill at learning new words—no greater *general* "reading readiness."[26] Both the Schramm and Himmelweit studies confirm the fact that children just beginning school who have been exposed to television have a larger vocabulary than children not exposed. However, by the time the viewers and non-viewers have been in school a few years, these vocabulary differences are erased.[27] Though youngsters say that they learn many things from television, and that it helps them in school by giving them ideas for themes or

[24] For a fuller discussion of broadcasting's contribution to Presidential power, see Samuel L. Becker, "Presidential Power: The Influence of Broadcasting," *Quarterly Journal of Speech*, XLVII (1961), 10–18.

[25] Alberta Engvall Siegel, "The Influence of Violence in the Mass Media Upon Children's Role Expectations," *Child Development*, XXIX (1958), 35–56.

[26] "Toward More Effective Educational TV: A Pilot Study of the Effect of Commercial TV on the Verbal Behavior of Pre-School Children" (Urbana: University of Illinois, Institute of Communications Research, December, 1958, dittoed).

[27] Wilbur Schramm, Jack Lyle, and Edwin B. Parker, *Television in the Lives of Our Children* (Stanford, California: Stanford University Press, 1961), pp. 86–88.

topics to talk about,[28] there is no evidence to validate these claims. This may be an area in which further research would be fruitful.

MEDIA IMPACT ON ATTITUDES

> [Movies] encourage goodness and kindness, virtue and courage.[29]
>
> The movies are so occupied with crime and sex stuff and are so saturating the minds of children the world over with social sewage that they have become a menace to the mental and moral life of the coming generation.[30]

These quotations exemplify the range of claims made about the effects of the various media on the attitudes of their audiences. The evidence is clear that most of such claims grossly overstate the case. Those who make such claims have apparently generalized the impact of the mass media on purchasing behavior to an impact on attitudes, or on voting behavior, or on basic values. These critics have failed to notice the essential difference among these various types of effects. When influencing purchasing behavior, the media are reaching an audience which is already interested in buying cigarettes, or soap, or some other product. This is an audience that tends to have no strong tie to one brand, and the various brands have little to distinguish them from each other. The important thing is to make the brand name salient, so that when one thinks of buying soap, for example, he instantly associates the felt need with the brand name. On the other hand, with voting behavior, or most other sorts of beliefs or behaviors for which individuals tend to have longer learning histories and which, in general, are most ego-involving, evidence indicates that the media have far less effect. This is not to say that they have *none*. Such a broad statement is obviously unfounded. The first generalization that we can make, on the basis of existing evidence, is that the impact of the mass media tends to be in *inverse* proportion to the importance to the audience of the issue involved.

Closely related to the variable of importance, though not necessarily identical, are the variables of degree to which one's attitude is structured, and the amount of relevant knowledge one has. Here, too, evidence indicates that the mass media have relatively greater impact when an attitude is unstructured or when an individual possesses

---

[28] *Ibid.*, p. 58.

[29] *World's Work*, March, 1913, p. 40. Quoted in Davis, p. 142.

[30] *Christian Century*, January, 1930, p. 110. Quoted in Davis, p. 231.

little relevant knowledge. Peterson and Thurstone,[31] for example, have found that the attitudes of junior and senior high school students who had little exposure to either Negroes, Chinese, or Germans, could be influenced by motion pictures. The anti-Negro film, *Birth of a Nation*, resulted in a striking increase in hostile attitudes, which was still apparent in sixty-two per cent of the cases five months after exposure to the film. Viewing a pro-Chinese film and a pro-German film resulted in more favorable attitudes toward these groups. Kraus,[32] more recently, found that rather simple dramatic films which featured a mixed cast of white and Negro characters could change attitudes of high school students who, again, had had relatively little exposure to Negroes. There is similar evidence from the study which I mentioned earlier that shows television's influence on stereotyping by children.[33] None of this would be especially important, except that the picture which youngsters get from the mass media about the world with which they have little direct experience is a distorted picture. As Barcus noted, after reviewing some 1700 studies of mass media content, "the media world is a white man's world. Not only is it white, it is a white American world."[34] Barcus found this to be true both in terms of the number of characters and their preferred status. He also found this bias to be consistent in movies, television, comics, and magazine fiction. Not only were minority groups badly underrepresented, relative to their true proportion in our population, they tended to receive unfavorable treatment as well. Though Barcus does not report the fact, there has been some change in media content in recent years, especially in the treatment of the Negro. Negroes are being shown more in non-stereotyped roles, both in advertisements and in dramas. Though they are probably not yet seen in anything approaching what would represent their proportion in the population, distinct progress is being made. And from what we know of learning theory, and from the aforementioned studies of stereotyping, this should have a positive effect on attitudes toward this minority group.

Research indicates pretty clearly that if those who are exposed to media messages which alter their attitudes do not find support for

[31] Ruth C. Peterson and L. L. Thurstone, *Motion Pictures and the Social Attitudes of Children* (New York: Macmillan, 1933).

[32] Sidney Kraus, "Modifying Prejudice: Attitude Change as a Function of the Race of the Communicator," *Audio Visual Communication Review*, X (1962), 14–22.

[33] Siegel, *loc. cit.*

[34] Francis Earl Barcus, "Communication Content: Analysis of the Research, 1900–1958 (A Content Analysis of Content Analysis)" (Unpublished Ph.D. dissertation, University of Illinois, 1959), p. 262.

these new attitudes in their interpersonal contacts or among their reference groups (the groups to which all of us look for cues as to how to behave or for support in our attitudes), they will quickly discount the messages. In other words, mass media messages seldom, if ever, are a sufficient cause of attitude change. They rather tend to interact with a complex series of other influences and predispositions.

In some cultures at least, and under some conditions, the media themselves can provide social suport for attitudes newly acquired through other means. The evidence is even clearer that those individuals who often provide this support (the so-called opinion leaders) receive much of their information and ideas from the mass media. Findings of this sort have led Katz and Lazarsfeld to coin the phrase, "two-step flow of communication."[35] The point is that the mass media of communication do not usually have a direct effect on the behavior of audiences, but rather tend to supply opinion leaders with the information which they use, in turn, to affect others.

Another type of attitude change is that related to the acceptance of a new idea or a new practice, such as the use of hybrid seed corn, certain health practices, or perhaps even birth control. For this sort of change, interpersonal communication has been shown to be relatively more important than the mass media, but the latter also play a critical role. As Katz[36] has indicated, when such changes are broken down into phases, we get a clearer picture of the function of the mass media in the change process. For example, we can break the diffusion process into the following phases:

Phase 1. An individual becomes aware of an innovation.

Phase 2. He becomes interested in it.

Phase 3. He considers trying it.

Phase 4. He tries it.

Phase 5. He decides to continue doing it.

Evidence indicates that mass communication, in general, is more influential in the early phases of the process, while interpersonal communication is more influential in the later phases. Thus, mass and interpersonal communication are complementary, each playing a major role at different stages of the change process.

---

[35] Elihu Katz and Paul E. Lazarsfeld, *Personal Influence, the Part Played by People in the Flow of Mass Communications* (Glencoe, Ill.: The Free Press, 1955).

[36] Elihu Katz, "Communication Research and the Image of Society: Convergence of Two Traditions," *American Journal of Sociology*, LXV (1960), 435–440.

Those who have studied the process by which new ideas or practices are accepted have also found that the so-called "innovators" —those who accept a new idea early—are more likely to have been influenced by the mass media than those who accept the idea later. The latter, again, are more likely to be influenced directly by other people whom they know.

In this section on media impact on attitudes, I have concentrated upon situations in which individuals have unstructured attitudes and/ or little knowledge about the attitude object. As I indicated earlier, where individuals have strong or ego-involved attitudes (as they do toward much of the content of the mass media), the media have little impact. The major reason for this limited impact appears to be what we might call the law of consistency. (This is what Heider calls "Balance theory."[37] Festinger calls "Dissonance theory,"[38] and Osgood and Tannenbaum call the "Congruity hypothesis."[39]) This is the pressure within individuals to be consistent—to keep attitudes consistent, to keep their cognitions consistent, and to keep their cognitions consistent with their attitudes. For example, an anti-Semitic attitude and the knowledge that some Jews are good people are inconsistent. An individual with such an attitude who is confronted with such knowledge must do something to avoid or reduce this inconsistency. If his attitude is not strongly held, he might change it. More likely, he will either avoid the information, misperceive or reinterpret or deny the fact, or he will conveniently forget the fact. These are what have been labeled selective exposure, selective perception, and selective retention. These are the psychological processes which sharply limit the often laudable efforts of people in the mass media to change destructive attitudes. For example Lazarsfeld,[40] who was one of the first to note the phenomenon of selective exposure, has described the incident of the radio series which was designed to better human relations. Each program told about a different nationality and the things it had contributed to American culture. It was hoped that the series would help to teach tolerance of other nationalities. The only problem was that the audience for each program turned out to be mainly from the

[37] Fritz Heider, *The Psychology of Interpersonal Relations* (New York: John Wiley and Sons, Inc., 1958).

[38] Leon Festinger, *A Theory of Cognitive Dissonance* (Evanston, Ill.: Row Peterson and Co., 1957).

[39] Charles E. Osgood and Percy H. Tannenbaum, "The Principle of Congruity in the Prediction of Attitude Change," *Psychological Review*, LXII (1955), 42–55.

[40] Paul F. Lazarsfeld, "The Effects of Radio on Public Opinion," in Douglas Waples, ed., *Print, Radio, and Film in a Democracy* (Chicago: University of Chicago Press, 1952), p. 69.

national group which was being discussed. Thus, there was little chance to teach tolerance or anything else because selective exposure resulted in an audience which already highly approved of what was being said. Another example of this phenomenon was the study done of the effects of the motion picture *Gentlemen's Agreement* on anti-Semitism. When one compared only the post-viewing attitudes of those who had gone to see the film with the attitudes of persons who had not seen the film, there were great differences. The average attitude of those who had seen the film was much less anti-Jewish than that of the latter group. The researchers would have concluded that the film had great impact, except that they also had attitude measures for the movie-goers before they had seen the film. These data showed clearly that those who chose to see *Gentlemen's Agreement* tended to be more favorable to Jews *initially*. Those on whom the film might have had the greatest impact, avoided it.[41]

The classic case of selective perception is that described by Kendall and Wolfe.[42] This was the study in which a series of cartoons featuring a very unattractive individual displaying his prejudices against minority groups was shown. The purpose was to show the stupidity of bigots. However, those at whom the cartoons were aimed—those who were highly prejudiced—tended to misperceive the point of the cartoons. Some with very strong prejudices even perceived the purpose of these cartoons as being to encourage prejudice.

There are a great many studies in which we can see evidence of the selective retention phenomenon; the tendency to remember the things which are consistent with our attitudes and to forget those which are not consistent. An example is Taft's study of Negro boys who, over a period of time, tended to forget the parts of a message about a Negro baseball player which were unfavorable to Negroes but remembered the parts which were favorable.[43]

Having noted these points about selective exposure, perception, and retention, we must avoid the erroneous conclusion that the media, therefore, have no effect on these strong attitudes. The conclusion is rather that those who disagree with a persuasive message *tend* not to expose themselves to it or, if exposed, *tend* to misperceive the

---

[41] Charles Y. Glock, "Some Applications of the Panel Method to the Study of Change," in Paul F. Lazarsfeld and Morris Rosenberg, eds., *The Language of Social Research* (Glencoe, Ill.: The Free Press, 1955), pp. 243–244.

[42] Patricia L. Kendall and Katherine M. Wolfe, "The Analysis of Deviant Cases in Communications Research," in Paul F. Lazarsfeld and Frank N. Stanton, eds., *Communications Research, 1948–1949* (New York: Harpers, 1949), pp. 152–179.

[43] Ronald Taft, "Selective Recall and Memory Distortion of Favorable and Unfavorable Material," *Journal of Abnormal and Social Psychology*, IL (1954), 23–28.

point or, if they perceive the point correctly, *tend* to forget that which is contrary to their prior attitudes. We must keep in mind that this means *some* who disagree with a mesage do expose themselves to it, do perceive it correctly, and do remember it. One of the important research jobs remaining to us is to study these so-called deviant cases to a greater extent, to find the conditions which cause them to deviate from the norm. Such findings will add immeasurably to our understanding of the mass media's impact on attitudes.

MEDIA IMPACT ON CULTURE

One of the questions which has interested scholars of communication, since at least the beginnings of the age of mass communication, is the effect which changing modes and media of communication have upon our culture. In considering this question, it is important first to recognize two facts. One is that this sort of causal relationship is impossible to establish with much certainty; historical data have severe limitations for the establishment of such relationships. There are too many factors which are confounded with the introduction of various media. To name only a few, innovation in media use has generally been accompanied by urbanization, an increase in literacy, and, often, even political changes. If anything, the evidence indicates a type of reciprocal relationship: certain levels of urbanization and literacy both facilitate and make necessary the development of mass communication and, once a mass communication system exists, it facilitates urbanization and further developments in literacy. A modern society is impossible without mass media. They are essential for the marketing of mass-produced products, both for diffusing information about such products and for establishing common tastes in style and type. In other words, the media are both indices and agents of cultural change.

The second fact to keep in mind as we consider the question of whether the media have an effect on our culture is that the question is, in a very real sense, tautological, for the media are an important part of our culture. Thus, any change in the media or in the pattern of media use, by definition, is a change in our culture.

Having noted these facts, there are still obviously some important unanswered questions. To what extent do the media, as they are operated in the United States, affect our tastes? To what extent do they hinder or aid the development of art products of greater artistic merit? Was Reinhold Niebuhr correct when he saw the effect of television as "a further vulgarization of our culture"?[44] Or is Neibuhr one of the disenchanted members of the intelligentsia of whom Paul Lazarsfeld speaks? These people fought and won the battle for shorter working hours and better wages for the American laborer, hoping that the workers would spend some of this extra money and time at Columbia University, only to find that they spent the time instead with the Columbia Broadcasting System. These are emotion-laden questions for most of us. I will try to examine them as objectively as I can.

> In general, cultural traits diffuse outward from the point of origin *along the most-used lines of communication* and contact; and those traits that are *objectively superior* or that come from a *more powerful or prestigious source* are especially likely to be taken over.[45]

These are the generalizations about cultural change which Berelson and Steiner believe can be made up on the basis of existing studies in the behavioral sciences.

It is certainly clear, even from casual observation, that the mass media, by facilitating communication, facilitate the diffusion of culture through space and time. The effects here are analogous to those of other mass-production industries or mass-marketing chain stores. These organizations have made a *greater variety* of products available to the average person but, conversely, have made pretty much the *same* choices available to all. Thus, social class, education, size of community, or part of the country (or perhaps even part of the world) have little effect on styles of clothing available in local stores to the average person, or the kind of music or drama to which one can expose himself at the local cinema, or on one's radio or television receiver. The exchange of records, films, and television programs between Great Britain and the United States has created a common culture. We see the same phenomenon in the fashion industry. Though international fashions are not a completely new phenomenon, they were once the exclusive province of the wealthy who moved physically back and forth among the continents. They are now the province of everyone. One travels to Paris via the mass media to learn what is being worn there and then buys the latest Paris fashions at Macy's in New York or Marx and Spencer in London or at comparable stores in other parts of the world. The elite "BBC speech" is slowly becoming the common dialect of Great Britain, just as General American has become more

---

[44] *Time,* February 7, 1949, p. 70. Quoted in Davis, p. 225.

[45] Bernard Berelson and Gary A. Steiner, *Human Behavior: An Inventory of Scientific Findings* (New York: Harcourt, Brace & World, Inc., 1964), p. 653 (italics added).

generally accepted in the United States since it became the standard pronunciation for most network radio and television announcers in this country. As the mass media increase the communication between our countries, we expect these two dialects to slowly merge.

Thus, Berelson and Steiner's first generalization, that "cultural traits diffuse outward from the point of origin along the most-used lines of communication," and my corollary generalization that, as these lines increase and extend, cultural products and practices can no longer remain the special province of a particular class or region or time, appear to be clearly supported. On the other hand, Berelson and Steiner's second generalization, that "those traits that are objectively superior or that come from a more powerful or prestiguous source are especially likely to be taken over," appears to me to be highly questionable. Unless one defines "objective superiority" and "powerful and prestiguous sources" circularly; i.e., by considering any trait that is adopted as necessarily superior, or the source that it came from necessarily powerful or prestiguous, this generalization cannot be supported. Judged by the media products to which most members of the American public expose themselves, there is little question that objective superiority has little effect on popular taste. The extent to which the mass media are responsible for the level of taste that exists is quite another question however. To what extent do the media follow taste? To what extent do they lead taste? The answer is probably that they do some of both, though hard evidence of either (especially evidence that the media lead taste) is hard to acquire. Historically, there is certainly no evidence that the media have lowered taste, for the taste of the "masses" has never been high. If anything, it is probably higher today than it ever was. Conversely, one cannot attribute this probable raising of taste to media influence, for the change has been accompanied by developments other than the growth of the media, most especially the extended formal education of most people who thus, presumably, learn more about literature, music, art, and theatre. The school orchestra, a relatively recent innovation in most schools, undoubtedly has had some influence on interest in certain types of music. Also, increased wealth and leisure for a larger proportion of the population are probably important factors in the development of taste. As Lazarsfeld and Merton pointed out:

> The effective audience for the arts has become historically transformed. Some centuries back, this audience was largely confined to a selected aristocratic elite. Relatively few were literate. And very few possessed the means to buy books, attend theatres, and travel to the urban centers of the arts. Not more than a slight fraction, pos-

sibly not more than 1 or 2 per cent, of the population composed the effective audience for the arts. . . .

Some forms of music, drama, and literature now reach virtually everyone in our society. . . . [But] the great audiences for the mass media, although in the main literate, are not highly cultivated. . . .

Whereas yesterday the elite constituted virtually the whole of the audience, they are today a minute fraction of the whole.[46]

Clearly, the majority of today's audience for whom the arts are available, choose art products that are less demanding. They prefer a western to *Death of a Salesman,* Norman Rockwell to Renoir, Lerner and Lowe to Wagner. On the other hand, attendance at museums, opera houses, and art museums has soared in the past decade or two. More people attended concerts in 1962 than went to all of the major and minor league baseball games.[47] The book has become a "mass medium" in a very real sense, in part because of the paperback revolution. The sale of books increased tenfold from 1950 to 1960.[48] This is roughly twice as high a rate of growth as population growth can account for.[49] The circulation of "high-brow" magazines has more than doubled since World War II.[50]

The role of the mass media in stimulating this involvement with the arts is clearly considerable. No individual can like something or want something if he does not know it exists. The mass media have helped to make the bulk of the public aware of a great variety of arts and entertainments. (Whether the media could have made the public aware of an even broader range is another question.) As Leonard Bernstein reported, after an extremely successful cross-country tour of the New York Philharmonic:

In Las Vegas, whose cultural opulence doesn't always run in traditional channels, and where no major symphony had performed before, a hall holding 7,000 was jammed. . . . These people were well aware of the Philharmonic. I doubt if awareness of the Philharmonic extended much beyond the Hudson 50 years ago.[51]

[46] Paul F. Lazarsfeld and Robert K. Merton, "Mass Communication, Popular Taste, and Organized Social Action," in Bernard Rosenberg and David Manning White, eds., *Mass Culture* (Glencoe, Ill.: The Free Press, 1957), pp. 466–468.

[47] *Concert Music USA* (New York: Broadcasting Music, Inc., 1961). Quoted by Frank Stanton, *Books and Television* (New York: New York Public Library, 1963), p. 9.

[48] "Currents," *Publishers' Weekly,* CLXXVII (May 9, 1960), 10.

[49] Dan Lacy, "The Economics of Publishing," *Daedalus,* XCII (1963), 47.

[50] Leo Bogart, *The Age of Television* (New York: Frederick Ungar, 1956), p. 140.

[51] Reported by Frank Stanton in a speech at Dartmouth College, November 26, 1962.

The New York Philharmonic's *Young People's Concerts*, carried on television, made the orchestra a familiar group in homes across the country. When the Philharmonic opened Lincoln Center in New York in 1961, almost 26,000,000 persons saw or heard some part of the two-hour concert on television.[52] Another mass medium which is contributing to an increased interest in music is the phonograph recording. The record industry sold in excess of 25,000,000 classical, long-playing records in 1962.[53] The mass magazines also play a role in familiarizing the public with the arts. *Life*, for example, publishes excellent color reproductions of some 500 art pictures a year.[54] After Henry James' *The Turn of the Screw* was dramatized on television, the entire Modern Library edition of the book was sold out.[55] Radio has widened public appreciation of good music by making it more readily available to more people.

I am not saying that the mass media changed people from art-haters to art-lovers, or even that they created active seekers-after-art from people who were totally oblivious to the arts before. Quite the contrary. The evidence indicates that those who were affected had either a prior propensity in this direction or that other forces were pushing them toward this new behavior.

> The importance of the radio as a source of music . . . lies in its ability to make other influences effective. The radio is seen to have its greatest success with those individuals who possess some basic predisposition toward listening. The main importance of the radio does not lie in its direct ability to create interests, but in its effectiveness as a follow-up for forces quite detached from it.[56]

The media here, as in some of the attitude areas, seem to be energizers, rather than change agents. This however does not change the basic point that there would be fewer people exposing themselves to these esthetic experiences, either first-hand or through the media, if the media had not existed.

Critics of the mass media not only berate the effects of the media on audience tastes, they also complain that a type of Gresham's Law has operated, so that the flooding of the market with mass art has driven out the class art. This point of view is difficult to reconcile with

---

[52] *Ibid.*

[53] Alvin Toffler, "A Quantity of Culture," *Fortune*, LXIV (November 1961), 127.

[54] Stanton, 1962.

[55] Stanton, 1963, p. 11.

[56] Edward A. Suchman, "Invitation to Music," in Paul F. Lazarsfeld and Frank N. Stanton, eds., *Radio Research 1941* (New York: Duell, Sloan and Pearce, 1941), pp. 172–173.

the statistics which I cited earlier on museum and concert attendance, reading and record purchases. Clearly, because there are more art products being produced, we must expect that the *average* quality of these products has gone down. But are there fewer high-quality symphonies being created proportionately to the total population? Fewer high-quality plays? novels? paintings? These are impossible questions to answer with certainty. Underlying all of these questions is the basic question of standards. What are the standards by which one labels an art product as "good" or "bad"? As "mass" or "class"? Whose standards are they? Is "good" art that which serves a need of the people as indicated by their use of it or preference for it? Or is "good" art that which passes muster with some authority? I do not have the answer to these questions, but I do believe that those who claim that standards are declining have an idealized picture of the past. When they point, for example, to the decline of the theatrical road show, they neglect to consider the quality of those shows. Toby and Susie shows have declined, as have the other second-rate road shows, but there are more good repertory theatres in America than there ever were before. As White indicates,[57] not only should we compare American mass media to Shakespeare's theatre, we should compare them to the bear-baiting entertainments which were popular in the Elizabethan age.

In addition to the idealization of the past, another factor in the perception of a decline in the arts or of culture in America is that there is less diversity of culture today than there was in earlier years; there is less difference among groups. The media, working together with universal education, have contributed to the more rapid assimilation of these groups into the American culture. Even when a group maintains some semblance of its own culture, it has knowledge of and access to the general culture of the country and more quickly assimilates it with its own. Thus, the unique "folk cultures" once so common throughout the United States are more difficult to find now, or at least to recognize.

Though the mass media have not had a negative effect upon our culture (as a matter of fact quite the opposite), it is possible that they could have a more positive effect. The precise ways in which this could be accomplished within our present mass communication system needs to be studied. This may well be one of our most important media research needs at the present time.

---

[57] David Manning White, "Mass Culture in America; Another Point of View," in Bernard Rosenberg and David Manning, eds., *Mass Culture* (New York: The Free Press of Glencoe, 1957), p. 14.

MEDIA IMPACT ON SOCIAL STRUCTURE

I indicated earlier that the mass media took many of the kinds of information (art, styles, etc.) to which only the privileged classes had access previously and made them available to all. This revolution began in the sixteenth century with the perfection of printing. This media impact was limited by literacy, however, until the development of photography, the motion picture, and, especially, radio and television. As the speech, dress, and knowledge of the Colonel's Lady and Rosie O'Grady became virtually indistinguishable, class lines began to waver and disappear. As the mass media made information equally available to a wider and wider circle of the population, the base of power widened from the few to a larger and larger group. This shift in power was recognized early in the development of the media. The licenser of the Press in London noted it as early as 1680.

> A newspaper makes the multitude too familiar with the actions and councils of their superiors and gives them not only an itch but a kind of colorable right and license to be meddling with the government.[58]

As late as 1958, Lerner[59] found evidence that radio and the motion picture were changing leadership patterns in the Middle East. In the villages, the grocer with a radio or the bus driver who has seen movies brings news from the outside world. These innovators are listened to. They become the new opinion leaders. There is evidence from a study of broadcasting and politics in Great Britain[60] that radio and television are changing the power structure of the political parties in that island country. Though elections are completely local (constituency), the mass media (and especially the broadcasting media) are essentially national. In addition, the broadcasting media tend to personalize the political parties in the image of the party leaders. Thus, the national leaders are gaining in strength relative to the other members of Parliament. This has happened to such an extent that one finds speakers and newspaper editorials in Great Britain inveighing against the trend toward "Presidential-type" elections. This phenomenon in Great Britain is related to the previously mentioned relative gain in the power of the President over the power of the Congress in this country.

---

[58] Roger L'Estrange, Licenser of the Press, London, 1680. Quoted in unpublished paper by Harry Ashmore, n.d.

[59] Daniel Lerner, *The Passing of Traditional Society* (New York: The Free Press of Glencoe, 1958).

[60] Samuel L. Becker, "Broadcasting and Politics in Great Britain," *Quarterly Journal of Speech*, Vol. 53 (February, 1967), 34–43.

In the modern societies, with an ever-increasing level of technology, there is a great deal of mobility—both social and spatial. The mobility is both effect and cause of urbanization, the disintegration of family ties, and the questioning of traditional religious faiths. These faiths and family relationships and interpersonal relationships within the small community were the cement which held society together. The media have become, to a large extent, the new cement for the modern society. The process by which they do this societal cementing has been described by Lasswell:

> (1) The surveillance of the environment; (2) the correlation of the parts of society in responding to the environment; (3) the transmission of the social heritage from one generation to the next.[61]

So it is no accident that the mass media have developed first and fastest in those countries with the highest technology and, thus, the greatest capability and the greatest need for these forms of communication.

Probably the most provocative hypothesis concerning the impact of the mass media on social structure is one that has been advanced by Lerner.[62] It grew out of his study of the role of communication in the social changes of developing countries. His hypothesis is that the media provide the people of these countries with the capacity to conceive of situations and ways of life quite different from those which they have experienced. This is an important state for social change. Until men can conceive of something different from their existing situation, it is difficult for them to become sufficiently motivated to change. It should be noted also that, assuming the hypothesis is confirmed, it would indicate again the special importance of radio, television, and the motion picture as opposed to the print media in much of the world. The visual and aural media are able to leap the barrier of illiteracy and bring information and ideas to those to whom interpersonal communication was, until recently, their only medium to the world outside their immediate experience. Data gathered by Lerner and others indicate that this is, indeed, what is happening.

Considering the impact which the mass media have had upon us, and considering our failure to recognize this impact by appropriate

---

[61] Harold D. Lasswell, "The Structure and Function of Communication in Society," in Lyman Bryson, ed., *The Communication of Ideas* (New York: Cooper Square Publishers, 1964), p. 38.

[62] Daniel Lerner, "Comfort and Fun: Morality in a Nice Society," *The American Scholar*, XXVII (1958), 153–165.

additions to or adjustments in our school curricula, the following parable seems to be the most relevant conclusion to this chapter.

> The story is told of an ancient tribe whose people lived a comfortable and unchanging existence. The children of the tribe were brought up in the traditions of their fathers and were taught how to fish in clear streams and how to hunt the sabre-toothed tiger. Then the snows came and the streams became muddy and the sabre-toothed tiger moved south. But the tribe preserved their traditional ways. They cleared a small part of the stream so that the children could continue to fish, and they stuffed a tiger's head so that they could learn to hunt. Then a radical young tribesman approached the council and asked why, instead, the children were not taught to fish in muddy streams and hunt the polar bear, which had recently begun to ravage the villages. But the council was angry. "We have always taught how to fish in clear streams and how to hunt the sabre-toothed tiger. These are the classical disciplines. Besides," they added, "the curriculum is overcrowded."[63]

---

[63] Stuart Hall and Paddy Whannel, *The Popular Arts* (New York: Pantheon Books, 1964), p. 1.